Sounds of Survival

The Press gratefully acknowledges the generous support of the AMS 75 PAYS Fund and General Fund of the American Musicological Society, supported in part by the National Endowment for the Humanities and the Andrew W. Mellon Foundation.

Sounds of Survival

Polish Music and the Holocaust

J. Mackenzie Pierce

UNIVERSITY OF CALIFORNIA PRESS

University of California Press
Oakland, California

© 2025 by J. Mackenzie Pierce

All rights reserved.

Library of Congress Cataloging-in-Publication Data

Names: Pierce, J. Mackenzie, author.
Title: Sounds of survival : Polish music and the
   Holocaust / J. Mackenzie Pierce.
Description: Oakland, California : University of
   California Press, [2025] | Includes bibliographical
   references and index.
Identifiers: LCCN 2024036116 (print) | LCCN 2024036117
   (ebook) | ISBN 9780520405929 (cloth) | ISBN
   9780520405936 (ebook)
Subjects: LCSH: Jews—Poland—Music—20th century—
   History and criticism. | Music—Poland—20th
   century—History and criticism. | Holocaust, Jewish
   (1939–1945)—Poland. | Antisemitism—Poland—
   History—20th century. | Socialism and music—
   Poland—History—20th century.
Classification: LCC ML3776 .P53 2025 ML297.5
   (print) | LCC ML3776 ML297.5 (ebook) | DDC
   780.89/9240438—dc23/eng/20240913
LC record available at https://lccn.loc.gov/2024036116
LC ebook record available at https://lccn.loc.gov/
   2024036117

GPSR Authorized Representative: Easy Access System
Europe, Mustamäe tee 50, 10621 Tallinn, Estonia,
gpsr.requests@easproject.com

34   33   32   31   30   29   28   27   26   25
10   9   8   7   6   5   4   3   2   1

Contents

List of Illustrations .... *vii*

A Note on Toponyms, Translations, Transliterations,
   and Archival Citations .... *ix*

Acknowledgments .... *xi*

Introduction: Imagining Cultural Continuity in the
Polish Bloodlands *1*

PART I. THE INTERWAR YEARS

  1. Musical Belonging and Its Limits *25*

  2. A Civil Society for Music *50*

PART II. WORLD WAR II AND THE HOLOCAUST

  3. The Nation Is Now a Matter of Life and Death *79*

  4. We Cannot Imagine Life without Music *108*

  5. We Must Restructure the Musicians into Soviet Thinking ... *137*

PART III. THE AFTERMATH

  6. Synthesizing Socialism *167*

  7. The Aesthetics of Loss *194*

Conclusion: A Generation in the Shadow of the Cold War ... *231*

Appendix 1: Cast of Characters 241
Appendix 2: Key Institutions 246
Notes 251
Bibliography 293
Index 323

Illustrations

FIGURES

1. Cartoon by Jerzy Srokowski, 1939 / *28*
2. Adolf Chybiński, Maria Szczepańska, Bronisława Wójcik-Keuprulian, and Hieronim Feicht, ca. 1925 / *39*
3. The musicians of the Warsaw Philharmonic, 1931 / *43*
4. Mateusz Gliński welcomes Édouard Ganche to Warsaw, 1927 / *45*
5. Piotr Perkowski lays a wreath on Chopin's grave in Paris, 1929 / *56*
6. Nadia Boulanger visits the Union of Polish Composers, 1967 / *59*
7. The Philharmonic of the General Government performs, 1944 / *89*
8. Still from the film *Forbidden Songs*, 1947 / *96*
9. Program of the Dom Sztuki café, September 1941 / *104*
10. Unearthing the Oyneg Shabes archive, 1946 / *110*
11. A singer performs on the streets of the Warsaw Ghetto, 1940 or 1941 / *116*
12. Józef Koffler, late 1930s / *148*
13. Zofia Lissa, late 1942 / *157*
14. Ruins of the Warsaw Ghetto, ca. 1945 / *170*
15. Nowy Świat street in Warsaw, ca. 1947 / *171*
16. Roman Palester, 1960s / *184*

vii

viii | Illustrations

17. The musical intelligentsia gathers in Cracow, 1945 / *188*
18. Nathan Rapoport's Monument to the Ghetto Heroes, 1948 / *223*

MAPS

1. Music schools in Poland, 1931 / *69*
2. The Warsaw Ghetto, 1940 / *112*
3. Occupied Poland, 1939 / *138*

MUSIC EXAMPLES

1. Roman Palester, *Mała uwertura na orkiestrę*, mm. 4–10 / *37*
2. Grażyna Bacewicz, Trio for oboe, violin, and cello, mm. 70–79 / *53*
3. Konstanty Régamey, Quintet for clarinet, bassoon, violin, cello, and piano, movement 2 (Intermezzo Romantico), mm. 1–11 / *98*
4. Niccolò Paganini, 24 Caprices for Solo Violin, No. 24 in A Minor, variation 9 / *102*
5. Witold Lutosławski, *Wariacje na temat Paganiniego*, mm. 130–33 / *102*
6. Józef Koffler, *Szkice ukraińskie*, movement 6, mm. 1–6 / *151*
7. Tadeusz Zygfryd Kassern, *Tryptyk żałobny za śpiew solowy z fortepianem*, "Płaczy dzisiaj duszo wszelka," mm. 1–14 / *200*
8. Roman Palester, *Polonezy M. K. Ogińskiego*, rehearsal no. 39 / *207*
9. Zygmunt Mycielski, *Ocalenie, pięć pieśni do słów Czesława Miłosza*, I. "Ty, którego nie mogłem ocalić . . ." / *215*
10. Roman Palester, Symphony No. 2, mm. 1–5 / *219*
11. Zbigniew Turski, Symphony No. 2 "Olimpica," mm. 721–39 / *225*

A Note on Toponyms, Translations, Transliterations, and Archival Citations

Toponyms pose challenges for scholars of eastern Europe because the official names of places were changed multiple times over the course of the twentieth century. To refer to a single place by its ever-changing name leads to confusion: "Zofia Lissa, born in Lemberg in 1905 and educated in her native Lwów in the 1920s, remained active during the Soviet occupation of Lvov. After the war, she decided against returning to her hometown of L'viv." For ease of reading, I use the English names of the key cities in this study: Warsaw, Lviv, and Cracow. I use the Polish names of cities that are not as well established in English.

All translations are my own unless otherwise specified. In the notes and bibliography, transliterations from the Ukrainian follow the Library of Congress system and those from the Russian follow the guidelines in the introduction to the *New Grove Dictionary of Music and Musicians*, second edition. In the text itself, I use the commonly accepted names of musicians and composers.

Citations of archival materials follow the standard Soviet and eastern European format: abbreviated name of the archive, collection number or name, file number, and title (or brief description) of the document(s).

Acknowledgments

This book would not have been possible without extensive personal, intellectual, and institutional support. Preliminary research and language study was underwritten by the Beinecke Foundation, Kosciuszko Foundation, and Cornell University. I conducted further research for the project thanks to fellowships at the Jack, Joseph and Morton Mandel Center for Advanced Holocaust Studies at the United States Holocaust Memorial Museum and the Polin Museum for the History of Polish Jews in Warsaw. The statements made and views expressed, however, are solely the responsibility of the author. Publication expenses were offset by a subvention from the School of Music, Theatre & Dance at the University of Michigan, Ann Arbor. I had the luxury of putting the finishing touches on the manuscript while in residence at the Summer Institute for the Study of East Central and Southeastern Europe, hosted by American Council of Learned Societies and the Center for Advanced Study, Sofia.

This book was improved from the feedback and lively discussion among a number of scholars who read it in its entirety, including Mark Clague, Kevin C. Karnes, Peter J. Schmelz, and Lisa Cooper Vest. Brian Porter-Szűcs's generosity strengthened the arguments of chapter 1 and what eventually became chapter 7, and the introduction was improved thanks to the late Charles Hiroshi Garrett. Lisa Jakelski's guidance, wisdom, and unflagging humanity have been indispensable at every level of this book's long gestation. Annette Richards not only shaped this

xii | Acknowledgments

research from its earliest days but was (and is) a model for what it means to live the life of the mind. Barbara Milewski first piqued my curiosity about Polish music studies and has offered a supportive ear and critical eye ever since. I am also grateful for feedback on various aspects of this project from James Webster, Roger Moseley, Andrea F. Bohlman, and the late Richard Taruskin. Its remaining faults are my own responsibility.

For conversations about various aspects of this research and its music, I wish to thank Ewa Bachmińska, Leah Batstone, Karol Berger, Xak Bjerken, Wayles Browne, Maria Cizmic, John Connelly, Dietmar Friesenegger, Lucy Fitz Gibbon, Beth Holmgren, Uliana Hrab, Kyrill Kunakhovich, Tony Lin, Ryan MacEvoy McCullough, Anne Shreffler, Martha Sprigge, the late Steven Stucky, David Tompkins, Bret Werb, and Andrew Zhou. At the University of Michigan I have benefited beyond measure from the support and comradery of Christi-Anne Castro, Gabriela Cruz, Inderjit Kaur, Joseph Lam, Charles Lwanga, Stefano Mengozzi, Diane Oliva, James Borders, Louise Stein, and Geneviève Zubrzycki, as well as the students in my courses.

I owe an immense debt to the musicological community in Poland, who have helped me in ways too many to name. I would especially like to acknowledge the late Leon Tadeusz Błaszczyk, Beata Bolesławska-Lewandowska, the late Michał Bristiger, Maciej Gołąb, Zofia Helman, Violetta Kostka, Marcin Krajewski, Alek Lachowski, Katarzyna Naliwajek, Irena Poniatowska, and Zbigniew Skowron. I am grateful to the descendants of Witold Baruch in Warsaw for preserving his papers and providing me access to them, and to the heir of Tadeusz Zygfryd Kassern for unequivocally supporting the discussion and publication of his works.

Dozens of archivists and librarians made this project a possibility. I am especially grateful to Magdalena Borowiec and Piotr Maculewicz at the Archive of Polish Composers for providing a wonderful working environment and for guiding me through the archive's immense collections. Izabela Zymer was indispensable at the Union of Polish Composers, and I am grateful to Mieczysław Kominek for granting me access to the union's archive. Przemysław Kaniecki and Kajtek Prochyra were immensely helpful at the Polin Museum. In Lviv, I was grateful for the assistance of Kristina Opaiets. A special thanks is due to the late Hans Wahl for the warm welcome, spare room, and lively conversation in Paris.

This book contains material that appeared in an earlier form as "Zofia Lissa, Wartime Trauma, and the Evolution of the Polish 'Mass

Song,'" *Journal of Musicology* 37, no. 2 (2020): 231–66, and "Sonic Transformations: Urban Musical Culture in the Warsaw Ghetto, 1940–1942," in *The Oxford Handbook of Jewish Music Studies*, edited by Tina Frühauf (New York: Oxford University Press, 2023), 240–60. I am grateful to the editors of these publications for shaping this work in its initial form.

I wish to thank Kathryn for pushing me to write with clarity and verve long before it was academically necessary and Leighton for instilling a love of the sonically odd and the oddly sonic. A word of thanks is also due to the village of Potsdam, New York, for providing a refuge from the world where, rather unexpectedly, the majority of this manuscript was composed. Last, and most of all, I wish to thank Erica not only for reading this book more times than is advisable, but for all the love.

Introduction

*Imagining Cultural Continuity in
the Polish Bloodlands*

From almost any perspective, World War II (1939–45) was an unprecedented cataclysm for Poland. About 16 percent of its population was killed during these years, including about 92 percent of Polish Jews, who were murdered in the Holocaust.[1] Warsaw was reduced to ruins. After the war, Poland's borders were shifted westward, its population was rendered ethnically and religiously homogenous for the first time in history, and its political system was forced into a Soviet mold. Despite these upheavals, many musicians in Poland believed that concert (or classical) music was a force of continuity across the midcentury. They interpreted the war as a paradoxically fertile time during which Polish composition continued to grow unharmed. Others asserted that the war had heightened the social and political significance of music to such a degree that it seemed vital to audiences in ways unimaginable a few years prior.

Sounds of Survival shows that promulgating such narratives of musical stability was a political and social undertaking of immense dimensions. Composers, music critics, and cultural officials mobilized a belief that music could help restore normalcy and remind listeners that they belonged to an enduring collective. Most significantly, their efforts downplayed the countless experiences of suffering that could not be reconciled with a vision of forward-directed musical progress. In so doing, they not only contained the effects of the wartime violence that were felt by nearly all musicians. They also marginalized the cultural aftermath of the persecution and murder of the hundreds of Polish

2 | Introduction

Jewish musicians who had for decades been central to Poland's musical culture, as performers, composers, organizers, and intellectuals.

Prior to World War II Poland was among the most ethnically diverse countries in Europe. In 1931 approximately 64 percent of the population were Poles, 10 percent Jews, and 16 percent Ukrainians, with the remainder comprised of Belarusians, Germans, and Lithuanians.[2] These statistics do not capture just how important Polish Jews were to the musical culture in Poland, however. Acculturated Jews—those who spoke Polish, belonged to the educated middle class, and generally understood themselves to be both Polish and Jewish—had been central to creating the sounds and institutions of classical music in Poland. Aleksander Tansman led a wave of renewed contact between Polish and Parisian composers in the 1920s. Józef Koffler was the first composer in Poland to use twelve-tone technique in his works. Mateusz Gliński edited one of the country's most consequential music periodicals, *Muzyka* (Music). The scholar Zofia Lissa was among the most precocious musicologists in Poland, publishing on topics from film music to music psychology. The conductor Grzegorz Fitelberg directed the most important orchestras in the country and championed Polish modernist compositions. Jews filled the stage and hall of the Warsaw Philharmonic, Jewish musical associations proliferated in large cities and small towns, and the Jewish press reported on countless concerts and recitals.[3] In the 1920s and 1930s the classical music world in Poland was an integrated Polish and Polish Jewish one, even if it was struck through with bias and discrimination.

The Nazi occupation cleaved this musical community in a fundamentally new way, dividing it into rigid racial categories that did not accord with musicians' own identities. As the Nazis sequestered Jews in the Warsaw Ghetto in the fall of 1940, Poles were revitalizing notions of music as a means of national survival. While Jewish musicians were being deported en masse to the death camps of Treblinka, Sobibór, and Bełżec in 1942, Polish musicians were continuing to perform in cafés and private apartments. After the war ended in 1945, while Poles were rebuilding their interwar musical organizations with help from the communist state, Jews faced continuing violence from their Polish neighbors and many emigrated, leaving their projects behind (or relaunching them abroad). In the more abstract realm of memory, too, Poles came to portray the war as a moment in which musical culture had flourished, while Jews began to question the value of musical performances in the ghettoes on the eve of the mass murder of the Jewish community. After the war, Polish music critics dismissed works that publicly aired grief and wartime loss while championing those that seemed to project the stability of the nation. Throughout this book I argue that Polish musicians' investment in continuity as an institutional, social, and aesthetic project created little space for acknowledging Jewish suffering, much less their own. Ultimately, *Sounds of Survival* not only reveals that the Holocaust was a—perhaps *the*—central event within modern Polish musical culture; it also shows why its musical aftermath has been difficult to hear.[4]

THE SOCIAL BASIS OF CONTINUITY AND RUPTURE

Examining Poland's musical community of the mid-twentieth century reveals how the meaning of suffering was constructed socially, molded in accord with the political, cultural, and aesthetic priorities of survivors. As the sociologist Jeffrey C. Alexander observes, "For traumas to emerge at the level of the collectivity, social crises must become cultural crises. . . . Trauma is not the result of a group experiencing pain. It is the result of this acute discomfort entering into the core of the collectivity's sense of its own identity."[5] Continuity and rupture are the two most extreme ways of conceptualizing how trauma impinges on a collectivity's sense of historical time. The former prioritizes a smooth ebb and flow of time, calling attention to what stays the same despite loss; the latter highlights instead the sharp, jagged edges of difference between now and then. Historical time is often imagined as a homogenous, linearly unfolding expanse, exemplified by the ever-ticking clock advancing from past into future. But how people experience time—how they imagine it to be parceled into periods of continuity and rupture—is more circuitous.[6] A rupture is not merely an event that has produced a massive body count, a new political system, or millions of cubic meters of rubble, but rather one that has generated the sustained belief that these deaths, revolutions, or ruins have fundamentally altered the collective to which they occurred.

The cultural production of continuity across the war and Holocaust in Poland required musicians to prioritize experiences that fit a forward-directed notion of progress and musical development. It also required them to marginalize experiences of loss, suffering, and destruction that did not. I trace this process of selection and omission in detail from the 1920s to the 1950s. This transhistorical perspective brings into focus multiple factors that informed the creation of cultural continuity. Some of these factors were grounded in the peculiar conditions of

4 | Introduction

the interwar period (1918–39), which emphasized the creation of small and tight-knit organizations, and of the occupation (1939–45), where cultural repressions produced new forms of musical sustenance. Some of these factors were ideological, including the growing influence of exclusionary ethnonationalism in the musical community before the war and the alliance between communism and Polish nationalism after it. Some reflected the practical realities facing Polish Jewish musicians, including the fact that announcing one's Jewishness had little benefit in an environment characterized by anti-Jewish rhetoric and violence.

One of my central claims, however, is that the musical continuities that spanned across the war emanated from a deeper, enduring mode of sociality shared by composers, music intellectuals, and some performers in midcentury Poland. This sociality was that of the intelligentsia (*inteligencja*), whose patterns of thought and action persisted across the traumas of war and political transformation. Chapter 1 will define the intelligentsia, its modes of action, and the limitations on its membership in greater detail. Suffice it to say here that this group, who were educated although not necessarily wealthy or politically influential, had emerged as the de facto political class during the mid-nineteenth century, gaining this position during a period of Polish statelessness.[7] It included both Poles and acculturated Polish Jews. Its modes of action and thought were premised on casting a wide variety of activities within a framework of national survival and development, which provided a model for enduring periods of persecution. Throughout this book I use the term *musical intelligentsia* as shorthand for the milieu of musicians who believed that the ethos, mindset, and mission of the Polish intelligentsia should be enacted within the domain of music, and, conversely, that music could play a key role in the construction of the intelligentsia's particular understanding of nationhood.

Casting themselves as capable of improving Poland musically, while aware of the precarious place of Poland in broader geographies of culture and power, the musical intelligentsia was an elite formation, albeit a particular one.[8] As the sociologist Shamus Rahman Khan observes, elites have "vastly disproportionate control over or access to a resource" and the ability to transfer or convert "that resource into other forms of capital."[9] Often impoverished or materially insecure, the musical intelligentsia in Poland did not possess the financial capital that shaped bourgeois musical culture of the nineteenth and twentieth centuries in western Europe.[10] Rather, they possessed cultural capital that allowed them to frame their actions as benefiting the nation and to be taken seriously when they did so. Educated and multilingual, they wielded discursive authority that could be converted into administrative influence over institutions, but often little more. Their position was a fragile one because it depended on rhetoric and recognition rather than on access to wealth or the levers of political power. Nonetheless, in the impoverished and socially stratified Poland of the 1920s and 1930s, they embraced elitism, seeing themselves as the leaders who would bring the rural, uneducated, and assumedly unmusical "masses" into European modernity.

Discourse and debate were the glue that held the musical intelligentsia together, allowing its members to form strong interpersonal connections and adapt to new political circumstances. For keen prose stylists such as Zygmunt Mycielski and Stefan Kisielewski, the words written about music mattered as much as its sounds. These men received little recognition as composers, but they both exerted enormous influence on the Polish music scene nonetheless due to their personal gravitas and their ability to define the stakes of the community's aesthetic and political debates. Beyond discourse, the fact that the musical intelligentsia saw themselves as national leaders led them to cast their small-scale actions as possessing a broad significance. Gliński, for instance, described his journal, *Muzyka*, as not only bringing "Poland's musical life into close proximity to the artistic currents of Europe" but also "caring for the development of Polish national art," thereby suggesting that what might seem like a modest publication was in fact a vessel of national progress.[11] Such rhetoric was not only hubris. It was also an assertion that Poland's musical ecosystem (*ruch muzyczny*) should be built through small-scale action, whether by organizing concerts for schoolchildren, publishing journals, or serving on the board of music associations.

The national framing that permeated the musical intelligentsia's debates and acts helped to form tight-knit social circles (*środowiska*), which were held together not only by personal amity but also by the belief that these relationships would help advance Polish musical culture.[12] Tadeusz Ochlewski, for instance, was far more than a concert promoter or publisher, although he was both these things. His sprawling correspondence with dozens of musicians reveals how he quilted together the members of the musical intelligentsia around the institutions he led, whether to organize concerts in the provinces in the 1930s or as head of the state music publisher after the war. Polish musical institutions of the midcentury—including journals, publishing houses, and music associations—coalesced around social circles and remained enmeshed in the politics of their creators. The survival of these social circles acted much like the stump of a cut-down tree, offering an enduring core from which new branches of musical activity could shoot, even after what might appear to have been a fatal felling. On one level, then, Polish musical culture seemed continuous to the musical intelligentsia because its leaders could point to how some of their key relationships and institutions spanned from the 1920s to the 1950s, even as many others had perished.

Continuity was also an ideological project, part of the musical intelligentsia's broader aim of securing support for concert music and shoring up their cultural relevance. They were a precarious elite, both because of their dependence on cultural capital and because they had staked their significance to concert music, an art form whose full import, they believed, much of Polish society had failed to grasp. A sense of musical inadequacy was, as Lisa Cooper Vest has shown, a powerful motivating idea in Polish musical aesthetics, driving the experimentation and fecundity of the new music scene for decades.[13] In the 1930s and 1940s, the presiding sense of musical crisis also had important practical implications for the musical intelligentsia, as I discuss in greater detail in chapters 2 and 6: it led them to seek alliances with the Polish state in the belief that its power could transform Polish musical culture.

Eager to consolidate influence and assert music's political and social significance, they aligned themselves with the aims of cultural stability and nation building, which in turn emphasized growth, development, and continuity, rather than rupture, across the midcentury. During the wartime occupation, they highlighted the continued productivity of composers and the eagerness of audiences to attend concerts, treating these phenomena as evidence of concert music's increased social worth. After the war, they argued that music would help rebuild Poland from the ruins of war and was thereby worthy of funding and prestige. By asserting that it could help direct audiences away from the losses of the war and toward a better, if hazily defined, future, they suggested that it was deserving of support from the socialist state, for whom rebuilding from war and the building of a new, socialist Poland were mutually reinforcing goals. Thus, the musical intelligentsia's abiding investment in the idea that music mattered did not lead them to champion sonic analogues for the experiences of loss, disruption, and trauma. Rather, it led them in the opposite direction: musical expressions of the unruly past had to be curtailed lest they destabilize the present and foreclose a future in which music would be a vital component of Polish society. The result was a musical culture in which everyone knew firsthand of the immense losses of the war and the Holocaust, but the musical traces of these events were often faint.

JEWISH ASSIMILATION AND THE POLISH CONCERT HALL

The Polish Jews who shaped classical music in Poland prior to World War II were in many respects exceptions. While most Polish Jews spoke Yiddish, were impoverished, worked as craftspeople or small shopkeepers, and lived in the small market towns of the Polish countryside, those at the center of Poland's classical music world spoke Polish, belonged to the educated middle class, and lived in larger cities.[14] They (or their parents or grandparents) were representatives of one of the most important social transformations to have occurred in Polish Jewish life, namely assimilation (*asymilacja*). *Assimilation* is a widely used albeit imprecise term that refers to several distinct changes within Jewish society from the mid-nineteenth century onward: it usually encompasses acculturation (how Jews adopted the language, culture, and beliefs of Poles), integration (how Jews entered into non-Jewish social circles and institutions), emancipation (how Jews gained civil rights), and secularization (how Jews rejected religious beliefs and customs).[15]

Concert music has long been acknowledged to hold particular salience for Jewish acculturation and integration in Europe. Ruth HaCohen observes that "music, with its unique spiritual potential, held a special attraction" for acculturating, well-to-do Jews in major European cities during the nineteenth century.[16] The historian Ezra Mendelsohn wrote of the "special role" played by classical music in Jewish integration, speculating that perhaps its status as an "international language" made it an appealing pathway for Jews on the margins of European society to perform their membership in various national cultures.[17] Focusing on Poland, Halina Goldberg has written of how Polish Jewish virtuosi, such as the violinist Izydor Lotto (1840–1927), demonstrated that Jews could "excel in new arenas" and "participate in the making of a national culture," thus turning these musicians into "poster children" for the promises of integration.[18] Acculturated and converted Polish Jews played a leading role in establishing Warsaw's musical institutions and patronizing them as audience members, strong evidence of their integration into Varsovian society. Henryk Toeplitz, Adam Münchheimer, Józef Wieniawski, and Ludwik

8 | Introduction

Grossman were all founding members of the Warsaw Music Society, inaugurated in 1871.[19] Several decades later in 1901, the Warsaw Philharmonic—the city's premiere concert institution—was founded thanks to the initiative of, among others, Aleksander Rajchman, a Jewish critic who published a popular cultural periodical, and Leopold Julian Kronenberg, a banker, industrialist, and amateur composer of Jewish background.[20]

The forces driving Jewish acculturation only intensified after the reestablishment of the Polish state in 1918, when more and more Jewish children attended Polish-language schools and otherwise interacted with state institutions.[21] By the early 1930s, Polish Jews constituted a significant portion of the urban professional classes that formed the backbone of the intelligentsia; for instance, in 1931 around half of all lawyers and 46 percent of doctors in Poland were Jewish.[22] Acculturated Jews were prominent in creative arenas too, including Polish-language literature, Polish-language cinema, and the cabaret, where integrated troupes performed for mixed Polish and Polish Jewish audiences.[23]

While some acculturated Jews (or their children) converted to Catholicism, acculturation and integration did not lead teleologically toward conversion. Indeed, many acculturated Jews retained investments in Jewishness as religious practice, ethnicity, and national identity, even if they spoke Polish with their friends, fell in love with the Polish literary canon, or made music in Polish orchestras.[24] In the censuses of 1921 and 1931, a notable minority of Polish Jews described their religion as Judaism but their nationality (in 1921) or their mother tongue (in 1931) as Polish.[25] So heavily Polonized were a subset of Polish Jews that they preferred to read their news and cultural commentary in Polish, which gave rise to a substantial Polish-language periodical press addressed explicitly to a Jewish readership.[26] There was even a small but significant literary movement whose authors endorsed a strong sense of Jewish national identity but wrote exclusively in Polish, since they knew neither Hebrew nor Yiddish.[27] As we will see, there were also robust discussions about Jewish music conducted by Polish Jews in the Polish language, as well as music organizations that identified as Jewish and served primarily Polish-speaking audiences. Thus, while Polish Jewish musical intellectuals such as Zofia Lissa or Józef Kofler are not representative of Polish Jewry writ large, they are representative of one of its core subcultures: those who negotiated both Polish and Jewish cultural spheres during a period of rapid social transformations.

It can be challenging to tell the stories of acculturated Polish Jewish musicians since the in-betweenness that defines their subculture is delicate and easily trampled.[28] Because many Polish Jewish musicians downplayed the Jewish aspects of their lives in order to survive in anti-Jewish environments, their connections to Jewishness can seem incidental, barely evident in the historical record. Because they wrote in the eloquent Polish of the interwar intelligentsia and framed their actions as serving Polish culture, it can be appealing to retroactively assimilate them into Polish nationhood, honoring them for their contributions to the nation that were often denied during their lifetimes. I have sought to push against this default to Polonization by making explicit the aporias around Jewish backgrounds and experience that are endemic in the primary sources that I draw on, and by considering how these omissions were foundational for the construction of a Polish musical culture in the first place. Jewishness—as ethnicity, religious practice, nationhood, and race—often haunts Polish musical culture, I suggest, even when it seems to be most absent.

ANTISEMITISM AND POLISH ETHNONATIONALISM

As Jews were acculturating into the Polish language and integrating into Polish institutions throughout the first decades of the twentieth century, more and more Poles were rejecting the possibility of a Polish identity that could encompass them. When I discuss antisemitism within Polish music circles, I refer to the belief that Jews were inherently foreign and therefore could not be assimilated into the Polish nation.[29] This was not the only prejudice Polish Jews encountered, but it was an important one because it took direct aim at Jewish acculturation, integration, and emancipation. Modern antisemitism had taken root in Polish discourse during the final decades of the nineteenth century and had begun to animate Polish politics a few years before many of the composers I discuss were born. Indeed, throughout much of the early nineteenth century, Polish activists had celebrated a somewhat inclusive national community, valuing patriotic action on behalf of the Polish political cause rather than "the description (or creation) of an ethnically and culturally homogenous social collective," as Brian Porter-Szűcs has argued.[30] But by the early twentieth century antisemitism had proven useful in mobilizing voters in an era of mass politics and in gaining political power.[31]

Antisemitism played a key role in consolidating Polish ethnonationalism, a right-wing view of the nation as ethnically homogenous, Catholic, and Polish speaking. Polish politics during the interwar years is often, if reductively, narrated as a conflict between the ethnonationalism of

Roman Dmowski (and his political formation, the National Democrats) and the civic nationalism of Józef Piłsudski, who gained power in a coup in 1926. Piłsudski endorsed a notion of Polishness grounded in citizenship, which was in theory open to the country's many ethnic minorities.[32] Dmowski and ethnonationalist activists, by comparison, treated Jews as a threatening foil against which to construct their own idealized vision of Polish nationhood.[33] Acknowledging that antisemitism was not only a prejudice against Jews but rather a core element of promoting a particular interpretation of Polish nationalism helps to clarify why antisemites frequently attacked acculturated Jews and Poles of Jewish background, including musicians. For ethnonationalists, the purportedly deleterious influences of acculturated Jews were hidden behind Polish language and customs, corrupting Polish culture from within.[34] Ethnonationalism was not the only conception of Polish nationhood at play in the interwar years. Nonetheless, it was Dmowski, observes Timothy Snyder, who "did more to determine the content of Polish nationality" than anyone else during the first half of the twentieth century. By 1914, his "definition of Polishness was all but hegemonic."[35]

Within musical circles antisemitism often took the form of a "cultural code," to borrow a phrase used by Shulamit Volkov in the context of imperial Germany.[36] It was a set of tropes, rhetorical figures, and concepts that served not only to denigrate Jewish musical acculturation but also to signal support for a broader politics of Polish ethnonationalism. Sometimes antisemitism took the form of the dismissal of Jewish music making as noise-like or inexpressive, partaking of a long tradition that HaCohen has described as the "music libel" against the Jews.[37] At other times it echoed Richard Wagner's assertions in "Judaism in Music" that Jews could not speak the musical language of the nation or that their compositions were derivative of the innovations of non-Jews. When Poles confronted Soviet power during and after World War II, antisemitism often took the guise of assertions of a quasi-conspiratorial connection between Jews and communism, a phenomenon encapsulated by the term *Żydokomuna* (Judeo-Bolshevism), through which Polish Jewish musicians were castigated for their purported complicity in Soviet rule.[38] While these tropes had roots stretching beyond Poland and predating the interwar years, their expression occurred within a historically and culturally particular context, forming a system of political speech that musicians could choose to promote, counteract, or acquiesce to.

None of this is to minimize the impacts of anti-Jewish politics on the lives and livelihoods of Polish Jewish musicians. Despite the Constitution of 1921 guaranteeing equal rights to religious and national minorities, Polish Jews faced routine and extensive discrimination from the Polish state as well as other political actors throughout the interwar years. The Polish state did not hire Jews for its extensive bureaucracy, and Jewish enrollments at universities declined across the interwar years from nearly a quarter of students in the 1921 academic year to about 8 percent on the eve of World War II.[39] Beginning in 1931, right-wing activists launched campaigns to spread anti-Jewish ideas among broad swaths of Poles and to encourage boycotts of Jewish-owned businesses.[40] Matters only worsened after the death of Piłsudski in 1935, when the ruling regime took a rightward swerve. In the 1935–36 and 1936–37 school years, right-wing students and activists demanded the segregation of Jewish students at universities through the creation of so-called "ghetto benches," which became common at Polish universities.[41] Major professional associations, including those for lawyers and doctors, either banned Jews outright or prevented the admittance of new Jewish members at this time. Increasingly, the Polish regime saw the only solution to the "Jewish question" as large scale emigration, even considering a far-flung plan for a Jewish settlement in Madagascar, then a French colony.[42] No wonder that many Polish Jews felt a sense of despair and hopelessness about their future in Poland.[43]

When it comes to understanding the contours of friendship and enmity that shaped the Polish classical music world, only rarely and with great caution is it possible to extrapolate from antisemitic musical discourse to the behavior of individual musicians. One of the most important instances where I do so is when I discuss antisemitic rhetoric as an administrative tactic in chapter 2. Ad hominem attacks on Polish Jews within musical institutions served to de-Judaize these institutions, in some cases with long-reaching implications. But in general, the links between musicians' words and their acts are too ambiguous and over-determined to insist on causality. Jerzy Waldorff, for instance, penned antisemitic diatribes during the late 1930s, but by 1946 he was coauthoring the memoirs of Władysław Szpilman (the protagonist of the 2002 film *The Pianist*), a decision to amplify the experiences of a Jewish survivor that would seem baffling if we assume antisemitism to be an immutable hatred of all Jews. As we will see in chapter 2, the musicologists Stefania Łobaczewska and Zdzisław Jachimecki wrote tracts that segregated Polish Jews out of narratives of Polish music, yet they also had close personal friendships with Polish Jews and, in the case of Łobaczewska, sheltered the Polish Jewish pianist Marian Filar in her

12 | Introduction

apartment during the Soviet occupation of Lviv.[44] Their actions are not excuses for their words, but rather reminders of the humanity mediating musicians' beliefs, written words, and actions.

The prevalence of both acculturation and ethnonationalism makes it difficult to situate musicians within the racial, ethnic, and national divisions of their day. On the one hand, many leading Polish Jewish musicians would have sought to circumvent the label of "Jewish." Some would have chosen to call themselves "Poles," others "Poles of Jewish background," and still others "Poles of the Faith of Moses," gesturing toward an older integrationist paradigm in which Jewishness would become a private, religious confession.[45] On the other hand, even those least tied to Jewishness had to confront antisemitism and, later, racial terror, whose perpetrators did not care about their subjective identifications. A well-meaning impulse to avoid sorting lived experience into neat categories can obfuscate the stark realities of racial persecution.

While there is no ideal solution to this conundrum, I have reluctantly chosen to label people in accord with the ethnonationalist division between Poles and Jews. Thus, I use the term "Polish Jew" (or "Polish Jewish") to describe Jewish citizens of Poland or recent descendants thereof, including acculturated Jews and Poles of "Jewish origin." I generally use the term "Pole" to mean non-Jewish, Catholic Poles.[46] Whenever possible I also show how musicians' own identities complicate such labels. When describing music and culture instead of people, by comparison, I use the term "Polish" is a broader sense, to mean discourse that was conducted in the Polish language and the music created by those working within a Polish-language ecosystem. Thus the phrase "Polish music" is definitively *not* a synonym for "music created by non-Jewish, Catholic Poles." Indeed, the tension between "Polish" as descriptive of a relatively open cultural project, which could be built by both Poles and Polish Jews, and of a narrower, ethnonationalist one, built by Poles alone, was a defining characteristic of the country's musical culture.

LISTENING FOR THE HOLOCAUST

The Holocaust, by which I mean the mass murder of European Jewry by the German state and its accomplices, encompassed a wide range of atrocities perpetrated against Jewish communities located across thousands of miles. Thus national, regional, and even local dynamics often matter far more to accounts of musical culture during and after it than might first meet the eye.[47] From the perspective of German Jewish musicians, for instance, the Holocaust was often understood to be the final, tragic end point of a longer history of the expulsion of Jews from German society that began in the early years of Nazi rule. Understandably, forced emigration plays a central role in how composers such as Arnold Schoenberg grappled with the Holocaust and its cultural impact, as musicologists including Joy H. Calico, Amy Wlodarski, and Pamela M. Potter have discussed.[48] In eastern Europe, by comparison, the Holocaust was perpetrated within the context of a rapidly imposed, brutal military occupation, which gave the vast majority of Jewish victims no feasible path to escape through emigration.[49]

The broader context of wartime occupation in eastern Europe also meant that the mass murder of the Jews took place alongside a vast slate of other wartime atrocities. Some of these were perpetrated by the Germans, including the mass murder of tens of thousands of non-Jewish elites, bombings of civilians, attempts to eliminate Poles and Poland, and the reduction of cities to rubble in retaliation for resistance. Others were committed by the Soviet Union, including the deportations of hundreds of thousands to the Gulag. So broad and interlocked were these atrocities that the historian Timothy Snyder has called for a reframing of this violence under a regional rubric. By treating eastern Europe as an arena in which multiple projects of state-directed violence were perpetrated, which he terms the "bloodlands," scholars can avoid interpreting these losses through competing nationalized narratives of Polish, Jewish, or Ukrainian (and so forth) victimhood. While few musicologists wish to work on such a broad geographic scale, Snyder reminds us that studying music of the Holocaust in eastern Europe requires accounting for the additive effect and interplay among atrocities while retaining a critical stance toward nationalized memory of them.[50]

For acculturated Polish Jewish musicians, the wartime context of the Holocaust meant that the Polish musical milieu to which they belonged was itself reeling, even as they were singled out for persecution that their non-Jewish colleagues were spared. Although Poles were not slated for elimination during World War II, they were treated with immense brutality by Nazi Germany, suffering a fate that was second in occupied Europe only to that of their Jewish neighbors. In Michael C. Steinlauf's classic formulation, the anti-Polish policies of the German occupation made Poles into "passive witnesses" of the Holocaust.[51] According to this view, they had no choice but to observe the murder of the Jews from an intimate vantage point, but they were largely bystanders who had no power to stop it. This image of Polish passivity has been complicated in

14 | Introduction

recent years by scholars who have examined the agency that Poles did possess and the actions that they took toward Jews, even while they were also being repressed. That Poles blackmailed Jews in hiding, murdered them in pogroms, expressed indifference to (or approval of) their murder, and gained materially from the expropriation of Jewish property while others aided Jews suggests that the classic division into perpetrators, victims, and bystanders of the Holocaust obfuscates the painful social dynamics surrounding atrocity. Poles were more than just witnesses or bystanders, even if the Final Solution was devised above their heads.[52]

Before long, the complexity that characterized Polish-Jewish musical relations during and shortly after the Holocaust would be overshadowed by heavy-gauge memory politics, promoted by the communist state. The predominant narrative of the communist era in Poland subsumed millions of Jewish deaths into a generalized Polish-centered account, in which millions of "Polish citizens" had been martyred by the Germans because of their purportedly "antifascist" views. The racial violence of the occupation and Holocaust was downplayed in museums, textbooks, and commemorative practices, allowing Poles to imagine themselves as the primary—and primarily innocent—victims of the war.[53] This narrative began to unravel only after the end of state socialism in Poland in 1989, when Poles began to encounter far different narratives of the war years. A key turning point occurred in the early 2000s, when the Polish-born, Princeton-based historian Jan T. Gross described how Poles murdered their Jewish neighbors in 1941 in Jedwabne, a village in eastern Poland. The publication of his book *Neighbors* was a "narrative shock" to Polish collective memory, which unsettled the dominant Polish-centered view of Nazi rule.[54]

I agree with Gross that "there are not two histories of the war and occupation—one Polish and the other Jewish" and that it is imperative to reject the application of ethnonationalist lenses to a region characterized by national and ethnic diversity.[55] To this end, I examine the interactions and interpersonal proximity between Polish and Polish Jewish musicians before, during, and after the Holocaust. I consider Polish aid to Jewish musicians, marriages that spanned the ghetto wall, and professional contacts that provided hopes of survival, but also instances of Poles blackmailing Jews in hiding and expressing indifference to Jewish suffering. In this regard I concur with Gross that "the fate of the Jews was at the center of the occupational experience of Polish inhabitants of every city or town," even when Jewish experience has not been given a prominent place in collective memory.[56] Indeed, as will become apparent, it is by keeping Polish and Polish Jewish experience in dialogue with one another that the omissions foundational to the narrative of Polish musical continuity across the war come into view.

BETWEEN SILENCE AND WITNESS

As I scrolled through reels of microfilm and paged through hundreds of archival folders to research this book, I often longed for sources that would illuminate a basic yet elusive question: what did it feel like to have lived the Second World War and the Holocaust through music? I hoped in vain that tape-recorded cassettes of Zofia Lissa would emerge from a dusty corner of the University of Warsaw Library, recordings in which she shared what she felt as she collected songs among Polish Jewish refugees in the Soviet Union. Perhaps a long-forgotten cache of letters would not only explain the pressures of performing in a café in occupied Warsaw but also capture the mental anguish of doing so. With the exception of chapter 4 on the Warsaw Ghetto, where prisoners had no choice but to confront terror and trauma directly, there are relatively few moments in this book where the immediacy of suffering comes through in the protagonists' own words. Those that do often stand as exceptions, indications of the private world of experience that was papered over in public discourse. I came to understand that the evasiveness of much of the historical record created by musicians in Poland was not an accident but reflected how they had chosen to respond to the war and its many forms of suffering. Collectively, they had produced countless articles, memoirs, and musical works that were at once about the war and not about it, as if they had tacitly agreed to discuss the war while also ignoring the profound impacts it must have had on each of their psyches. This texture of avoidance, of eliding the personal and the subjective, was the foundation on which they built an uninterrupted sense of Polish musical culture.

The musical intelligentsia's commitment to cultural continuity produced reactions to the war and Holocaust that frustrate some of the main categories that scholars of the last few decades have used to describe the aftermath of these events. They did not ignore the war's myriad impacts on listeners and composers, and it does not make sense to describe their responses as "silences."[57] But their responses rarely meet definitions of "witness" or "testimony" either. Amy Wlodarski has written eloquently of compositions from Schoenberg to Steve Reich

16 | Introduction

that respond to the Holocaust by "promot[ing] the perception that a 'sense of the real' lays buried somewhere beneath the veneer of language and thus imbues the work with a sense of moral, ethical, and historical agency," an aesthetic she terms "musical witness."[58] But for the most part the musical intelligentsia did not wish to convey a sense of "the real" or to make claims about atrocity grounded in the moral authority of suffering. Their reactions are often indirect, ambiguous, and ambivalent. I sometimes describe their relationship to suffering through the lens of absence, using language such as marginalization, downplaying, omission, and aporia to draw attention to what might have been expressed but was not. In other instances I explore without resolving the simultaneous presence and absence of wartime trauma in musical works and the discourse about musical culture. No doubt, Avery F. Gordon would describe much of the Polish musical intelligentsia's response to the war and Holocaust as one of "haunting," characterized as it is by reminders of the unresolved nature of the past that emerge unexpectedly, as if ghosts of past violence.[59]

To some degree, the musical intelligentsia's responses to mass suffering are products of a particular moment in the formation of Holocaust and war memory. Shortly after the war in Europe, victimhood and survivorship held less moral weight than they did decades later, and the survivors of mass atrocity were generally portrayed in collective, often negative, terms.[60] Nor was there much value assigned to public displays of loss. Frank Biess has described an "emotional regime" in postwar Europe, east and west, defined by the "juxtaposition of ubiquitous and quite strong emotions with a cultural injunction against their open and free expression."[61] Scholars of Holocaust memory likewise caution against applying ideas born of the late twentieth century to the 1940s. After all, what Annette Wieviorka termed the "era of the witness," in which first-person accounts of genocide were accorded high moral and historical value, took several decades to emerge through the legal, artistic, and political cultures of the postwar era.[62]

When viewed within the context of other Polish artistic communities, however, the musical intelligentsia's reticence surrounding the experience of the war and its memorialization is more surprising. From the late 1940s onward Polish film makers turned their camera lenses to the war and the Holocaust, producing an extensive body of visual witness to these traumas.[63] The Polish literary community also did not shy away from engaging with the moral tumult of these years. Polish writers considered the quandaries of witnessing the Holocaust, as evinced in poems such as Czesław Miłosz's "A Poor Christian Looks at the Ghetto" and Jerzy Andrzejewski's novella *Holy Week*.[64] I have drawn much inspiration from Marci Shore's sweeping and elegant collective biography of the Polish literary intelligentsia that survived the war and built postwar Stalinism, many of whom were Jewish. But unlike the musical community who were their exact contemporaries and of similar social standing, the Polish literati understood their writing as inextricable from the subjectivity of history. Shore's is a story of "lived experience," an approach made possible because the literary intelligentsia's life writings bear witness to history in aching personal ways.[65]

Of course, music often expresses trauma in a manner that literary and visual cultures do not, confounding the tropes and chronologies developed around other art forms, as scholars including Maria Cizmic, Martha Sprigge, and Jillian C. Rogers have observed.[66] This is especially true of textless instrumental music of the type most often championed by the Polish musical intelligentsia. Without words to name victims, perpetrators, or even events, instrumental music written in the aftermath of tragedy can evade the issue of whether trauma can or should be represented.[67] Symphonies, string quartets, and overtures can sound mournful and tragic, while through the abstraction inherent to these genres they refuse to name their political or commemorative stakes. Thus, in addition to the social and political factors shaping the musical intelligentsia's responses to the war, their evasiveness about its traumas might also be seen as an affordance of the medium in which they had chosen to work. Instrumental music was useful in downplaying the suffering of war and intuiting a sense of continuity because it seemed to convey profound emotional truths without defining these truths with precision.

BIOGRAPHIES OF SURVIVAL

To tell the story of continuity and change across World War II, I focus on the generation who were young adults when the war began. I describe them as a "generation" because this was one of the main conceptual frameworks that they used to situate themselves in relation to historical and aesthetic change.[68] By foregrounding those whose lives spanned the war, I move away from a historiography grounded in the archives of the postwar Polish state. Because the records of the Polish state rarely predate 1944, relying on them inadvertently reinforces the belief that the war was a fundamental turning point in musical culture.[69] Indeed, as the

18 | Introduction

Cast of Characters and list of Key Institutions in the appendixes make clear, not only did many musicians display remarkable resilience across the war, but so did several of the country's major musical institutions, which were relaunched after 1944 by those willing to adapt them to the postwar political environment.

These musicians were born around the first decade of the twentieth century, began their careers during the turbulence of the Second Republic (1918–39), were well established by the beginning of the war in 1939, and played the leading role in reconstruction after the war. By the late 1950s and early 1960s, this wartime generation had been eclipsed by a younger generation of avant-garde composers, although many maintained significant stature as professors, mentors, and cultural critics despite the shifting aesthetic winds.[70] The wartime generation has often been portrayed as a missing link in narratives of Polish music, a bridge connecting the romantically inclined modernism of Karol Szymanowski, who died in 1937, with the avant-garde compositions of Krzysztof Penderecki and Henryk Górecki of the 1960s.[71] Treating them as an intellectual, political, and aesthetic force in their own right, by comparison, reveals how their interwar sensibilities for social activism and their orientation toward the building of Polish musical culture became the central paradigms through which they made sense of the destruction of the war.

To tell their story, I begin in the interwar years during which they came of age. Chapter 1 introduces readers to the social, aesthetic, and political dynamics of the Polish music scene during the 1920s and 1930s. A key source of unity for these protagonists was the belief that they should take up the mantle of the Polish intelligentsia, the educated classes who had long played an outsized role in Polish politics as the de facto leaders of the nation. The resulting community, which I term the *musical intelligentsia*, was both a social network and an ideological project. Its members often knew each other, debated with one another, and formed institutions together. They subscribed to a hierarchical vision of Polish society in which they would help edify the "masses" and thereby turn Poland into a more musical nation. Women and gay men played a central role in the musical intelligentsia. By comparison the boundaries between Poles and Jews within the community proved to be fraught. Indeed, some in the musical intelligentsia asserted that the deficiencies of Polish musical culture should be attributed to the role that Jews had played in building it over the prior decades. At the same time, some Jewish members of the musical intelligentsia criticized the assumption that music should be a vector of Jewish acculturation, and they sought to define Jewish music independently from the dominant Polish culture in which they had been raised. The chapter thereby highlights the tension between the musical intelligentsia's aspiration to create a more musical Poland and the political, social, and national diversity of the citizenry on whose behalf they claimed to act.

The musical intelligentsia's belief that small-scale action was the key to musical progress led it to develop a rich, variegated civil society around music in the interwar years. These organizations often had sweeping mandates that stretched from internationalist exchange to the development of audiences in the most remote and impoverished corners of the Polish republic. This musical civil society would form an armature for musical activism that persisted not only through World War II but also, in some cases, into the early postwar years as well. Understanding the interwar roots of Polish musical organizing, I argue in chapter 2, is imperative because of how these organizations and the discourse around them reflected the increasingly discriminatory political atmosphere of the time. Commentators debated whether Polish Jews could successfully represent Polish music abroad, while key musical organizations, such as the Polish Music Publishing Society, undermined the participation of Polish Jews in Polish musical life. By the eve of the war, calls for better organization of Polish musical culture had grown into endorsements of fascist and totalitarian systems of cultural patronage among a significant minority of commentators. Thus right-wing thought was not only an aspect of Polish musical discourse during the interwar years but was also embedded in the institutions that played the central role in shaping the country's musical culture.

The three wartime chapters consider how musicians grappled with the racial, national, and political violence that was promulgated during the German and Soviet occupations of Poland. Chapters 3 and 4 focus on Warsaw, which emerged as the main center for the musical intelligentsia's activities in German-ruled Poland. Chapter 3 is based in Polish Warsaw, the area of the segregated city outside of the ghetto. Here, the Nazi occupiers took aim at Polish high culture, which they believed was essential to Polish national identity and survival. They shuttered musical institutions and limited performances of art music to German-sanctioned ensembles and to a small number of cafés. The suppression of musical performance in national terms had the unintended consequence of underscoring the significance of classical music and imbuing acts of listening and composing with heightened national consequence.

20 | Introduction

At the same time, the interpersonal networks that had animated interwar musical organizations became integrated into one of the largest resistance movements in German-occupied Europe, the Polish underground. The underground gave Polish musicians both financial support and a sense of moral community that could help them navigate the dire circumstances of the occupation. While Poles in occupied Warsaw suffered immensely, these material conditions, alongside the reemergence of powerful beliefs about the centrality of music to Polish nationhood, allowed musicians in Polish Warsaw to find a paradoxically positive dimension to the occupation. Music seemed to finally matter.

Chapter 4 focuses on music making in the Warsaw Ghetto. It traces the roots of the ghetto's musical culture in the prewar city and the sonic transformations forced onto Jewish Warsaw under Nazi rule. I focus on several key venues and institutions, including the Jewish Symphony Orchestra, concerts in courtyards, and performances in cafés. Polish Jewish musicians who had once played a central role in the city's classical music life, including members of the Warsaw Philharmonic, continued their work under the auspices of the Jewish Symphony Orchestra. These performances were interpreted through the lens of the centrality of concert music to Jewish assimilation. Meanwhile, the city's dense housing stock and courtyards became the sites of hundreds of musical performances, which organizers hoped would help establish a Yiddish-aligned public sphere. The ghetto's dozens of cafés also emerged as central sites of performance, indexing fraught concerns over wealth and poverty in the ghetto, as well as the antagonisms between Yiddish and Polish as languages of Jewish culture. The chapter calls attention to the multiple senses of proximity—cultural, spatial, and interpersonal—that connected imprisoned musicians to their Polish colleagues, as well as to the fundamental traumas that separated the ghetto from Polish Warsaw.

When scholars and memoirists have written about music in wartime Poland, they have traditionally focused on the territories under Nazi rule and most often on the cities of Warsaw or Cracow. But dozens of members of the musical intelligentsia found themselves under Soviet rule for all or part of the war. Like their counterparts in Warsaw and Cracow, they were forced to engage with a regime that sought to shape musical culture for political ends. Chapter 5 considers the long arc of this Polish-Soviet wartime experience, from the early years of the war, when Nazi Germany and the Soviet Union were allies, through the German-Soviet war beginning in 1941, into the establishment of the postwar Polish state in summer of 1944. It posits Lviv as a wartime counterweight to

Warsaw—a city that quickly emerged as a center of musical activity under Soviet rule. While the German occupation in Warsaw sought to suppress musical culture, the Soviets in Lviv instead championed performances, treating these as emblems of communist progress over the now defunct Polish republic. Although the Soviets did not impose the racial violence that defined the German occupation, their rule did change interethnic relations. For instance, Soviet policies led to the advancement of Polish Jews and Ukrainians in musical institutions. Most significantly, the Soviet Union was a refuge for tens of thousands of Polish Jews from Nazism and the Holocaust, including a handful of prominent musicians who helped relaunch Polish musical life after the war.

The last section of the book is devoted to the musical aftermath of the war. Chapter 6 examines how reconstruction further cleaved the musical intelligentsia along lines of Jewishness and Polishness. Jews had to contend with pogroms that led many to question whether rebuilding in Poland was feasible. At the same time, reconstruction was an unprecedented opportunity for Polish musicians and cultural officials to shape the country's musical future. I trace the alliance formed between the musical intelligentsia and the postwar state, showing how its members integrated their projects into the newly created institutions of state socialism. Prewar projects that focused on music publishing and popularizing music among the masses found renewed support at this time, as they were now cast as part of vital efforts to create a more democratic Poland and to distance its people from the trauma of war. Thus, for many Poles in the musical intelligentsia, reconstruction confirmed the continuous nature of Polish musical culture, as they observed familiar projects from the interwar years being revitalized. For Polish Jewish members of the musical intelligentsia, by comparison, the violence of the early postwar years led to additional displacement, disaffection, and marginalization.

Chapter 7 takes readers into the height of the Stalinist period during the late 1940s and early 1950s. I trace the solidification of the musical intelligentsia's influence as it sought to define the aesthetic implications of the war. The book's arguments come together here: we will see how memory of the war and of Jewish loss circulated informally, echoing the proximity of Polish and Jewish music making during the occupation. At the same time, the musical intelligentsia also began to craft a narrative of the war that conveyed the recent past in selective terms, focusing on those elements of the war that bolstered the status of classical music while downplaying the harsh realities of the occupation. Such selection

22 | Introduction

served to create a view of Polish musical culture as essentially continuous, a task to which discussions of musical aesthetics would also contribute by calling for topical silence about the war. This winnowing of war and Holocaust memory into the imagined stability of national tradition was further cemented in 1949, when communist officials demanded the creation of works that celebrated wartime heroism and triumph instead of loss. The musical intelligentsia and state officials alike cooperated to create a vision of Polish musical culture that stressed the perdurance of nation over the more unruly experiences of loss, even when the latter permeated the lived experience of the early postwar period.

In the conclusion I reflect on the paradoxical legacy of the wartime generation. On the one hand, their work to rapidly rebuild from the war and their insistence on a deep cultural basis for Polish new music had long-lasting effects: they helped to erect the institutional and ideological groundwork for subsequent generations, including the Polish avant-garde of the 1960s (and beyond). On the other hand, they soon slid into obscurity, and the extensive labor they performed to contain wartime trauma and to delimit memories of Poland's interethnic musical scene have largely been forgotten. I suggest that one of the main reasons for this obscurity is that their actions during the 1940s fit awkwardly into later Cold War paradigms that defined the prestige of Polish compositional styles and shaped the historiography of Polish postwar composition. The Cold War was characterized by cultural competition between East and West, and the question of music's subservience to, or friction with, communism became the main lens for evaluating Polish composition for decades to come. This perspective overshadowed the significant moments of cooperation between the wartime generation and communist officialdom after the war. It also obscured the fundamental fact that the most consequential trauma of the midcentury for Polish Jewish musicians was not the establishment of communist rule in Poland, but rather the Holocaust.

PART I

The Interwar Years

I

Musical Belonging and Its Limits

As World War I swept across eastern Europe and revolution consumed the Russian empire, the composer Karol Szymanowski fled from his family's estate in Tymoszówka (today Tymoshivka, Ukraine) to Warsaw. When he arrived in 1919, the capital of the newly independent Poland appeared grim and disappointing.[1] "The European atmosphere of my art is simply indigestible in the midst of the provincialism here," he bemoaned to the musicologist Zdzisław Jachimecki in 1920. His cosmopolitan outlook—cultivated prior to the war through travels across Italy, North Africa, Persia, and Greece—seemed out of place in a city still reeling from the war.[2] Yet he also saw in this state of affairs an impetus to act. "There remains only one thing: to shake off one's personal life fundamentally, and to take one's place in the lowliest ranks of devoted, honest workers, beginning to build the nation from its foundations."[3]

Szymanowski's reactions to the disruption of war and to the reestablishment of the Polish state were shared by many of his colleagues in the Polish musical community. Similar views found support from classical musicians with a number of professional identities who were dispersed throughout Poland's major cities and who subscribed to a variety of aesthetic viewpoints. Like him, these musicians asserted that they were at once more culturally advanced than average Poles yet also obliged to serve the nation, as they cast themselves as capable of building Poland in musical terms. Those who held such hierarchical visions of Poland's musical culture were inspired by the ideals of the intelligentsia, a relatively

25

small, largely self-proclaimed vanguard of the educated who believed they could lead and transform Poland. This chapter theorizes the emergence of a musical equivalent to this social stratum, a musical intelligentsia that exercised broad influence on twentieth-century Polish musical culture.

By focusing on the people and social practices of the musical intelligentsia, I develop an alternative to a "nation-centered" historiography of Polish music while also foregrounding how nationalism was among the most important ideologies shaping the actions of musicians in Europe in the first half of the twentieth century. As Brigid Cohen usefully observes, the discipline of musicology has since its founding privileged nation as a category for organizing the musical past, sorting concert music into competing schools such as "German romanticism" or "French neoclassicism" and interpreting these styles as expressions of their respective national collectives.[4] Nation has often served as a homogenizing abstraction, flattening out power dynamics of the musical scenes within a country's borders and downplaying musicians' nonnational identities. By analyzing the musical intelligentsia as the key agents working to define and promote concert music in Poland, I return our attention to the people who were acting in relation to ideas about nation. They show that "Polish music" was a contested, fragmented category, populated by individuals with differing ideas of community, citizenship, and even nation itself.

This chapter maps the forces of inclusion and exclusion that coursed through the musical intelligentsia in the interwar years. The musical intelligentsia bridged with relative ease the geographic divides among the regions of interwar Poland, with members in the major cities of the Second Republic, such as Warsaw, Cracow, Lviv, and Poznań. It could incorporate members with a wide variety of professional identities, including composers, scholars, critics, publishers, and some performers. Its members also held a variety of political views, from communists on the far left to National Democrats on the far right. Some women, especially female musicologists, could partake in it, and gay men were among its most important representatives. One of its main fault lines concerned the desirability of Jewish acculturation and integration through music. Many still held that concert music could underscore Jewish belonging to Polish institutions and culture, but others began to question this belief: on the one hand, influential Polish musicians asserted that Polish music was to be built by, and to serve the creation of, an ethnically homogenous collective in which the country's myriad minorities would play little role. On the other, some acculturated Jewish musicians and intellectuals wished to build a Jewish musical culture of their own that would be distinct from Polish music, thus rejecting a core tenet of musical acculturation and integration. Jewishness was not only a fundamental aspect of Polish musical culture of the interwar years but also fraught with competing investments as to its meaning and significance.

CREATING A MUSICAL ELITE

After concerts of the Warsaw Philharmonic during the 1920s, the city's leading composers and critics congregated in the Nowa Gospoda (New Tavern), located a short distance from the concert hall. Passing below a sleekly lettered neon sign and entering an interior replete with mirrors, tiled walls, and art deco lamps, they filled two tables. The "conservative" proponents of nineteenth-century romanticism took their seats at one, while the younger, modernist-aligned "progressives" surrounded the conductor Grzegorz Fitelberg at the other.[5]

The deep fissures separating the conservative and progressive tables spoke to the aesthetic stakes of new music in interwar Poland, which were captured by the cartoon in figure 1. The conservatives included composers such as Piotr Rytel (1884–1970) and Eugeniusz Morawski (1876–1948), who held sway in the city's musical institutions. They believed that new compositions ought to continue a tradition of German-inspired symphonism, endorsing a harmonic language that rarely extended beyond that of the late romantic era. Rytel's 1918 tone poem *Legend of St. George*, op. 9 (*Legenda o św. Jerzym*), for example, would have been more than at home in the 1860s. The progressives held more wide-ranging musical views. Most of them were educated after World War I (or shortly before), making them younger than the conservatives, who had established themselves around the turn of the century. They were unified in rejecting the conservatives, yet their musical aesthetics cannot be easily placed into any one of the major movements of European interwar modernism.[6] They had a respect and fascination for the works of Karol Szymanowski, who served as their de facto elder statesman, but their own compositions did not always draw inspiration from either his early luscious romanticism or his turn to Polish folk sources in the mid-1920s.[7] Many progressives—including Grażyna Bacewicz, Antoni Szałowski, and Zygmunt Mycielski—were drawn to Paris and the studio of Nadia Boulanger, while others sought inspiration in the music of Paul Hindemith. Twelve-tone composition, although discussed

FIGURE 1. The main aesthetic division in interwar Polish concert music was between the progressives (left, represented by Jerzy Waldorff, Konstanty Régamey, and Zbigniew Drzewiecki) and the conservatives (right, Stanisław Kazuro, Piotr Rytel, and Eugeniusz Morawski). The progressives hear angelic sounds in this concert of modernist composition during the annual festival of the International Society for Contemporary Music, while the conservatives hear the same performance as grating cacophony. Cartoon by Jerzy Srokowski, *Kurier Poranny*, 16 April 1939. Used by permission of the estate of Jerzy Srokowski.

in progressive musical circles during the late 1930s, found few adoptees outside the composer Józef Koffler, based in Lviv.[8]

Although the conservatives and progressives saw themselves as locked in an irresolvable conflict over Poland's musical future, their side-by-side congregation in one of Warsaw's cafés suggests that they perhaps had more in common than it might at first appear. Indeed, by the 1920s cafés had become not only meeting points for the educated but also a metonym for the Polish intelligentsia's ambitions. It was the venue in which artistic movements were born and collapsed, a place where intimate discussions held among an artistic elect could portend the direction of national culture writ large.[9] That the new-music world flocked to such venues to socialize and argue over music suggests that its members shared a distinct social milieu, despite the clamorous fissures between progressives and conservatives: that of the Polish intelligentsia.

The Polish intelligentsia (*inteligencja*) was a relatively small group—at most about 6 percent of the Polish population in the interwar years.[10] It was comprised largely of those with an education, including bureaucrats, teachers, and those in the free professions, such as lawyers and doctors. Despite its small size, the intelligentsia wielded outsized influence in Poland because it had cast itself as the nation's de facto leaders from the late nineteenth century onward. At this time there was no independent Polish state—the Polish-Lithuanian Commonwealth had been partitioned by Prussia, Russia, and Austria in the eighteenth century and subsumed into these empires. Because Poles had limited access to levers of official power (especially under Russian rule), the intelligentsia believed it could act as an alternative, non-state-based social stratum that would help to preserve the nation and advance Polish interests. As the historian Jerzy Jedlicki has noted, it saw itself as having "a pioneering and missionary role to play."[11] Its emergence against the backdrop of adversity in the nineteenth century would portend the role it would play among musicians during the far worse conditions of the Second World War.

While the term *intelligentsia* shares roots with the French term *intellectuel* and the English *intellectual*, it is importantly distinct from these terms. The French *intellectuel*, a term that gained popularity in the 1890s in response to the Dreyfus affair, connoted a literary and academic avant-garde that believed it could critique the status quo thanks to its distance, if not autonomy, from society itself.[12] By comparison, the Polish intelligentsia saw autonomous critique as less significant than acting on the nation's behalf. Its members encouraged economic development, promoted literacy, and developed hygiene programs.[13] Nor was membership in the Polish intelligentsia limited to an artistic or literary avant-garde: notaries, provincial doctors, and schoolteachers could partake in this form of national leadership in addition to renowned poets, scholars, and composers.

In viewing themselves as national leaders, the intelligentsia claimed the authority that previously had been wielded by the hereditary nobility or gentry (*szlachta*), Poland's historical political class. As the agrarian gentry economy collapsed in the 1860s (due to land reforms, the emancipation of the peasantry, and the failure of gentry-led national uprisings), impoverished gentry moved to cities, where they formed the core of the new intelligentsia.[14] One result of this widespread relocation, as the historian and anthropologist Longina Jakubowska has shown, was that the intelligentsia's "cultural genealogy, that is, its system of values, practices, and objectives, was modeled after the historically accumulated noble heritage," a genealogy that manifested itself in a focus on patriotism, sovereignty, history, and other traditional gentry

30 | Chapter 1

values in artwork and literature.[15] Nonetheless, membership in the intelligentsia was not limited to the impoverished gentry, and it included both those of nongentry background as well as acculturated Jews.[16]

The ideals of the intelligentsia took on renewed significance for musicians during the protracted instability following World War I. The war had been brutal for territories that would become the Second Republic, whose population declined by around 12 percent, or 3.7 million people, between 1914 and 1918.[17] The war had also precipitated the collapse of the empires that had ruled Polish lands since the late eighteenth century. In their wake, the Second Polish Republic was established in 1918. Because Polish lands had modernized under three different empires during the nineteenth century, newly independent Poland faced discrepancies in everything from its legal codes to the gauges of railway tracks.[18] Numerous political parties and governments attempted to govern the country until Józef Piłsudski's coup in 1926 established the Sanacja (literally, "healing") regime, which brought some measure of stability to Polish politics, albeit at the cost of authoritarian rule.

The intelligentsia's authority derived primarily from its cultural capital rather than from its proximity to financial capital or its wealth. It was not an outgrowth of the bourgeoisie or middle class. Poland remained highly agrarian and underindustrialized in comparison to western Europe well into the twentieth century, and as late as 1931 less than 1 percent of the country could be counted as part of the bourgeoisie.[19] Few members of the intelligentsia controlled economic capital, and many of its members did not even enjoy basic material stability.[20] Rather, the intelligentsia saw itself as an elite that was neither reducible to the gentry nor derived its clout from economic station alone. The creation of the intelligentsia as a stratum capable of national leadership that would fill the void of the collapse of the gentry was a decades-long process, one that relied on discourse about the direction of the nation and the narration of countless acts in terms of their purported national significance.

Membership in the musical intelligentsia was signaled not only through musicians' beliefs, but also through their commitment to engaging in public discourse about music, whether in cafés or in print. By examining Polish musical culture through the lens of the musical intelligentsia, we will see connections among Poland's musicians that might otherwise seem perplexing. The musical intelligentsia as a social-analytic tool brings into relief the outsized role played by individuals who did not fit into the more traditional roles of composers, critics, or performers yet played a fundamental role in creating the institutions of

Polish music, such as Tadeusz Ochlewski, a music publisher, and Piotr Perkowski, who founded numerous mutual aid organizations for musicians but whose career as a composer was rather undistinguished. In a time when regional divides created by the partitions were still powerful in Poland, the members of the musical intelligentsia were based in several cities, with Warsaw (in former Russian-ruled Poland) and Lviv (in former Austrian-ruled Poland) emerging as the major foci of their activities. Its membership stretched across the political spectrum. Its members were men and women, Poles and Polish Jews.

Perhaps no individual as fully embodied the aspirations of the musical intelligentsia as did Zygmunt Mycielski, a composer, critic, and diarist with broad musical and cultural interests. While not all members of the musical intelligentsia were of gentry origins, Mycielski was. In his unpublished memoirs he traced his lineage back to the eighteenth century through some of Poland's most powerful gentry magnates, including the Tarnowski, Potocki, and Wielopolski families.[21] This was an elite background that he shared with his major composition teachers: Szymanowski and—in Paris—the renowned pedagogue Nadia Boulanger. At times, their backgrounds provided a shared set of values, too. For instance, when he exclaimed to Boulanger that Szymanowski "is so noble in everything that is essential and profound—*so European* in the best sense of the word," he evoked a conception of class and culture that he implied all three shared.[22]

Mycielski was also a gay man, as were several prominent members of the musical intelligentsia, including Szymanowski, the critic Jerzy Waldorff, and writer Jarosław Iwaszkiewicz. It might seem remarkable that their sexual orientations did little to foreclose their clout as cultural tastemakers. It is worth noting, however, that homosexual acts had been decriminalized in Poland in 1932, although homosexuality was pathologized by the Polish medical establishment and was far from normalized. More significantly, the foundational assumption of homophobia—that homosexuality was an inherent quality of an individual rather than a sexual act—had yet to percolate uniformly through Polish territories in the 1920s and '30s.[23] In some cases homosexuality could even be allied with the nationalist underpinning of the intelligentsia into what Kamil Karczewski describes as a "homonationalism." Indeed, not only had Szymanowski written the first openly homosexual novel in Polish, *Efebos* (1918), but in it he cast Poland as a homophilic nation in the tradition of the ancient Mediterranean (and insinuated that Jews were responsible for introducing homophobia to Poland).[24] In

32 | Chapter 1

these conditions, sexuality could be trumped by the class standing and educational background of the intelligentsia, allowing those of Mycielski's social standing to obtain significant influence on matters of culture.

And indeed, Mycielski's writings about musical culture in the 1930s endorsed the view that national culture was created by a small group of artists and listeners who stood above the lower classes. "What always matters is the elite," he wrote in 1934. "Bartek Zwycięzca," the peasant protagonist of the eponymous novel by Henryk Sienkiewicz, "will not raise the level of our musical culture."[25] If Mycielski was explicit in his belief that an artistic elite should create national culture, others in the musical intelligentsia more delicately articulated their hierarchical imaginations of Polish social space by highlighting the role of the intelligentsia in raising the "people" into culture. This latter approach became especially clear in the 1930s, a period of deep economic pain during which the musical intelligentsia began to routinely endorse the idea that Poland's musical culture was in a state of crisis.[26] "Music must go to the wide masses," declared Teodor Zalewski in an essay on this topic, while Bronisław Rutkowski called similarly for the "musicalization of the wide masses of society."[27] Such claims, ubiquitous by the 1930s, painted the "masses" as an undefined and homogenous social group on which the intelligentsia could act. The term *musicalization* (*umuzykalnienie*), used by Rutkowski and common throughout the 1930s, set up nonelite listeners as an object to be worked upon by being transformed from "unmusical" to "musical."[28] Others believed that much like Poland had been provided with the infrastructure for electricity (a process known as *elektryfikacja*), so too could the country undergo a process of *muzyfikacja*.[29]

For some commentators, such as the choral director and composer Stanisław Wiechowicz, the imperative to create a "mass" musical culture had grown out of practice: he was a leader of the amateur choral movement in western Poland and had regularly directed and composed for choirs of peasant and working-class musicians.[30] For others, the concerns with the musical edification of the lower classes represented a return to older ideas about "organic work" that had animated the intelligentsia in the late nineteenth century, in which they had sought to educate and gradually improve the living conditions of the impoverished as an alternative to political revolution. When members of the musical intelligentsia called for "artists to become socially active" (*uspołecznienie artystów*) or for its individual members to assume the role of the "artist-activist" (*artysta-społecznik*) they likely had these older models in mind.[31] Such calls might appear to represent a democratic or antihierarchical impulse and contrast with Mycielski's skepticism of the masses. Yet commentators such as Zalewski and Rutkowski were not claiming that the intelligentsia should forfeit its leading cultural role as much as they were suggesting that it ought to expand its domain of action to include rural and impoverished areas of the country.[32]

TOWARD A MIDDLEBROW MODERNISM

From the 1920s into the 1950s, the musical intelligentsia expressed a recurring anxiety about the boundaries between "elite" and "mass" culture, asserting that the "masses" should be led away from popular musical genres and toward those of the concert hall. Such concerns were by no means unique to Poland. As Christopher Chowrimootoo and Kate Guthrie, among others, have discussed, the midcentury saw the rise of an aesthetic category of the "middlebrow" across Europe and the United States. The middlebrow was represented by artists and cultural promoters who sought to mediate between "lowbrow" audiences, "whose imagined desire for mindless entertainment was supposedly exploited by shamelessly commercial companies," and "highbrow" artists, who purportedly shunned "the offerings of mass culture in favor of aesthetic autonomy, originality, and difficulty."[33] The "brow"-based terminology was not, to my knowledge, used in Polish musical circles of the mid-twentieth century. However, a similar concern for the relation of aesthetics to social hierarchy was a common theme of the musical intelligentsia's debates and was filtered through their long-standing concerns for national action and improvement. They understood the ascendance of a commercial, mass culture as especially threatening to their social authority, premised as it was on elite-led edification of the "masses."

The musical intelligentsia's hope that they could bring the "people" into classical music had to contend with the evolving listening habits of Poles during a period of rapid urbanization and modernization between the world wars.[34] In the 1920s and 1930s Poland saw an explosion of music in genres such as big band, swing, and dance as Polish-speaking musicians attempted to break into what Beth Holmgren has described as the "'big time' of at once elemental and sophisticated world music."[35] Supported by a nascent recording industry and radio broadcasts, the tango, foxtrot, and rumba were propelled into the popular imagination by bands created by the likes of Artur and Henryk Gold, Henryk Wars, and Szymon Kataszek.[36] It was this music—performed in revues, dance

34 | Chapter 1

halls, cinemas, restaurants, cafés, and cabarets—rather than the new works for the concert hall, that had arguably demonstrated an ability to achieve mass appeal at the time. It was also this music that resonated especially strongly with the urban professional classes that more broadly defined the intelligentsia.[37]

The members of the classical music world often had negative views of the primacy that popular music (*muzyka lekka*; literally, "light music") seemed to be gaining over classical genres (*muzyka poważna*; literally, "serious music"). Some, such as the violinist and publisher Tadeusz Ochlewski, saw light music as confirming the erasure of individuality by mass taste. "The essential cause of the atrophy of musical culture [*ruch muzyczny*] seems to me to be the atrophy of individuality," he asserted in 1934. "A person's individual feelings have been forced into the frame of collective life, the life of the crowd," a development caused by "jazz," "mechanical music," and, ultimately, the "vegetation of spiritual life."[38] Others, such as the composer and critic Konstanty Régamey, focused on the supposed simplicity of light music. It is "tragic," he claimed, "that *only* banal and superficial music can seize larger masses for whom true and serious art remains entirely foreign."[39] Nor were such worries limited to the decaying tastes of the "masses" alone. In Jan Maklakiewicz's view, the "worst is with the intelligentsia" itself, whose taste he thought was limited to such hits as the 1932 tango "Jesienne róże" (Springtime roses), by Artur Gold and Andrzej Włast.[40] For some commentators these dismissals were no doubt also rooted in anti-Jewish prejudice, since Polish Jewish musicians were among the most prominent creators of interwar popular song.

Within this environment, characterized by both skepticism of light music and envy of its mass appeal, younger "progressive" composers could stake out aesthetic terrain that attempted to reimagine the audience and sonic possibilities of contemporary composition. The compositions and criticism of Roman Palester are indicative of the ambivalence that some in the musical intelligentsia felt toward light music. The son of a prominent specialist in infectious disease, Palester had trained in music in Lviv and Warsaw. By the early 1930s, he had established himself as one of the leading younger talents among the progressive composers, and his reputation was growing beyond Poland's borders as well. His reputation was established with a performance of *Muzyka symfoniczna* (Symphonic music) during the International Society for Contemporary Music (ISCM) festival in Oxford in 1931, a peripatetic, annual festival that was a meeting ground for modernist composers from across Europe.[41] Underscoring his commitment to the modernist musical cause, he played a prominent role in the Polish section of the ISCM and claimed to be largely responsible for realizing the programming at the ISCM festival's Polish iteration, held in April 1939.[42]

His views from the 1930s endorsed ideas common to the progressive wing of the musical intelligentsia about the responsibilities of the artist to society and the superiority of serious composition vis-à-vis light music. In a 1932 article titled "The Crisis of Musical Modernism," he portrayed modernist music as the telos of classical music's historical development and claimed that new composition was increasingly isolated from a broad listenership. He criticized composers who lacked even "the smallest feeling of social responsibility."[43] These deficiencies, he believed, meant that Polish music needed a stronger "social foundation" and that composers must "think concretely about what can be done here in Poland, to whom one addresses with one's music, how to raise [*wychować*] a cadre of listeners."[44] Two years later he made these claims more concrete, asking musicians to move beyond addressing urban concertgoers alone with their compositions and instead to develop connections with "rural and working-class youth."[45] This broader engagement was, however, to take place decisively according to the terms of high art: "We all know what horrendous kitsch today's 'light' music is—that jumble of tangos, foxtrots, and waltzes," he cautioned. "This music is vulgar; it spoils the taste of the broad listening public and causes incalculable damage to the essence of musical culture."[46]

Even as Palester wrote with condescension about tangos and foxtrots, however, he proved himself adept at working within a "light" musical language. In the 1920s and '30s he often deployed this idiom while writing music for fourteen films. Indeed, his best-known composition from the 1930s was a foxtrot: the song "Baby, ach te Baby" (Girls, oh girls), sung by Eugeniusz Bodo in the 1933 film *Zabawka* (Just a toy), about a cabaret dancer and her amorous misadventures. Polish sound films of the 1930s often included songs written by light-music composers, the most prolific of whom was Henryk Wars.[47] Palester was working within this framework. Woven throughout the film, the song "Baby, ach te Baby" reveals that he understood the conventions of big band music and was willing to engage musically with the subject of the cabaret, one of the prime venues in which light music was created and performed.[48]

Rather than interpreting the contradiction between Palester's elitist views and cabaret-friendly music as hypocritical, it is more accurate to see it as outlining an intellectual and musical space between high and low

36 | Chapter 1

genres in which progressive composers could work. The composition that most clearly demonstrates Palester's comfort in this terrain is his 1935 *Mała uwertura na orkiestrę* (The little overture for orchestra).[49] Palester does not draw directly on elements of big band in the composition. Rather, the overture is characterized by an incessant forward-directed energy and propulsive dynamism that obscure aspects of the musical language that otherwise would have been tagged as modernist. Its clear, easily graspable orchestration also contributes to such an assessment: brief moments of seeming disorientation, most notably in the introductory phrase and the concluding section, give way to an orderly exposition of thematic material, such as the entrance of the main theme, given in the bassoon with banjo countermelody, as shown in example 1. The inclusion of the banjo, one of the most sonically striking aspects of the *Little Overture*, is doubtless a nod to American vernacular music.

Palester's colleagues in the progressive wing of the musical intelligentsia were primed to hear the work in terms of their commitment to socio-musical betterment. For Michał Kondracki, the *Little Overture* showed Palester searching for "the path and means for popularizing unpopular 'modernism' among a wider public," a mission that he believed the work easily fulfilled.[50] Régamey likewise praised the overture's fidelity to modernist concerns. "Despite a certain 'accessibility,' the work does not include anything cheap. . . . It is a popularization of modern music, but not a modernization of popular music."[51] Of course neither Palester's *Little Overture* nor these comments about it meant that the boundary between high and low musical genres had been eradicated, or even significantly lessened, in interwar Poland. Yet they do suggest how the intelligentsia's focus on social mission, alongside their awareness of the emergence of new forms of popular culture, could open a fecund cultural space in which to create new musical idioms. For at least some in the musical intelligentsia, progressive composition and modernism more broadly were not to be understood as rejections of contemporary taste, but rather as idioms capable of more fully realizing the social mandate that the musical intelligentsia had envisioned for itself. What resulted might be called, somewhat anachronistically, a search for a Polish compositional middlebrow. This aesthetic self-consciously prized listenability in ways that the musical intelligentsia hoped would mediate across a starkly hierarchical society without, however, dismantling this social hierarchy. The hope that the elite musical intelligentsia would create a truly popular modernism would be a lodestar as its members searched for relevance during and after the war.

EXAMPLE 1. Roman Palester, *Mała uwertura na orkiestrę* (The little overture for orchestra), mm. 4–10. Polskie Wydawnictwo Muzyczne.

38 | Chapter 1

MUSICOLOGY, SOCIAL THOUGHT, AND GENDER IN THE MUSICAL INTELLIGENTSIA

Of the many professional identities that together comprised the musical intelligentsia, musicology possessed a surprising centrality. Not just scholars or historians, musicologists such as Adolf Chybiński and Zofia Lissa shaped the institutions and politics of Polish new music across a period of decades. Indeed, it was often musicologists who arrived at the most imaginative accounts of musical culture. Musicology had been established as an academic discipline in Poland with the opening of musicology programs at universities in Austrian-ruled Poland, first by Zdzisław Jachimecki in 1911 in Cracow and then by Chybiński in 1912 in Lviv.[52] These programs, as well as the one opened in Poznań in 1919, trained dozens of students during the interwar years. For some musicologists, such as Chybiński, musicological research served a nationalist program: the discovery and publication of medieval and renaissance compositions from Polish archives, he believed, would help to legitimize Polish culture vis-à-vis that of other nations.[53] For other musicologists, the discipline was a space to explore, promote, and at times push beyond the assumptions of the musical intelligentsia. Often, the musicologists who developed the most interesting aesthetic and political positions were women.

That a handful of female musicologists could attain intellectual visibility within the musical intelligentsia reflected, at least in part, broader changes to the academic and social culture of interwar Poland. By the first decades of the twentieth century a full-blown feminist movement was underway, centered in Warsaw, which emphasized female education, employment, and equal rights.[54] Women gained the franchise in 1918, and the interwar years saw a proliferation of women's associations and social activism that often promoted ideas about social improvement and feminism simultaneously.[55] Within this environment composers such as Anna Maria Klechniowska, Helena Dorabialska, Władysława Markiewiczówna, and Ilza Sternicka Niekraszowa attracted the attention of the press.[56] Their music was performed at women's congresses and promoted as emblems of female progress in Poland.[57] At the same time, elite women in Poland were gaining greater access to higher education. Although Polish women had been traveling abroad for education since the late nineteenth century, in the 1920s and '30s they made up around a quarter of domestic university enrollments, and over half of all humanities students.[58] Similarly, in Poland's musicology programs

FIGURE 2. While the founders of Polish musicology were all men, women were prominent in the subsequent generations of scholars. Adolf Chybiński (left), founder of the Lviv musicology institute, with his students Maria Szczepańska (center left), Bronisława Wójcik-Keuprulian (center right), and Hieronim Feicht (right), circa 1925. BUP, Rkp802 II/2, karta 42.

women made up around a quarter to over half of all graduates; at the Jan Kazimierz University in Lviv, which had the highest number of female musicology graduates, thirteen of the twenty-two degrees in the discipline were earned by women.[59] Thus, while the founders of academic musicology in Poland were all men, the subsequent generations of Polish musicologists were significantly feminized.[60]

The star scholar of this second generation was Zofia Lissa. She was born in 1905 in Lviv to a family she described as "Polish of the faith of Moses," a phrase commonly used by acculturated Jews.[61] Her father was a professional photographer and her mother was an accomplished pianist. Educated under Chybiński, she departed sharply from her mentor's focus on early music to pursue topics of a contemporary bent. She described her "deepest" musical experiences as hearing Berg's *Wozzeck* and Schoenberg's *Verklärte Nacht*, compositions in which, she explained, "one's whole self resonates with that which flows toward us from the work."[62] Such sympathies are also evinced through the painstaking musical analyses in her 1929 dissertation, which argued that premonitions of twelve-tone technique could be discerned in Scriabin's harmonic language.[63] Her writings on atonality, polytonality, and twelve-tone

40 | Chapter 1

music were among the most in-depth considerations of these topics to be written in Polish between the wars.[64] Her exploration of these topics around 1930—perhaps prompted in part by her attendance at the 1928 ISCM festival in Siena, where Zemlinsky's String Quartet No. 3, op. 19, and Webern's String Trio, op. 20, had been raucously received—preceded by a half decade the extended polemics about twelve-tone technique in the pages of *Muzyka* and *Muzyka Polska*.[65]

Lissa maintained her modernist aesthetic commitments as her research expanded toward the sociology and psychology of music and, eventually, as she turned to political communism. Her early work brought an empirical and psychological lens to topics of musical education, which were of widespread interest in musical circles at the time.[66] This work gave way to a focus on the sociology of culture and an engagement with of-the-moment topics. In 1932, a mere six years after the Polish Radio began broadcasting, she wrote about the impact of radio on musical culture.[67] In 1937, she published a book on music and film, a topic rarely discussed in musicology at the time.[68] In it, she engaged with sound film at a time when Polish sound film had recently attained new sophistication and barely eight years after the first talking picture was premiered in Poland (*The Singing Fool*, screened in 1929).[69] By the late 1930s she was working as a courier and copyist for the Communist Party of Western Ukraine, which began her turn toward political communism.[70] Her thinking often brought a Marxist angle to well-established topics in Polish musical discourse. For instance, while many Polish commentators spoke of the need for improving the musicality of the "masses," Lissa argued that the inaccessibility of new music was an outcome of the class stratification of society and pointed to the need for the proletariat to create its own forms of musical culture.[71]

Lissa was not the only female musicologist to have leftist commitments. The musicologist Helena Dorabialska was an avowed socialist and the music critic for the Polish Socialist Party's daily, *Robotnik* (The worker), although her views on musical aesthetics were more conservative than Lissa's.[72] Stefania Łobaczewska, who had also trained in musicology in Lviv, shared Lissa's modernist proclivities, and her interest in popularizing musical culture was also wrapped up in her socialist sympathies.[73] She also saw Poland's female composers, performers, musicologists, and educators as playing a key role in pushing musical culture to reflect the "spirit of the present." The work of Polish women musicians, she declared, had "headed first and foremost in the direction of experimentation, placing the accent on the intellectual rather than emotional aspect."[74]

The scholarly fervor of interwar Poland's female musicologists, however, rarely translated into prestigious academic employment or influence over musical institutions. Although it was sometimes possible for women to gain temporary, assistant positions at universities (of which around 13 to 15 percent were held by women), they had less success at achieving the habilitation degree, which was needed to lecture at a university, much less at being appointed as professors.[75] Often the sexism of the interwar Polish academy was painfully personal. Chybiński, the head of the Lviv musicology institute, undermined the careers of some of the very women he had trained. He discouraged the editors of some of the most important Polish music periodicals from publishing Lissa's work (although this was also due to his antisemitism, to which I return in the next chapter). In 1933 he publicly accused Łobaczewska of lacking knowledge of medieval music, and he deployed a similar argument when refusing to support Bronisława Wójcik-Keuprulian's habilitation degree.[76] Even after Wójcik-Keuprulian did manage to receive her habilitation by pursuing it at a different university (an unusual step at the time), Chybiński continued to act against her. He was able to foil her ambitions of founding a musicology institute at the University of Warsaw by successfully elevating a younger and seemingly less-qualified male candidate for the position instead. "I—unfortunately—am *Mrs.* Keuprulian," she noted in a letter about the incident before explaining how she was told that Chybiński's chosen candidate was "dangerous competition for me because I have the misfortune of belonging to the lower sex."[77] She did eventually manage to lecture at the university level in Cracow, but she never became a professor or founded a musicology institute. Indeed, female leadership in Polish musicology only became a reality after World War II, when Lissa and Łobaczewska received their habilitation degrees and Lissa founded what would become the Warsaw Institute of Musicology in 1948. (Wójcik-Keuprulian had died in 1938.)

IN SEARCH OF JEWISH MUSIC

As I discussed in the introduction, more and more Jews were understanding themselves to be Polish during the interwar years, at the same time that more and more Poles were treating the same people as anything but. The simultaneous growth in acculturation and antisemitism was strongly felt in the musical intelligentsia. Not only were Polish Jews particularly active in the concert hall, but modern antisemitism struck

42 | Chapter 1

at deep connections between Jewish acculturation and concert music that had developed since the late nineteenth century.

Consider the Warsaw Philharmonic. It had been founded (in part) by prominent Polish Jews, between a quarter to a third of its musicians were Jewish (see figure 3), and Jews frequently attended its performances.[78] In his memoirs published in 1933, Leopold Julian Kronenberg, a founder of the philharmonic of Jewish background, noted, "In Poland, the most numerous amateurs and lovers of music were (and are) Jews; and they also entirely filled the hall of the philharmonic."[79] This gave them a certain amount of clout, Kronenberg explained, which they used to boycott the institution in 1911: Grzegorz Fitelberg, himself a baptized Jew, caved to pressure from the right-wing National Democrats, who claimed that there were too many Jews in the ensemble, by dismissing many Jewish musicians from it. The abysmal concert attendance prompted by the boycott forced Fitelberg to be replaced by Zdzisław Birnbaum, also of Jewish background, who hired more Jewish personnel. According to Kronenberg's dispassionate recounting, "there thus arose a situation that perhaps has existed nowhere else: a religious matter determined the success or failure of such a cultural institution."[80]

By the 1930s, claims about the deficient status of Poland's musical culture were ubiquitous across the musical intelligentsia irrespective of political orientation, but not all viewed the roots of this problem in the same way. For some, the problems with Polish musical culture could be attributed, at least in part, to the role that Jews had played in creating it over the prior decades. For instance, the composer and critic Jan Maklakiewicz quipped about the "complete indifference of Polish society" to classical music and declared that "Jewish musical spheres support only their own artists," implying not only that "Polish" and "Jewish" were mutually exclusive categories but that Jews possessed a solidarity lacking among Poles.[81]

It can be tempting to filter antisemitism through the lens of compositional aesthetics. Since antisemitism was common among those supporting conservative, right-wing politics it might seem logical that it was also widely endorsed by aesthetically conservative composers. To be sure, Piotr Rytel, the most prominent of the aesthetically conservative composers, was also among the most antisemitic. He was aligned with the right-wing National Democrats and was the music critic for the *Gazeta Warszawska* (Warsaw gazette), a National Democratic paper, for which he wrote reviews drenched in vile antisemitic tropes.[82] But antisemitism was also at home in the "progressive" wing of the

FIGURE 3. A composite photograph of the musicians of the Warsaw Philharmonic, created in 1931 to celebrate the thirtieth anniversary of the founding of the institution. The exterior and interior of the hall are visible and portraits of individual musicians fill out the space. USHMM, Photograph Number 29425.

musical intelligentsia, which championed musical modernism. Szymanowski, the leader of the progressive group (and Rytel's archenemy), subscribed to disturbing views about Jews. In an unpublished essay titled "The Jewish Question" from 1922, he claimed to reject all forms of "ideological or merely political antisemitism," but he also considered the "question of the racial origins of artists to be a matter of first importance." Further, he endorsed the idea that Jewish musicality was rote and derivative: "Only the *Aryan genius* has discovered new terrain that has yet to be examined, whereas Semitic *talents* have exploited this terrain in a more or less worthwhile manner."[83]

Nor was Szymanowski an exception. The music critic Jerzy Waldorff, pictured in figure 1, weighed in repeatedly in favor of modernist composition and vehemently attacked Rytel on aesthetic grounds, all while penning ominous invectives about the "complete creative impotence at

44 | Chapter 1

the very foundations of the Jewish psyche."[84] The aesthetically progressive periodical *Muzyka Polska* (Polish music) published reviews replete with anti-Jewish prejudice while expunging Jewish names from its pages (discussed in greater detail in chapter 2). A 1935 review of performances at the Warsaw Philharmonic by Jascha Horenstein, a renowned conductor of Jewish background who had been expelled from Nazi Germany, noted that "the bizarre movements and cheap tricks of Horenstein will perhaps please unrefined listeners from vicinity of Nalewki Street"—a major Jewish thoroughfare in Warsaw—"but judging from the reports in the press, he also delighted our so-called music critics."[85] The anonymous critic here telegraphs well-established caricatures of Jewish musicality as superficial and unrefined, which are applied equally to Horenstein as to the audience he attracted.[86] While the critic implicitly delineates Polish ("our") critics from the Jewish conductor and audience, he also uses the trope of Jewish unmusicality as a cudgel against these Polish critics (that is, the "so-called" critics). The subtext of this claim is that the purported weakness of Jewishness has also infiltrated Polish musical culture, undermining it from within.

At the same time that some Poles were attempting to excise Jewishness from Polish musical culture, Polish Jewish intellectuals were exploring a widening range of Jewish identities in music. Although the majority of Jewish members of the musical intelligentsia were acculturated (and some had converted), this did not mean that Jewishness was irrelevant to them. Indeed, in interwar Poland a substantial minority of Polish Jews embraced both Polish language and culture and a Jewish sense of self, as the robust circulation of Polish-language daily papers aimed at a Jewish readership, such as *Chwila* (The moment) or *Nasz Przegląd* (Our review), makes clear.[87] At the same time, the ideas of the "new Jewish politics," movements such as Zionism and Bundism (a socialist, mass labor movement that valued secular Yiddish culture), encouraged Jews to understand Jewishness as based on "peoplehood," or ethnic belonging.[88] The intersection of these trends—namely, increasing acculturation, the rise of modern antisemitism, and new models of Jewish peoplehood—underwrote discussions among Polish Jews about the future of Jewish music.

For some, such as the critic, editor, and conductor Mateusz Gliński, highlighting the Jewishness of musicians was less of a priority than seamlessly integrating them into the intelligentsia-led project of cultural betterment in Poland. He endorsed values typical of the musical intelligentsia when founding his periodical *Muzyka* (Music) in 1924, which

FIGURE 4. Mateusz Gliński's periodical *Muzyka* sought to build connections to western Europe and to integrate Polish new music into wider orbits. Here, Gliński (far left) welcomes the French musicologist Édouard Ganche (center) to the periodical's office in Warsaw in 1927. Ganche is flanked by luminaries of Polish new music: Ludomir Różycki (center left), Karol Szymanowski (center right), and the pianist Zbigniew Drzewiecki (far right). Narodowe Archiwum Cyfrowe.

he modeled on periodicals such as the French *Signale* and *Courrier musical*: he aimed at nothing less that "the awakening and fueling of a healthy musical instinct, a fight with analphabetism and disorientation in the field of music"—all to be accomplished by publishing accessible yet well-informed articles about classical music.[89] Indeed, he initially conceived of the journal as the unofficial mouthpiece of the Polish section of the International Society for Contemporary Music (ISCM), which had been founded in 1924 with Szymanowski as its president and Gliński its secretary.[90] As such, *Muzyka* was not only to develop audiences, but also to place Polish composition into broader European conversations. Gliński solicited essays about the state of musical culture in Poland from prominent Polish Jewish composers, such as Aleksander Tansman and Józef Koffler, something that *Muzyka*'s competitor—*Muzyka Polska*—did not.[91] Although he was certainly aware of these contributors' Jewishness, he did not identify them as Jewish on *Muzyka*'s pages and remained focused instead on their contributions to Polish (and, indeed, European) musical culture.

46 | Chapter 1

Others highlighted Jewish identities while emphasizing the role of Jews in creating local, Polish, and European musical culture. Alfred Plohn's 1936 article "Music in Lviv and Jews," for instance, presented a seemingly boundless list of Jewish musicians who partook in nearly every aspect of the city's musical life over the preceding century.[92] To some degree, Plohn's focus on how Jewish musicians built the musical culture of Lviv reflected the well-established idea that classical music was an avenue of Jewish acculturation.[93] For other writers engaging in similar projects, however, the focus on the successes of Jewish musicians was an urgent refutation of antisemitic claims that Jewish artistic culture was vacuous. Artur Mehrer's tributes to the composers Jacques Halvéy and Georges Bizet in *Nasza Opinja*, for example, were intended to "give the lie to the assertion made by enemies of Jewry that among Jews there are only performers and not original composers."[94]

If musicians such as Gliński and Plohn implicitly celebrated integration and acculturation, others saw the historical arc of Jewish music making as pointing toward the creation of a distinctly Jewish musical style. Among the thinkers to most fully explore this position in Polish was the musicologist Józef Reiss, who in a 1928 essay titled "The Soul of Jewry in Music" declared that the compositions of the Jewish composer should be "based on a national foundation" so that "his music will be a manifestation of the national soul," thereby asserting that Jewishness was a national identity that should form the basis for art-music composition.[95] A Jewish national music, Reiss believed, should be based on Jewish scales and folk sources. The model for such music, he believed, had been provided by composers such as Joel Engel, Mikhail Gnessin, and others who had been associated with the Society for Jewish Folk Music, founded in St. Petersburg in 1908. These composers had taken the idea, common throughout the late nineteenth century, that a "national music" could be created through the synthesis of folk and art music and extrapolated it to Jewish music and nationhood; they had collected Jewish folk music and transformed it into compositions for the concert hall.[96] The ideas of the Society for Jewish Folk Music resonated in interwar Poland, not only as evinced in Reiss's essay, but also through the founding of several associations modeled on it, including the Warsaw-based Society for the Promotion of Jewish Music (Towarzystwo Krzewienia Muzyki Żydowskiej), founded in 1928, and the Cracow-based Jewish Music Society (Żydowskie Towarzystwo Muzyczne), founded in 1930.[97] These organizations brought works of Russian Jewish composers to audiences in Poland and aimed to cultivate a sense of distinctly Jewish cultural identity among audiences who were mostly acculturated, committed to European high art, and Polish speaking.[98]

In addition to endorsing a turn toward the Jewish folk, Reiss's essay partook in a longer intellectual tradition in which antisemitic ideas about Jewish distinctiveness were reinterpreted as evidence of Jewish nationhood, understood in a positive sense.[99] Reiss saw the rise of antisemitism in the nineteenth century as having prompted a renewal of Jewish composition since it forced Jews to confront their purportedly inherent distinctiveness from other Europeans. Likely influenced by the ideas of scholars such as Lazare Saminsky and Abraham Tzvi Idelsohn, Reiss gave Richard Wagner's antisemitic screed "Das Judenthum in der Musik" (originally published in 1850 and reissued in 1869) a central role in his narrative.[100] Wagner's polemic, he believed, had "awakened creative strengths that previously had lain dormant in the soul of Jewry, muffled by the influence of foreign culture," as he cast doubt on the possibility or desirability of Jewish assimilation through music.[101] Indeed, both the idea of Jews as forming a "nation" and a "race" play a leading role in Reiss's essay, although what he means by these words is not entirely clear: "Where there is no national consciousness, where there is no feeling of race, artistic work will always be cold, cut off from life," he cautioned.[102]

Those who shared this view of a new Jewish music saw Poland as one node within a transnational network of musicians that stretched from Moscow to New York and who were working to revitalize—if not to create outright—Jewish musical culture. This network is perhaps best exemplified by the composer and piano virtuoso Juliusz Wolfsohn. Born in Warsaw in 1880, he trained at the Moscow and Warsaw conservatories before settling in Vienna and establishing himself as a leading virtuoso and interpreter of Chopin.[103] In 1928 he became a founding member of the Vienna-based Society for the Promotion of Jewish Music (Verein zur Förderung jüdischer Musik), and he committed himself to cultivating a sense of distinctly Jewish music—to the "cultivation of *Jewish music* and not the works of Jewish musicians," he explained.[104]

In a manner redolent of the ideas endorsed by Reiss and Reiss's Russian Jewish models, Wolfssohn's compositions interlaced Jewish folk and dance music—described in an exoticizing manner by the Viennese press as the music of the "*Ostjuden*" or "East Jews"—into virtuosic paraphrases typical of early twentieth-century pianist-composers. His *Hebrew Suite*, op. 8 (1926), which he often performed in a now-lost orchestral version, frames Jewish folk materials in a variety of virtuosic

48 | Chapter 1

textures, for instance. As an admired virtuoso, Wolfsohn had a platform to promote his vision of Jewish music by combining performances of canonic works, such as the Chopin piano concertos, with his own Jewish-themed compositions.[105] In Poland he was the star attraction of a concert of the Jewish Music Society in Cracow in 1930, held in the city's Old Theater, where he played the *Hebrew Suite* in a performance that "fascinated both the Jewish and non-Jewish members of the audience."[106] In 1933, he gave lectures in Warsaw on the "New Jewish Music," illustrated with his own compositions.[107]

The various approaches toward Jewishness that I have discussed were neither static nor uncontested. For some, the salience of Jewishness changed in response to the increasingly anti-Jewish environment of the 1930s. For instance, while Gliński had attempted to focus on building Polish culture in the 1920s while ignoring ad hominem attacks against him, he acknowledged in his memoirs that this broader context spelled the downfall of the journal *Muzyka*. Even writing decades later while living in Canada, he went out of his way to avoid blaming his colleagues for their prejudices, instead painting antisemitism as an essentially non-Polish phenomenon: "From Poland's western border [that is to say, Nazi Germany] ultra-chauvinistic and fascist-racist tendencies permeated into Poland," where they were "systematically instilled in artistic life," leading in part to "*Muzyka* finding itself on the 'index' of [the two major] state authorities," he wrote. "Looking soberly at the political situation and foreseeing the coming catastrophe [of the war], I understood that fighting to defend *Muzyka* had become increasingly pointless."[108]

In other cases, disagreements about the best way to support Jewish music pivoted on how Jewishness was to be defined in the first place. In 1936, for instance, the Jewish Artistic-Literary Society in Lviv organized a concert of Jewish performers who played a variety of classical compositions not by Jewish composers. The group believed that they were responding to the reality that "not all Jewish musicians have the possibility of full and free artistic fulfillment" in other venues, likely an allusion to the discrimination they faced.[109] This approach was met by a vociferous response from Józef Koffler, a composer and the Polish representative on the Advisory Council for the World Centre for Jewish Music.[110] He asserted that "on the Jewish concert not a single work of a Jewish composer was performed, and not one specifically Jewish composer, such as Engel, Weprik, or others was heard," evoking again the Russian Jewish composers associated with the Society for Jewish Folk Music.[111] The polemic thus recapitulated the central dynamic among the Polish Jewish musical intelligentsia: was Jewishness to be understood as an incidental part of an artist's identity, or, rather, was Jewishness the foundation on which a new music ought to be built?

THE SOCIALITIES OF MUSICAL LEADERSHIP

The musical intelligentsia cannot be divorced from powerful ideas about social hierarchy, nation, Jewishness, and gender in interwar Poland. Its members sought to interpret their commitments to contemporary classical music through the lens of nation and service, turning to the inherited legacy of the intelligentsia as a source of musical identity. While this sense of elite leadership was the common denominator among members of the musical intelligentsia, they subscribed to diverse and contentious views about the future of music in Poland. There was little agreement about aesthetics, as the conflict between "progressives" and "conservatives" suggests, nor about "light music," nor even about the boundaries of belonging and exclusion within Polish nationhood itself. Despite these fractures, the musical intelligentsia's hierarchical imagination would prove to be powerful. Its ideas about leadership and action were not only theoretical conceits but also provided the groundwork for forming institutions that shaped and supported Polish musical life, animating its concert halls, professional unions, publishing houses, and journals. Turning from the intellectual and social worlds of the intelligentsia to the interpersonal networks and organizations its members built, we will see how they attempted to enact their ideas of national leadership in ways reflective of the fissures that defined their milieu. These organizations—along with the dreams and prejudices of their creators—would, in some cases, persist long after the demise of the Second Republic.

2

A Civil Society for Music

To survey interwar Poland's musical life is to be confronted with a seemingly endless patchwork of musical organizations. These small self-governing groups—known as "associations" (*stowarzyszenia*) or "societies" (*towarzystwa*)—aimed to advance a wide slate of cultural, political, and economic aims that their members endorsed, from improving local concert life, to organizing amateur performances, to training musicians, to advancing the economic interests of professionals. Indicative of the scale of such organizing, the historian Sylwia Jakubczyk-Ślęczka has identified nearly eighty Jewish musical associations in the region of Galicia alone—a tally that includes neither the dozens of non-Jewish musical organizations in Galicia nor the hundreds of musical organizations, Jewish and otherwise, that were active elsewhere in Poland.[1] These organizations could range in size from a few dozen to a few hundred active members, who paid modest monthly membership dues.[2] Some, such as the Polish Music Society (founded in 1838 in Lviv as the Gesellschaft zur Beförderung der Musik in Galizien) and the Warsaw Music Society (founded in 1871), had roots stretching back decades, while others had been established more recently.[3] Their ubiquity suggests that small-scale organizing was the engine driving the fragmented, localized musical life of interwar Poland. Founding a musical society or association was often the most feasible path to enacting a vision of leadership and musical progress core to the musical intelligentsia.

50

Together, these associations formed a vibrant civil society organized around music. The topic of civil society, or the body of institutions that exist independently of the state, has attracted a great deal of attention from scholars and activists concerned with Poland's political trajectory throughout the twentieth century. The focus of such commentary has usually fallen on the Polish People's Republic (1952–89) and on whether this unpopular, authoritarian regime created a "social vacuum" in which a chasm separated individuals and their kinship circles from the institutions of the state, with which Poles rarely identified.[4] Civil society, however, looked very different in the 1930s, 1940s, and even the early 1950s from the point of view of the musical intelligentsia. They had an abiding faith in the creation of institutions, whether independent or state backed. In the interwar years they founded these associations on a wide scale. During the occupation of World War II, some of these same institutions were retooled, becoming spaces of refuge that promised to preserve musical culture until peacetime. After the war, these activists and a few of their projects became integrated into the postwar state, enjoying the support and prestige of which their leaders had only dreamed in the 1930s. While the musical institutions of the postwar years were not a mirror image of the interwar years, they did have roots in the people and practices of that earlier period.

I tell this longer story of growth and adaptation in chapters 3 and 6. For now, suffice to say that evaluating continuity and change in musical institutions across the war requires treating them not as bounded, named entities, but rather as their organizers and leaders saw them: as sites of social investment, where friendships and professional relations coalesced around a shared set of ideas and debates. Polish musical institutions of the midcentury were nodes within the musical intelligentsia, formalized structures that helped to solidify a social circle around a shared purpose. The fact that they were small and closely tied to their members' viewpoints afforded these projects resilience, enabling them to survive as long as their core members did.

This chapter examines the interpersonal dynamics and cultural ideologies driving some of the most important musical organizations of interwar Poland. I treat these organizations as what the sociologist Karl Mannheim has termed "generational units," that is to say, groups within the young generation of the musical intelligentsia whose members "work[ed] up the material of their common experience in different specific ways."[5] Broadly understood, these groups partook in what Lisa Cooper Vest has described as the intertwined impulses of "modernism"

52 | Chapter 2

and "modernization" in Polish music, in which aesthetic concerns for innovation helped to reinforce the imperative of building musical culture from the ground up.[6] The Association of Young Musician-Poles in Paris aimed to facilitate Polish composers and classical performers studying in Paris, contending that Polish music required exposure to western Europe to grow, while the Polish Music Publishing Society and the Organization for Musical Culture both focused on building audiences within Poland's border. While these three organizations had different aims, they also had overlapping memberships drawn from the progressive musical intelligentsia and held a shared commitment to the edification of Poland's musical culture.

The members of these organizations contested not only how to modernize Poland musically, but also whose artistic expressions and organizational acumen should be endowed with national significance in the first place. The idea of a French-Polish musical synthesis evoked an essentialist, racialized notion of Polishness, which cast Polish Jews as racially other and thus undermined the legitimacy of acculturated Polish Jews in the creation of Polish modernism. Other associations attacked Jewish musicians and excluded them from the project of musical modernization. By the late 1930s, calls for the organization and rationalization of Polish musical life among the musical intelligentsia took on an increasingly right-wing tone, as some Polish musicians openly supported fascist and totalitarian arts policy. Thus, on the eve of World War II, the musical intelligentsia's aims of organizing musical culture became compatible with the idea of a centralized, powerful state, which some of them envisioned as enacting an ethnonationalist conception of Polishness.

NATION AND RACE, AT HOME AND ABROAD

By the mid-1920s, Paris had emerged as the epicenter of Polish musical modernism.[7] Dozens of composers and classical performers arrived in the city for stays that ranged in length from a few months, to several years, to, in a handful of cases, permanent immigration. The main institution that supported Polish musical studies and travels to Paris was the Association of Young Musician-Poles in Paris (Stowarzyszenie Młodych Muzyków Polaków w Paryżu).[8] Founded in late 1926 by the composer Piotr Perkowski, it grew from 37 members at its founding to 111 members by the end of 1935 (and remained active, albeit at a reduced scale, until 1950). It helped to facilitate studies abroad, provided introductions for

EXAMPLE 2. Grażyna Bacewicz, Trio for oboe, violin, and cello, mm. 70–79. Polskie Wydawnictwo Muzyczne.

recently arrived students, organized concerts, and even offered loans to struggling students, many of whom lived together in a single dormitory.⁹ Many of the most prominent members—including Bolesław Woytowicz, Zygmunt Mycielski, Grażyna Bacewicz, and Tadeusz Szeligowski— studied with the renowned pedagogue Nadia Boulanger and would go on to have major careers in Poland.¹⁰

For the composer Grażyna Bacewicz, studies in Paris portended an escape from Warsaw's dated aesthetic dichotomies and a discovery of new potentials within the vast category of contemporary composition. "Paris is an ideal city for work," she explained in a 1935 interview, whereas in Warsaw, she said, "the atmosphere is not conducive to

54 | Chapter 2

work—rumors, envy."[11] Her Trio for oboe, violin, and cello, premiered in 1936, reflected the sense of expansion and musical discovery that she saw in Paris. The first movement is a compact exercise in contrast and synthesis between the material presented in the freely meandering oboe melody of the opening and passagework that by this period was associated with a neoclassical aesthetic. It is replete with quasi-baroque gestures, usually presented in sequential or stepwise patterns. In line with a modernist reimagination of baroque grammar, however, this material also at times spins out of control, seeming to unexpectedly pause the musical discourse, as shown in example 2.

Grounded within the compositional techniques of the neoclassical style, works such as Bacewicz's were interpreted by critics in Poland as part of a developing style that was both grounded in Poland and partaking in European modernism beyond the country's borders. The musicologist Zofia Helman has observed that the neoclassic aesthetic offered Polish composers an alternative to the late romantic styles of "conservative" composers, who continued to hold sway in Poland's conservatories and concert halls.[12] Yet progressive composers and critics did not necessarily see the neoclassical idiom as tantamount to a full-scale rejection of the traits of romanticism. In 1928, for instance, the composer Tadeusz Marek claimed that it was "entirely possible to share the views of neoclassicism, aspiring to 'absolute,' clear musical content," yet also "to draw from sources that reflect subjective experience" in ways he believed were typical of romanticism.[13] The emphasis on the expressive and subjective remained a core aspect of the reception of neoclassicism during the 1930s in Poland. In reviewing Bacewicz's trio, for instance, the composer Michał Kondracki heard in it not only "freshness of invention" but also an "engaging honesty of expression."[14] For Régamey, the focus on expression among Polish composers by the late 1930s—what he termed the "emotional potential" in their works—had helped to rework neoclassicism into a new "Polish style," which he described as a "new romanticism that is free from pathos, immeasurably discrete, and almost wholly uses classical phrasing."[15] This link between Polish compositional style and emotional expressivity would remain a core theme of musical aesthetics shortly after the war in Poland and would resonate into the Polish avant-garde as well.[16] The coding of emotion in national terms also reveals that while neoclassic composition is sometimes considered a "universal" style—what Richard Taruskin termed a "musical Esperanto"—the aesthetic still coursed with nationalized investments.[17]

The alacrity with which Poland's musicians traveled to Paris in the 1920s and 1930s was underwritten by the conviction that it was here that a synthesis between the "national" and the "universal" could be carried out. This idea had been popularized by the composer Karol Szymanowski, who encouraged young composers to travel to Paris and had constructed a myth that contemporary Polish composition ought to take up where Fryderyk Chopin had left off a century prior: "Let [our music] be 'national' in its racial identity, yet let it aspire without fear for its values to become universal [ogólnoludzkimi]; let it be 'national' but not 'provincial.' . . . Let all of the currents arising from universal art also run freely through our [art]. . . . We should not lose the organic ties with universal culture, because only on this level can significant, great art grow, and thus national music. And we possessed this once—formerly—in the work of Fryderyk Chopin."[18] These were exciting words for dozens of young Polish composers because they authorized them to take seriously European-wide trends without forfeiting their investments in national identity. Indeed, a major appeal of Szymanowski's ideas lay in their aesthetic flexibility. He did not insist on a rigid set of compositional criteria through which the "universal" and "national" were to be reconciled, but rather he established discursive parameters with which composers might engage.

Even as he argued for a liberal vision of Polishness that could embrace a wide range of influences, his ideas were shot through with a racial imagination. In interwar Europe "race" was frequently used to describe European groups, and national-racial epithets such as the "Polish race" or "French race" were common in nonscholarly discourse. These existed alongside scientific attempts at racial-biological classification, which flourished in interwar Polish anthropology.[19] It is tempting to describe Szymanowski's racial terminology as a rhetorical flourish, an embellishment on the perhaps more comfortable terminology of "nation" that he also used.[20] But this is to misread an important part of his project and, indeed, an important aspect of Polish musical discourse of the interwar years: namely, that appeals to "race" could anchor discourse of nationhood. Broadly speaking, race could provide a political justification for the existence of nation by positing the inherent physical and intellectual qualities of "the people," which purportedly informed their heritage, customs, and even psychology and thus nationhood.[21] And, indeed, in Szymanowski's writing, race often serves to underscore the innate and inherited qualities of national expression in music. "Musical creation is too directly connected with the individual qualities of the artist for it

FIGURE 5. Poland's modernist composers saw themselves as following in the footsteps of Fryderyk Chopin, who had emigrated to Paris about a century prior. Here, the composer Piotr Perkowski, the founder of the Association of Young Musician-Poles in Paris, lays a wreath on Chopin's grave in Père Lachaise Cemetery in Paris in 1929. Narodowe Archiwum Cyfrowe.

not in the end to be based on his racial foundation," he asserted.[22] In other moments, "race" underscored the historical depth and timelessness of Polishness, such as when he asserted that Chopin "instinctively aspired to a super-historical perspective, so to speak, one that expressed the depths of his race."[23]

For members of the Association of Young Musician-Poles in Paris, the idea that Polishness was an inherent racial quality could strengthen the argument that their organization could serve the nation at home and abroad. Note how Zygmunt Mycielski, who studied in Paris between 1928 to 1936, endorsed a similar idea of race as national essence when justifying the association's existence to a Polish readership: "An over century-old tradition demonstrates to us that true talent only profits from contact with western culture. The greatest masters of central Europe searched for this contact. Goethe and Chopin, Wagner and Stravinsky did not lose their racial qualities in Paris or Italy. To date, there has never existed an artist without influences or tradition. What matters is the choice of this environment. We believe that basing Polish music with one leg in Paris will only benefit it. Such is, in a few words, the genesis of the association and the reason for its existence."[24] In Mycielski's view, race underlies national-universal synthesis, guaranteeing that individuals will not lose their sense of national distinctiveness even as they take on influence from western Europe. The concept of race thus allowed him to endorse western Europe as the center of musical culture with which Poles must engage while also implying that the Polishness of those traveling abroad would remain unimpeachable.

Others sought to justify the focus on France by asserting that both France and Poland partook of a shared "Latin culture." In the manifesto of the Association of Young Musician-Poles in Paris, its members declared that their aim was to "establish close contact with Latin culture" while distinguishing themselves from the "prewar generation of musicians, who were educated chiefly in Germany."[25] Feliks Łabuński, then the association's president, made a similar point, claiming that "for a long time, the voice of our great bard [Chopin] remained without an echo, and the ensuing generations of Polish musicians directed themselves to other musical centers of Europe, to environments that are more foreign to us than France and Latin culture."[26] Mateusz Gliński echoed this idea, albeit in different terms, when in an article on the association and French influences on Polish music, he asked rhetorically if "it was necessary to prove that Gallic ideology, tied inextricably to the collective psyche of the French nation, is closer to our emotional tendencies and tastes than the German style?"[27]

These evocations of "Latin" culture certainly reflected a desire to move beyond the influence of partition-era cultural politics by finding a point of reference free from associations with German, Austrian, or Russian rule. It was especially convenient, in this regard, that French music critics had already been evoking the "Latinism" of French composition in an effort to distinguish it from German composition, an idea that Polish commentators adopted with ease.[28] More ominously, the idea of defining Poland as a "Latin" country had resonances with various forms of right-wing politics. In Poland, the historian-philosopher Feliks Koneczny had influentially theorized Poland as a bulwark of "Latin civilization"—by which he meant it was an essentially Catholic nation—while denigrating "Jewish civilization" as inferior and a baleful influence on Poland.[29] The term also had resonance on the French right, where writers such as Charles Maurras and Maurice Barrès used it to evoke an unbroken civilizational continuity between modern France and the classical world, intending in this manner to excise the influx of foreigners that had begun in earnest in France during the nineteenth century.[30] The term had also been used in debates concerning the desirability of different immigrant groups to France, a context Polish musicians in France would have doubtless understood. Within these discussions, Poles were often seen as the most "Latin" of the Slavs. "Latinness" implied not only cultural affinity to France, but also an ability to partake in the French national and racial project.[31] The use of this term in Polish musical discourse thus argued for Franco-Polish affinity by insinuating that Poland was a Catholic nation, at the expense of the religious and ethnic diversity that in fact characterized the Polish Second Republic.

While evoking ideologies of race and Latin culture to justify the significance of Paris for Polish new music, the association also underscored that its ultimate objective was the transfer of musical innovations back to Poland. As its members wrote in 1930, "we feel that we are a part of [Polish] society; we are not, after all, emigrants. Each of us remembers the fact that there will come a moment when we will be obligated to return to Poland in order to display the benefits that were attained abroad, and to transplant them onto Polish ground."[32] The assertation that not all members intended to emigrate was an exaggeration (Antoni Szałowski, Michał Spisak, and Szymon Laks all remained more or less permanently in Paris). But by describing themselves as non-emigrants, the members differentiated the association from the influx of hundreds of thousands of working-class Polish emigrants to France, as well from the numerous Russian émigrés who had made Paris their home after the revolution.[33] Such rhetoric also underscored that the success of the association and its members had to be evaluated in terms of their impact on Polish musical culture at home. The international project of the association was to be measured with the yardstick of domestic progress.

The notions of the "Polish race" and a Catholic-centered "Latin culture" that coursed beneath the surface of Franco-Polish musical synthesis also suggested that non-Catholics and those outside the "Polish race" could not engage fully in such synthesis. This was the message conveyed by one reaction to a 1928 competition hosted by the Association of Young Musician-Poles in Paris. The competition was open to all Polish citizens, and the entries were anonymously judged by a prestigious panel consisting of Maurice Ravel, Albert Roussel, Florent Schmitt, and Arthur Honegger, who awarded several prizes to Poles of Jewish background. An anonymous writer in the Poznań-based *Przegląd Muzyczny* exclaimed in response, "A shadow, however, clouds the bright fact of this accomplishment, a shadow that perhaps not all can

FIGURE 6. Studies in Paris could lead to lifelong friendships, such as that between Zygmunt Mycielski (left) and his composition teacher Nadia Boulanger, pictured here during her visit to the Union of Polish Composers in Warsaw in December 1967. Tadeusz Marek (Żakiej) looks on from the center. Photo by Andrzej Zborski, from the Archive of the Polish Composers' Union/POLMIC.

perceive. This shadow is the surnames: in the first column [of winners] we have the names of Fitelberg, Kassern, Lachs [sic], while in the second we find Kondracki, Wiechowicz, and Jarecki. This opposition speaks for itself. All of these composers are Poles, but not, however, of the same race.... Young, *ethnically Polish* composers should draw from this fact the appropriate conclusions and take to heart this shameful defeat."[34] In this instance, race divides Polish new music, excising Polish Jewish composers from the national project while simultaneously suggesting that "ethnically Polish" composers had been defeated by their purportedly inferior counterparts.

Other commentators attempted to draw a clear distinction between the Franco-Polish synthesis carried out by "truly" Polish composers and that executed by Polish Jewish ones. While the former could be seen as drawing from abroad while maintaining their inherent national qualities, the latter were at times cast as losing all national footing, falling into a kind of unrooted cosmopolitanism. In the very same article in which Régamey praised an emerging Polish style that had synthesized French elements, he dismissed the composer who had arguably had

60 | Chapter 2

some of the greatest international success in so doing: Aleksander Tansman. Tansman had moved to Paris in 1919 and found success thanks to the support of Maurice Ravel. In 1927 he wrote that he wished his compositions to display a "marvelous synthesis of Polish sensibility filtered through French clarity and moderation," which he believed Chopin had accomplished nearly a century earlier.[35] According to the exhaustive research of Renata Suchowiejko, Tansman was perhaps the most important promoter of Polish music in the French press during the 1920s, garnering more attention from French critics that the association did.[36]

Despite this, Régamey dismissed Tansman as an "artist absorbing in his works almost all the spoils of new European music." Due to this supposed eclecticism, Tansman was unable to fulfill the role of an "intermediary between Polish and European music," Régamey asserted, because he "brings no original values" to his works, yielding instead to "affectedness and cheap flashiness."[37] Such views partake in a long history of dismissing Jewish musicality as superficial and uninspired, and they are all the more striking because of the similarity of Tansman's aesthetics to the works that Régamey had chosen to celebrate. That Régamey had to begin his essay with an elaborate dismissal of Tansman (whom he also acknowledged was the most internationally successful Polish composer after Szymanowski) in order to arrive at his claims of synthesized, Franco-Polish music makes evident his insecurity about who could belong to the Polish nation in the first place. Nor, according to Tansman's memoirs, was this the only attack to which he had been subjected in Poland. "The [Polish] press was unleashed on me, with racist allusions in each article. And yet, rightly or wrongly, no composer since Chopin had done as much to promote Poland as I had. . . . But the sonority of my name, which does not end in '-ski' or '-itch,' humiliated my compatriots in a manner that is difficult to understand in the West."[38]

The musicologist Stefania Łobaczewska extended this race-based categorization of positive and negative internationalism in an article that implicitly segregated Polish composition along the lines of Jewish heritage. In one group she lumps together Tansman, Koffler, Rathaus, Jerzy Fitelberg, and Palester, and claims that they reject the influence of the "Polish milieu or Polish nationality," while denigrating Tansman as reliant on "rhythmic schemata" and Fitelberg as possessing the "personality of an essentially international type." She then contrasts these Polish Jewish composers with non-Jewish Poles studying or composing abroad. Woytowicz, for instance, possessed in her view a "typically Slavic physiognomy, a Polish physiognomy, whose lyricism always searches for its own means of expression," a quality that was only heightened by his extensive studies in Paris.[39]

A racialized understanding of Polishness led other commentators to assert that Polish Jewish composers living abroad ceased to have any legitimate connection to Poland at all. Zdzisław Jachimecki, a musicology professor at the Jagiellonian University in Cracow, grouped Polish Jewish composers into a single category, overlooking their considerable stylistic differences, only to dismiss their claims of Polishness wholesale: "In the group of composers that consists of Rathaus, Tansman, Klecki, Gradstein, Jerzy Fitelberg, and Koffler, strong progressive tendencies are evident, which arise from intersecting influences of the Russian, German, and French schools. With the exception of Koffler, all of these composers are permanently living abroad. They underscore, either resolutely or more delicately, their affiliation with Poland, whether because they happened to have been born on the territory of Poland or out of a feeling of Polishness. However, their activities are connected more strongly with every other musical culture than with that of Poland."[40] Recycling the trope of the Jew as rootless cosmopolitan, Jachimecki here reduces the composers' connections to Poland to a mere subjective feeling or to accidents of happenstance.

What is particularly noteworthy in these examples is how even a liberal discourse about culture building through international exchange could have embedded within it an essentialist notion of a racial Polishness. There certainly were more virulent instances of right-wing and antisemitic thought at the time, some of which we will encounter below. Yet the discourse surrounding interwar musical internationalism in Poland shows how the idea of inherited, essential national qualities guided and impinged on interwar projects. In Szymanowski's vision of Chopin's synthesis of the national and universal, the concept of a deeply engrained, racial Polishness purportedly provided Poles with the ability to aspire to the "universal" and allowed them to advance the national cause irrespective of how geographically distant they were from Poland. It is also racial thinking, however, that underwrote descriptions of Polish Jewish composers as incapable of such synthesis and as inherently susceptible to unrooted imitation.

INSTITUTIONALIZING ANTISEMITISM

The second major institution I will consider, the Polish Music Publishing Society (Towarzystwo Wydawnicze Muzyki Polskiej), makes clear how

62 | Chapter 2

the musical intelligentsia sought to navigate a period of relatively weak state involvement in the arts. The correspondence preserved among its members also shows how antisemitism was amplified through the interpersonal dynamics of the association, shaping the institution and its priorities from within. If the Association of Young Musician-Poles in Paris understood musical innovation as flowing from western Europe, and thus requiring synthesis and exchange between Paris and Warsaw, then the Polish Music Publishing Society prioritized the development of musical culture within Poland's borders. Despite its name, it embraced a wide variety of subgroups and projects. Its roots trace to December 1926, when the violinist Tadeusz Ochlewski, organist Bronisław Rutkowski, and lawyer and pianist Teodor Zalewski formed the Warsaw-based Association of Enthusiasts for Early Music (Stowarzyszenie Miłośników Dawnej Muzyki), a group dedicated primarily to the performance of baroque compositions.[41] After a couple years of growing audiences at these performances, they launched the Polish Music Publishing Society in 1928.[42] The members of the group understood that music publishing could help build a national public sphere devoted to music, as had occurred in German lands over the prior century. This would, in turn, cultivate both audiences and sustained engagement with musical culture.[43]

Publishing early music was a major part of its activities, but the Polish Music Publishing Society would also shape the interwar musical intelligentsia more broadly because it created major forums in which the intelligentsia's musical discussions could play out. It published a musicology journal (*Kwartalnik Muzyczny* from 1928; *Rocznik Muzykologiczny*, 1935–36) and a broader-circulation music periodical aimed primarily at the musical intelligentsia (*Muzyka Polska*, 1934–39). Indeed, the society became especially important to the younger "progressive" composers.[44] Many of its members had also been active in the Association of Young Musician-Poles in Paris. Not only was the society one of the few organizations to distribute the works of progressive composers, but *Muzyka Polska* became one of interwar Poland's main venues to discuss new music.[45] The journal's editorial team included such progressive champions as Kazimierz Sikorski (a composition professor who trained many of the progressive composers), Stefan Kisielewski (a contrarian figure who regularly weighed in on debates about new music), and Konstanty Régamey (a composer and major commentator on Polish new music). Reflecting progressive priorities, the pages of the periodical regularly featured articles with titles such as "Is Atonality Really Atonal?" and "On the Directions of Contemporary

Polish Music."[46] In 1935 the society further increased its support of new music by organizing concerts with the Polish section of the International Society for Contemporary Music and creating the Commission for Contemporary Music.[47] Reflecting the wide-ranging ambitions of the group, the Polish Music Publishing Society renamed itself the Polish Music Society in 1939, just months before World War II.[48] As we will see in subsequent chapters, its projects would persist in various forms during and after the war.

The society positioned itself as carrying out the tasks of culture building that the Polish state was unable or unwilling to fulfill. From the regaining of Polish independence in 1918, there was consistently a state apparatus to support the arts, but it was hampered by frequent bureaucratic reshuffles that downgraded the power of the arts bureaucracy. Most significantly, in 1922 the Ministry of Art and Culture was disbanded and its prerogatives folded into the Ministry of Religious Denominations and Public Education (Ministerstwo Wyznań Religijnych i Oświecenia Publicznego). Musicians and other artists objected, fearing (correctly) that patronage of the arts would become a subsidiary goal of an already overextended ministry whose priorities were religious affairs and public education.[49]

Precarious funding for the arts was an even greater concern than weak bureaucratic structures. As early as 1919, employees of the Ministry of Art and Culture had complained about inadequate funding for carrying out their remit.[50] After the integration of arts funding into the Ministry of Religious Denominations and Public Education, complaints about the small budget for the arts only intensified, and it was often pointed out that less than 1 percent of the ministry's budget was devoted to the arts—fine arts, music, theater, and literature combined.[51] In 1929, the writer Juliusz Kaden-Bandrowski quipped that the budget for acquiring new works of art, for example, could purchase only seven medium-sized paintings.[52] But matters only worsened during the Great Depression, and by the late 1930s artists were complaining that funding was little more than "symbolic pennies."[53] Matters at the Fund for National Culture, the other major state-backed funder of the arts, were hardly much better: by 1936 its budget had declined by 97 percent from the time of its founding in 1928.[54]

While funding for the arts and culture in Poland in the 1930s was rather dismal, the Polish Music Publishing Society was able to grow the scope of its activities thanks to close connections to officialdom and to the two main state-backed funding organizations for music, the Ministry

64 | Chapter 2

of Religious Denominations and Public Education and the Fund for National Culture. The society's relationship with the Fund for National Culture proved especially lucrative: indeed, Rutkowski's contacts with the fund's director, Stanisław Michalski, secured the funding needed to launch the Polish Music Publishing Society. The society's leadership continued to have Michalski's ear, with the musicologist and society member Julian Pulikowski boasting that Michalski "discussed all musical matters" with two of its members, Teodor Zalewski and Rutkowski.[55] The various arms of the publishing society received each year between a third and nearly 80 percent of all the monies that the Fund for National Culture dispensed to musical institutions.[56] Considering the diversity and scale of musical organizations in Poland, this was a remarkable consolidation of state resources. The publishing society further cemented its financial position in fall 1934, when the musical representative in the Ministry of Religious Denominations and Public Education agreed that the ministry would support the society by denying subventions to its competitors.[57]

While all the society's members aimed to build Polish musical culture, some of its leaders also subscribed to an ethnonationalist, and antisemitic, vision of Polish musical culture. Indeed, the founding of the society's flagship journal, *Muzyka Polska*, was wrapped up in the politics of anti-Jewishness. *Muzyka Polska* had been conceived as an alternative to the journal *Muzyka*, edited by the Polish Jew Mateusz Gliński, whom the society's members painted in a negative light. Correspondence by members of the publishing society that discussed Gliński sought to denigrate him as a Jew merely pretending to be a Pole by evoking with scorn his birth name, Hercensztajn. Chybiński, for example, wrote, "The editor Gliński forgets that from the moment someone is named Gliński he should stop using the methods of the former Herzenstein [*sic*]," insinuating that Jews lacked the ethical compass of Poles.[58] More broadly, members of the society painted Gliński as someone who "knew how to pander to the young" and who "competently steer[ed] his 'business'" while attacking *Muzyka* as "salon-like and socialite" and trading in "ephemeral-current trash."[59]

The mounting difficulties that Gliński faced in maintaining the journal reflected the growing antisemitic environment in which he operated.[60] Indeed, from as early as 1930 the Fund for National Culture denied funding to *Muzyka*, likely in accord with the antisemitic beliefs of its director, Stanisław Michalski.[61] Then, in 1934, the new director of musical activities in the Ministry of Religious Denominations and Public Education decided to remove all its funding from *Muzyka* in favor of funding the Polish Music Publishing Society exclusively, a decision that the society's leadership greeted with great excitement.[62] It was this change that allowed the society to begin publishing *Muzyka Polska*—a journal that explicitly differentiated itself from *Muzyka* by the inclusion of the national epithet "Polska" in its title. "The ever-active editor of *Muzyka*," noted Zalewski in his memoirs, "would have liked to be regarded as the foremost opinion maker within the contemporary Polish musical environment and to have an influence on matters of Polish music. Our group wished to clearly oppose this, not seeing in Mr. Gliński an activist who was honestly and disinterestedly devoted to matters of Polish music."[63]

Correspondence among the editors of *Muzyka Polska* reveals how they eliminated the contributions of Polish Jews from their pages. The musicologist Adolf Chybiński played a key role in these exclusionary acts. As a professor and editor for the society, he held clout with its members, which he used to prevent the publication in *Muzyka Polska* after 1934 of work by his own musicology student, Zofia Lissa, who was Jewish.[64] A few months after this request, he received confirmation from Rutkowski that *Muzyka Polska* was "slowly cleansing itself of foreign and unnecessary elements," and that even the straightforward chronicle of musical events excluded "names that are to us foreign and hostile," an allusion to the removal of Jewish names that ensued.[65] Underscoring his motivations in a 1937 letter, Chybiński stated that he "would be very happy if *Muzyka Polska* united all the ethnically Polish writers on music, in the same way as under my strong pressure it expelled all jews[66] and crypto-jews. Otherwise, we won't win in musical matters here."[67]

Nor were these concerns limited to *Muzyka Polska*. Julian Pulikowski, Chybiński's protégé, was even more explicit about the matter, wishing to make the society's publications "*rassenrein*" (German for "racially pure") and claiming that the Fund for National Culture would provide more funding if they were to do so.[68] Chybiński also bemoaned that "jews and jew-like people [*żydoidy*] are beginning to lounge around the *Kwartalnik Muzyczny* and are pushing through the doors and windows."[69] In turning *Muzyka Polska* into a bastion for Poles, narrowly understood, Chybiński believe that Gliński's *Muzyka* would become the journal of last resort for these "non-Polish" Poles: "[*Muzyka*] will be to an ever-greater degree a basin of jews and jew-like people since we have swept away with an iron hammer all that is non-Polish from *Muzyka Polska*. Muzyka* has come back to life thanks to some money from an

66 | Chapter 2

unclear source, supported by jews and Freemasonry in Poland. We, however, will continue to sweep away international and Jewish influences."[70] *Muzyka Polska* did restrain itself from publishing virulent antisemitic views, limiting itself to coded anti-Jewish positions in its pages, which were just a glimmer of the views that the editors expressed in private correspondence.[71]

Not all members of the publishing society shared Chybiński's views. The society also published and distributed works by composers of Jewish background such as Tadeusz Zygfryd Kassern (who had converted to Catholicism as a young man), Marian Neuteich (who would become an organizer of the Jewish Symphony Orchestra in the Warsaw Ghetto), and Roman Palester (whose father was a Jewish convert).[72] Stefan Kisielewski, whose mother was Jewish, led the editorial office of *Muzyka Polska* from 1936 to 1938, despite antisemitic slanders from Pulikowski, the right-wing member.[73] Nonetheless, the society's politics of anti-Jewish exclusion were not lost on outside observers. An unsigned 1937 article in the Lviv-based *Echo*, edited by the Polish Jewish composer Józef Koffler, described a "fear of certain names—a doctor would say 'nomenfobia,'" behind *Muzyka Polska*'s excision of Jewish names from its pages. The critic described how *Muzyka Polska* had reprinted a report of a concert organized by the Polish ISCM section in London but had removed all the Polish Jewish composers and performers from it, including Koffler, Karol Rathaus, and Leopold Münzer. In response, the critic mockingly underscored the centrality of Jews to Polish musical culture, noting that "if all the worrying names are removed, Lviv would be musically equivalent to a podunk town." He also, however, objected to the state support that enabled *Muzyka Polska*'s anti-Jewish posture: "Is it not a waste of Polish citizens' money (since all of this is paid for by subventions) on such a foolish game?"[74] The phrase "Polish citizen" signals his allegiance to a notion of Polishness grounded in citizenship rather than ethnicity, one that would be open to Jews. This was the model of national belonging that *Muzyka Polska* and Chybiński had sought to extirpate.

MUSICALIZING THE MASSES

The musical intelligentsia's belief that they were a culturally advanced elite who would bring the people of Poland into the concert hall was exemplified by the Organization for Musical Culture (Organizacja Ruchu Muzycznego, or ORMUZ), a wing of the Polish Music Publishing Society. Launched in 1934 and led by Tadeusz Ochlewski, it aimed to "musicalize" the Polish provinces and eastern borderlands by organizing thousands of concerts of classical music in schools and other venues for those lacking access to live classical performances. ORMUZ operated on a broad scale: by the end of 1937 it had organized about 2,300 performances.[75] The group elucidates several of the tensions of the musical intelligentsia of the interwar years, including that between elite and non-elite listeners, between "serious" and "light" music, and between urban musicians and the ethnically diverse populations of Poles, Jews, and Ukrainians living in the eastern Polish provinces. While ORMUZ was inspired by programs in the Soviet Union that brought classical music to rural and proletarian audiences, it was also ideologically distinct from these.[76] It had virtually no interest in left-wing social transformation or in mitigating class-based inequality but rather dedicated itself to more widely disseminating classical music within a social structure left intact.

The musicians who performed with ORMUZ and supported its mission tended to subscribe to both "progressive" musical aesthetics and a sense of social responsibility that defined the intelligentsia. "The task faced by musicians of the younger generation," Rutkowski declared in a founding statement about ORMUZ, "is the creation of a wider riverbed for musical culture [*ruch muzyczny*] in Poland. Then it will be possible to discuss the development of Polish musical culture and its deepening."[77] Its musicians included those with international careers such as the pianists Henryk Sztompka and Stanisław Szpinalski, the violinist Eugenia Umińska, and the soprano Stanisława Korwin-Szymanowska (Karol Szymanowski's sister) as well as progressive composers such as Grażyna Bacewicz, Witold Lutosławski, and Bolesław Woytowicz (who performed on their respective instruments).[78] Idealism aside, they were attracted to ORMUZ because unemployment among musicians had soared during the 1930s, reaching as high as 60 percent by one estimate.[79] Thanks to numerous performances strung together over a multi-week tour, ORMUZ allowed the performers to earn "a considerable sum and live easily for several months," as the violinist Umińska recalled.[80]

ORMUZ also capitalized on a wider realignment within the progressive branch of the musical intelligentsia that heightened the salience of small-scale actions on behalf of Polish musical culture. Karol Szymanowski played a crucial role in reorienting modernist musical circles toward the provinces, recapitulating the role of ideological leadership that he had played a decade prior in directing composers toward France. His 1930 essay "The Educational Role of Musical Culture in Society"

68 | Chapter 2

was especially influential. Overflowing with idealist descriptions of music's power to unify the *polis*, the essay concludes that musical culture must be built from the ground up. "I should like to show that an artist's individual work really can take flight when it has as a springboard a common artistic culture which prevails throughout society."[81] Here, too, Szymanowski was measuring Polish musicality against western Europe, although he had in mind not Paris, but rather the amateur choral societies and broad-based, participatory musical culture that had grown in German lands over the prior century. In underscoring the dependence of elite artists, such as himself, on "society" as a whole, he ultimately placed the onus for improving Poland's musical conditions on his colleagues, who, in his view, must engage in "unremitting work and unceasing effort" to lay "the foundation of our national, social, and state life."[82] Such slogans also alluded to the ideas of the Warsaw positivists from the 1860s and 1870s, who had believed that through small-scale actions to improve education, hygiene, and agricultural practices among Poland's peasantry and lower classes, the nation would embark on a gradual course of economic and social betterment.[83] In any case, Szymanowski was not repudiating the modernist aesthetics for which he consistently advocated, but rather he was calling for their integration into a broader project of social service.

ORMUZ's founders believed that the eastern borderlands of the Polish Republic, known as the *kresy*, were the country's most musically deficient region and thus held great potential for national reinvention. Map 1, published in 1931, reflected this mindset, showing the stark geographical divides within Poland's classical music culture. While there was a plethora of music schools (for both amateurs and professionals) in Warsaw, Lviv, Poznań, and Vilnius, entire provinces in the east had no formal music education. Such numeric descriptions of the borderlands' musical culture did not tell the entire story, however. At the same time that the *kresy* were impoverished, musically undereducated, and staggeringly illiterate, they were also romanticized as a bastion of Polish national culture, since it was here that many gentry families had their estates.[84] The *kresy* were also the Second Republic's most diverse regions. Poles in the region were often a minority, and the region was characterized by Jewish towns and Ukrainian peasantry.[85]

ORMUZ was one of many cultural and political organizations that sought to assert Polish cultural authority over this diverse and unruly borderland.[86] It described its work in militaristic terms, casting the borderlands as a region in need of forced civilizing. In an article entitled "The

MAP 1. A map of music schools in Poland in early 1931 reveals vast regional differences in the distribution of formalized musical education in the Second Republic. Members of the musical intelligentsia saw the paucity of musical institutions in several of the eastern territories as evidence of musical underdevelopment in the region. The map documents different types of schools, including general music schools (*szkoły ogólno-muzyczne*), vocal academies (*szkoły śpiewu*), organ schools (*szkoły organistowskie*), and schools for dance and rhythm (*szkoły rytmiczne*). The map indicates three state music schools (*szkoły państwowe*), in Warsaw, Poznań, and Katowice, and two higher schools of music (*szkoły wyższego typu*), both in Warsaw. The shaded squares indicate the number of students who attended each school. Janusz Miketta, "Ze statystyki szkolnictwa muzycznego," *Kwartalnik Muzyczny*, nos. 10–11 (1931): 156–169.

70 | Chapter 2

Knights of ORMUZ," the composer Michał Kondracki explained how performers were undertaking a "peacetime cultural offensive."[87] Expanding his bellicose metaphor, he described how "the army of musicians occupied the entire territory of the Republic, conquered all the hamlets and towns!"[88] Others described Ochlewski's organizational acumen in militaristic terms. He tracked the "musicalization" of various provincial outposts on a map of Poland with color-coded flags to indicate the status of a town's developing musical culture.[89] Dispatched in accordance with this plan, the teams of musicians felt like they were part of "ORMUZ's military staff" operating under "Ochlewski's command."[90] If the provinces belonged to the Polish state, such comments implied, they were also foreign, potentially hostile, and in need of centralized control.

Others saw the provinces as a wellspring of cultural renewal. Color pieces written by ORMUZ musicians exoticized the terrain they visited, describing muddy roads and harsh weather, as well as the bearskins, peasant sleighs, and horse-drawn carriages required to navigate them.[91] In underscoring the cultural distance between urban musicians and provincial audiences, however, these tropes could also be inverted to suggest that the provincial audiences were untutored, sincere, and thus the ideal raw material for a future musical public. Some described a "direct connection between artists and listeners" that they felt was missing in Warsaw.[92] The pianist Henryk Sztompka claimed to prefer the audiences in the provinces to those of major cities, because in the provinces "we feel needed by everyone, by the people of all of Poland, and not only by a small handful of snobs and by the even fewer who are truly devoted to music."[93]

In equating the provinces with the "people" of Poland, Sztompka elided the more complex issue of how those living in the *kresy* understood their identities and relation to the Polish state. Intriguingly, ORMUZ musicians almost never described the ethnic or religious makeup of their audiences, despite traveling through a diverse region and performing in many towns that were Jewish population centers, such as Szumsk, Łuck, and Równe.[94] The archives of the Association of Young Musicians in Cracow, who for several years organized concerts with ORMUZ, however, suggest that Jews often attended the performances. A concert in Nowy Sącz, for example, could not be scheduled on a Jewish holiday since, as a local official pointed out, "without the participation of the Jewish public, attendance at the concert would be so small that it would be impossible to cover the costs."[95] A local organizer of a concert in Mielec (near Rzeszów) likewise explained that the town was 60 percent Jewish and that therefore a concert could not be organized on a Friday evening.[96] That local organizers had to explain basic tenets of Jewish observance and local demographics suggests a disconnect between urban musicians and the realities of cultural life in provincial towns. Nor did ORMUZ choose to collect information about its audiences' religious or ethnic identities, although it did administer extensive surveys about audiences' musical preferences.[97] Perhaps they believed the makeup of the audience was irrelevant to their mission of musicalization. It is also possible that they wished to keep in check the antisemites among the Polish Music Publishing Society's members and funders.

ORMUZ's claim that it was bringing music to the "people" also obscures the extent to which it remained a project of and for the intelligentsia. In an early essay on the organization, Rutkowski was explicit that it aimed to meet "the cultural needs of the *inteligent* who lives in Suwałki, Święciany, Janów, and hundreds of other towns."[98] Its organizational work also privileged contact with the intelligentsia; ORMUZ aimed to capitalize on the extensive network of intelligentsia-led social organizations that grew under Sanacja and to convince these organizations that music should be supported.[99] Much of Ochlewski's time was spent corresponding with these various social associations (such as the Women's Union for Citizenship Work), as well as with schools and cultural associations that could host the concerts and visiting musicians.[100] As a result, when musicians arrived in the borderland towns, they interacted most directly with people from a familiar social stratum—the notaries, town clerks, and other members of the provincial intelligentsia who acted as their hosts. "Different local notables fought over us," Umińska recalled. "Each wanted to host us for lunch or dinner."[101]

The repertoire ORMUZ programmed partook of the musical intelligentsia's distrust of "light" or entertainment-focused forms of artistic expression. Rutkowski believed that provincial listeners only had access to genres such as operetta, cabaret ("the refuse from the cabarets in major cities"), and operatic arrangements offered by touring opera groups ("the worst operatic trash").[102] Ochlewski, meanwhile, believed that jazz was a factor in the spiritual crisis and the emptying of the concert halls.[103] At other times, ORMUZ's artists worried about how radio and sound recording were making music more accessible, yet in ways that they believed undermined the listening experience of attending a live concert (and threatened the livelihoods of performing musicians).[104] At times, ORMUZ portrayed the towns it visited as if no music were ever heard there, as "massive blank spots on the map of cultural life."[105] But

72 | Chapter 2

it is more accurate to view ORMUZ as attempting to influence how people were consuming music in a period of rapid modernization by attempting to replace more popular genres with highbrow ones, and mechanically reproduced sound with live performance. As a result of these priorities, ORMUZ focused on shorter works that still bore the imprimatur of the classical canon. During one concert, for example, the soprano Stanisława Korwin-Szymanowska and pianist Henryk Sztompka performed arias by Mozart, Stanisław Moniuszko, and Domenico Scarlatti, Liszt transcriptions of Wagner and Chopin, a selection of Chopin works (including his Ballade No. 1 in G Minor), and mélodies by Gabriel Fauré and the French-Venezuelan composer Reynaldo Hahn.[106]

While ORMUZ hoped that these performances would convey an "aesthetic experience, a direct feeling for music," it also focused on the more didactic work of socializing audiences in concertgoing expectations.[107] Students made up a major part of their audience, in part because the Ministry of Religious Denominations and Public Education had effectively required that schools offer live musical performances. This policy had likely been crafted with ORMUZ's knowledge, if not cooperation, underscoring the significance of state backing for the ostensibly independent organization.[108] Over several years of visits, students were to progress from concerts that focused on more accessible musical forms to performances that focused on individual composers and time periods. There were units on contemporary music (works of Ravel, Honegger, Hindemith, Schoenberg, and Stravinsky) as well as contemporary Polish music (Paderewski, Niewiadomski, Walewski, Lipski, Szymanowski, Różycki, and Maklakiewicz).[109] Other performances focused on topics such as religious music, Polish national opera, sonata form, Polish music after Chopin, or Polish dance.[110] Framed by introductory lectures that could take up a third of the recital, the ORMUZ programs suggested that aesthetic experience alone was insufficient for engaging an audience that lacked relevant expectations and musical background.

TOWARD TOTALISM AND FASCISM

The examples of the Association of Young Musician-Poles in Paris, the Polish Music Publishing Society, and ORMUZ reveal how institutions were sites of dynamic social investments. Organizing musical life was a key part of what it meant to belong to the musical intelligentsia. Networks of individuals built institutions that they cast as being of tantamount significance to the nation. This interweaving of social circles, formalized institutions, and a broader sense of national mission defined both the musical intelligentsia and the contemporary classical music scene in interwar Poland, which developed against the backdrop of strong ideas about national culture but with relatively weak institutions of the state. As we will see in the remaining chapters, the social circles and discourses created by the musical intelligentsia would reappear in several different forms over the following years.

By the late 1930s, the idea that a strong, centralized state should exert a more powerful role in Polish music had become a common refrain among members of the musical intelligentsia. There were both Poland-specific and international factors driving this shift. Within Poland, following Józef Piłsudski's death in 1935, the ruling Sanacja regime lurched toward the right, making overtures to the right-wing National Democrats whom Piłsudski had once shunned. Antisemitism and ethnonationalism became integrated into the ruling platform, and Polish Jews increasingly despaired for their future in Poland.[111] For the next few years there were debates within ruling circles between supporters of an openly totalitarian model of governing that prioritized discipline and cohesion, such as Edward Rydz-Śmigły and Adam Koc, and those who defended Sanacja's more liberal roots.[112]

The musicians associated with the Publishing Society and *Muzyka Polska* were also looking abroad and often saw Nazi Germany, fascist Italy, and, to a lesser degree, the Soviet Union as models worth discussing, if not emulating. An especially appealing institution for them was the German Music Chamber (Reichsmusikkammer), which had been created in 1933 in Nazi Germany and was instrumental in expunging Jewish musicians from the profession in the Reich.[113] Polish plans for creating the Music Chamber (Izba Muzyczna) generally called for the state to deputize legal force to a body of musicians, perhaps even an already-existing union or association, who would then be tasked with limiting access to the profession to qualified professionals, much like the regulatory bodies that governed doctors and lawyers.[114] In this regard, the Poles found the idea of the Music Chamber appealing for many of the same reasons as musicians in Weimar and Nazi Germany had: a centralized governing body would help limit those seeking employment as musicians, decrease competition from amateurs, and improve its members' wages and job security.[115] Unlike in Germany, these plans remained hypothetical in Poland.

By 1937, the focus on the regulation of the profession had given way to considerations of openly totalitarian approaches to organizing

74 | Chapter 2

musical culture. *Muzyka Polska* asked leading composers and intellectuals to write short articles about whether they endorsed a "totalistic" (or totalitarian) organization of musical life. In establishing "totalism" as a topic of debate, the periodical was inviting its associates to compare Poland to Nazi Germany, the Soviet Union, and fascist Italy, and to comment on whether the commitments of these countries to the "dissemination and spreading of cultural-artistic values" and to "subordinating culture and art to a given ideology" were worth emulating.[116] The results of the survey indicated a mixed verdict. While some were skeptical about totalism's ideological impositions, most respondents wished to embrace the promises for better organization and greater state funding that they believed were the norm in totalist societies. Zygmunt Mycielski supported stronger organization of Polish musical life, but he was also skeptical of emulating the models put forth by other countries.[117] The pianist Stanisław Szpinalski and composer Tadeusz Szeligowski were both more open to totalism. They thought that the proposed Music Chamber should have expansive powers to organize concerts, oversee education, and even impose taxes to improve musical culture in Poland.[118] Even so, Szeligowski made it clear that he did not wish to cede power to the state, but rather he wished for the state to delegate its authority to elite musicians: "Of course, decisions about musical policy should be entrusted to the most important musicians in the country," a group in which he no doubt would have included himself.[119]

It is no surprise that some musicians in Poland found fascism to be appealing; after all, the ideology enjoyed support from intellectuals across the continent, including composers such as Stravinsky and Schoenberg.[120] That the intellectual center of support for such arts policy would be the Polish Music Publishing Society is equally unsurprising. Its members had already demonstrated success at channeling state resources to advance its goals and had shown a tolerance, if not open support, for right-wing politics. By calling for a more strong-handed state, some musicians associated with the society were likely calculating that a stronger state would continue to bolster their own influence over musical matters. The warmness toward totalitarian values among some members of the musical intelligentsia was in this sense a logical, albeit troubling, extension of their long-standing focus on organizing and improving musical culture in Poland.

On the eve of the war, in 1938 and 1939, several commentators began to embrace Italian fascism and Nazism in ways that moved beyond the more measured discussions of rationalization and organization of the previous year. On the pages of *Muzyka Polska* the critic Jerzy Waldorff declared himself a "totalitarian" and claimed that totalitarian dictatorship was the surest way to defeat the "leftist-Jewish enemies," an antisemitic slur against the Soviet Union and communists more generally. He wrote in glowing terms about Mussolini's Italy, praising its support for artists and claiming that the government interfered little with its artists.[121] Elsewhere he asserted that "there is no Jewish creative output in art" and railed against the alleged power that Jewish critics, whom he terms "Jewish artistic *tzadiks*," held over Poles, who are subjected to a "ritual beating," he asserted, with "all available means, which the chronically rich Jews have in abundance."[122] Szeligowski eliminated doubts about his sympathies when he published an essay in *Muzyka Polska* titled "Freedom and Gagging" in which he described, without objection, Germany's official antisemitism and expulsion of Jewish musicians. He further argued that the Nazis had created a popular high art, and he praised how the "factory workers brought together in the 'Kraft durch Freude' participate in concerts of the highest level."[123] In a later essay he compared ORMUZ to the methods of popularizing music among the masses practiced in fascist Italy and Nazi Germany.[124]

The costs of Poland's increasing authoritarianism and antisemitism were high for Polish Jewish musicians. We have already seen the impacts of institutionalized antisemitism within the Polish Music Publishing Society and on Gliński's *Muzyka*. The composer Józef Koffler wrote in a 1937 letter to the Czech composer Alois Hába that he feared that antisemitism in the education system would soon deprive him of his teaching position and force him to emigrate; he did not do so, although he did leave the Jewish community at around this time.[125] Even the Association of Young Musicians in Cracow—founded on the belief that membership should be allowed irrespective of a musician's "gender or confession," succumbed to these forces.[126] In 1938, it was taken over by a new administration that limited membership to those of "Polish nationality" and promised schools that they could "guarantee to supply exclusively Christian performers."[127] The result was the resignation en masse of the association's many Jewish members. Mieczysław Drobner, a founding member, berated the takeover in a long letter, asserting that "the association has embarked on a path that has broken with all its fundamental principles."[128] Unsurprisingly, some Jewish musicians turned to Jewish musical associations for employment after opportunities in Polish institutions were foreclosed.[129] Conditions were, however, about to worsen beyond all imagination.

PART II

World War II and the Holocaust

3

The Nation Is Now a Matter of Life and Death

The seventeenth annual festival of the International Society for Contemporary Music (ISCM), held in Warsaw and Cracow from April 14 to 21, 1939, was supposed to confirm that Poland had definitively arrived on the European new music scene. Although Poland's composers had sought to host the prestigious festival since 1931, it had taken them several years to obtain enough clout within the ISCM to do so.[1] Indicative of the high hopes pinned on the event, the editors of *Muzyka Polska* believed that guests who traveled from across Europe to Poland for the week of concerts would leave convinced that "our music does not end with Chopin, Szymanowski, and a few of the younger composers. Alongside the vigorous growth in contemporary composition, we also have beautiful musical traditions reaching back to the sixteenth century." These historical roots were exemplified by concerts of early Polish music and Polish folk music, held in Cracow's famed St. Mary's Basilica, in addition to the standard ISCM fare of contemporary classical compositions.[2]

In reality, the 1939 ISCM festival confirmed that composers and audiences alike were unable to escape the tumultuous political events propelling Europe toward war.[3] On April 1, two weeks before the festival was to begin, the organizers learned that Germany, who just weeks prior had declared the Protectorate of Bohemia and Moravia, would not allow thirteen Czechs, including Alois Hába, to attend the festival.[4] Around the same time, the Italians withdrew from the festival, claiming

80 | Chapter 3

that they had been slighted with too few performances on the program, although the Polish organizers suspected that the real reason was the growing Italian-German alliance.[5] A few days later the United Kingdom and France pledged to support Polish independence. On April 5, shortly after British assurances to Poland had been made and a mere nine days before the festival began, Edward Dent, the former president of the ISCM, exclaimed, "It is just the moment for an Englishman to be welcomed in Poland!"[6] But many guests decided against traveling under these conditions, whatever political significance their presence might have conveyed.[7] With numerous cancellations at the eleventh hour, seven works had to be pulled from the program, including Anton Webern's string quartet and Roman Palester's saxophone concertino, which was to be performed by Sigurd Raschèr.[8] Despite this turbulent backdrop, the festival continued. "One can say, without exaggeration, that Poland's 'roof is burning above its head,' yet it managed to organize a week of music," noted the Hungarian composer Sándor Jemnitz with approval.[9] Indeed, for Polish musical commentators the 1939 ISCM festival had succeeded in projecting normalcy in the face of the brewing storm. It had proved that "traveling to Poland in the current moment is not madness," according to Konstanty Régamey: "Here a greater calmness reigns than anywhere else."[10]

Even before the ink had dried on Régamey's pronouncement, this calm faltered. On April 28, a week after the festival concluded, Hitler unilaterally renounced the Polish-German declaration of nonaggression of 1934 and renewed German territorial claims over Polish land, portending war. A few months later, on August 23, 1939, Nazi Germany and the Soviet Union signed the Molotov-Ribbentrop Pact, a nonaggression agreement that included a secret protocol that would divide Poland between them in case of a war. "By August 31, 1939, everyone in Warsaw was already certain that war with the Germans was unavoidable," recalled the pianist and composer Władysław Szpilman.[11] But the barbarism of the invasion that began the next morning was unexpected. Hitler had told his senior military commanders before the invasion to "close your hearts to pity. Act brutally."[12] They did exactly that.

Cities across Poland were bombed from the sky. Warsaw—including its civilians and non-military assets—was targeted in ruthless aerial bombing campaigns, the first time in history that an air force had systematically bombed a major European city. "About every hour, the silver bodies of bombers appeared high up in the cursed, blue sky of that autumn," recalled Szpilman. "In this roulette of destruction, one had to

The Nation Is a Matter of Life and Death | 81

expect to die if the bomb, like a roulette ball, landed on the number of the house where one was sheltering."[13] On September 26, after seventy-two tons of firebombs were dropped on the city, the concert hall of the Warsaw Philharmonic burned to its foundation.[14] Thousands of civilians fled east, while German pilots shot at the refugees from the sky. Among them were Grażyna Bacewicz and her family. They only narrowly avoided being killed when German bombers appeared over the village of Garwolin, where they were staying. "A couple of minutes later, Garwolin had ceased to exist," she recalled.[15] All told, some 25,000 civilians were killed in the bombardment of Warsaw, a staggering number, although one soon to be dwarfed.[16]

On September 17 the Soviet Union invaded Poland from the east, acting on the secret agreement of the Molotov-Ribbentrop Pact. Nazi Germany and the Soviet Union had partitioned Poland, with the USSR seizing much of the eastern territories of the collapsing Second Republic. This second invasion came as a surprise. Adolf Chybiński, the musicologist based in Lviv, was incredulous when Soviet troops, instead of German ones, occupied his city.[17] For Zygmunt Mycielski, who had recently joined the Second Regiment of the Podhale Riflemen as an infantryman to defend Poland, the Soviet invasion spelled the end of any possibility of immediate victory. Soon after it, he crossed the border into Hungary.[18] "All that I can tell you is that I am still alive," he wrote on a postcard to Nadia Boulanger dated September 22, 1939. "But I don't know anything about the fate of my family and friends—of my brothers, mother, family, not to speak of everyone, of the entire country."[19] Soon he made his way to France, where he joined the Polish Army being assembled there.[20] "I didn't know anything about our army here [in France], but I had decided to serve in any army that was fighting with Germany or Russia," he explained to her. "We are defending mankind. All that is not mankind—all that is beyond humanity—must be destroyed."[21]

As dire as conditions were in the fall of 1939, they would only deteriorate over the next five and a half years. The Germans attempted to destroy Poland through capricious violence and mass murder. Einsatzgruppen, Nazi paramilitary death squads, were ordered to eliminate the intelligentsia and governing classes of Poland by murdering tens of thousands of Polish citizens.[22] By fall 1940 the Germans were carving ghettos from cities and imprisoning Jews in them. Then, in June 1941, Germany broke the nonaggression pact with the Soviet Union and invaded, turning on its onetime ally. In the months that followed, the Nazi murder of Jews, which

82 | Chapter 3

had characterized German rule in eastern Europe from its first days, reached a new, previously unthinkable pitch. Millions of Jews were systematically murdered in the Nazi death camps, including Treblinka, Sobibór, and Bełżec, or were shot in town squares and ravines. Then, during the last years of the war, two uprisings—the Warsaw Ghetto Uprising of 1943 and the Warsaw Uprising of 1944—were brutally suppressed by the Germans, leading to the deaths of tens of thousands of Varsovians and to the systematic destruction of the city. All told, by the end of the war more than 90 percent of Polish Jews had been murdered, while a still staggering 7 to 10 percent of the country's non-Jewish population had also perished.[23] These are numbing statistics, almost incomprehensible in their scope. Behind them lie the stories, struggles, and hopes of millions of individuals, each of whom lived their own life and died their own death.

The three chapters in this section consider how musicians grappled with the political, national, and racial violence that was promulgated by the Germans and Soviets. I begin in the area of Warsaw outside the ghetto before turning to music making in the Warsaw Ghetto (chapter 4) and in Soviet-ruled eastern Poland (chapter 5). During the occupation, the physical location of the musical intelligentsia's members came to play a defining role in their activities, the scope of their actions shaped by vastly different policies applied in Polish Warsaw, the Warsaw Ghetto, and under Soviet rule. As a result, the musical intelligentsia's activities took on a more local character, and its ambitions as a leading elite that spanned the territories of the republic were put on hold.

There is no simple way to name the area of Warsaw outside the ghetto, which is the focus of this chapter. For most non-Jewish Varsovians, they were simply living in "Warsaw," as they had prior to the war. Using this broad designation in scholarship, however, can suggest that claims made about non-Jewish Varsovians apply equally to the Warsaw Ghetto, since the Ghetto, too, was part of Warsaw. At times I call this area outside the ghetto the *aryjska strona* (Aryan side), a term frequently used by Jews who hid outside the ghetto and in discussions of Jewish rescue and aid. The term *aryjska strona* conveys the terrorizing, racialized geography experienced by Polish Jews and reminds us of the dangers posed by both Germans and Poles to Jewish survival outside the ghetto. But it makes less sense when talking about Poles, who did not identify with this Nazi moniker. I thus call the area of Warsaw outside the ghetto "Polish Warsaw," although this is also a simplification: not all who lived and hid there were non-Jewish Poles, and many Jews in the ghetto also considered themselves to be Polish.

One of the main themes of this chapter is how German cultural policy in Polish Warsaw inadvertently reinforced the musical intelligentsia's investments in the political and national significance of music. This occurred, I suggest, because the Germans implemented policies premised on the assumption that music held a profound political significance, but which were also ineffective at curtailing the musical intelligentsia's activities. Kazimierz Wyka, a probing analyst of the social conditions of occupation, observed a related phenomenon in a 1945 article on the informal economy of the occupation. Poles learned to evade the strict rules and extreme penalties of the occupation, he claimed, "faster than the Germans noticed that their dam was scarcely even a sieve." What resulted was "a gap in the fiction from below. A gap that was accessible to everyone, verified by experience, and inviting risk that usually paid off."[24] Within the musical intelligentsia, the many gaps in German cultural policy allowed them to continue to organize and make music, while the German attacks on Polish music making gave their actions a new sense of urgency. At the end of the chapter, I consider some of the ways that this invigorated paradigm of national leadership within the musical intelligentsia was also a narrow one, rarely extending a sense of comradery to the Polish Jews segregated into ghettos or forced into hiding by the Nazis.

A CITY DIVIDED

During the occupation Warsaw became an even more important center of activity for the musical intelligentsia than it had been before the war. Dozens of Polish musicians from western Poland relocated to Warsaw after being expelled from cities such as Łódź and Poznań, where they had once lived. These cities, along with much of western Poland, were incorporated directly into the German Reich and were intended for the exclusive inhabitation of Germans or ethnic German Volksdeutsche.[25] As a consequence of these expulsions, the once dispersed musical intelligentsia became more concentrated.[26]

Warsaw, along with Cracow to the south, were ruled under an administrative structure called the General Government, which was headed by Hans Frank, the general governor. The General Government was treated as a colony that would serve the economic enrichment of the Reich. Poles of all classes were to be reduced to a "leaderless pool of unskilled labor."[27] They were to become "a kind of eternal seasonal migrant laborer with a permanent home in the areas around Cracow,"

84 | Chapter 3

who would be denied both civil society and national identity.[28] The intelligentsia was targeted for persecution, and tens of thousands of them were murdered.[29] There was to be no rebuilding, resistance was to be destroyed, and assets of value were to be sent to the Reich.[30] Hundreds of infractions carried the death penalty, from minor acts of black market trade to serious ones of armed resistance. The administration of such "justice" was arbitrary and chaotic, leaving those in Warsaw fearful that any encounter with the occupational authorities would end in death.

While Poles and Jews alike were treated with violent disdain in the General Government, the roots, nature, and extent of this violence differed. As John Connelly has argued, the German occupiers attacked Poles not out of racial animosity but rather because they posed a political and practical barrier to rule over the east, and anti-Polish policies were implemented in response to ever-growing Polish defiance of Nazi rule.[31] As a result the Germans made no overtures toward state-level collaboration in Poland. Poland has been described as a country "without Quislings," in which high-level officials were given no chances to serve Nazi policy, although this did not mean that the actions of Poles did not serve Nazi ends.[32] By comparison with this somewhat haphazard anti-Polishness, antisemitism was at the very heart of the Nazi worldview. From the first days of the occupation Jews were treated with unmatched violence: they were targeted and harassed, forced to wear armbands, and murdered at random.

A handful of Polish Jewish musicians were able to escape Poland altogether. Mateusz Gliński, the founder of *Muzyka*, secured a fake invitation from the Brazilian ambassador to conduct—with no small irony—Wagner operas in Rio de Janeiro. Exit visa in hand, he escaped instead to Italy, where he became a music critic for the Vatican's newspaper.[33] Others fled east during the first weeks of the war prior to the capture of Warsaw. They soon fell under Soviet rule. The composer Andrzej Nikodemowicz recalled many Polish Jewish students enrolling at the Lviv conservatory during this time, most of them refugees from the General Government.[34] Others crossed between the German and Soviet occupations for a variety of reasons. The composer Tadeusz Zygfryd Kassern, a converted Jew, had initially evacuated to Lviv from Poznań, but in October 1940 he fled to German-controlled Cracow (and later Warsaw), likely fearful that as a former Polish public servant he would be deported to the Soviet interior if he remained.[35] While Kassern went into hiding under a false identity and thus remained out-

The Nation Is a Matter of Life and Death | 85

side the ghetto, other Polish Jews who made a similar journey from the Soviet to German territories, such as the pianist Marian Filar or singer Wiera Gran, moved into it.[36]

On October 12, 1940, the Germans mandated the creation of the ghetto in Warsaw, where Jews were forced live, and they sealed the ghetto off from the rest of the city on November 16, 1940. Following this decree, tens of thousands of Jews were forced to move into the ghetto while a slightly smaller number of Poles were forced to move out. As a result, around four hundred thousand Jews were crammed into just over fourteen hundred buildings in the ghetto. Food was scarce, poverty was rampant, and disease spread unchecked. These conditions worsened until the so-called Grossaktion in summer 1942, when the majority of the ghetto's inhabitants were deported to Treblinka and murdered in gas chambers.[37] In April 1943, surviving Jews in the ghetto launched the Warsaw Ghetto Uprising, one of the most significant acts of armed Jewish resistance to Nazi rule. The uprising was crushed in May and the Great Synagogue on Tłomackie Street was blown up in retaliation. By the liberation of Warsaw in January 1945, what had once been the ghetto had been reduced by the occupiers into little more than mounds of rubble.

When discussing the wartime experiences of Polish Jewish musicians, it is imperative to note that not all musicians who were persecuted as Jews by the Germans saw themselves as Jewish. Indeed, Nazi policy in the General Government from mid-1940 onward defined a "Jew" as anyone who had two Jewish grandparents, anyone who had belonged to the Jewish community on September 1, 1939, and anyone with a Jewish spouse. This was a broad definition, even by Nazi standards: the Nuremberg Laws, which had been applied to German Jews, defined Jews as people with three or four Jewish grandparents.[38] The stricter definition that was applied in the General Government was especially consequential to members of the musical intelligentsia who had lived on the border between Polishness and Jewishness prior to the war: acculturated Jews (those born to Jewish parents but who adopted the practices of Polish culture), converts (born Jewish but baptized), and even some of "Jewish background" (whose parents or even grandparents had converted) were all now considered "Jewish" and persecuted as such. The composer Roman Palester, for instance, was Jewish in this sense. His father had converted from Judaism to Catholicism—thus giving Palester two Jewish grandparents, even though he did not see himself as Jewish. If, for members of the musical intelligentsia, Jewishness

86 | Chapter 3

and Polishness had long been cultural categories whose boundaries were contested, fluid, and often overlapping, then under occupation Nazi racial principles ran like a knife stroke through these ambiguities. Individuals were sorted into hardened groups to which they did not always see themselves as belonging.

COMPOSITION AS RESISTANCE

The occupation transformed musicians' creative practices and quotidian existence in equal measure. Not only had the halls of the Warsaw Philharmonic and Warsaw Opera been destroyed during the bombing of the city.[39] The occupiers also banned concerts, halted conservatory instruction, and shut down musical organizations.[40] Attempts by musicians from the Warsaw Philharmonic to reopen the ensemble were rebuffed by the Germans.[41] Musicians who had once performed in ensembles or taught in the conservatory had to find new ways of making ends meet, often turning to café performances to eke out a living.[42] Nor were the occupiers' cultural repressions limited to live performance: they also banned the possession of radio receivers and destroyed the Polish record industry, carting away extant recordings of folk songs and Chopin as scrap to Germany.[43] These policies were far more severe than the ones the Germans adopted in occupied western Europe, where concert life was tolerated, if not encouraged, to bolster support for Nazi rule.[44]

The Nazis believed that by banning Polish culture, art, and education, Polish society would be destroyed from within.[45] "The Poles should only be provided with those means of education," Goebbels explained to Hans Frank, the general governor, "that show them the hopelessness of their national destiny."[46] For most of the occupation musical performances were banned unless they took place in purportedly entertainment-focused locales, such as cafés, restaurants, and cabarets.[47] This policy was codified in 1940, when the Ministry of Public Enlightenment and Propaganda (Abteilung für Volksaufklärung und Propaganda) created the so-called "cultural-political guidelines" (*kulturpolitische Richtlinien*) decreeing that Poles be allowed "cultural activity in so far as it serves the primitive need of amusement and diversion." The guidelines had sections concerning theater, cinema, literature, painting, Polish national emblems—and also music: "Permission is granted for Polish musical productions if they aim only at amusement. Concerts whose select program is intended to provide the audience with an artistic experience [*ein künstlerisches Erlebnis*] are to be forbidden.

Of Polish music the following are to be banned: marches, folk songs, national songs, and all classical pieces [*alle klassichen Stücke*]."[48] Consequentially, the policy drew a stark division between art and entertainment, ordering that music that promised an artistic experience was to be banned whereas the purportedly less consequential modes of entertainment were to be allowed. "Art" music thus occupied a special position in Nazi cultural repression, where it was placed alongside music with clearer militaristic, national, and political overtones.

Polish commentators understood the suppression of Polish culture as an attempt to deny Poles sovereignty and nationhood. "The fundamental aims of the German occupational powers in regard to Polish cultural life," read a report from 1940 compiled by members of the underground, is that "Poles will be provided with the possibility of work that is in accordance with their 'national character.' . . . [According to the occupiers,] the 'national character' of the Poles predisposes them to agrarian, craft, and technical-professional work on a low and middle level. However, leadership roles, the sphere of historical-political ambition, and the entire domain of higher spiritual culture will be closed to them."[49] Another report summarized that the "barbarous destruction and theft of spiritual goods [*dóbr duchowych*] is intended to deprive the Polish nation the support of its own culture" and to "degrade Poles to the role of farmhands of Germanness in 'Hitler's New Order.'"[50] It was through this lens that Polish musicians responded to the opening of an exhibition about Chopin organized by the occupiers in 1943, which recast him as a composer of German origin whose musical language was derivative of German composers.[51] The exhibit was an attempt to "undermine Polish society's trust in its own culture," noted one observer in a clandestine publication.[52]

Both Nazi cultural policy and the Polish response to it shared the assumption that artistic culture was a fundamental component of nationhood. This was hardly a new idea. Since the mid-nineteenth century, Polish intellectuals had asserted that music, literature, and visual culture were vessels for preserving the Polish nation while Poles were ruled by Austria, Russia, and Prussia.[53] Meanwhile, in German lands, intellectuals had long asserted that the existence of a canon of German classical music was proof that Germans were a "people of music" and thus a coherent nation despite the fractured nature of German political life in the nineteenth century.[54] Nazi cultural policy in the General Government was a violent inversion of this belief: if classical music traditions were instrumental in turning people into nations, then repressing a nation's classical music might weaken the bonds of nationhood, turning

88 | Chapter 3

nations back into mere amalgamations of individuals. The stakes of making music—or censoring it—were thus high.

Polish musicians were incessantly exposed to these principles because they informed the extensive censorship of nearly all public performances. In theory, every performance had to receive approval from the Ministry of Public Enlightenment and Propaganda. Special scrutiny was paid by the censors to both Polish compositions and to classical works, which were allowed in only a handful of venues.[55] Works were expunged from programs for a variety of reasons, including the political connotations of song texts, racial principles (that is, works by "Jewish" composers), and overly strong links to national identity, although the policies were unevenly and even inaccurately applied.[56] Janina Godlewska-Bogucka, who liaised with the censor's office on behalf of the café Sztuka i Moda, recalled that two-thirds of the Polish compositions she proposed were struck by the censor.[57] Bolesław Woytowicz, who ran the café Dom Sztuki, recalled that he could program some Polish composers, but that those with strong national significance were banned, including Chopin and Paderewski. So extensive were these efforts that even street performers were, at least in theory, required to have proper authorization and to have their repertoire approved by the censor.[58]

Polish musicians were also exposed to the German national discourse around classical music because many participated in German-led institutions that aimed to project the Germans as bringers of culture to a land purportedly devoid of it.[59] The most prominent musical institution of this type was the Cracow-based Philharmonic of the General Government (Philharmonie des Generalgouvernements), which was established by Hans Frank in May 1940 and performed over two hundred concerts during the occupation.[60] Prior to the war, many of its musicians had played in premier Polish ensembles, such as the Warsaw Philharmonic, Warsaw Opera, and Polish Radio Orchestra, and they had joined the Philharmonic of the General Government either under threat or due to promises of better conditions.[61] They performed a repertoire drawn primarily from the German classical canon under German conductors and soloists, a structure that itself suggested clear national hierarchies.[62] Indeed, Frank intended for the ensemble to project German cultural superiority in the East, noting in a conference with the philharmonic's first director, Hanns Rohr, that the ensemble was a "most important cultural and 'political instrument' in the hands of the general governor."[63] Poles were not ignorant of these aims. One observer noted that the ensemble was trying to convince foreigners and Germans that

FIGURE 7. The Philharmonic of the General Government performs in 1944 under a statue of Copernicus in the Collegium Maius of the Jagiellonian University in Cracow. The German occupiers saw the city's Gothic and Renaissance architecture as proof that Polish culture was derivative of the Germans and claimed Copernicus for modern German nationalism. Narodowe Archiwum Cyfrowe.

"prior to German rule, Poland had lacked the foundations of musical culture; only the Germans enabled the cultivation of symphonic music in Poland.... When Poles are left to their own initiative, only café music exists; serious music can only be cultivated in institutions that are led by Germans."[64] In this view, the suppression of Polish performances of art music was the logical complement to the attempts by the Germans to paint their rule over eastern Europe as a civilizing force.

Paradoxically, Nazi cultural policy reinvigorated the belief among Polish commentators that culture was, in fact, a core element of nationhood. Numerous articles published in underground periodicals returned to this point.[65] In one, titled "Music at a Turning Point," the author claimed that the war had made the question of nationhood in music inescapable: "With perhaps the greatest clarity, the current war has demonstrated that culture is the most essential and durable element in the life of nations. It has shown that to a certain degree, culture is the foundation on which the very concept of nation is based. Hard historical necessity has forced even the most indecisive individuals to define their relation toward the problem of the nation. This problem has become again for all a matter of life and death; it has ceased to be only a topic of

90 | Chapter 3

voluntary discussions."[66] The author is no apologist for the brutality of Nazi rule or its arts policies, but he does come close to celebrating the war as a nationalizing experience, one that has reminded composers of the significance that their work should have always possessed.

The Nazi occupation certainly led to new emphasis on nationalist themes in music, as is often the case during modern warfare.[67] Yet the violence of occupation, which was conceived in national terms, also allowed Polish commentators to assert that cultural continuity was itself a form of resistance. Evidence of such thinking may be detected between the lines of numerous wartime musical activities. Consider, for instance, the "Instructions for Culture Workers" issued by the underground as part of plans for "civilian struggle" (*walka cywilna*) with the occupiers. According to these instructions, a core component of civilian struggle was for artists to continue making art and to maintain their cultural organizations to the maximum extent possible.[68] The boundaries between continuing to make art and making art that fought with the occupiers had been collapsed. A similar logic underwrites the propensity to document musical productivity in both personal letters from the occupation and underground reports, in acts of both formal and informal cataloging.[69] "Ten symphonies, four symphonic poems, four piano concerti, four violin concerti, eleven string quartets, two quintets, three sonatas, four violin works, thirty-seven piano works," reads one report tallying new compositions created between 1939 and 1942, as if evidence of anonymized musical productivity was itself relevant to Polish political leaders, who had fled the country at the beginning of the war.[70] In another example of the great lengths some went to demonstrate the continued vitality of composers in Poland, several newly composed works—by Palester, Padlewski, Régamey, and Wiechowicz—were microfilmed, smuggled out of the country, and published and performed under pseudonyms in London.[71] As Palester recalled, the aim of the project was "to demonstrate that composers in Poland were not wasting their time."[72] Thus, while the occupation was a time of severe limitations on musical life, it also confirmed, at least for some observers, that the musical intelligentsia had been correct to argue—as it had for decades prior—that classical music was fundamental to the nation and its civic existence.

THE ARMATURE OF SURVIVAL

For music to serve as an emblem of the nation's survival, musicians needed time, opportunities, and material support to continue their art, which was no small task under German rule. If one aspect of the cultural continuity between the interwar period and the occupation concerned the idea that music making was a civic project, then another was the systems of mutual aid among members of the musical intelligentsia. Not only did some of the most prominent interwar organizations continue their activities despite the occupation, but their leaders were quickly integrated into one of the largest resistance movements in Nazi-occupied Europe, known as the underground (*podziemie*).

The term *underground* can refer to a wide variety of activities undertaken in resistance to German rule in wartime Poland—including, but not limited to, illegal university instruction, hiding Jews from persecution, and participating in armed resistance. It can also denote the highly formalized structures of resistance that were subordinate to the remnants of the Second Republic, whose leadership had fled the country and reconstituted a government-in-exile, which was based in London for most of the war. Sometimes referred to as the underground state, it was an extensive, albeit illegal, governing system that existed just below the surface in German-occupied Poland. Armed resistance and the preparation for an uprising against the occupiers was an important aspect of the underground; it fielded an army (initially called Związek Walki Zbrojnej, Union of Armed Struggle, and after February 1942 the Armia Krajowa, AK, or Home Army) of about 350,000 members. But there was also an extensive underground civilian administration, known as the Delegate's Bureau, with a range of departments devoted to issues including internal affairs, security, and culture and education. It, too, reported to the London government-in-exile.[73] The imperative for underground preservation and resistance spoke with pronounced clarity to members of the Polish intelligentsia, who had traditionally been committed to national continuity under duress. Indeed, it was often members of the intelligentsia who assumed key positions in underground politics and activism.[74]

Members of the musical intelligentsia integrated themselves into underground activity in a variety of ways. Some became Home Army soldiers or aides. The music critic Konstanty Régamey, for example, worked as a courier for the Delegate's Bureau, traveling between Warsaw and Budapest on his (neutral) Swiss passport to avoid arrest.[75] The Delegate's Bureau also sought to form underground cells of musicians. This work was led by Stanisław Lorentz, the former director of the National Museum in Warsaw, who coordinated with two groups of musicians, one led by Edmund Rudnicki, the former director of the

92 | Chapter 3

Polish Radio, and the other by Piotr Perkowski, a composer and founder of the Association of Young Musician-Poles in Paris.[76] The Delegate's Bureau provided funding to musicians, which supplemented their meager incomes from café performances or savings.[77] In turn, musicians relayed reports to the London-based government-in-exile concerning musical conditions on the ground in occupied Poland.

While the occupation paused legal musical organizing, it did not spell the demise of Poland's musical organizations as much as it forced them into a more tentative stance. The people and interpersonal relations that had animated these organizations before the war reemerged during the occupation. Perkowski, for instance, who led one of the major groups of underground musicians, arranged loans to musicians who were in financial need and facilitated employment opportunities, recapitulating the role played by Association of Young Musician-Poles in Paris in a very different context over a decade earlier.[78] Tadeusz Ochlewski continued the work of the Polish Music Publishing Society, the umbrella organization whose mission had included publishing scores, running the ORMUZ concert organization, and performing early music. He commissioned musical and scholarly manuscripts that could be printed after the war, which in turn allowed him to distribute funds to musicologists and composers.[79] Of special importance for him was a multivolume set of analyses of Chopin's works.[80] Other projects included the publication of Szymanowski's letters, several volumes of early music scores, and a historical dictionary of musicians.[81] The concert-organizing venture ORMUZ, which had operated under the auspices of the society, also took on an occupation-era mandate. It was the model for recitals that were organized without German approval in trade schools for women, which reached an estimated eight thousand students.[82] Bronisław Rutkowski, a longtime editor of *Muzyka Polska* (the society's journal) likewise began laying the groundwork for a postwar continuation of the periodical: "We are continuously working and we believe that our work could pay off in the future. We have many projects, and it seems as if all of them are important and realistic. Among others, we are thinking about 'MP' [*Muzyka Polska*]. We have already begun to collect materials for it," he wrote in a letter of 1942.[83]

Through their commitments to institutional continuity, Perkowski, Ochlewski, and Rutkowski were also positioning their musical institutions as civically and political relevant after the war. Perkowski's group, for instance, devised a number of committees, the majority of which were directed toward rebuilding musical culture after the war concluded: there were committees on rebuilding the Warsaw opera house, on rebuilding the Warsaw Philharmonic, and the organization of a "music council."[84] These were not culturally insignificant projects for the group to consider. The Warsaw Philharmonic and opera house were arguably the two most important institutions of Poland's classical music culture. This planning was pragmatic and practical, addressing issues such as where the opera's library would be located and which rehearsal halls would be used for the ballet and which for the orchestra.[85] Strikingly, about half of the philharmonic, burned in 1939, had been rebuilt during the war, although this work would be undone by the Warsaw Uprising of 1944.[86] The commission devoted to the "music council" is also notable, since this replicated an idea that had first gained momentum in the late 1930s, when members of the Polish Music Publishing Society had envisioned a similar organization, the Music Chamber, as a way of controlling and "rationalizing" Polish musical life.

The underground also possessed a high level of moral authority, which it used to set norms that defined acceptable interactions with the occupiers.[87] It had a powerful megaphone to shape public opinion against those who were seen as accommodating the Germans thanks to its word-of-mouth networks and clandestine periodical, the *Biuletyn Informacyjny* (Informational bulletin), which was published in a print run of tens of thousands of copies and had an even larger informal circulation.[88] When the conductor Adam Dołżycki was seen as "bootlicking the Germans" before and during his performances, the underground condemned him by threatening the soloists who worked with him, calling for boycotts of his performances and denouncing him in the *Biuletyn Informacyjny*.[89]

The underground provided guidance and support when musicians were forced to make decisions about cooperating with the occupiers. Ochlewski, Rutkowski, and Rudnicki all oversaw the delicate balancing act around the Philharmonic of the General Government, both attempting to shield musicians from forced participation in the ensemble and also using membership in the orchestra to protect other individuals from persecution and deportation.[90] In other cases, members of the underground sanctioned appointments to German institutions if it was believed that doing so would help protect Poles with Jewish spouses: this was the rationale that led to Walerian Bierdiajew conducting the official orchestra of the Warsaw City Theater (Theater der Stadt Warschau) and Irena Barbag-Drexler (who was, conveniently, Viennese) serving as the secretary at the Warsaw Conservatory while her

94 | Chapter 3

husband was hidden in a tuberculosis hospital.[91] The underground's members also provided aid for musicians who were forced into compromising performances, such as when they helped the violinist Eugenia Umińska pass herself off as a chicken farmer to avoid a propagandistic performance before the German governor of the Radom District.[92]

Thanks to its political and moral authority, the underground allowed its members to exploit German musical institutions in ways that, without such guidance, would have been condemned as collaboration. Many musicians wished to reopen the Warsaw Conservatory in September 1940, for instance, because doing so would allow students to continue their educations, shield them from deportation, and employ the conservatory's instructional staff. But doing so required accepting German leadership of the school. Faced with this dilemma, Kazimierz Sikorski, who had been put forth as the new director, first consulted with members of the underground, including Rutkowski and Rudnicki, who approved of his cooperation with the occupiers in this instance. After reopening (purportedly as a low-level trade school), the conservatory effectively taught the prewar curriculum in an environment with little German oversight and without "any programmatic or ideological conditions" other than that there could be no students or teachers "of Jewish background."[93] Underground reports on the conservatory emphasized the "Polish character" of the institution, noting not only that students were studying Polish music but also that only six of the four hundred students at the conservatory did not "belong to the Polish nationality, and these are Russians and Ukrainians. There are no Germans or Volksdeutsch among the students."[94] Even while underground reports describe the reopening as a clever manipulation of a German-sanctioned institution, they made recourse to ethnonational categories to describe the "Polishness" of the institution, brushing aside the requirement that no students of Jewish background be allowed. Given that in 1931 about 20 percent of the conservatory's students had been Jewish, this was no minor omission.[95]

SOUNDS OF THE UNDERGROUND

The idea of the underground also offered musicians a metaphor for a social space that existed outside the confines of the German-ruled public sphere. The hundreds of concerts held in private apartments were often described in these terms.[96] Such concerts were organized on a systematic, near weekly basis by musicians associated with the underground.[97] Often, the income from the events was given to unemployed or impoverished musicians.[98] Nor, despite their private nature, were the events always small: some of the apartments qua concert halls were the spacious quarters of prewar industrial barons that could hold up to eighty people.[99] Assembling such a crowd without arousing suspicions required a delicate choreography, and audience members would begin to drift slowly into the apartment several hours before the performance began.[100] Despite being illegal, the concerts were relatively safe: there were no reports of them being raided.

The intimate, clandestine nature of the performances epitomized the idea that Polish art music would survive the war, an interpretation aided by the fact that the concerts were uncensored and the organizers routinely programmed works by Chopin, Szymanowski, and contemporary Polish composers.[101] At a concert held in 1942 in honor of Szymanowski (who had passed five years prior), the writer Jarosław Iwaszkiewicz delivered introductory remarks: "We have gathered together here," he noted, "in secret, like the first Christians in the catacombs, in order to celebrate in hiding the memory of our great artists. And we have even greater trust in our future now that we must hide our cults. Our secret cults of great people will have to kindle the bonfire, the great bonfire of true culture."[102] Here, Iwaszkiewicz endows Szymanowski with a Christlike aura, recasting the oppression of the occupation as a promissory note for future cultural strength. The listeners, in this metaphor, become the true believers whose commitment is the spark from which future musical culture will be ignited.

A similar idea is demonstrated by the 1947 film *Zakazane piosenki* (Forbidden songs), Poland's first postwar feature film, which narrated the war through the song culture of occupied Warsaw. In a central scene the film shows audiences attending a secret Chopin concert, pictured in figure 8. A voiceover states that the audience has attended the concert, because "for an hour or two, they were in Poland and not in the General Government. This was the miracle of Chopin." The scene of silent and full attention to Chopin's "forbidden" music is juxtaposed with the next scene, which features publicly available "light music." Cuts between saxophonists, dancers' bare legs, roulette tables, and German soldiers dancing with local women conjure not only "low" genres of popular music, but also the salacious, compromised, and collaborationist behavior that the film suggests accompanied such music in the censored, German-dominated public sphere.[103]

In addition to making such hard-edged claims for underground concerts as sites of national survival, composers and music critics also

FIGURE 8. The 1947 film *Forbidden Songs* depicts a clandestine concert of Chopin's music, held in a private apartment in occupied Warsaw. The pianist is Jan Krenz.

believed that the venues could serve as central nodes for the airing and discussion of new music. Most notable in this regard were the series of private concerts titled Concerts of Wartime Compositions, which began in December 1941 and continued through 1944.[104] In sum, these concerts included premieres of around twenty-five compositions in chamber genres by fifteen composers, including Grażyna Bacewicz, Roman Palester, and Konstanty Régamey, among others. Writing shortly after the war concluded, Régamey sang the praises of such underground concerts, claiming, "Never in the prewar times could one encounter such a receptive audience, so full of enthusiasm, as one did in these modest private gatherings."[105] He was especially positive about the concerts that premiered new compositions, claiming that "these concerts attract an elite of Polish artists, and never in other circumstances could composers count on such a select listenership and on such intimate contact with the listener, nor, for that matter, on such a quick performance of their new works."[106]

Régamey's claim that the underground concerts were in fact improvements on prewar performances because of their select and intimate nature reflects a veneration of elite listenership that had deep roots in the musical intelligentsia. He also suggests that the war had led to a focusing and concentration of a new-music community that had been more ideologically and geographically diffuse prior to the war. Such views were rooted in his experiences premiering his works during the occupation. Indeed, Régamey made his compositional debut during the war, after many years spent as a critic and editor. The most widely discussed of his wartime works was his Quintet, for clarinet, bassoon, violin, cello, and piano, which was premiered in 1944. The performance reportedly had "created a sensation," according to Jan Krenz, who had turned pages at the premiere.[107] Régamey wrote in a letter shortly after the performance that he found himself "completely disoriented by this success."[108]

The work was especially striking for its blending of twelve-tone technique with tonal harmony, one of the few Polish works composed during the war to engage with such techniques. As Alicja Jarzębska has demonstrated, the second movement is based on three twelve-tone rows.[109] Although the composition is based in atonal techniques, Régamey arranges his twelve-tone material so as to provide frequent anchor points in triadic harmonies, as shown in example 3. The initial row, presented in measure one, is partitioned into four chords that provide an ostinato for the opening phase. The first beats in each measure are diatonic, second-inversion triads, while the bass spells a chromatic ascent from B to D. The second row, introduced by the violin in measure four, is likewise composed of a number of thirds and fourths, which imply tonal relationships. Perhaps it was these elements of a tonal musical language that led Stefan Kisielewski, one of the few to dislike the work, to accuse Régamey of "betraying contemporary music, diminishing it by returning to the filth of the nineteenth century."[110] What is most noteworthy here is not the content of the views per se, but rather the way in which underground concerts of new music could engender such debates about new music in the first place. In this sense, private concerts served as a stand-in for discursive spaces that the musical intelligentsia had long cultivated. Although their periodicals, concert halls, and music organizations were officially shuttered, their commitment to a small cultural elite debating and leading musical life remained in place.

MUSIC IN PUBLIC: THE WARSAW CAFÉS

There was also a robust public musical life in Polish Warsaw, much of which occurred in cafés. Their role within narratives of national

EXAMPLE 3. Konstanty Régamey, Quintet for clarinet, bassoon, violin, cello, and piano, movement 2 (Intermezzo Romantico), mm 1–11. Polskie Wydawnictwo Muzyczne.

continuity and resistance to German rule was less clear than that of the underground concerts or clandestine organizing, however. In the first months of the occupation numerous cafés offering musical performances were established in Polish Warsaw, and by late 1940 it was estimated that around five hundred musicians in the General Government found employment through them.[111] As discussed previously, German occupation policy presumed that by confining musical performance to cafés, listeners would be limited to consuming "low," entertainment-centered genres, which in turn would undermine their sense of national legitimacy. This policy, however, was premised on an erroneous understanding of the cultural significance of cafés in Warsaw prior to the war. Indeed, as discussed in chapter 1, Polish intellectuals had flocked to cafés in the 1920s and '30s, which they viewed as quasi-avant-garde spaces in which new literary movements could be birthed and aesthetic principles debated. The idea that the café could be more than a space for socializing, entertainment, and casual performance was ingrained in the intelligentsia's imagination.

Like their prewar counterparts, the occupation-era cafés were diverse in their approaches to art, performance, and music. In some, musical performances were background to conversation and socialization. Régamey recalled that as a café pianist he was "obligated to improvise quantities of slow fox-trots, tangoes, and so forth," and he was so bored by the task that he was able read books concurrently.[112] Other cafés, such as the composer Piotr Perkowski's café Lira (The Lyre), aimed to help struggling musicians eat and connect them to employment.[113] Still other cafés appealed to an audience of the concertgoing and theatergoing public who wished to see their favorite performers. For example, at U Aktorek (The Actresses' Café) guests were served by actresses and singers who had refused to perform on official German-sanctioned stages and now worked as waitresses instead. A major draw of this venue was the promise of up-close interactions with once inaccessible (and primarily female) stars of the Polish stage.[114] Whatever their cultural offerings, most cafés attracted small groups of devoted attendees, which could balloon when well-known musicians performed.[115]

Cafés provided musicians with income and proof of employment, a crucial certification in German-ruled Poland. Earnings in cafés were not high: according to a report written in late 1941 or early 1942, earnings could vary from between four to twenty złoty a day for café performers, although stars attracted higher rates.[116] This was not a lot of money, but it was not an exceptionally low income either. For comparison, the average Warsaw city employee made around 250 złoty a month.[117] Such wages were in themselves not sufficient to live on, since the price of food had risen sharply during the occupation; by early 1942 a kilo of flour on the black market cost seventeen złoty, about thirty-three times the prewar price.[118] Musicians' low earnings in cafés help to explain the appeal of employment at the conservatory or the Philharmonic of the General Government, both of which paid wages of five hundred złoty a month.[119] But even if wages were low at cafés, proof of employment was a certification without which one could be sent to a concentration camp or to forced labor in the Reich.[120] Aware of this benefit, some impresarios such as Bolesław Woytowicz, who ran the café Dom Sztuki (House of Art), sought to maximize the number of musicians featured in his concerts so as to protect as many as possible.[121]

Even as the finances of many café employees and patrons had become perilous, several of the cafés offered patrons a sense of connection to the ornate, cultured environment of the prewar city. U Aktorek began operations in a palace belonging to the Radziwiłłs, perhaps the most powerful family of Polish noble magnates, and paintings of the family adorned the rooms where guests ate.[122] Although lacking in noble ties, the café Sztuka i Moda (Art and Fashion)—or SiM as it was commonly known—had made a name for itself by appealing to a world of cultured elites. Before the war, its owner recalled, it was a "very exclusive venue" where painters, sculptors, and poets could have their works displayed and interact with their upper-crust patrons. These encounters took place in the elegant surroundings of a converted orangery, complete with expansive glass windows, modern furniture, and statuary.[123] During the occupation it offered around 1,300 performances, or around five concerts per week.[124] Suggestive of the role envisioned for SiM as a cultural institution, it had an artistic director, Mieczysław Jerzy Erhardt, who was in charge of programming and published a monthly calendar of these events.[125]

Musical performances in cafés sated the wide cultural tastes of the urban intelligentsia by offering performances that ranged from the established stars of the operatic stage to the fast-growing world of popular music. Patrons at U Aktorek could hear regular performances from the internationally renowned operatic soprano Ewa Bandrowska-Turska, several salon-jazz orchestras, and three performances a week by Mieczysław Fogg, the most famous Polish crooner.[126] The then little-known composers Witold Lutosławski and Andrzej Panufnik explored this eclectic aesthetic in their composing or, more accurately, arranging: they formed a piano duo that performed in several cafés, including U

Aktorek and SiM. Sometimes their performances were background music, in which they performed "light, jazz, and popular music," and they also improvised in these styles. They also drew from the classical canon. They performed Debussy's two piano arrangement of the *Prelude to the Afternoon of a Faun*, as well as their own versions of Ravel's *Boléro*, a Bach organ toccata, Bizet's *Carmen*, Tchaikovsky's *Nutcracker Suite*, and waltzes of Schubert, Brahms, and Mozart.[127] Of the duo's approximately two hundred arrangements, the majority were only informal notations in scores that helped to guide their performances, while about a dozen were fully written out with an eye to postwar publication. Almost all of these arrangements were lost during the Warsaw Uprising in 1944.[128]

One work that has survived is Lutosławski's *Variations on a Theme by Paganini*, based on Paganini's twenty-fourth Caprice for Solo Violin. Lutosławski's composition is a virtuosic tour de force, revealing the immense pianistic skill and compositional ability that the duo could bring to Warsaw's cafés. One of the main compositional feats of the work is to reimagine the virtuoso techniques of the violin for the piano. Of course, if transcribed literally for two pianos the original caprice would lose all of its technical challenges. Lutosławski instead seeks out pianistic equivalences of violin virtuosity, which are faithful to the variation techniques that Paganini employs. An especially clear example of this virtuosic reimagining occurs in the ninth variation, which in Paganini's caprice requires the violinist to alternate notes that are bowed by the right hand with those plucked by the left, which is simultaneously stopping the string at the proper pitch (see examples 4 and 5). (These pizzicatos are indicated with a "+" above the note in the score.) Needless to say, this technique is extremely difficult on the violin and cannot be replicated on the piano. Lutosławski instead captures the slightly jolting, off-kilter rhythm the technique produces, as evinced through the before-the-beat grace notes in the *secunda* part. The sense of rapid back-and-forth between pizzicato and bowed notes in Paganini is also evoked by the interlocking rests and attacks of chords spread across octaves in the two pianos. With its attention-grabbing virtuosity, this piece was by no means the music of background listening. But since it is the only surviving of the duo's pieces, we cannot say with any certainty whether it was representative of their wartime performances.

Of all the cafés of the occupation era, it was perhaps Woytowicz's café, Dom Sztuki (House of Art), that came closest to transforming the purportedly entertainment-centered venue of the café into a substitute

EXAMPLE 4. Niccolò Paganini, 24 Caprices for Solo Violin, No. 24 in A Minor, variation 9.

EXAMPLE 5. Witold Lutosławski, *Wariacje na temat Paganiniego* (Variations on a theme by Paganini), mm. 130–33. Polskie Wydawnictwo Muzyczne.

concert hall. Since 1924 Woytowicz had been a professor of piano at the Warsaw Conservatory and also a respected composer, having studied with Nadia Boulanger from 1930 to 1932. When the Warsaw Conservatory was shuttered in 1939, he was approached by Irena Bielińska, the director and co-owner of the Dom Sztuki antique dealership, who wished to open a concert hall devoted to classical music. After protracted back-and-forth with the occupation's cultural officialdom, they received permission not for a concert hall but for a café instead. Known as either Dom Sztuki or Kawiarnia Prof. Woytowicza (Professor Woytowicz's Café), the café was one of a handful that was authorized to perform classical repertoire.[129] Exploiting this status, it became a de facto concert hall, offering performances of works such as the Brahms Piano Quintet, Debussy Cello Sonata, and Liszt Piano Sonata in B Minor, as shown on the program for one month in figure 9. Despite performances five or six days a week, seats in the café had to be reserved up to six weeks in advance and it was not uncommon for 150 or 200 people to attend a concert. Respecting traditional concert etiquette, audiences came to listen in silence, not to eat, drink, or talk.[130]

In Polish Warsaw there were as many reasons for attending café performances as there were audience members, and many listeners and performers alike saw café performances as a way of escaping the dreadful reality of the occupation.[131] When Woytowicz wrote about Dom Sztuki in the 1960s, he unequivocally asserted that the classical performances were "resistance to the Germans who had condemned Poles to only trashy, worthless so-called music."[132] Given the high stakes of performing art music under the occupation, others no doubt shared this view. Wartime evidence, however, shows a higher level of ambivalence about the musical cafés than Woytowicz recounts. Some contemporaries questioned the degree to which the cafés had successfully subverted German limitations on the performance of high culture. Although a handful of oft-mentioned cafés—such as Dom Sztuki or SiM—did manage to preserve a place for well-rehearsed classical music, they were not necessarily the norm. A contrasting perspective emerges from a report compiled by the underground, which noted that "with few exceptions, the level of musical production in cafés is generally low."[133] A different article in an underground periodical claimed that "cafés—with only a few exceptions—do not give musicians the possibility of practicing their art on the highest level."[134] Others went further. Performing in the cafés was a "humiliating artistic compromise" for musicians, according to another anonymous writer, in large part because of the repertoire

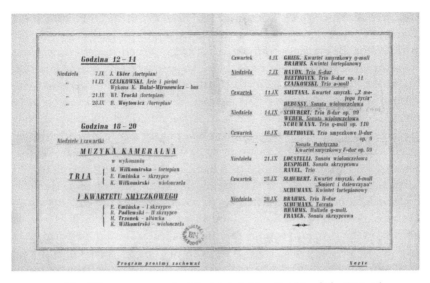

FIGURE 9. Detail from a program for Woytowicz's Dom Sztuki café for September 1941. The front and back of this one sheet of paper show the repertoire for the entire month and implore listeners to "please save the program" at the bottom. In this month a concert took place every day except Mondays, with two performances each Sunday. The 6 p.m. start time of the evening concerts ensured audiences had time to return home before curfew. Polona/Biblioteka Narodowa.

performed there.[135] For such observers, the strictures limiting music to cafés and to "light" genres had been largely effective, even if Dom Sztuki, SiM, and U Aktorek were notable exceptions.

The public nature of the café also meant that German officials often attended the performances. The most infamous example of this was the Lardello Café, where the conductor Dołyżcki was widely condemned for his subservience to German audiences, as mentioned previously. But even cafés where musicians avoided such displays of deference had to contend with the presence of Germans in their audiences, some of whom were educated devotees of classical music. Lutosławski recalled that the "least pleasant" days at SiM were Sundays because the café would be flooded by German officers, many of whom came specifically to listen to his duo perform. "Unfortunately, it is necessary to note that, as far as musical listeners go, they were a select group," he recalled.[136] Woytowicz likewise described numerous visits from musically inclined Germans in his cafés. The changing strictures on whether Germans could attend performances at Dom Sztuki was a continual source of stress for him. When

The Nation Is a Matter of Life and Death | 105

they were allowed, a group of around twenty German officers, many of them medics, attended the performances of chamber music.[137] Thus, even if café performers and impresarios believed their performances were resisting German rule, they were also entertaining their enemies.

Cafés were also dangerous places to spend time. Of course, nowhere was truly safe in occupied Warsaw, but cafés were specifically targeted by the occupiers because the intelligentsia was known to gather in them. Indeed, the Germans had decided to allow cafés to continue to operate in part because they believed doing so would make it easier to monitor and control the intelligentsia.[138] German agents would routinely carry out raids of cafés, arresting those who happened to be in attendance.[139] Lutosławski and Panufnik only avoided falling prey to one such arrest when the owner of the café vouched that they were his employees.[140] Roman Jasiński recalled that he was lucky not to be performing on the day that SiM was raided but that his less fortunate colleagues and some audience members were sent to Auschwitz.[141] Palester was less lucky: on May 8, 1940, he was in Café Club, at the corner of Jerozolimskie and Nowy Świat streets, passing the time before he began performing at Gastronomia, a café across the street. Off work, he was arrested in a roundup and spent six weeks in the notorious Pawiak prison before being released thanks to the combined efforts of his soon-to-be wife, Barbara Podoska, and his family.[142] As these experiences suggest, the assertion that cafés undergirded Polish musical sustenance and national preservation has to be weighed against the reality that they were a key site of German control and violence against Polish elites.

POLISH CONTINUITY, JEWISH ABSENCE

The musical ecosystem that took shape in Polish Warsaw was hardly the emaciated version of musical life that Nazi policy envisioned for the Poles. There were both cultural and material reasons for this vitality. The occupiers' attempts to extirpate Polishness in the cultural arena conjured up well-established scripts of action for the intelligentsia, leading it to reiterate its view of culture as a source of national continuity. Materially, music making continued in part because the Germans did not eliminate underground resistance. Thus, the Delegate's Bureau could supply musicians with funds, and the leaders of prewar musical organizations drew on their networks of contacts to help create an infrastructure for wartime mutual support. Even the German policy of confining performances to cafés in an attempt to deprive Poles of "artistic experiences" had the unintended consequence of pushing performance into private spaces and reinforcing the artistically heterogeneous nature of the public café.

I do not mean to present a rosy vision of the occupation or to dismiss the suffering experienced by virtually all Varsovians. All who lived in occupied Warsaw experienced terror. But this chapter's examination of musical continuity into the war period does help us to grasp a prominent, if confusing, aspect of how these years have been remembered by non-Jewish, Catholic Poles who lived through them: namely, a belief that the war was a period of musical growth and development. For instance, in a letter composed in 1942 (which he published in 1979), the music critic Jerzy Waldorff endorsed the view that the war was "a few years' time for solid work, free from diplomatic receptions, ministerial teas, celebratory premieres," and similar distractions. Not only, he claimed, "were all composers [in 1942] working no worse than before the war, but in many cases we were working more intensely than before the war."[143] To illustrate this point he lists all the composers who had reached new levels of productivity during the occupation, including Ludomir Różycki, Régamey, Palester, and Bacewicz. Palester endorsed a similar view, describing the occupation as "time given by God, in the sense that we were free from all types of marginal activities and could attend exclusively to creative work," although he added that only "people with very strong nerves" could capitalize on this newfound time.[144] Perhaps no one captured this ambivalence as clearly as the pianist Roman Jasiński: "Despite the horrors experienced in occupied Poland, I was somehow in my own way happy then. I understand that this sounds strange, at the very least . . . but despite the fact that each of us were threatened with death—or maybe precisely because of this—I felt a strange peace. . . . Music was then the main current of my life."[145] Such memoirs are not only back shadowing: we have seen extensive contemporary documentation that likewise cast the war as having elevated the social significance of music.

These reactions among non-Jewish, Catholic Poles raise the fundamental question of who belonged to the Polish musical community in the first place. If productivity was proof of cultural survival, then whose productivity mattered? The answer to this question, put bluntly, is that their arguments for continuity in institutions and practices ignored the suffering of those confined to the Warsaw Ghetto. No one in the ghetto would have chosen imprisonment over even the dullest of ministerial teas or celebratory premieres. The narrative of cultural continuity—

undergirded by the institutions of Polish survival in occupied Warsaw—was also a myopic one, as it did not extend a sense of comradeship across Nazi racial segregation. I do not mean that there was a conscious, overt animosity that led non-Jewish Poles into this stance. As we will see in the next chapter, non-Jewish musicians did aid their Jewish colleagues and were aware of their plight. Rather, the reemergence of powerful narratives concerning Polish cultural survival against the backdrop of unprecedented segregation and anti-Jewish violence simplified the fraught, and multiple, meanings of nation that had animated the musical community before the war. To imagine a national community grounded in the past that would survive the war, the musical intelligentsia also simplified who belonged to that nation. Insisting on musical performance as an emblem of their survival and their own vitality, they reified Jewish absence, placing Jewish music making outside the boundaries that defined the Polish musical community.

4

We Cannot Imagine Life without Music

The Warsaw Ghetto was an inescapable presence in the city during the occupation, even for those who did not explicitly mention or discuss it. It was carved out of north-central Warsaw, and it was here that dozens of musicians attempted to survive ever-worsening conditions. The Warsaw Ghetto's relation to both the prewar city and Polish Warsaw were complex. Internees could not leave the ghetto, at least not easily and certainly not legally. It was cut off from the city by walls and barbed wire, and the entry points were guarded by Jewish and Polish police, as well as German forces. Poverty, hunger, and infections were rampant, and thousands died monthly of disease and starvation between when it was sealed in November 1940 and when the mass deportations to death camps began in July 1942. Yet there were also reminders that the ghetto prisoners were still living in Warsaw; there were postal deliveries, tram services, telephone connections, and continuous smuggling across the ghetto walls, on which the internees depended to survive. As the historian Barbara Engelking has noted, the ghetto existed "behind a 'half-drawn curtain'"; its prisoners still lived in the city of Warsaw, but a city remade in countless horrifying ways.[1]

The musical culture that took shape in the Warsaw Ghetto was likewise an outgrowth of the city's prewar music making, albeit one subjected to the shock, violence, and widespread poverty that defined existence in the ghetto. A symphony orchestra comprised of members of the city's leading prewar ensembles performed, even as its musicians starved.

Cafés flourished as sites of artistic and social activity, even if they were often inaccessible. Cabaret performers offered musical-social critique, now directed at the strictures of ghettoization rather than the foibles of urban interwar life. Even the courtyards of the dense housing stock of northern Warsaw had a role to play in the ghetto's musical life, as they became the de facto stages on which hundreds of musicians performed.[2]

These traces of the familiar within the radically new environment of the ghetto underscore what the historian Amos Goldberg has identified as the central challenge facing scholars of the Nazi ghettos: "How is it possible to write the history of *helplessness*," he asks, "without sliding into heroization on the one hand, or obscuring the magnitude of the crisis on the other, but also without [helplessness] becoming a sanctified and melodramatic icon?"[3] A focus on continuities in culture between the prewar city and the ghetto can imply a false resilience among internees that ignores the myriad ways trauma shaped their sense of self. But it is also possible to go too far in the other direction by aestheticizing the victims' experiences and the newness of the ghetto itself. Musicologists have been especially attuned to this second tendency, because music of the Holocaust has sometimes been programmed and marketed in ways that suggest that it is uniquely posed to offer audiences access to Holocaust experience.[4] To avoid these dual pitfalls, Goldberg urges scholars to examine transformations in the ghetto, attending to the ways in which the practices of meaning making were at once familiar and remade in it. Indeed, we will see several ways in which music in the Warsaw Ghetto remained a site on which the conflicting pressures that had long defined Jewish modernity continued to be heard and contested.

In addition to focusing on the Polish-speaking musical intelligentsia within the ghetto, I also sketch a broader account of the musical ecosystem of the ghetto, examining some of the key institutions, activists, and spaces of music making in it. I do so in part because the ghetto forced acculturated Polish Jewish members of the musical intelligentsia to confront their relationship to Jewish culture, identity, and language in ways they had not always done so prior. But I also do so in order to make explicit the absence of the ghetto's music in both Polish wartime and postwar accounts: music mattered as much, if not more so, in the ghetto than it did in Polish Warsaw, and it was supported by some of the same types of institutions, including cafés and mutual aid organizations. Despite this, the traces of the Warsaw Ghetto's music making beyond its wall and after its destruction were often few and far between.

FIGURE 10. Michał Borwicz and Hersz Wasser (right) unearthing part of the Oyneg Shabes archive from the rubble of the Warsaw Ghetto on September 18, 1946. Photo by PAP/Władysław Forbert.

The omnipresent horror of the ghetto led some of its witnesses to create a historical record characterized by an immediacy of observation that is markedly different from the accounts of music making in Polish Warsaw or, for that matter, in early postwar musical discourse. Ghettoized writers had much more to say about practices of listening, the experiences of audiences in new venues, and the texture of everyday life than did musicians in Polish Warsaw, perhaps because everyday life was fundamentally different than it had been before the ghetto. This is especially true of the essays written for the Oyneg Shabes archive (also known as the Ringelblum archive), several of which I draw on here. This was a secret archive situated in the ghetto and named after the traditional Sabbath gathering of members of the community, reflecting the fact that its organizers held their regular, clandestine meetings on the Sabbath.[5] Although one of the most significant sources concerning the Warsaw Ghetto, it has seen little attention from music scholars. Begun by the historian Emanuel Ringelblum in its earliest form in October 1939, it preserves thousands of contemporary documents, mostly in Polish and Yiddish, which in 1942 and 1943 were buried in metal boxes and milk canisters below the ghetto and partially recovered after the war, as shown in figure 10.[6] Because the archive's dozens of associates believed that evidence drawn from everyday life in the ghetto would help create a postwar history of Jewish persecution, the reports it commissioned and collected preserve keen observations about the catastrophe engulfing Jewish Warsaw. They are profound documents of witness.

INSIDE THE WARSAW GHETTO

The area of Warsaw in which the ghetto was established, slightly north of the city center, had been a center of Jewish inhabitance before the war, but it was not exclusively a Jewish neighborhood, and Jews had also lived elsewhere in Warsaw. In April 1940 the German authorities mandated the building of a wall around Jewish-inhabited areas under the false pretense of containing a typhus pandemic. The ghetto was officially decreed on October 12, 1940, at which point Jews were required to live within its arbitrary boundaries and Poles were required to leave said territory. The decreeing of the ghetto unleashed a frenzy as Jews attempted to find apartments within the ghetto boundaries; all told, 138,000 Jews and 113,000 Poles had to change their residence (a process that would be repeated as the ghetto's boundaries were changed several times over the following years). By the time the ghetto was sealed in November 1940, nearly 400,000 Jews were confined to an area of about 1.3 square miles, shown in map 2. The ghetto also saw the influx of around 150,000 refugees who had been deported to the ghetto from elsewhere and who were among the ghetto's most destitute. Even before the so-called Grossaktion Warschau—when, from July 22 to September 21, 1942, more than 300,000 ghetto prisoners were deported and murdered in Treblinka—thousands of internees were dying every month of starvation and disease.[7]

In the decades prior to the Holocaust, Warsaw had a Jewish population of over 300,000, making it one of the world's largest Jewish metropolises.[8] The political and cultural heterogeneity of this population was reflected in the ghetto itself, in which dozens of Jewish identities, political parties, and artistic programs continued to hold sway. Although the majority of the ghetto spoke Yiddish, there were also many cultural figures interned in it who primarily spoke Polish. Recall that in Warsaw the German occupiers considered people to be Jews if they had two or more Jewish grandparents, and thus many acculturated Jews were forced into the ghetto. They had often participated in Polish cultural institutions before the war, understood themselves as helping to build Polish musical culture, and often had extensive professional and

112 | Chapter 4

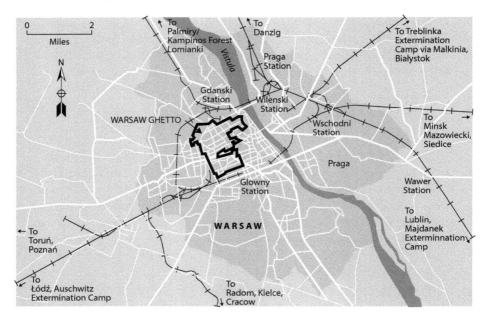

MAP 2. The Warsaw Ghetto (1940), to which hundreds of thousands of Jews were confined, was carved out of the urban fabric of the city.

personal connections to non-Jewish Poles outside the ghetto. The decision of acculturated and even converted musicians to move into the ghetto was not illogical: in 1940, when the ghetto was created, the deportations to death camps were unforeseeable, and for many Jews it seemed safer to relocate to the ghetto than risk being blackmailed, caught, or exposed for living illegally outside it. Those who remained in Polish Warsaw had to pass completely as Poles.[9]

This was the case with the family of Roman Palester. His father, Henryk, a renowned doctor, had continued to work as the director of the Society for Preventative Medicine during the first weeks of the occupation. Soon, however, a senior official in the city hall called Henryk's wife, Maria, to inform her that a list of all Jews employed by the city would soon need to be compiled. Sensing the danger that including Henryk on such a list would hold for the family, the official proposed an alternative plan: Henryk would cease working and his wife, Maria (Roman's stepmother), would work for the city instead. She could lead the milk kitchen, or cafeteria, division as long as she used her maiden name. This plan was decisive for the family's survival since it helped mask their Jewishness, allowed them to remain in their apartment, and provided the family with a much-needed source of income.[10] In addition, the family altered the name of Henryk's mother from the Jewish "Goldenberg" to the German-sounding "Gödenburg" on a crucial marriage certificate.[11] Thanks to this foresight in the early days of occupation, they could use their apartment in Warsaw's Mokotów neighborhood to help the less fortunate: they offered refuge to numerous Jews, who hid in their apartment for periods of months to years.[12]

For acculturated musicians who did relocate to the ghetto, the sealing of the ghetto often led to a sudden break in ongoing artistic projects that had previously crossed racial boundaries. The pianist and composer Władysław Szpilman, for instance, had performed with non-Jewish musicians in a café in Polish Warsaw up until the sealing of the ghetto.[13] In the other direction, the Jewish Symphony Orchestra situated in the ghetto had been hiring non-Jewish wind players to fill out its roster up until the moment entry to the ghetto became highly restricted.[14] The breaking off of these performances by the ghetto wall was a rapid act of forced isolation in which nearly overnight the premise that Poles and Polish Jews were coparticipants in the city's musical culture was shattered.

In other cases connections across the ghetto wall continued, albeit in constrained form. Wiera Gran, one of the most prominent singers in the ghetto, claimed that her non-Jewish admirers would sneak into the ghetto to hear her perform.[15] Polish underground organizations, discussed in chapter 3, also had connections with the ghetto: Piotr Perkowski, a leader of the musical underground in Polish Warsaw, claimed to have a network of contacts extending into the ghetto through which he heard about the artists performing there.[16] Mixed marriages proved crucial in these cross-wall connections. One of Perkowski's intermediaries was Gerard Gadejski. A non-Jewish Pole, he was married to the Jewish Irena Neumark, who lived in the ghetto and was the secretary for one of its main concert organizations. Gadejski had a pass allowing him to enter the ghetto, which he used to visit his wife, attend performances several times per week, and consult with ghetto musicians about how to obtain permission from the occupiers for performances.[17] Around the time of the mass deportations in summer 1942, connections such as Gadejski's outside the ghetto became a matter of life and death: a musician's professional network, marriage, or contacts with non-Jewish Poles was often a decisive factor in escape and hiding on the *aryjska strona* (Aryan side), as we will see.

114 | Chapter 4

While the complete isolation of Jews was a major aim of the occupiers, German interference in the ghetto's cultural life was arguably less severe than it was in Polish Warsaw. Performances in the ghetto were censored, although according to different criteria than those in Polish Warsaw. While the Nazis aimed to ban performances of art music and pieces with Polish national connotations in Polish Warsaw, ghetto performers were restricted to performing only "Jewish" music, as was the case in the Jüdischer Kulturbund in Germany.[18] The Nazi understanding of Jews as racially inferior meant that purportedly Jewish music in the ghetto was not seen as threatening to Nazi rule as was Polish music, and thus the priority remained on its containment and cultural isolation. Musicians in the ghetto did have to submit their programs to censorship, and there is extant documentation that the aid organizations organizing concerts and cafés did so.[19] But there was also evidently less concern for these strictures in the performance spaces themselves. So lax was the enforcement that the ghetto's Jewish Symphony Orchestra played works by non-Jewish composers for nearly two years before this violation came to the attention of the authorities and the orchestra was forced to cease performances, although this was quite possibly a pretext.[20] True, the orchestra took the precaution of not printing the repertoire on advertisements and instead announcing the pieces from the stage, but their performances were also reviewed in the official paper, where the titles of the "non-Jewish" pieces were given.[21] A final consideration is that the punishment for playing forbidden music paled in comparison to the widespread misery, starvation, and death that were the everyday reality of the ghetto. As Stanisław Różycki, a commentator writing for the Oyneg Shabes archive, asked, "Are we allowed to perform works of non-Jewish composers and authors? . . . I don't know. Maybe we are, maybe not. I only know that whether it is allowed or not the people of the ghetto will do it all because without it they won't survive even one day, because without it they cannot imagine life. . . . We don't know what's allowed, or rather we know that nothing is allowed and therefore everything is allowed."[22]

SONIC TRANSFORMATIONS IN THE WARSAW GHETTO

The traumatic remaking of the city through ghettoization was painfully audible to those writing in or about the ghetto. Witnesses observed how the collapse in musical employment meant more and more musicians were performing on ghetto streets. Stanisław Gombiński, who was a police officer in the ghetto, mentioned in the first chapter of his memoirs from April 1944 that the "noise of the ghetto street was loud."[23] His ear was drawn not only to people begging and selling wares but also to the less expected sounds made by musicians. "Singing and music with every step, on the street, blocking traffic, in courtyards, on squares," he wrote. Some of what he heard were beggars singing for alms, but he also described the sounds of trained musicians. "Again, scales of the most varied types—singers, excellent opera arias and beautiful songs, voices, which had sung in concert halls and opera houses. Verdi, Puccini, Meyerbeer, Moniuszko, Niewiadomski, and—oh Jewish impudence—Schubert, Schumann, and Wagner."[24] The repertoire that Gombiński heard (or chose to list) included Italian, Polish, and German composers that far exceeded the "Jewish" music the ghetto prisoners were supposed to perform exclusively. Beyond this, his description of such sounds early in his memoirs conjures the aural newness of the ghetto, underscoring how ghettoization had dislocated music from the concert hall onto the street.

The *Gazeta Żydowska* (Jewish newspaper) gave this phenomenon a positive veneer. It described how "with the lyre in her hand, Polyhymnia, the muse of music, has left behind those venues that are today no longer needed. She has left the stifling and always crowded venues of the nighttime dance halls as well as the serious temples of this art. She has gone onto the cobbled street in order to survive the difficult period of the war."[25] This statement should be interpreted within the context of its publication in the *Gazeta Żydowska*, the official paper of the Jewish community in occupied Poland, which was published in Polish. Although this periodical is an important source about musical life in the ghetto because of its extensive concert reviews, it was also widely despised by ghetto prisoners for promoting German propaganda and downplaying the severity of ghetto life.[26] The article quoted above, titled "Art on the Street," was written less than a week before the ghetto would be sealed from the city, at a time when thousands of Jews had just been forced into the ghetto and others were desperately attempting to find apartments in it. The writer euphemizes ghettoization by describing it as the "difficult period of the war" and paints the mass unemployment among musicians, which was the reason musicians went into the streets in the first place, as a quasi-democratization of art. The critic's attempt to project normalcy onto the transformation of the ghetto's aural spaces suggests, if nothing else, that the changing sounds of the ghetto street were becoming ubiquitous, and so difficult to ignore, that they called for a euphemistic interpretation.

FIGURE 11. An opera singer, identified as Dotlinger, performs on the streets of the Warsaw Ghetto in 1940 or 1941. USHMM, Photograph Number 05518.

One of the most notable attempts to address this crisis in musical employment was the organization of a symphony orchestra in the ghetto, which began performing shortly after the creation of the ghetto and remained in operation until April 1942. The orchestra primarily performed canonic European repertoire, including many works by banned non-Jewish composers, including Mozart, Bach, and Beethoven.[27] By summer 1941 the orchestra was operating under the auspices of the Judenrat (Jewish Council) and under the honorary patronage of Adam Czerniaków, the head of the Judenrat, and his wife, Felicja. At this point the orchestra assumed the official name of the Żydowska Orkiestra Symfoniczna (Jewish Symphony Orchestra).[28] From its origins, the orchestra was seen not only as a way of meeting the "cultural needs" of internees in the ghetto, but also as a way of supporting unemployed musicians.[29] Audiences were encouraged to attend the events and to promote the concerts as an act of charity. The concerts were popular, and they regularly filled or exceeded the capacity of their performance spaces.[30] Even this well-attended ensemble, however, could do little to counteract the dire conditions facing its musicians. Pay was low. In March 1941, for instance, a violinist was paid ten złoty and was due another six złoty for two concerts and two weeks of rehearsals—at a time when a loaf of bread cost nine złoty.[31] (By comparison, recall that the wages for non-Jewish musicians in German ensembles and at the

Warsaw conservatory were five hundred złoty a month, a rate about fifteen times higher than that of the Jewish Symphony Orchestra violinist.) According to Marcel Reich, "the majority of musicians in our orchestra were then faced with extreme poverty and often came to rehearsals or concerts having not eaten anything all day."[32]

Reich was well positioned to observe the orchestra's activities. In the ghetto he worked for the Jewish Council, where he translated correspondence with the occupiers. He was also a music critic for the *Gazeta Żydowska*, writing under the pen name Wiktor Hart.[33] Shortly after the war concluded, he wrote an extensive report about the Jewish Symphony Orchestra, which he deposited with the Central Jewish Historical Commission in Warsaw. In it, he described how the orchestra was able to recruit string players but was faced with a dearth of wind players. Before the ghetto was sealed, the orchestra brought in non-Jewish Poles to play these parts. After this was no longer possible, more creativity was required. The clarinet, trumpet, and trombone parts in the classical compositions were played by jazz musicians, with oboe parts also played on the clarinet. The orchestra leaders found their first flutist because he had been busking on the street. Unable to find any French horn players, the orchestra instead played these parts on the saxophone.[34] Never before, claimed Reich, had the famous horn calls of Beethoven's Fifth Symphony been played by saxophones. Parts and sheet music were also scarce: sometimes parts were smuggled from Polish Warsaw, but more often parts for the sixty to eighty musicians had to be copied out by hand from the score, a laborious process. Heating and lighting in the performance halls was, at best, inconsistent.[35]

Audiences faced other perils. Attending the concerts could be dangerous because they had to traverse the ghetto, thereby exposing them to German roundups. "Every time I left my house to go to a concert, I didn't know if I would make it to the hall. Many times, young supporters of music paid for their love of the art by lifting heavy furniture or chopping wood," Reich claimed, after they had been forced into labor by the Germans. "But nonetheless," Reich concluded, "the huge hall was always full: the Jewish youth could not deprive themselves of the one cultural entertainment that ghetto life then made available."[36] In his view, the dire material conditions of the ghetto were a foil not only to the dedication of the audience, but also to that of the musicians themselves, who rehearsed challenging compositions that were rarely performed in prewar concerts in the city, including arrangements of Beethoven's Grosse Fuge and Verdi's String Quartet in E Minor.

118 | Chapter 4

The sponsorship of the ensemble by the Jewish Council raises the question of how, if at all, the ensemble was implicated in the politics of Jewish leadership within the ghetto. The Jewish Council was a controversial organization both during the time of the ghetto and in the subsequent historiography.[37] Consisting of members of the Jewish community, it was established by the Germans and tasked with being the liaison between the ghetto and the occupation authorities. Because it was the designated head of the Jewish community in Warsaw, it appeared to internees to be the government of the ghetto, but in fact it had little power to act beyond the strictures imposed by the occupiers.[38] Most significant for a consideration of the Jewish Symphony Orchestra, the Jewish Council was attacked by many in the ghetto for being Polish speaking and assimilationist. Some of its members were Catholic converts, who, it was reported, could not speak Yiddish, the language of the ghetto's multitude they were tasked with leading. As the historian Katarzyna Person has noted, the Jewish Council was "perceived by the majority of the ghetto as an alien, German-induced body, composed almost entirely of the assimilated strata."[39]

The orchestra aligned with the assimilationist stance of the Jewish Council insofar as the ensemble was cast as a continuation of prewar Polish ensembles that had played a noted role in Jewish integration and acculturation over the preceding decades. The crisis in musical employment to which the ensemble responded was primarily one caused by the ghettoization of musicians who had once performed in Polish musical institutions: according to one description, the Jewish Symphony Orchestra was comprised of "former members of the [Warsaw] Philharmonic and Great Warsaw Opera" as well as members of the Radio Orchestra, glossing over the big band musicians who were also employed by the ensemble.[40] As the historian Marian Fuks has observed, the core group of organizers behind the orchestra had been members of the Warsaw Philharmonic prior to the war.[41] The trio of conductors who led the ensemble were also acculturated: Szymon Pullman, a violinist based in Vienna (and who had the distinct misfortune of visiting his parents in Warsaw when the war broke out), Marian Neuteich, a graduate of the Warsaw Conservatory and a member of the Warsaw String Quartet (from 1929), and the cornetist Adam Furmański, who had performed with the Warsaw Philharmonic (and declined conversion to Catholicism).[42] The orchestra itself had at least one convert as well, the violinist Witold Hugo Baruch (1889–1946).[43] He had studied with Stanisław Barcewicz at the Warsaw Conservatory and had held positions in the

Warsaw Philharmonic, in the orchestra of the Polish Radio, and as a soloist.[44] He had been baptized in 1920, likely when he married the (non-Jewish) pianist Zofia Dutkiewicz, who remained outside the ghetto.[45] Baruch attended mass at one of the churches in the ghetto and bemoaned spending Christmas in 1941 away from his wife.[46] "I am not alone here," he wrote to her, "but I don't feel anything for these people who are supposedly close but entirely foreign to me; sometimes it seems to me that I never had anything in common with them."[47]

Several observers went further in interpreting the ensemble through the lens of musical acculturation. Rachel Auerbach, a major Yiddish literary figure, quipped in her 1943 memoirs that the orchestra included many musicians "who had been reminded by the Germans that they were Jews."[48] Writing about Furmański, she claimed that he "was in reality more Pole than Jew."[49] Both of Auerbach's turns of phrase paint the categories of Pole and Jew as mutually exclusive and imply that the acculturated were not fully Jewish. Reich in some ways agreed with this assessment of the ensemble, but he gave this aspect of its cultural politics a more positive valence. For him, the performances of classical repertoire—especially German classical repertoire—by Jews gave lie to the absurdity of Nazi racial rule and reaffirmed Jewish belonging to European musical culture: "In the ghetto, which had been created and walled off by German decree, the masterworks of the greatest German composer [Beethoven] were performed under the direction of a Viennese musician-Jew [Szymon Pullman], by Jewish musicians, who were marked as such by the Star of David, which they were required to wear."[50] Reich's contrast between German culture and German barbarity reflected his own recent past: born in Poland, he had spent the formative years of his youth in Germany, where he became enamored with German literature and music. It was only in 1938, when he was expelled from Nazi Germany for being a Jew (and a Polish citizen), that he was forced to relocate to Warsaw.[51] The Jewish Symphony Orchestra in the ghetto thus might be considered as the final chapter in the long history that linked the institutions of the symphonic orchestra with Polish Jewish acculturation.

MUSIC OF THE COURTYARDS

In addition to playing on the streets or in the Jewish Symphony Orchestra, unemployed musicians began touring among the ghetto's courtyards, offering makeshift concerts in these large spaces that were enclosed by the

120 | Chapter 4

ghetto buildings. These performances began in the first months of the occupation, before the ghetto was created, at a time when a "fever for entertainment" swept Jewish Warsaw, according to the actor and impresario Jonas Turkow, who wrote an essay in Yiddish on this topic in 1941.[52] The courtyards became venues for performances in part because Jewish life turned away from public spaces, and the courtyard became a focus of socializing for those living within a building. The predominant housing stock in the ghetto consisted of large buildings that could house hundreds of residents, if not more. These buildings became a basic unit of social organization in the ghetto, and most of them had a house committee dedicated to various self-governance tasks.[53] Turkow described how, as the dangers of the street grew during the occupation, "in almost every house [in Jewish Warsaw] there are either nightlong parties, or, at the very least, ones lasting until curfew."[54] These events were often organized by the house committees, and they could be rather formal, advertised through posters that listed performers and dates.[55] Unemployed musicians and actors could earn some money pooled from the inhabitants of the building.[56] "People who for years occupied renowned places on global stages now travel from courtyard to courtyard in order to not die from hunger and often captivate us with their splendid sounds," Turkow observed.[57]

The creation of the ghetto briefly paused, but did not stop, this fervent artistic activity. Turkow described the newness of the sealed ghetto by recounting the sounds and sights of its street, much like Gombiński and the critic writing for *Gazeta Żydowska* had done, albeit in more gruesome terms: "A few steps further—there is a corpse covered with paper, from which a hand or leg sticks out; next to it—a violinist, who with a trembling hand and faded eyes bows the strings; a little farther, a woman with a small child in a pushcart, singing opera arias to the accompaniment of her child's cries; next to her, a cantor with a child in hand singing liturgical melodies . . . such scenes take place along all the streets and passages [of the ghetto]."[58]

The courtyard performances and events organized by the house committees were, as Turkow described, set away from the misery of the street. That he saw the courtyards and houses as part of an emerging semipublic artistic space in the ghetto is further suggested by his concern with shaping these performances. He worried not only that organizers were passing their parties off as charitable fundraisers, but also that the events were of low artistic quality and conducted in Polish rather than Yiddish.[59] Turkow's concern with the language of performance in the ghetto reflected an enduring prewar interest, namely in treating Yiddish, the vernacular of the Jewish masses in eastern Europe, as a foundation for a national Jewish culture.[60] Indeed, before the war, Turkow, along with his brother Zygmunt, had been especially influential in the movement among Jewish intellectuals to reform the Yiddish theater and turn it into a venue for high art.[61]

Turkow was able to act on these concerns because in September 1940 he had been put in charge of the newly created Centralna Komisja Imprezowa (Central Commission for Entertainments), or CKI. The CKI was intended to regulate the performances organized in the ghetto houses, a task it could carry out because it operated under the auspices of the Żydowskie Towarzystwo Opieki Społecznej (Jewish Society for Public Welfare), under whose aegis the house committees also operated.[62] The idea was that every performance to be organized in the houses first had to be vetted by the CKI, who would use this power, Turkow hoped, to "raise the cultural level of events" and "to fight with assimilation by supporting Yiddish during performances and events, to create in this manner a center of Jewish culture."[63]

In addition to approving events, the CKI also organized its own performances, some in coordination with house committees and others in the extensive network of soup kitchens and orphanages run by the self-help organization.[64] Turkow claimed that the CKI organized 1,814 performances (not all of them musical).[65] This volume of performances allowed him to enact the regulation and betterment of artistic life that he believed was needed. Over 250 artists registered with the CKI, turning it into what he described as a "clandestine professional union," and this in turn allowed the CKI to gain "control over all the events" and "in most cases decide on the program," while also "engag[ing] the most serious artists performing in Yiddish and performers of Jewish music."[66] Nor must we only take Turkow's word: the extant archives of the CKI confirm that it operated on a wide scale.[67] Suggestive of the volume of musical performances that it facilitated, in one representative month, May 1941, thirty-nine musical programs were to be performed on twelve different days. Most of these concerts involved singers, violinists, or pianists.[68] Virtually no lists of repertoires are preserved in the CKI's archive, but one exception is a June 1941 program of the singer Dina Turkow, the wife of Jonas, who went by the stage name Diana Blumenfeld. Her program was primarily in Yiddish, with songs by Mordechai Gebirtig, Dawid Bajgelman, and Iso Szajewicz, among others.[69]

Not all artists in the ghetto saw Turkow's vision for control, regulation, and the Yiddishization of musical performance in a positive light.

122 | Chapter 4

Gran, one of the most famous singers who performed in Polish in the ghetto, viewed him rather as a "censor." In her memoirs she claimed that her refusal to join his professional union had been the root of his attempts to tarnish her reputation after the war. (In 1945 he had allegedly helped circulate rumors that she was cozy with Gestapo agents, she asserted. No concrete evidence was ever established for these accusations, and she was acquitted of them multiple times.) "He could not forgive me for being the single professional artist who was not registered with his 'artistic' bureau, and thus the only one who did not pay tribute money to the censor," she claimed.[70] Lurking behind these accusations were interpersonal rivalries and the politics of language. Turkow, for his part, was dismissive of Jewish artists in the ghetto who had prior to the war "worked their whole lives for Polish culture," had "steered clear of Jews, emphasizing at every chance their 'Aryan-ness,'" and to whom "it never occurred that someday they would be forced to change over to Jewish bread, although they had never turned down Jewish money."[71] Gran, meanwhile, performed in Polish and believed that Turkow's dislike of her was also due to the fact that his wife, Blumenfeld, did not have access to "any of the self-respecting ghetto cafés" because she performed exclusively in Yiddish. Even in some of the most fraught interpersonal polemics, the question of the language of the ghetto's public life remained inescapable.

Turkow's essay does not acknowledge such tensions, as he frames his actions in terms of regulating, shaping, and bettering the ghetto's public. His essay is not only a description of the artistic "chaos" that he saw prevailing in Jewish Warsaw, but it also documents his attempts to transform the new performances in the ghetto in line with his commitment to highbrow artistic production and Yiddish culture.[72] In asserting that the CKI was successful in this endeavor, he painted a picture of a new Jewish public coming into focus around the events: "In contrast to other venues and private ventures, the broad crowds of the Jewish masses and intelligentsia attended the events organized by the Central Commission for Entertainments. These audiences had finally found a place where they could gather in a warm, cultured atmosphere and listen to artistic performances of recitations, songs, and music while not being exposed to the company of the so-called new 'elites.' These events enjoyed a good opinion in the better environments of Jewish society and were attended by them on a wide scale."[73]

The clear optimism in this passage is in no small part due to the time at which the essay was composed and the period it covers; late 1940 into early 1941 was the high point of the house committees' activities.[74] Even so, we see him here placing the CKI within the ghetto's social worlds, positioning its events as bridging masses and intelligentsia while implicitly excluding the smugglers, criminals, and others who had become wealthy in the ghetto and formed its "new elite." In defining the CKI against the exclusivity of both "private ventures" and spaces frequented by the half-world of criminals, he alludes to the emergence within the ghetto of other publics, to which he was opposed but over which he could exercise little control. The most significant of these spaces was the ghetto café.

OVERHEARING THE GHETTO'S CAFÉS

Whereas the CKI and house committee performances grew out of the ghetto's social welfare organizations, the dozens of cafés in the ghetto operated on a commercial rather than charitable footing.[75] By one estimate there were nearly one hundred cafés in the ghetto.[76] Most of these were small venues, with just a couple of rooms. They had been created from what had once been apartments or offices.[77] In their competition for patrons, café proprietors turned to performers, as "each hall attempted to surpass its competitors with the best the ghetto had to offer in terms of shows or music," as Turkow recalled.[78] In the minds of many commentators, these venues were associated with the so-called new elites who had gained wealth in the ghetto from the dangerous and lucrative yet essential work of smuggling food and goods into the ghetto. Some ghetto chroniclers, such as Ringelblum and Turkow, claimed that the cafés depended on protection from the Jewish police and Gestapo, too.[79] For others the cafés epitomized the disregard shown by the wealthy for the plight of their immiserated neighbors, since the seven to nine złoty typically spent on coffee and cake was a fortune to the impoverished.[80] Chaim Kaplan wrote in his diary, for instance, about the contrast between "the lavishly dressed crowds enjoying the music, pastries, and coffee [in a luxurious café]" and how "sometimes at the very entrance of one of these elegant cafés [a visitor] might stumble on the corpse of a victim of starvation."[81] Guided by such remarks, prior scholarship has pointed to the cafés as an example of how access to musical performance had become restricted within the ghetto.[82]

A more ambivalent view of the ghetto cafés is presented by Stanisław Różycki in his essay "Kawiarnie" (Cafés), written for the Oyneg Shabes archive. Little is known about Różycki, although he was likely a high

124 | Chapter 4

school teacher in Warsaw before the war, and in 1939 he fled to Soviet-occupied Lviv before returning to the Warsaw Ghetto in October 1941.[83] His essays for the Oyneg Shabes archive are written in an elegant Polish. They focus on the Jewish street, documenting the atrocious sights, smells, and dangers of the ghetto's most public domain. In reading his essay about the cafés, we should keep in mind that, as discussed previously, cafés were far more than places to drink coffee or eat cake for Poland's intellectuals. Indeed, Warsaw's prewar cafés had been mythologized as a public sphere in which forward-looking artistic movements of the 1920s and 1930s had been born.

A trace of the idea that the café performed a social function exceeding its culinary one is evident in the very opening of Różycki's essay. In the second and third sentences, he observed:

> The ghetto cafés play a very significant role, not only in the ghetto's social life, but also in its public life due to the lack of clubs, unions, associations, markets, parks, cinemas, fields, dance halls, and so forth. The café thus substitutes for the theater, the cabaret, the variety show, the cinema—but not only—because alongside cabaret and music, the café is also a grocery store and restaurant, illicit trade occurs here, smugglers meet here to discuss their business, exchanges take place, goods are offered and searched for, there are rooms for lovers, and trade in living wares also finds protection here, not to mention that prostitution—as always—is rife in bars.[84]

In these two dizzying, list-filled sentences, Różycki underscores the simultaneous narrowing and widening of the café's role in the ghetto. He first distinguishes, and then immediately collapses, the difference between social (*towarzyski*) and public (*publiczny*) life in the ghetto, suggesting that the cafés had now been asked to fulfill the role formerly played by institutions of the public sphere, such as professional unions and voluntary associations. On the cafés writ large he reserves judgment, underscoring the essential social function they serve while enumerating, in the same breath, their sordid aspects. In concluding his essay on the cafés, he returned to this point. He noted that "the existence of venues of this type is not in itself bad." Rather, he wished that the cafés would "not only be for snobs and layabouts, smugglers and speculators, but also for working people, office workers, the working intelligentsia, the proletariat."[85] While the promise of the café as public space was valid, he believed, the ghetto conditions prevented the cafés from fulfilling their potential.

Różycki's views on the ghetto café were further developed against his observations on the collapse of Jewish public spaces, much like Turkow had also done. To leave one's apartment was a treacherous undertaking that required navigating children begging for food, strangers infected with typhus, and dead bodies.[86] In essays written for Oyneg Shabes with titles such as "Street Scenes from the Ghetto" and "Morality of the Street," he described streets littered with human waste and a collapse in public decency.[87] He saw the elitism of the cafés, which offered shelter from these conditions, as reflecting this broader collapse. "Because—if such a general and shameless public demoralization rules," he wrote, "such places [as the cafés] must exist and are only a natural emanation of the general conditions."[88]

Różycki describes the interiors, people, and sounds of the ghetto cafés in order to paint a picture of the differences among the ghetto's various well-to-do subgroups and their reactions to ghettoization. Despite the many reasons that led patrons to the cafés, he noted, "All have or wish to have the delusion that the atmosphere of the café separates them from the reality of the street, from the darkness of everyday life."[89] To make this point when he visits L'Ours, one of the ghetto's larger cafés, he calls attention to the difference between the trappings of the cafés and the conversations of its patrons. "There are no traces of the war, imprisonment, the ghetto. The faces are not at all haggard, rather the opposite—they look normal, well fed."[90] The patrons are, as he describes, a mix of those who still have savings and those who have become rich off of illicit activity in the ghetto. But as he listens more intently to the patrons, he notes that "the topics of conversation are the same, reduced to a common denominator [zglajchszachtowany]. What's new, when's the offensive, how are you doing today with bread? . . . Neither the content nor the form is different from all our everyday, identical, stubbornly repeating questions that stubbornly repeat themselves, the answers to which are monotonously sad and hopelessly desperate."[91]

Różycki repeatedly evokes music in the essay to describe the patrons and atmosphere of each venue. When he visited the café Arizona, which he claimed was almost exclusively frequented by smugglers, his description of the café's music paints its patrons as isolated from the everyday concerns of the ghetto. They "dance, and dance with verve, with temperament, with humor, speeding up, stamping their feet to the beat, demanding encores."[92] When one of the musicians sang about a poor orphan begging for bread on the street, Różycki describes how one of the richest patrons, Jerzyk Kupfer, began to cry. "The asshole indeed shed a teardrop and quickly poured a drink of advocaat as consolation, though it made no difference."[93] Różycki's description of Kupfer's single teardrop points to the chasm separating him from the ghetto's realities:

126 | Chapter 4

his reaction is trite compared with the immense misery of the ghetto, Różycki implies, while his attempt to ameliorate the emotion through expensive alcohol is as futile as it is self-centered.

If Różycki described the song about the orphan to cast into relief the distance between street and café, elsewhere in the essay music serves to underscore the distance between the present reality of the ghetto and memories of the pre-ghetto life. When visiting the café Splendid, where Artur Gold played with what Różycki considered to be the best jazz band in the ghetto, he wrote that the "wild rhythm of the unbridled jazz orchestra, playing in a negro tempo, is a dissonance, a clash with the slow, monotonous life, entirely ruled by everyday dullness. And this expresses, this creates a kind of unnatural, sick atmosphere; it appears as something unreal, not from this world. The contrast is too brutal."[94] He was more sympathetic to the music that he heard in the café Fontanna, which offered performances by Leon Boruński (a laureate of the 1932 Chopin Competition), Erwin Wohlfeiler, and songs from the soprano Marysia Ajzensztadt (the daughter of a Jewish choir director). But here, too, music seemed to express to his ears first and foremost a disjunction between sound and reality: "The mood that dominated here was as if in essence people had escaped to hell to listen to music, to raptly take in melodies, to remind themselves of the content of songs on which they had once been intoxicated."[95]

That Różycki discusses the music of each café he visited not only confirms that the cafés were a major venue in which music was made. It also suggests that music played a central role in how he grasped the café's function in the ghetto. In some instances he turns to music to sharpen the distinction that he draws between interior and exterior, bringing into focus the distance between the café audiences and the street. At other times music serves as an emblem of the past, appearing to him to conjure the audiences' links to and desires for the world before the ghetto. Put differently, the contradictions that Różycki believed defined the ghetto cafés were as much heard as they were seen. Similar to Gombiński, who chose musical and sonic terms to evoke the newness of the ghetto street, Różycki heard in music a way of describing the café as social space, a sonic marking of the distance between audiences' hopes and their reality.

WEALTH, POWER, AND SATIRE IN THE CAFÉ SZTUKA

No café sheds light on the interplay between acculturation, musical performance, and elite patronage in the ghetto as does the café Sztuka (Art, not to be confused with Sztuka i Moda or Dom Sztuki, cafés in Polish Warsaw that were discussed in chapter 3). This café was frequented by the Polish-speaking intelligentsia interned in the ghetto. They would have been familiar with the cultural touchstones of the prewar intelligentsia, such as the famous literary café Ziemiańska, the journal *Wiadomości Literackie* (Literary news), and the witty and urbane Qui Pro Quo cabaret. Turkow and Różycki both wrote with disdain about Sztuka, a stance that at least in part reflects larger concerns among those working with the Oyneg Shabes archive about language and assimilation within the ghetto.[96] Turkow quipped about how "Yiddish grated unpleasantly on the ears" of Sztuka's audiences.[97] Różycki went even further, describing Sztuka's audience as "converts, educated bourgeoisie" who were "proud that before the war they had been rich . . . [and] can't stand the fact that they have been made equal with the 'scabs, Yids' [*zglajchszachtowani z 'parchami, Żydłakami'*], that they share a common fate."[98] These scathing observations represent one point of view on Sztuka, but such quick dismissals of the experiences of the ghetto bourgeoisie and its Polish-speaking internees perhaps say more about the authors' priorities than about the café itself.

What is beyond dispute is that the venue catered to a well-to-do clientele. We have unusually detailed insight into the operations of Sztuka because its surviving co-owners and staff were called as witnesses in the postwar trials of Wiera Gran, the café's star performer. Owned jointly by seven or eight stakeholders, the café had initially been founded so that the co-owners could "have lunch and dinner," but the venue in which they spent long hours working also became something more. As Maciej Czarnecki, one of the co-owners, noted, "The café was my home but not only my home: it was our home."[99] To sustain their business, community, and lives, the owners catered to what one early co-owner of the café termed the "financial aristocracy" of the ghetto.[100] While some Sztuka patrons relied on dwindling prewar savings, others had become wealthy through questionable financial activities in the ghetto. "Almost daily, so-called 'dangerous guests' came to Sztuka, from 'the Thirteen' and others suspected of collaboration with the Gestapo," explained Romana Wajnkranc, a co-owner and the maître d'.[101] "The Thirteen" was the colloquial name for the Office for the Prevention of Usury and Speculation, named for the street address of its headquarters on 13 Leszno Street. Its members engaged in economic exploitation in the ghetto and reported directly to the Nazi governor of Warsaw, thus forming a wealthy ghetto elite whose power depended on their close relations

128 | Chapter 4

with the occupiers rather than on the Jewish Council.[102] Members of the Jewish police force were also regular patrons of the café.[103] Wajnkranc claimed that "the basis for the café's existence was these suspect people, who incurred enormous bills."[104] And because of both this financial dependence and their power in the ghetto, "it was impossible to kick out any of the suspect people from the café," according to Czarnecki.[105] Such descriptions of the café's financial footing from its co-owners reveal how Sztuka's existence depended on wealth that the owners themselves believed had been unethically obtained. They also underscore how various ghetto subgroups shared a tense coexistence in cafés, spaces that provided refuge for artists and the nouveau riche alike.

The power imbalance between the wealthy patrons of ghetto cafés and the staff living on the edge poverty was often painfully on display. In some cafés, waitresses were expected to perform sexual acts that were demanded by the patrons.[106] In other instances, café artists were forced into musical performances for powerful figures in the ghetto whom they did not wish to entertain. Gran, for example, was compelled to perform at a party held by a prominent member of the Thirteen, an experience she was reported to have described shortly after it occurred as a "nightmare in her life."[107] In still other instances, the pressures facing artists were social in nature. At many cafés there was an expectation that artists would mingle with the patrons and sit at their tables after a performance, likely flirting with the patrons or otherwise entertaining their whims.[108] Sztuka was able to mitigate these pressures to some degree, in part because its owners saw the café as a venue for artistic expression. Indicative of this orientation, they rebuffed one co-owner who had wished to give the café "a very cabaret-entertainment character and allow for a certain familiarity between the personnel and café patrons," as was common in other venues.[109] The contracts between Sztuka and its performers specified that the artists were free to leave after their performances, and Gran, the café's most famous performer, did precisely that.[110] She was "always rather haughty," recalled Gadejski, keeping her distance from those with whom she was not friends.[111] And, indeed, she had no financial need for flirting or fraternizing with the wealthy since she earned around one hundred złoty a day from her performances alone.[112] This was a staggering sum in the ghetto and, for that matter, outside it.

Many of the performers at Sztuka had cut their teeth in prewar Warsaw's cabaret scene, including Boruński, Gran, Pola Braun, and Władysław Szlengel. The prewar cabaret had been distinguished by its topical commentary, satire, and quick-paced production schedules in performances that integrated Jewish and Polish performers who played to a mixed audience. This Polish-language cabaret was also noteworthy for combining music—especially "light" music of internationally popular dance genres—with scenarios penned by some of the most eminent Polish poets, such as Julian Tuwim.[113] The artists at Sztuka did not abandon these values when they were interned in the ghetto. One audience member, Mary Berg, a teenager imprisoned in the ghetto, described in her diary that at Sztuka, "one can hear songs and satires on the police, the ambulance service, the rickshaws, and even the Gestapo in a veiled fashion." Perhaps she had in mind Szlengel's *Żywy Dziennik* (The living newspaper), a literary-artistic satire on events in the ghetto. In discerning such meanings, Berg believed that the songs of Sztuka carried a significance that could not be reduced to escapism or nostalgia: "It is laughter through tears, but it is laughter. This is our only weapon in the ghetto—our people laugh at death and at the Nazi decrees."[114] Such critiques were risky given that some targets of the satire were also the café's financial lifeblood, and performances required a delicate touch, in which allusion and implication ruled. As Michał Borwicz observed in an early postwar account of Sztuka—which he based in part on interviews with Gran—the "jokes [told in Szutka] had to be limited to derivative and peripheral elements while evading the central, fundamental issues." But he also noted that audiences became adept at interpreting even seemingly banal songs about greenery or forests as implied commentary on the ghetto.[115]

We gain a sense of what Berg and Borwicz might have had in mind by turning to one of the extant works premiered at Sztuka: a musical composition titled *Jej pierwszy bal* (Her first ball), which was originally premiered as part of one of the *Living Newspaper* performances.[116] The piece for voice, accompanied by two pianos, is around fifteen minutes long and includes narrative recitation as well as singing. The text was written by Szlengel, a prominent poet in the ghetto and the key figure behind *The Living Newspaper*. Its music was composed by Władysław Szpilman, a stalwart performer at Sztuka. Before the war he had established himself as a respected interpreter of Chopin and a composer of classical music, having studied during the early 1930s with Franz Schreker in Berlin.[117] It was sung by Gran, who had risen to fame before the war by performing in the Warsaw cabarets while still a teenager, and whose popularity ballooned in the ghetto.[118] "Every locale in the ghetto fought for her performances, since she was the reason for the complete

130 | Chapter 4

success of events," as Gadejski described her fame.[119] Nonetheless, she chose to perform almost exclusively in Sztuka, where Szpilman, and his duo partner Andrzej Goldfeder, accompanied her.

Her First Ball is a series of variations on a waltz from Ludomir Różycki's opera *Casanova* (1922). (The waltz had also recently appeared in Poland's first sound film, *Moralność pani Dulskiej*.)[120] The title *Her First Ball* alludes to the plot of a French film, *Un carnet de bal* (1937), in which the widowed protagonist revisits the fates of her suitors twenty years after her debut ball. To reflect the varied life paths of the suitors, Szpilman composed each variation in a different musical style, including a slow foxtrot, rumba, tango, Tyrolian waltz (complete with yodeling), and a mazurka "à la Chopin."[121] The work's blending of genres—drawing from opera, film, the dance hall, Chopin, and even pseudo–folk music—evinces an interest in blurring high-low divides that was also characteristic of the prewar Polish-language cabaret.[122]

For many listening closely to *Her First Ball*, the piece was likely more than a lighthearted commentary on the foibles of past flirtations. Consider this following passage, sung about the final suitor, a "melancholy composer":

Bicie naszych serc,
W nokturn się zmieniło.
Będzie dłużej żył,
Niż nasza miłość.
Rytmy, rytmy łzy,
Ścielą się pod stopy.
Umrze może wielka miłość,
Lecz zostanie Chopin.

The beating of our hearts,
Turned into a nocturne.
It will live longer,
Than our love.
The rhythm, rhythm of tears,
Flows under our feet.
Perhaps great love will die,
But Chopin will remain.

The music here transforms from a waltz into a mazurka, both dances that share the same triple meter but have distinct rhythmic profiles. Audiences would have doubtless understood that the interpolation of the mazurka was no accident; indeed, it was the genre of Chopin's that had become most closely associated with Polish national identity.[123]

Within the context of occupied Warsaw, the piece's allusion to Chopin in both text and music was daring. Outside the ghetto, his music was banned for much of the occupation because of its strong associations with the Polish national cause.[124] Meanwhile, inside the ghetto, Jews were ostensibly banned from performing all non-Jewish music, although this ban was routinely ignored. Interpreted against this background, the line "But Chopin will remain" was not only a claim that musical works are more enduring than youthful love. It was also a suggestion that Chopin—and perhaps Polish nationhood along with it—would endure the latest cataclysm visited upon it. Gran, who sang the piece, recalled that audiences understood the weight of the Chopin allusion. She described how it felt risky to include the line and how it brought Sztuka's audiences to tears.[125] In this brief musical moment, the connections between the Szutka performers and the prewar milieu of the Warsaw cabaret, defined by double meanings and social commentary, comes to the fore. But we also gain a glimpse of how Sztuka's artists and audience understood themselves in terms of the Polish musical and literary culture to which they had long belonged and which, for years prior, they had been integral to creating.

THE ENDS OF WARSAW'S MUSICAL CULTURE

I have discussed both the sonic traces of prewar culture in occupied Warsaw and the radical transformation of them under German rule. In broad terms there are similarities between the musical cultures on both sides of the ghetto wall: across the city, music was integrated into social and political movements, whether that of the Polish underground, the Jewish self-help organizations, or the Jewish Council. Both Polish Warsaw and the ghetto saw new private and semiprivate spaces emerge for musical performance, such as the courtyard, the private apartment, and—perhaps most importantly—the café. On both sides of the ghetto wall, the repertoires of the cafés were eclectic, pushing the boundaries between entertainment and art. In both places, the café assumed an ambivalent valence in cultural politics as a venue that both promised continuity in performance culture and also exposed the fragility of life under German rule. Across Warsaw, music remained a dynamic part of both political and cultural life.

Yet we also see emerge within the ghetto a way of listening that is less evident in Polish Warsaw. While the Polish commentators outside of the ghetto were, to a degree, successful in narrating the destruction of war

132 | Chapter 4

within a framework of national resilience, ghetto commentators reveal that the noisy, chaotic, and immiserated street was never far from listeners' ears. The misery of the ghetto was the ever-present counterweight to artistic performances in concert halls, courtyards, and cafés. As Reich—the ghetto's music critic and translator—wrote in his memoirs in the 1990s, "Weighing upon [all in the Warsaw Ghetto], whether young or old, whether clever or stupid, was a dark and terrible shadow from which there was no escape—the shadow of the fear of death."[126]

Any tentative similarities across the ghetto wall came to a definitive end with the so-called Grossaktion Warschau, when from July 22 to September 21, 1942, more than three hundred thousand ghetto prisoners were terrorized in roundups, crammed into cattle cars, and murdered in Treblinka. For those who remained in the ghetto, the mass murders inaugurated a new phase in public life in which the reality of imminent death was impossible to avoid. They were also the prelude to the largest and most significant act of Jewish armed resistance to Nazi rule, the Warsaw Ghetto Uprising of 1943.[127] But before the uprising, most musicians had either fled or had been murdered. Of the more than four hundred performing artists in the ghetto, only around a dozen survived, Turkow believed. Those who did relied on a combination of luck and connections beyond the ghetto to join what Paulsson has described as a "secret city" of an estimated twenty-eight thousand Polish Jews living clandestinely on the *aryjska strona* of Warsaw.[128]

To escape, Jews required contacts outside the ghetto, so non-Jewish Poles often played a decisive role in their survival. The Polish Jewish relations that had long been embedded in the musical intelligentsia could offer a lifeline for a handful of prominent musicians. Szpilman was first saved when he was recognized in line at the Umschlagplatz during the Grossaktion, and in February 1943 he escaped from a work brigade thanks to the help of the Polish singer Janina Godlewska-Bogucka and her husband, the actor Andrzej Bogucki.[129] He became one of a handful of Jewish musicians who went into hiding thanks to the help of the Polish underground musicians' organization.[130] Professional networks also aided other Polish Jews, including several who never moved into the ghetto. The musicologist Seweryn Barbag, for instance, had evacuated from German-occupied Lviv to a small town outside of Warsaw, where he was hidden with help from musicians in a hospital for tuberculosis patients under the false identity of Franciszek Brachuciak. There he contracted tuberculosis and died in September 1944.[131] The cellist Kazimierz Wiłkomirski hid Halina Kowalska-

Trzonkowa, the Jewish wife of his quartet's violist Henryk Trzonek, for several weeks before she moved in with violinist Eugenia Umińska. (Henryk had been shot in a street execution.)[132]

In other cases marriages and familial relations proved decisive. Gran was able to escape thanks to her husband, who had remained on the *aryjska strona*, and she spent several months hiding in different apartments in the city before leaving it.[133] She was separated from her other family members, who were murdered. On July 28, 1942, as the Grossaktion was in full swing, Baruch, the violinist from the Jewish Symphony Orchestra, expected the worst and wrote farewell to his (non-Jewish) wife outside the ghetto: "I'm writing only a few words because I cannot completely collect my thoughts; dearest Zofia, you likely know our situation. Perhaps God the Lord will allow us to see each other again, but if not—remember my only child—that I only had one love in my life. I idolize you and I am not in a state to describe the love, attachment, and longing for you, my dearest Zofia, that are overflowing from my heart."[134] Shortly thereafter he was smuggled out of the ghetto through the courthouse on Leszno Street (which served both the ghetto and Polish Warsaw) by his brother-in-law. The two pretended to be German and took the German-only commuter rail car to the town of Reguły, a suburb of Warsaw, where he stayed with the brother-in-law's family.[135] Once he had escaped he took on the identity of Aleksander Laskowski, a book binder, a name he used until his death in 1946.[136]

The dependence of Jewish escapees on the goodwill of non-Jewish Poles, however, also exposed the limited nature of Poles' sympathy toward Jews and the realities of their collaboration with the occupation. While Poles could almost always count on their neighbors to turn a blind eye toward clandestine concerts, supporting the Home Army, or hiding armaments, the same did not go for hiding Jews, which made this a dangerous form of resistance. The social bonds of the underground often did not extend uniformly to Jews, who were, in the eyes of many, perceived as either a threat to the Polish national community or not an integral part of the nation in need of protection.[137] Indeed, the increase of Jews in hiding after the Grossaktion led to a surge in blackmail, resulting in Poles attempting to extract money or other valuables under the threat of turning over Jews and their protectors to the Gestapo. Thousands in Warsaw made money by threatening Jews and their Polish helpers with murder in this manner.[138]

The family of the composer Roman Palester was blackmailed twice, once in late 1940 and a second time in 1943. The second blackmail was

134 | Chapter 4

a decisive moment for them. While the family was still in bed on a Sunday morning, two civilians and one police officer knocked at their door. The subsequent negotiations lasted many hours. It was at this moment that Małgorzata, Roman's fourteen-year-old half sister, realized for the first time in her life that she was Jewish (she had been away during the first, shorter blackmail). After paying off the blackmailers, Henryk, Roman's father, had to move out and stay with friends on the other side of Warsaw, across the Vistula, and the Jews who had been sheltered in the apartment also had to relocate. The blackmail also inaugurated the family's shift toward more formal involvement with the underground. They began to work with the Council for Aid to the Jews, code name Żegota, that had been formed in December 1942 as an arm of the Delegate's Bureau.[139] They worked closely with Irena Sendler, who played a leading role in this organization and is best known for her work smuggling children out of the ghetto, hiding their identities, and placing them with Polish families and convents, actions that saved as many as 2,500 children.[140] The Palesters were among the most active in finding new families and hiding places for these children, and they also helped distribute food, money, and medicine.[141]

What was the composer Roman Palester's relation to this deepening activism? We know that he was in close contact with his family for much of the occupation, although he grew more distant from them after the war. His 1943 identification document (*Kennkarte*) is registered to his family's address, and he wrote in his memoirs that "we were very close to one another, and, up to the time of my father's death [in November 1944], their home on Łowicka Street in Warsaw was also my home."[142] Echoing this view, one of his half sister's closest friends recalled to me in 2016 that Palester remained in contact with his family throughout the war and visited them several times shortly after it. After his arrest in 1940 he kept a low profile, claiming to be concerned that his prominence in the Polish ISCM section could attract Gestapo attention.[143] He spent much of his time in the countryside. By leaving Warsaw he found favorable conditions for composition: in the small town of Jędrzejów, north of Cracow, where he stayed with family friends, he completed his Violin Concerto and began work on the Symphony No. 2, a work that would come to define early postwar aesthetics. Even so, Roman did return to Warsaw several times, including in June 1942, when he and Barbara Podoska were married. Subsequently, in fall 1942 and 1943, the couple stayed with Barbara's family in Żerosławice, a village south of Cracow.[144] Thus, while Roman was not living with his family for the entire occupation, it is difficult to imagine that he was not aware of their actions.

His wartime and postwar writings do not mention his family's survival, their activism, or the Jewish background that endangered them all in the first place. In his "Fragments of a Memoir from the Years 1939–1945," written several decades after the war, he focused on his musical-stylistic evolution, describing how the war led him toward a "deepening of expression" in his compositions.[145] Shortly after the war, too, he remained focused on musical-aesthetic developments. He mentioned in a generic way the "exceptionally difficult situation during the war" for composers before describing the occupation as a nonevent for their music: "If someone were to analyze the works of our composers over the last fifteen years up to the present moment [1946], this analysis would in no sense lead one to suspect that the world had experienced certain rather deep-reaching shocks in the course of these years."[146] Music, he baldly asserted, floated above suffering. He soon came to exemplify Polish compositional productivity and national survival during the war, an interpretation aided by his imposing productivity: during the war he had completed his Violin Concerto (1939–41), Piano Sonatina for four hands (1940), Symphony No. 2 (1941–42), Concertino for piano and orchestra (1942), a cantata titled *Kołacze, poemat weselny* (Wedding cake, epithalamium, 1942), String Quartet No. 3 (1942–44), two études for piano (1943), and an arrangement of polonaises by Michał Ogiński for string orchestra (1943). In 1944 he had begun work on an opera, based on Wacław Berent's novel *Żywe kamienie* (The living stones, 1918).

Palester's evasiveness about his family shows that stories of Jewish survival within the musical intelligentsia could vanish into thin air, leaving only the faintest traces in the historical record. Indeed, I discovered the story of his family by accident when I stumbled on a cryptic allusion in a 1959 letter to Roman from his friend Tadeusz Przypkowski. In the letter, Przypkowski stated that Małgorzata Palester was offended that Roman had forgotten her address, "much like he had forgotten about them in 1945."[147] This glancing mention of a falling out between Palester and his half sister augured a hidden drama, one never mentioned in Roman's published writings, autobiographical reflections, or extant correspondence. Unlike Roman, Małgorzata had decided to document her family's activities. She sat for three hours of videotaped testimony with the USC Shoah Foundation in 1998, during which she spoke of their survival and their work with Żegota in detail. Her words in the

136 | Chapter 4

interview do not clarify what Roman thought or felt during the Holocaust. Rather, they underscore how the composer who would come to define Polish musical continuity during the war was never more than an arm's length away from Jewish activism and survival. His story reveals how Jewish and Polish Warsaw were both a world apart and intimately intertwined.

5

We Must Restructure the Musicians into Soviet Thinking

The third wartime cataclysm that would shape the musical intelligentsia was the seizure of much of the eastern territories of the Second Republic by the Soviet Union. On September 17, 1939, just over two weeks following the outbreak of war, the Red Army invaded Poland in accord with the Molotov-Ribbentrop Pact. In October of that year the occupied territories were incorporated into the Soviet Union through sham plebiscites. About twelve million citizens of Poland thus ended up under Soviet rule (see map 3).[1] The rapid Sovietization that followed the invasion was a shock to the musical ecosystem of this region, as major institutions were reorganized to match the imperatives of Soviet cultural policy.

Soviet rule did not last long. Less than two years later, on June 22, 1941, Germany invaded the Soviet Union in Operation Barbarossa, conquering territories that had been occupied previously by the Soviet Union. The inhabitants of this region experienced what Timothy Snyder terms a "double occupation," a whiplash between Soviet and German rule. This region—including Lithuania, Latvia, and the eastern territories of the former Polish republic—saw brutal anti-Jewish violence perpetrated by locals, usually with tacit German approval. *Żydokomuna*, the myth that Jews were inherent supporters of communism, was a key factor in this violence: local non-Jews murdered their Jewish neighbors in part because they scapegoated them for the social upheaval and violence of the Soviet rule, an equation of Jews with communism that the Nazi occupiers were eager to support.[2] Jews not killed in these waves of

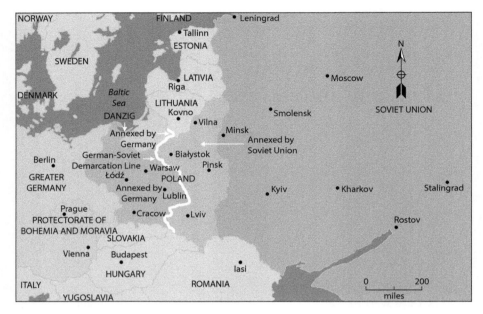

MAP 3. In September 1939, acting on the secret protocols of the Molotov-Ribbentrop Pact, the Soviet Union occupied the eastern territories of the Polish Second Republic, including the academic and cultural center of Lviv.

pogroms were forced into ghettos by the Germans, and most were soon murdered.

It has been a challenge for scholars and other commentators to recognize the significance of this double occupation to Poland's musical culture, despite the fact that Lviv was a major cultural center prior to the war and the eastern borderlands were a site of intense musical activism during the 1930s, as discussed in chapter 2. In part, the historiography reflects the politics of remembrance in postwar Poland. The taboo during the communist era against describing the Soviet Union as a malicious or occupying force meant there was less space to discuss the music of Soviet occupation than there was for that of the German occupation, which could fit more easily into a model of "antifascist" resistance.[3] An added challenge is that the experiences of musicians in this region were defined by displacement. The Soviet Union deported hundreds of thousands of Polish citizens to the Soviet interior, meaning that Polish musical activities often unfolded over vast distances among geographically dispersed communities. After the war, the territories occupied by the

Soviet Union in 1939 were reabsorbed into the Soviet Union, and many Polish musicians left their hometowns for cities such as Warsaw, Cracow, Poznań, or Wrocław, which lay within the new borders of the postwar Polish state. Those who remained often formed new communities within the Soviet Union while losing contact with the Polish intellectual circles they had previously belonged to, as these relocated westward.[4]

The double occupation matters, however, to understanding how the musical intelligentsia sustained itself across the war and how its members were able to imagine Polish musical culture as continuous. Indeed, continuity looked different in the eastern territories of the former Second Republic than it did in Warsaw or Cracow. While the Soviet occupation of 1939–41 was brutal and authoritarian, the Soviets supported the institutions of musical life and of Polish music, while at the same time forcing them into a Soviet mold. Soviet rule thus did not create space for the nationalized resistance that defined German-occupied Warsaw. In addition, the Soviet occupation was many musicians' first encounter with Soviet power, ideology, and administrative tactics of the sort that would become common in the postwar Polish People's Republic. Musicians began to understand how to navigate the Soviet-style regime, in which culture was ascribed a central ideological role. As we will see near the end of this chapter, the formation of postwar cultural institutions began within Soviet-ruled territories, led by musicians with extensive experience with Soviet power.

In addition to this political-administrative schooling, the double occupation also had profound impacts on Polish Jewish musicians. From 1939 to 1941 Soviet rule helped to remove some of the barriers to Jewish (and also Ukrainian) participation in musical institutions, offering a modicum of equality against a backdrop of authoritarian rule and immiseration. The Soviet occupation also saved many Polish Jews from near certain death at the hands of the Nazis, including over a hundred thousand Polish Jews who had been involuntarily deported deep into the Soviet Union. As I will discuss in the second half of this chapter, these Polish Jewish refugee communities in the Soviet interior offered a venue for testing the fusion of Polish nationalist symbolism and communist politics through music, as would be common after the war. Ultimately, for the musical intelligentsia, the wartime Soviet Union was an occupying force, a refuge, and a harsh introduction to communist cultural politics.

140 | Chapter 5

THE SOVIETIZATION OF LVIV'S MUSICAL LIFE

If Warsaw had emerged as the center of Polish musical activity under the German occupation, then Lviv played an analogous role under the Soviet occupation. As we saw in chapter 1, the city had long been an important center for the musical intelligentsia, in part thanks to its musicology institute, where Adolf Chybiński had trained scholars that included Zofia Lissa and Stefania Łobaczewska. It also had a robust circle of musicians dedicated to new music, as evidenced by the founding of a local branch of the Polish ISCM section in the city in 1930.[5] If anything, the cultural significance of Lviv ballooned in September 1939, when prominent intellectuals, writers, and musicians fled from the German advance on Warsaw to what they perceived to be the relative safety of Lviv.[6] These included stars of the light music stage, such as Henryk Wars, Wiera Gran, Eugeniusz Bodo, and Albert Harris.[7]

The Soviet occupation aimed to remake Lviv into a Soviet—and Ukrainian—city. The occupation was, according to Soviet propaganda then flooding the city, a liberation of Ukrainians from the despotic rule of capitalist Polish lords. To deliver this message, the Polish language was replaced by Ukrainian on the city's signs, and plaster statues of Lenin and Stalin were erected in the city's public spaces.[8] Although Ukrainians had faced discrimination in interwar Poland, it soon became clear that Soviet rule was not necessarily better. Standards of living collapsed, people went hungry after large estates were seized, factories and other large enterprises became state property, and private savings were wiped out through currency manipulation.[9] The Greek Catholic Church—which had been central to Ukrainian identity in the Second Republic—had its land confiscated and its role in public life severely limited.[10] Inhabitants who were deemed potentially disloyal faced an even more dire fate: four waves of deportations, orchestrated by the People's Commissariat for Internal Affairs (NKVD), removed prewar civil servants, members of former local government, family members of prisoners, Jews, and those who had fled from German-occupied Poland into the Soviet Union.[11] It is estimated that these deportations sent between 315,000 to well over one million Polish citizens into Soviet labor camps thousands of miles from their homes.[12] For those who avoided deportation, civil society was dismantled, political parties were banned, and the city's rich array of nonpolitical associations and media outlets was shut down.[13]

Despite these repressions, the Soviet occupation did not attempt to curtail concert music in Lviv as the Germans had done in Warsaw.

Rather, the Soviet occupiers sought to support and fund musical performance as an emblem of communist progress over "capitalist" Poland.[14] A radio orchestra held auditions, the philharmonic was put back to work (reportedly employing some 250 musicians), and by 1940, 450 choirs, 143 orchestras, and 97 dance ensembles were established in the newly annexed territories.[15] Premiere Soviet artists such as David Oistrakh, Yakov Zak, and Emil Gilels visited the city to concertize, contributing to a paradoxical situation in which, as the composer Andrzej Nikodemowicz recalled, the quality of musical life improved even as the inhabitants were terrified of the next oppressive measure.[16]

Soviet arts policy kept musicians employed, a crucial distinction between the Soviet and German occupations. This point was noted by Warsaw-based musicians who conveyed rumors of conditions in Soviet-occupied Poland to the London government-in-exile: "Polish music has ceased to exist as an independent, characteristic expression of national culture in the territories occupied by the bolsheviks [*sic*]. Polish musicians, however, continuing to work in these territories in their profession—albeit in foreign and difficult conditions—have one advantage: they have not lost their professional skills."[17] Such an opinion reflects the increasing narration of Polish musical culture through a lens of ethnonationalism and resistance, as we saw in chapter 3. It also suggests a degree of envy that at least musicians under Soviet rule were spared the day in and day out struggle for employment that defined musical life in Warsaw.

Another key difference between the occupations was that there was little space to opt out of the institutions of Soviet musical life. As Jan T. Gross has shown, inhabitants of Soviet-occupied territories had few ways of avoiding a Soviet-dominated political sphere that demanded their frequent participation in elections, ideological schooling, and propagandistic meetings.[18] Musical life unfolded predominantly in the public sphere, and there were few analogues to the semiprivate and private performances spaces found in Warsaw. If musicians did perform in cafés or clandestine concerts in Soviet Lviv, these events have left virtually no trace in the historical record. Musicians who were active in the city had to contend with censorship of their public performances. Wiera Gran, who had fled to Lviv near the beginning of the war (before returning to Warsaw), recounted how the censor bristled at lyrics about "little gold chains" in her songs, which he dismissed as "bourgeois trash." Nonetheless, she managed to perform extensively at two theaters in the city.[19] Others adapted to the need for ideologically attuned

142 | Chapter 5

performances. In 1941 Henryk Wars's ensemble performed a composition titled "Music on the Street," a three-act work that told the story of an unemployed group of musicians who travel from the United States, across all of Europe, to Lviv in search of employment, eventually finding that their talents were best recognized in the Soviet Union.[20]

The contours of musical life in Soviet-occupied Lviv were further shaped by the fact that no equivalent to the underground state could be established on Soviet territories. Nascent resistance movements under the Soviet occupation were quickly extirpated by the NKVD, which had greater experience in infiltrating and undermining these groups than their German counterparts.[21] If musicians formed underground unions or committees in the Soviet zone, they would have risked near-certain arrest. As a result, musicians lacked the support provided by the underground in Warsaw: they did not have an institution to help mediate interactions with the occupiers, nor the connections to a broader social movement afforded by the underground, nor the material support provided by the government-in-exile to artists.

The pressures facing musicians to participate in Soviet-backed institutions during the occupation are made especially clear by the Lviv State Conservatory, which was opened in 1940. The conservatory was formed by consolidating the faculty of Lviv's musical schools along with the university's musicology institute, which had been transferred from the university to the conservatory as part of this reorganization over Chybiński's objections.[22] As a result of this centralization in musical instruction, many of Lviv's leading musicians, musicologists, and pedagogues found themselves employed by the same institution. The aim of the new conservatory was nothing less than the ideological transformation of its students and faculty, as its administrators reported after the first academic year: "The primary remaining difficulties lie in the need to restructure the mental state of students and teachers. Their complete reorganization into the Soviet way of thinking and the Soviet system of work is neither a simple nor easy task."[23] While this task was never accomplished, the very fact that transforming the ideological outlook of the students was a goal of the conservatory strongly contrasts with the policies adopted under German occupation. As discussed in chapter 3, a German figurehead had been installed at the Warsaw Conservatory, but Polish musicians reported few attempts to interfere with the curriculum or teaching.

To carry out the reorganization of the Lviv Conservatory, a team of professors from Kyiv was sent to the city. They installed an administration comprised of both local figures and those brought in from Soviet Ukraine. The first director of the conservatory was Vasyl Barvinsky, a Lviv resident who had previously led the Ukrainian Lysenko Institute, but the vice-director was a musicologist from Kyiv, Oleksandr Breskin. Ukrainians held the main leadership positions within the conservatory, but the majority of students and teachers came from institutes that had served Poles and Polish Jews prior to the war.[24] Administrative work was carried out in Ukrainian, while the language of instruction varied.[25] Further, Lviv's composers and musicologists were to be integrated into the Soviet musical apparatus. For instance, a delegation from the Lviv State Conservatory was sent to the Conference of Composers and Musicologists in Kyiv in spring 1941.[26]

The establishment of the Lviv State Conservatory did not erase the interpersonal politics or research directions that had dominated Lviv musicology prior to the war. Lissa, who had previously worked at a now-closed music school, joined the city's only musicology division, as did Łobaczewska. Despite Lissa's communist credentials, however, she failed to unseat Chybiński, who was appointed to head the music history department. Chybiński recalled that Lissa and Łobaczewska then "became dependent on me," replicating his former position of power.[27] Lissa's subordinate role was balanced, however, when she was appointed as dean of the history, theory, and composition division, a position that entailed reporting to the central conservatory council on her division's activities.[28] Nor did the occupation lead to major changes in the research topics of scholars in the division. Individual scholars continued to research prewar topics, including fifteenth-century polyphony, music of the Polish baroque, and the folk music of the Podhale region.[29] At the same time, several Polish doctorate degrees—including Lissa's—were declared invalid because of their provenance outside the Soviet system, thereby forcing their holders to redefend their theses.[30]

Chybiński's postwar writings provide intriguing evidence concerning the pressures that he and others faced. He was displeased with the Soviet occupation and reluctantly fulfilled his duties in the conservatory. In department meetings, for example, he declined to present new scholarly work.[31] Indeed, in postwar correspondence he pointed to such recalcitrance—along with his refusal to forfeit prewar decorations and awards—as evidence of his refusal to cooperate with the Soviet occupation. These activities, he believed, were enough to have him slated for deportation to the east, a fate he was saved from only by the German invasion on 22 June 1941.[32] He also admonished Lissa and Łobaczewska,

144 | Chapter 5

claiming that they "worked obstinately on Moscow's orders, not to discuss that com[rade] Lissa was a . . . [*sic*] dean (read: informer) in the Derżawnej [*State*] Lviv Conservatory."[33] Chybiński's inability to refuse work in the conservatory despite his rejection of the institution's politics underscores the narrow ambit for action that musicians held under the Soviet occupation.

MUSIC AND THE POLITICS OF NATION IN LVIV

Lviv had long been a multiethnic city. In 1921 its population was about 62 percent Poles, 28 percent Jews, and 10 percent Ukrainians, while the rural areas outside the city were overwhelmingly Ukrainian.[34] Although Ukrainians were a minority in the city, it was a center for the emergence of modern Ukrainian national identity under Austrian rule in the late nineteenth century and home to key Ukrainian institutions, such as the Shevchenko Scientific Society.[35] Relations among Poles, Ukrainians, and Jews had grown fraught by the end of World War I, when Poles and Ukrainians fought for control of the region of Galicia as Austro-Hungary collapsed. On November 1, 1918, Ukrainians seized Lviv, declaring the city the capital of the short-lived West Ukrainian People's Republic, only to be repelled by Poles twenty days later.[36] Shortly thereafter, Poles perpetrated a pogrom against the city's Jews, whom they viewed as supporting the Ukrainians. Over three days, at least seventy-three Jews were killed, while Jewish businesses and homes were pillaged and burned. It was the worst atrocity that the city's Jews had experienced so far.[37] This violence set up uneasy relations between all three groups during the interwar period. Ukrainians understandably saw themselves as repressed by Polish rule. Indeed, the Polish authorities imprisoned about seventy thousand Ukrainians after securing Galicia and, in the 1920s, they imposed limits on the use of the Ukrainian language in education, despite the Polish constitution and Treaty of Versailles guaranteeing minorities equality.[38] Jews and Ukrainians routinely faced discrimination in Polish institutions, especially in the civil service and universities.[39] Nonetheless, the city remained an important intellectual and cultural center for Poles, Jews, and Ukrainians alike.[40]

The Soviet occupation did not impose the type of draconian racial rule that defined the German occupation, but it did reshape both the national discourses around music and the hierarchies that had placed Jews and Ukrainians in subordinate positions during the Second Republic. The occupiers sought to underscore the Ukrainianness of the city and to promote Ukrainians, who were now the titular nationality.[41] This pro-Ukrainian stance was the most recent instance of the Soviets manipulating Ukrainian national ambition—of supporting Ukrainian national identity when it was useful to the empire and then repressing it when it seemed to threaten Moscow's hegemony.[42] In Soviet-occupied Lviv, the musical press portrayed the invasion as a liberation of Ukrainian composers from the oppression of Poles.[43] The Lviv Opera began performing in Ukrainian, which Barvinsky wrote was a first for the institution.[44] In April 1941, the history, theory, and composition division of the conservatory was asked by the Kyiv State Conservatory to help provide musical examples for a textbook on the history of Ukrainian music and agreed "to reduce as much as possible the examples of non-Ukrainian composers who worked in Ukraine."[45] Since their region had in fact been the home of Ukrainian, Polish, and Jewish composers, this proposition amounted to a demand to write a historically inaccurate, ethnically purified account of the region's musical history that would accord with the official valorization of Ukrainian culture.

The city's concert programming during the occupation, however, suggests a more complicated picture. The European classical canon and Polish compositions were regularly performed in addition to works by Soviet composers and Ukrainian ones, such as Barvinsky, Stanislav Lyudkevych, Borys Lyatoshynsky, and Viktor Kosenko.[46] The Lviv philharmonic performed a Beethoven symphony cycle, a series of concerts of Soviet composers, and works of Mahler, Debussy, Borodin, and Schmitt.[47] The occupiers' policies on Polish music were also fluid. Early propaganda in the city had been decidedly anti-Polish, although at no time were performances of Polish music banned. The philharmonic even opened its 1939 season with a performance of a Chopin piano concerto.[48] After the summer of 1940, Soviet policy began to embrace Polish cultural figures and to celebrate them within a framework of equality purportedly offered by Soviet rule.[49] This change was evident in the city's musical programming and criticism, too. In early 1941 concerts featured contemporary Polish composers, including works of locals like Koffler and Sołtys, as well as compositions by Kazimierz Sikorski, Szymanowski, and Piotr Perkowski. Reviews of these performances claimed that Soviet rule was in fact supporting Polish culture.[50]

Other critics twisted the period of Russian rule over Poland in the nineteenth century into a time of Polish-Russian friendship and thus a historical antecedent to Soviet occupation. One of the most blatant examples of such revisionism were the reviews of performances of *Cud*

146 | Chapter 5

mniemany, czyli Krakowiacy i Górale (The would-be miracle, or the Cracovians and Highlanders). Since its premiere in 1794 on the eve of the anti-Russian Kościuszko Uprising, this vaudeville had been interpreted as a thinly veiled allegory for Polish rebellion against Russian dominance and had played an influential role over the following decades in coding stylized folk music as nationalist resistance.[51] In Soviet-ruled Lviv, however, critics sidestepped the work's anti-Russian message to focus on its protorealist use of dialect and its folk-inspired dance numbers.[52] Even music written in opposition to Russian imperialism could be recast in service of Soviet expansion.

The embrace of Polish music within Lviv's concert programming underscores a fundamental distinction between music making under German and Soviet rule. Both occupiers accorded music an important role in their political agendas. However, the German occupation attempted to constrain, if not extirpate, Polish artistic expression, which the occupiers saw as a core component of Polish nationalism and, by extension, a threat to their imperial rule. While the Soviet occupiers were also in the business of empire building, they were amenable to Polish performances as long as they could be recast to support Soviet expansion over Polish lands and communist progress over the "capitalist" Second Republic.

Beyond concert programming, the occupation upended the dominant position long enjoyed by non-Jewish Poles in the city, opening the way for Jews and Ukrainians to gain greater standing within institutions. This dynamic was especially clear in higher education. Prior to the war the Polish state had limited the enrollment of Jewish and Ukrainian students in universities, such that on the eve of the occupation nearly 77.8 percent of students at the university in Lviv were Polish, 12.9 percent Jewish, and 6.7 percent Ukrainian. Under Soviet rule these percentages changed drastically: by April 1941 enrollments stood at 22.4 percent Polish, 44.2 percent Jewish, and 33.4 percent Ukrainian.[53] Matters were somewhat different at the Lviv State Conservatory, because it had been created by combining several music schools, each of which had their own enrollment profiles. For instance, the two largest music schools in Lviv—at least according to data from 1931—enrolled about 58 percent Polish, 27 to 32 percent Jewish, and the rest "other" students. But the Lysenko Institute, a Ukrainian music school, had only two Polish and six Jewish students among its 236 students in 1931, the rest presumably being Ukrainian.[54] These issues aside, the occupation-era Lviv State Conservatory had a high percentage of Jewish and

Ukrainian enrollees: 53 percent of all students were Jewish (a rate higher than the Jewish population of the city as a whole), 24 percent were Ukrainian, and 20 percent Polish. In all but one of the conservatory's divisions Jews were the largest group, and in each and every division Poles were in the minority.[55] (The conservatory's faculty consisted of twenty-two Poles, twenty-three Jews, and thirty-two Ukrainians.)[56] Many of these Jewish students were likely refugees who had fled from German-occupied Poland to Lviv.[57]

The reactions of Polish Jewish musicians to these changes can be read between the lines of their public pronouncements. Lissa praised the Soviet occupation not only for bringing communism—which she supported prior to the war—but also for its promises of greater equality: "The chauvinist policies of the [prewar] Polish Radio led to Ukrainian broadcasts for only an hour on Sunday (!). Of Jewish broadcasts, there can be no discussion. Numerous 'Aryan paragraphs' and antisemitic policies shut access to the radio to both Ukrainian and Jewish composers and performers. Today, all of this, fortunately, has left forever."[58] As we saw in chapters 1 and 2, Jewish musicians, including Lissa herself, had faced discrimination prior to the war. There had also been complaints among Polish Jews about the lack of airtime devoted to Jewish topics and culture.[59] It is also possible that Lissa's enthusiasm for the Soviet occupation reflected her own professional advancement, as it allowed her to leave behind her position at a private music school to join the city's only musicology division, something that Chybiński had not allowed prior to the war. At the same time, however, her statement should be read within the propagandistic context of the occupation. The Soviet occupation was ruinous for the city's Jewish inhabitants and broke apart their communities, just as it hurt Poles and Ukrainians, even if it allowed a degree of improvement for their careers and access to education.[60]

The Polish Jewish composer Józef Koffler, pictured in figure 12, likewise toed the line between recounting prior discrimination and acquiescing to Soviet power in a short statement he wrote that lauded Soviet rule. He wrote that, prior to the Soviet period, "the Warsaw Philharmonic and the Polish Radio ignored me as a composer, and I could solely hear my works performed far away from Poland's borders. It is not surprising that an idea had taken root: leave everything and emigrate. But then came the unforgettable September of 1939. The Red Army arrived, and everything changed. I was given a chance to live and work as a free and happy man."[61] While this statement is comically

FIGURE 12. The composer Józef Koffler in the late 1930s. Narodowe Archiwum Cyfrowe.

pro-Soviet, it is based in a germ of truth: in 1937 Koffler had contemplated emigration in response to the worsening antisemitism in Poland.[62] Further, throughout the interwar period his music had gained limited traction within Poland, whereas he had professional success beyond the country's borders.[63] Several of his works were published by Universal Edition in Vienna, he was an important protagonist in attempts to revise the bylaws of the ISCM during the mid-1930s, and he was the Polish representative on the Advisory Council for the World Centre for Jewish Music.[64] (He left the Jewish community in 1937.)[65] In occupied Lviv, his position seemed to improve somewhat: he served as a professor of composition and the vice-rector of the conservatory. He was also a member of the Union of Composers of Soviet Ukraine, and he organized per-

Restructure Them into Soviet Thinking | 149

formances under its auspices in Kyiv, where his compositions were also performed.[66]

Not all saw the advancement of Jews and Ukrainians in a positive light, however. For Poles who subscribed to right-wing views, the improved positions of Jews and Ukrainians seemed evidence that they were complicit in the occupation. Chybiński exemplified this trend. Writing while the war was still ongoing, he described how on the first day of the occupation, "already Ukrainian patrols, made up of Ukrainian students, stood in front of the university. . . . Our administration had left, and in its place a Soviet one arrived that worked with a newly created 'student committee' consisting mainly of Jewish and Ukrainian students."[67] The occupiers—in his view—were both ethnically and politically other. The most noxious form of this view held that Jews were inherently susceptible to communism and that, therefore, they bore the responsibility for Soviet rule.[68] Although this trope of *Żydokomuna* had been well entrenched in Polish right-wing politics for several decades, it saw a resurgence under the Soviet occupation as a way of scapegoating Jews for Soviet policy.[69]

Chybiński's private reflections on this period echoed this idea. He described the murder of his Polish Jewish colleague, Koffler, in the following terms: "It seems that Koffler has left this world (in the bol[shevik] time he bossed around musical Lviv). He escaped to Wieliczka and there, apparently, all the circumcised were circumcised completely. . . . I heavily doubt whether after 1939 even a single musical work was composed, except for Koffler's *Joyous Overture*, written to greet the 'krasnej armii' [red army], and for the songs written to honor bat'ki [father] Stalin, written by jews [*sic*] and ukr[ainians] [*sic*]."[70] In this ugly passage of correspondence, Chybiński links perceived sympathies toward the occupation with ethnicity: the improved standing of Koffler is due to "Bolshevik" rule; he further dismisses the occasional—and, in his view, politically compromised—compositions of his colleagues by glossing them in Russian; and he labels non-Polish ethnic groups with lowercase names.[71] By claiming that compositions of this era were only created by non-Polish composers, he suggests—inaccurately—that Poles did not participate in the occupation's musical culture. Such remarks suggest that Chybiński had shifted the blame for the occupation from the Soviet Union itself onto the local non-Polish population, who, he insinuated, allowed Soviet power to take hold.

Koffler's compositions from the Soviet period present a more nuanced picture, one not easily reducible to the polarity of collaboration or

150 | Chapter 5

resistance that Chybiński endorsed. Consider in this regard his 1940 composition *Ukrainian Sketches*, a set of six miniatures for string quartet, which was published in Kyiv in 1941.[72] The title of the work—along with its allusions to Ukrainian folk music throughout—clearly aligns it with the new focus on Ukrainian culture in the city and calls in the Ukrainian-language musical press, notably in *Radians'ka Muzyka* (Soviet music), to embrace folk music in composition.[73] Its musical techniques, on the other hand, suggest intriguing continuities from Koffler's prewar compositional outlook. Since the mid-1920s he had based his compositions on twelve-tone technique, but by the mid-1930s he had been experimenting with ways of blending dodecaphony with diatonicism.[74]

The technique used in the *Ukrainian Sketches* derives from this period: throughout the composition, diatonic melodies are accompanied by their twelve-tone complements. That is to say, the pitch classes absent from the melody are used as the basis of the accompaniment. In the final sketch, for instance, the opening melody clearly establishes A minor (consisting of the pitch classes C, D, E, G♯, A, and B), while the accompanying pizzicato in the cello and viola fills in the remaining pitch classes (C♯, D♯, F, F♯, G, and A♯; A is repeated in both melody and accompaniment). (See example 6.) Koffler had previously deployed this technique in his *Variations sur une valse de Johann Strauss*, op. 23 (1935), which subjected Strauss's *Emperor Waltz* to a series of twenty atonal variations.[75] Yet whereas the Strauss variations take a familiar tonal melody and make it less so, the *Ukrainian Sketches* consistently maintain the diatonic intelligibility of their melodies. The opening of the sixth sketch, for instance, reinforces A minor: the only pitch class shared by both (tonal) melody and (twelve-tone) accompaniment is that of A, which is further emphasized in the accompaniment because of its placement on the downbeat. By comparison, the pitches outside the key of A minor—such as D♯, F♯, and B♭—are placed on the weaker offbeats. (The prominent C♯s in the accompaniment are a modal inflection, offering a hint of A major.)

It may seem surprising that a twelve-tone composition—even one written in a highly tonal, folk-inflected manner—could be published in the Soviet Union in 1940–41. We should keep in mind that, despite the antimodernist stance of the Soviet musical establishment at this time, the centralization of Soviet aesthetic doctrine within the Union of Composers was still a work in progress during the first years of the war, and the German invasion of the Soviet Union in summer 1941 would lead to a period of relative ideological liberalism in Soviet music.[76] What was

EXAMPLE 6. Józef Koffler, *Szkice ukraińskie* (Ukrainian sketches), movement 6, mm. 1–6. Copyright by Bote & Bock GmBH. Reproduced by permission of Boosey & Hawkes.

happening in Moscow or Leningrad did not necessarily translate to Lviv. Koffler likely understood the *Ukrainian Sketches* as meeting a Soviet imperative for modernizing folkloric composition. The topic of folk music had been widely discussed at the Organizing Committee of the Union of Soviet Composers, a weeklong event that Koffler attended in spring 1940 in Kyiv, which featured dozens of performances and numerous talks. According to the published summary of the event, the speakers arrived at the conclusion that, although straightforward arrangements of folk music were valuable, "the main task consists in the deep, artistic transformation of folk music. It should be reflected through the prism of the composer's individual perception to create works of a new, higher quality that are based on folklore."[77] The *Ukrainian Sketches* fit such a mandate, bringing Koffler's idiosyncratic compositional techniques to bear on Ukrainian folklore. Nor was he the only Ukrainian composer to do so. For instance, Lyatoshynsky had

152 | Chapter 5

also composed a number of Ukrainian folk-inspired works during the war.[78] Koffler's composition thus underscores how the city's music making became enmeshed within the Soviet political project, as individuals attempted to reconcile their long-standing aesthetic interests with the occupation.

LVIV UNDER GERMAN RULE

Operation Barbarossa, the invasion of the Soviet Union launched by Germany on June 22, 1941, would have momentous consequences for the millions living in its path. The shelter that Soviet rule provided to Jews quickly collapsed. In Lviv, Ukrainians greeted the arrival of German forces on June 30 with enthusiasm, erroneously believing that they would help create an independent Ukrainian state.[79] Indeed, Ukrainian nationalist militias and organizations had allied themselves with the Germans for this reason. When they discovered that thousands of Ukrainians had been executed in the city's prisons by the NKVD in the final days of Soviet rule, they held Lviv's Jews collectively responsible, asserting that the Soviet NKVD was controlled by them. In the pogrom that followed, Ukrainian militiamen wearing blue and gold armbands beat and tortured the city's Jews. Between four and eight thousand were murdered while the Germans looked on with approval, filming the pogrom for propaganda purposes. Later that July the German authorities authorized three days of pogroms—the so-called Petliura Days— during which Ukrainian police, peasants, and some Poles again tortured, killed, and robbed Jews, targeting the Jewish intelligentsia in particular. An additional two thousand Jews were murdered.[80] In November 1941 the city's remaining Jewish population was ordered into a ghetto located in the city's Zamarstynów neighborhood. By the end of 1942 around 80 percent of the Jews who had been in the city in summer 1941 had been murdered, and by the end of 1943 nearly all of them were dead.[81]

The arrival of German forces in the city spelled the end of Soviet-led musical life. The philharmonic and symphony orchestra were shuttered.[82] The conservatory was requisitioned by the Wehrmacht's Transportleitung Osten, and requests from the conservatory's former director to reopen the school came to naught; only a single lower-level music school for Ukrainian students remained in operation.[83] From the point of view of Polish musicians, these changes were frustrating and humiliating. Adam Sołtys, a onetime director of the prewar conservatory, became a schoolteacher.[84] Chybiński tried in vain to gain a teaching position at the university, or at the very least to recover his personal library, which had been requisitioned by the Soviets.[85] When this failed, he instead worked long hours for a social insurance program, which left little time for musicology.[86] Many musicians, he reported in 1942, now "'bureaucratize,' that is, they have temporarily changed their profession from musician to a 'bureaucrat.'"[87] In comparison to Warsaw, where he had heard that musical life continued, Lviv had become a musical "Sahara," he complained. "*No one is composing here.* Musicians sit behind desks so as to make ends meet," he wrote in April 1943.[88]

The fate of Jewish musicians was incomparably worse. That the atmosphere of profound anti-Jewish violence permeating the city was also directed toward the city's dozens of Jewish musicians is revealed by the insidious rhymed verse "Poem about Music," published in the *Gazeta Lwowska* by an anonymous author.[89] The author asserts that during the Soviet occupation the city's musical life was ruled by Jews, echoing the notion of *Żydokomuna*. Now, with the Soviet army expelled, he implores "lovers of music" to pay attention to "the small anthology enclosed in this poem" of Jewish musicians, whom the author describes as a "herd" galloping past:

> Here they are. So many of them!
> Mr. Josel [*sic*] Koffler leads the pack.
> He advertised great invention,
> But was an impotent talent.
> Among us, he was not much understood,
> But in London, he was valued.

Koffler is subjected to the anti-Jewish tropes of artificial creativity and cosmopolitanism. But most of the poem is a list of names of Jewish musicians, an inversion of prewar publications that had listed, in a positive sense, the myriad Polish Jews who had built Lviv's musical culture. The ominous motivation for this list emerges at the poem's conclusion, when the author encourages readers to act against those named: "Dears, do what you like; you won't sully the art!!"[90]

Violence against Jewish musicians was immense and immediate. According to Jan Gorbaty, a pianist who survived and wrote testimony on the topic in 1945, many Jewish musicians were murdered in the first days of German rule, including the former staff members of the Lviv conservatory such as Henryk Günsberg, Artur Hermelin, and Edward Steinberg. He recalls how one young pianist, a certain Heisman, asked

154 | Chapter 5

the Germans to "relieve him from physical work because he was a pianist," but instead "they smashed each of his fingers with a hammer before shooting him."[91] Koffler fled to Wieliczka and survived the liquidation of the ghetto there only to be murdered along with his family near Krosno.[92] The piano professor Leopold Münzer was interned in the Janowska labor and murder camp, where he played in the camp orchestra before being murdered.[93] Others in the ghetto perhaps joined the orchestras run by Jakub Bard and a certain Mr. Schildhorn.[94] It is likely that of the twenty-three Jews who had been employed by the State Conservatory between 1939 and 1941, only three survived the Holocaust: Gorbaty, Lissa, and the pianist Piotr Łoboz. "Where were those in the underground, who 'helped'?" asked Gorbaty in 1945. "Had envy blinded them, or chauvinism?"[95]

COMMUNITIES OF DISPLACEMENT

As I mentioned at the beginning of this chapter, the experiences of the musical intelligentsia in Lviv were defined not only by whiplash between Soviet and German rule, but also by displacement, often deep within the Soviet Union. This geographic discontinuity has made it difficult to grasp how pivotal their encounters with Soviet power were to their postwar music making. In this and the following section, I describe two major ways in which displacement created an alliance between music, nationalism, and communist administrative politics, focusing first on the song repertoires of Polish and Polish Jewish communities in the USSR and then on the role of refugees in the Soviet-backed, postwar governance of Poland. In this way I locate the roots of the musical intelligentsia's postwar activities not only within Warsaw, as we saw in chapter 3, but also in the vast interior of the Soviet Union, which became a harsh schoolroom in Soviet-style communism.

A tortuous history brought vast numbers of Polish Jews into the Soviet interior, saving them from dying during the Holocaust. Indeed, the Polish Jews from the Lviv region who survived most often owed their lives to sheer chance: the vast majority of the survivors had been deported from the region in the years prior and sent to the Gulag system. Between 1939 and 1941 at least 315,000 citizens of the Second Polish Republic were deported to the Soviet interior. Of these, between 101,000 and 115,000 were Polish Jews.[96] After the German invasion of the Soviet Union in June 1941, the status of these prisoners changed immensely. After Soviet officials restored relations with the Polish government-in-exile and signed the Sikorski-Maiskii Pact of July 30, 1941, these prisoners were granted amnesty. The pact also called for the formation of a Polish army within the USSR that would combat the Germans.[97] Hundreds of thousands of Polish citizens—both Poles and Polish Jews—were slowly freed from the Gulag. They were now, in the eyes of the Soviet state, a useful resource in the war effort.

The main hope of leaving the Soviet Union for these refugees was provided by the Anders Army, a Polish fighting force named for its leader, the general Władysław Anders, who was released from Moscow's infamous Lubyanka prison in the amnesty himself. It was a core institution of Polish existence in the Soviet Union, with around seventy thousand members (which included both soldiers and civilians). In spring and summer 1942 its members were evacuated through Iran and British-ruled Palestine, and then they fought in the Italian Campaign.[98] The Anders Army was, however, often hostile toward Polish Jews. It routinely excluded them from joining its ranks, despite the large number of such individuals who reported to its recruitment posts.[99] This did not stop it from becoming a home to some of leading Polish Jewish light music stars in the USSR, including Henryk Wars, Jerzy Petersburski, and Henryk Gold, who performed in revues for the army's members.[100] Following the evacuation of the Anders Army in 1942 from the Soviet Union, a main center of Polish activity within the USSR became the Union of Polish Patriots and its associated army, the First Division.

Unlike the Anders Army, the Union of Polish Patriots and First Division were clear ploys of the Soviet Union. The Union of Polish Patriots was created by Stalin in February 1943 in anticipation of a breakdown in relations between the Soviet Union and the Polish government-in-exile, which occurred in April of that year.[101] By this point in 1943, it was increasingly evident that the Soviet Union would defeat Germany and would liberate Poland from German rule. The Union of Polish Patriots was an attempt to dislodge the London-based Polish government-in-exile as the legitimate representatives of Polish refugees in the USSR and to replace it with a Soviet-backed organization instead.[102] Led primarily by Polish communists, it sought to consolidate a Polish diaspora that was largely distrustful of the Soviet Union and to create the appearance that the union, and by extension Soviet leadership, spoke on behalf of a genuine Polish population.[103] The union had over 233,000 members, about 44 percent of whom were Jewish.[104] It was the core institution of Polish refugees in the Soviet Union during this time.

156 | Chapter 5

In an attempt to sustain these refugees, the Union of Polish Patriots organized musical and cultural events among its hundreds of thousands of members. The group had around 650 point people in different cities who were in charge of local cultural activities; these helped run 640 Polish-language libraries as well as 463 different artistic groups that had a combined membership approaching 6,000.[105] Musical performances were a part of many of these events. By April 1945 the union boasted seven instrumental ensembles, eleven dance troupes, and sixty-eight choirs in operation in Russia, Kazakhstan, Uzbekistan, Ukraine, Tajikistan, Turkmenistan, and Georgia, as well as a number of smaller instrumental ensembles.[106]

These events were cast by organizers as capable of unifying the refugees and connecting them to an imagined sense of Poland. Radio broadcasts, including of Polish music, were seen as especially important in connecting refugees spread across these vast distances.[107] Handwritten reports sent to the Union of Polish Patriots' headquarters in Moscow highlighted the impacts of these performances. A report from Pavlodar, Kazakhstan described a performance of five Polish song and dance groups: "An oasis of Polish colors and sounds flowered in front of the audience's eyes on the boundless steppe of Kazakhstan. Audience members could . . . fill themselves with the melody of the Polish fields, woods, and rivers through songs. For a few hours, the listeners were transported to their fatherland."[108] In the mind of the organizers, the union's cultural activities could have higher stakes still. As the official guidelines for the Week of Polish Word, Song, Dance, and Music in 1944 explained, "The battle for maintaining Polish cultural achievements is a battle for the existence of the nation itself."[109] What is left unsaid in such reports is the ethnic makeup of the refugees, who are portrayed as unified around the symbols of Polish nationhood.

The fraught relationship between Polish and Polish Jewish refugees was more evident in the Polish Army in the USSR (also known as the Kościuszko Division and, later, the First Division), which was formed in spring 1943 from Polish citizens who had been unable to join the Anders Army. Klemens Nussbaum, a Polish Jewish officer in the army who later wrote a dissertation on the topic, has shown that a core issue facing the army was the tension between the Jewish members, many of whom were officers, and Polish soldiers. He estimates on the basis of the army's archives that the army was around a fifth Jewish.[110] But of its officers who were Polish citizens (many officers were Soviets, who had been brought in because of staffing shortages), around half were Jewish, in

FIGURE 13. Zofia Lissa, as pictured on the document allowing her to leave Uzbekistan for Moscow in late 1942. AKP, D-Lissa II/2.

large part because educated non-Jewish Poles had managed to leave the USSR with the Anders Army. The majority of the editorial staff for the division's newspaper, its actors, and its newsreel division were also Jewish.[111] These Polish Jewish members often had uncompromising views of Germany, and the army offered them a chance for advancement in military rank that had been denied to them in interwar Poland. At the same time, anti-Jewish sentiments were common among the lower-level soldiers, who saw the large numbers of Polish Jewish officers in the Soviet-backed army as evidence of Żydokomuna.[112] To address these tensions around politics and between the Polish and Polish Jewish

158 | Chapter 5

recruits, the army leadership leaned on rather blatant Polish symbolism: the division's namesake was Kościuszko, the leader of an eighteenth-century revolt against Russia; it used the Polish flag and eagle; and it tolerated Catholic songs, even holding masses with the participation of atheist communist officers.[113]

It fell on the musicologist Zofia Lissa to help organize the musical activities of both the Union of Polish Patriots and the First Division. Since we last encountered her, she had fled from Lviv. As I have discussed elsewhere, she survived the Holocaust in large part thanks to her communist credentials and her standing in the Lviv State Conservatory, which allowed her to flee eastward in advance of the Germans (and pogroms) through Kyiv, Kharkiv, and Baku before eventually arriving in a small village outside of Namangan on the Great Fergana Canal in Uzbekistan. Here she spent seventeen months teaching the basics of Western music to Uzbek children.[114] Life was extremely difficult for her in Uzbekistan, and she implored her left-wing Polish contacts—many now living in Moscow and close to the Kremlin—for support.[115] These entreaties came to fruition in early 1943, when she was summoned to Moscow by Wanda Wasilewska, a Polish confidant of Stalin who was integral to organizing the Union of Polish Patriots. Once in Moscow, Lissa was tasked with leading the music division of the union.[116] She was to "supply Polish centers and organizations in the USSR with musical materials and to promote Polish music in the USSR," a task she undertook with enthusiasm.[117]

At the Union of Polish Patriots, Lissa aligned her communist politics with the sounds and symbols of the Polish nation. Between June and early August 1943, she was dispatched from Moscow to the army in order to document what seemed to be a notable use of song and music by the soldiers.[118] Indeed, songs have often existed at the crux of Polish political movements, and the army in the USSR was no exception.[119] Officers such as Marian Naszkowski described the singing of prewar Polish military songs as one way in which the "wall of distrust" between officers and soldiers could be mitigated.[120] Others believed songs helped to lessen the cultural and physical distance the members felt from Poland.[121] Lissa treated these songs as the oral culture of the army, transcribing them as performed by the soldiers and editing them into a songbook.[122] Her *Śpiewnik żołnierza polskiego* (Songbook of the Polish Soldier) both preserved and capitalized on the robust and politically effective musical culture of the First Division.[123]

Many of the songs that resurfaced in the collection date from the period of Polish statelessness (1795–1918), when songs decrying tyranny and injustice helped preserve a sense of Polish nationhood. Anti-German songs from the Prussian partition zone proved particularly popular since they aligned neatly with the army's goal of dispelling the World War II–era German occupation of Poland. The song "Pieśń z nad Odry" (Song from the Oder), for example, is based on a poem by Maria Konopnicka that commemorated the school strike in Września against Germanization between 1901 and 1904. By comparison, Lissa treated partition-era songs with an anti-Russian bent more carefully. Problematic verses were removed from songs such as "Warszawianka 1831" (Song of Warsaw, 1831) and "Bartoszu, Bartoszu" (O Bartosz, o Bartosz). In addition, the book includes a dozen contrafacta in which a new text is given to a well-known tune. One of the best loved of these songs was "My, Pierwsza Dywizja" (We, the First Division), written for the army by the poet Leon Pasternak to the tune of "My, Pierwsza Brygada" ("We, the First Brigade"), a calling card of Józef Piłsudski's Legions from the time of World War I.[124] Here, Pasternak updates a song associated with the Polish struggle for independence during World War I to fit the context of World War II:

Nad krajem słońce znów zaświeci,
Na szwabskie karki spadnie miecz.
Już idą kościuszkowskie dzieci,
By wygnać Niemców z Polski precz!

Over our country the sun will shine again,
On the Krauts' necks the sword will fall.
Kościuszko's children are on the march,
To drive away the Germans from Poland once and for all!

By portraying this panoply of patriotic songs as the oral culture of the army, the *Songbook of the Polish Soldier* suggested that the communist-led and Soviet-created army was continuing Poland's earlier battles, whether of World War I or of the nineteenth century. For a diaspora that was shot through with political tension and conflict between Poles and Polish Jews, it provided an emblem of unification toward a communist future, underwritten by a century-old tradition of national struggle. In this manner, Lissa's work with songs and refugees in the Soviet Union foreshadowed the allegiance between nationalism and communism that would define the postwar Polish state and its musical life.[125]

160 | Chapter 5

REFUGEES, LIBERATION, AND THE FRAMEWORK OF POSTWAR MUSICAL LIFE

The refugees in the Soviet Union provided not only a laboratory in which to test the fusion of Polish musical cultures with communist politics. They also contributed more directly to the building of postwar socialism because some of their most prominent members led the state-backed artistic institutions that became fundamental to the artistic life of the postwar period. Often these leaders were, like Lissa, intellectuals with leftist (if not outright communist) leanings who acted as what Patryk Babiracki has described as "willing interpreters" of Soviet policy for Poland.[126] In July 1944 in Moscow the Polish Committee of National Liberation (Polski Komitet Wyzwolenia Narodowego, PKWN) was created as a communist-led seed government for postwar Poland. Once the Soviet army crossed over what Stalin considered to be the new border of Poland in July 1944, the PKWN was transplanted to Polish territory, and by December 1944 it was presented as the new interim government of Poland, with its capital in the eastern Polish city of Lublin. Inspired by Soviet models, it had a Department of Culture and Art, as well as departments focusing on topics such as economics or information and propaganda.[127] The Department of Culture and Art was the earliest attempt to bring music and the arts more generally under the purview of the postwar state, and it would form the basis for the Ministry of Arts and Culture, which was created in January 1945.[128]

Those chosen to lead the artistic subdivision of the Department of Culture and Art had usually spent much of the war in the Soviet Union, and several had been active with the Union of Polish Patriots or the Polish Army in the USSR.[129] Such was the case with the newly appointed head of the music division within the Department of Culture, Mieczysław Drobner. We last encountered Drobner as a founder of Cracow's Association of Young Musicians, who, himself Jewish, had resigned when the association was taken over by a board that had attempted to expel Jewish members. A member of the Polish Socialist Party (PPS) and son of the prominent socialist organizer Bolesław Drobner, he had spent time in Romania and Lviv during the war before fleeing into the heart of the Soviet Union.[130] In May 1943 he joined the Polish Army in the Soviet Union and directed the army's amateur ensembles and accompanied its choirs.[131] By August 1944 he had been summoned to Lublin, where he worked out of a shell-damaged room, attempting to open music schools, create orchestras and choirs, and form professional unions for artists.[132]

Drobner worked to restart musical life on a fine-grained, local level. His department attempted to establish branches in various cities and towns throughout Lublin Poland (as the liberated territories west of the new Soviet frontier were known).[133] These local versions of the department would capitalize on the initiative of musicians in the city, reporting back to the central office while overseeing and aiding in the establishment and funding of theaters, orchestras, choirs, art galleries, music schools, and so forth.[134] Prospective candidates were encouraged to get to work immediately; later, a CV with a description of wartime activities could be sent for confirmation. This "work first, confirm later" policy suggests that the immediate reactivation of cultural activities outweighed considerations of an individual's pro-communist political credentials and even of whether they had collaborated with the German occupiers.[135]

In some cases, prewar institutions were nationalized (*upaństwowienie*) as they were reopened. For instance, the Stanisław Moniuszko Music Institute in Lublin, which had been part of the Lublin Music Society before the war, became the State Stanisław Moniuszko Music Institute when it resumed pedagogical activities in September 1944.[136] In other cases, orchestras and choirs were assembled from musicians in the region, but these did not appear to have any formal prewar roots. Music schools and orchestras of this type had begun operations across the liberated territories, including in Rzeszów, Białystok, and Lublin itself.[137] In other cases, the department's aim of creating new musical institutions ran ahead of local initiative. Drobner had organized the Union of Polish Composers, but there were only four members in the union (including himself), and the group's concert was in fact organized by the department as well.[138] Despite the somewhat chaotic nature of these organizational efforts, the PKWN did institute significant changes in musical life. Joining the Union of Polish Composers or Professional Union of Musicians allowed musicians to receive rations.[139] The PKWN also began to redefine the relationship between the state and musical ensembles, which were now to fall under the "care" of the PKWN.[140] It quickly implemented subsidies for small, geographically dispersed ensembles, substituting state patronage for the kinds of activity that, prior to the war, would have been supported through voluntary associations.[141] There is no evidence, however, to suggest that Drobner or the PKWN were concerned with influencing the programming or ideological direction of the ensembles. The focus was on a return to musical performance.

162 | Chapter 5

THE POLITICS OF JEWISH OMISSION

It can be tempting to assume that Polish Jewish musicians like Lissa and Drobner helped build the Soviet-backed postwar Polish state not only out of political conviction, but also because the Soviet Union had saved their lives. We do know that the Holocaust often led Polish Jews to recognize a fundamental distinction between German and Soviet rule: while both occupations were brutal, they knew that only the Germans were an existential threat to Jewish life writ large. This was a perspective not always shared by Poles, who could see both occupations as similar attempts at destroying Polish sovereignty.[142]

It is not clear if Lissa, Drobner, or other Polish Jewish leaders of musical life in the USSR shared this perspective. Neither Lissa nor Drobner commented on this interlacing of survival and political conviction. Drobner's memoirs, published in 1985, are an occasionally humorous account of administering music in Lublin as the war was nearing its end. He offers florid insight into life as a Polish bureaucrat circa 1944 but says nothing about what it felt like to have survived Nazism or to have been recruited as a Polish Jew to relaunch Poland's musical life.[143] When Lissa returned to Poland in 1947 (after spending two years at the Polish Embassy in Moscow, where she worked on cultural diplomacy), she spearheaded the introduction of Soviet-derived aesthetics and genres, such as the mass song.[144] Her enthusiasm for Stalinism was intense and sincere, conveyed through a large body of tightly argued, intellectually intimidating scholarship that she published at an unflagging pace through the late 1940s and early 1950s. Even long after paeans to Polish-Soviet "friendship" were no longer de rigueur, she remained proud of her work with the Union of Polish Patriots.[145] One never learns from reading her recollections, however, that nearly half the union's members were Jewish, nor of the Polish Jewish tensions within the army, whose song culture she documented. Indeed, as far as I am aware she never wrote about the relation between Jewishness and survival in the USSR, despite producing hundreds of articles, recollections, and books, including an article that theorized the significance of the German occupation for Polish music.[146] Although she had written about Jewish topics prior to the war, participated in Lviv's Jewish-identified musical circles of the 1930s, and praised Soviet rule for counteracting antisemitism, Jewishness is absent from the work she published after the war.

What to make of such omissions? There were countless reasons that individuals did not wish to revisit the wartime past or highlight their experiences during it. In this case, however, it is also imperative to remember the broader political context: *Żydokomuna*, the myth that communism was a Jewish conspiracy, put communists who were, in fact, Jewish in a bind. In the eyes of some Poles, the existence of Jewish communists confirmed that communism was doubly foreign—a Soviet and "Jewish" imposition onto Poland. Communist officialdom, meanwhile, had to tread carefully around the fact that there were a small number of prominent Polish Jews within their ranks, lest powerful figures such as Hilary Minc (an economist and member of the politburo of Polish communist party) and Jakub Berman (head of the Stalinist security apparatus) solidify in the eyes of the populace the "foreignness" of the postwar political system.[147] While Lissa was never as visible as Minc or Berman, she was no doubt aware of their precarious position. The links between communism and Jewishness plagued her later in life, too. They were the subtext behind a physical attack on her in 1955, during which her teeth were knocked out, and behind insinuations from colleagues that she ought to leave the country for its own good.[148]

In this manner the experiences of Lissa and Drobner point to another factor influencing the marginalization of Jewishness within Polish musical narratives, in addition to those discussed in the prior two chapters. For Polish Jewish musicians who were most active in building the institutions of postwar musical life, to acknowledge the categorically different experiences of Jews and Poles under Nazism could have called attention to their own Jewishness and, in turn, undermined their claims of national belonging in the eyes of Poles who thought in exclusive, ethnonationalist categories. To describe the Soviet occupation from 1939 to 1941 as a time of shelter from Nazism and as an amelioration of interwar discrimination would suggest, at least to some Poles, that communism favored Jews and, by the illogic of conspiratorial thinking, that it was itself Jewish. Thus, the downplaying of Jewishness as a core component of their wartime experience was also likely a strategy of self-preservation. It was a condition for individuals like Lissa and Drobner to continue the musical intelligentsia's project of building musical culture and musical institutions.

PART III

The Aftermath

6

Synthesizing Socialism

As performers were returning to concert halls in the liberated territories around Lublin, one more large-scale act of resistance and tragic loss of life was playing out in Warsaw. On August 1, 1944, the Home Army launched an armed insurrection against the German occupiers in Warsaw, an event known as the Warsaw Uprising. The aim was to wrest control of the city from the Germans before the Soviet army arrived in the hopes that this would bolster the underground's claim to postwar legitimacy. By the time the Home Army surrendered on October 2, at least 150,000 civilians had been killed.[1] Following this defeat, the surviving civilian population was forced out of the city, and it was systematically destroyed by the German forces in retaliation for Polish defiance. Archives, libraries, and historic buildings were accorded special wrath.[2] Between the bombardment of Warsaw in 1939, the pacification of the Warsaw Ghetto Uprising in 1943, and the systematic destruction of the city in retaliation for the Warsaw Uprising in 1944, 85 percent of its buildings were destroyed.[3] Some musicians, such as Rutkowski and Régamey, participated directly in the Warsaw Uprising only to end up in POW camps after it. Others lost family members who were soldiers or unlucky bystanders.[4] As Warsaw was razed after the uprising, most musicians fled or were deported, but others stayed. Szpilman lived in the ruins, fearful of outing himself as a Jew.[5] Piotr Perkowski, a composer and key organizer of musical life during the occupation, remained in the city until October 25, more than three weeks after the Home

167

168 | Chapter 6

Army surrendered, working with the Polish Red Cross to evacuate those wounded or trapped in the remnants of the city. "I still cannot forget the uncanny impression left by the empty, depopulated ruins and the ominous silence," he wrote in 1967. After finally leaving the city he joined dozens of others who set out in search of new homes. "Dejected to the extreme, we wandered further into the unknown."[6]

Many, including Perkowski, headed south to Zakopane, a town situated in the Tatra Mountains. Here they met the musicologist Adolf Chybiński, who had left Lviv in March 1944 after learning that his name had appeared on a list of enemies of Ukraine.[7] Waiting out the end of the war while living in the Tatra Museum, he completed his memoirs and began a diary in which he tallied the losses and survivals of Poland's musicians following the Warsaw Uprising. In late November 1944, he learned that Piotr Perkowski, a main organizer of musicians in Warsaw, had survived when he appeared in town. "One more is saved! It's lighter on the heart," he recorded.[8] The composer Andrzej Panufnik passed through Zakopane too, and Chybiński soon learned that the composer Witold Lutosławski was safe in Cracow.[9] One morning in December 1944, he was woken by a knock on the door:

> When I replied, "Come in!" and lit the lamp on my bed stand, a handsome young man entered and began to apologize for his arrival at such an early hour. "I am Palester!" [he said.] I was overrun with such a joy that even though I had never seen him with my own eyes, I said reflexively, "At last!" I don't know how he understood this, but perhaps from our further conversation he figured out that my words expressed a feeling of joy that such a very eminent musician had exited the war in one piece and was far from the Warsaw adventures. After the first couple of sentences of our conversation I asked him if he had rescued his works. Except for a few small ones, he rescued all of the larger works with the help of his wife. My joy doubled—no, it increased manyfold!!![10]

Palester had survived the Warsaw Uprising (the "Warsaw adventures") because he had kept a low profile in the countryside. His family was less fortunate: his stepbrother had died a Home Army soldier in the uprising and his father, who had provided medical assistance to the wounded in Warsaw until the last moments, was run over by a truck in a refugee camp outside the city. Separated from his family, Palester ventured south to Zakopane, hoping to find safety during the war's final days. Chybiński's enthusiasm for his arrival reveals how the survival of composers and their compositions had acquired renewed weight at a time when the musical intelligentsia began to contemplate the future of

Polish music. Each who survived was not only a link to the past but also offered hope that a new musical future could be constructed out of the country's devastation.

The physical destruction that faced Poland's musicians in January 1945—when Warsaw was liberated from German rule—was immense. Seen from the sky, Warsaw's urban core was little more than "empty, burnt-out boxes grouped together into some kind of gigantic honeycomb," observed the musicologist Zofia Lissa as she arrived by plane for a visit from Moscow.[11] Even the buildings that had survived were heavily damaged. "In Warsaw there are no buildings that have 'survived' in the colloquial meaning of that word," observed the music critic Jerzy Waldorff. "All are more or less mutilated, slashed with shrapnel. If one says that a certain building in Warsaw has 'survived,' that means only that the most important part of the building is intact, the foundation for rebuilding."[12] Even so, this destruction was not even: while remnants of structures were still to be found in Polish Warsaw, what had once been the Warsaw Ghetto had been reduced to mounds of rubble, as shown in figures 14 and 15. Varsovians hoping to find what remained of their book collections or manuscripts required special passes to the enter the city's remnants, where they searched for traces of their former lives.[13] Understandably, much of the musical intelligentsia chose to regroup in Cracow, which had been the seat of the General Government and whose medieval city center was spared destruction.[14]

Reconstruction was an opportunity, a moment during which the future that would rise from the ruins of war had to be debated and defined. It required mass mobilization, including the broad participation of nearly all Polish citizens to remove the rubble from the streets and restore a sense of normalcy, however tentative. For the Polish communist authorities, it was a chance to turn Poland into a socialist state.[15] Indeed, reconstruction of ruined cities such as Warsaw was a popular project, one led by communist officials but also supported by a population that was in other respects skeptical of Soviet power in Poland.[16] So intense was the social transformation of reconstruction that the historian Katherine Lebow has argued that the period was defined by a "new popular understanding of citizenship" in which "it was work that *gave* meaning to individual and collective existence."[17] By the end of the decade, building had become a key metaphor in Polish discourse, an idea that "would bind together a social and political body that had been blasted apart by fascism and war."[18] For the musical intelligentsia, reconstruction was an opportunity to codify and formalize the

FIGURE 14. The Warsaw Ghetto was reduced to a sea of rubble. One of the few ghetto buildings to survive was the Church of St. Augustine, which towers above what had once been a dense urban environment. Narodowe Archiwum Cyfrowe.

authority that they had strived for since the 1920s. Possessing clout among their peers and an ethos of service, they took the reins of newly built or relaunched musical institutions, gaining access to the centralized, state-funded institutions that had been chimerical prior to the war. As we will see, reconstruction was also a time during which divisions between Polish and Polish Jewish members of the musical intelligentsia

FIGURE 15. Life eventually returned to the ruins of Warsaw. Here a woman sells ice cream next to a news kiosk on Nowy Świat street, a central thoroughfare, circa 1947. Narodowe Archiwum Cyfrowe.

continued to harden, in part because of continuing antisemitism, anti-Jewish violence, and emigration.

By positing reconstruction as a key project shared by both the musical intelligentsia and the Polish state, this chapter intervenes into debates about the agency of musicians during a period in which communist control over the state was being consolidated. Music histories have generally taken their cues from political history, positing an early period of relative openness and liberalism (1944–47), followed by a sharp crackdown on culture with the consolidation of communist authority in 1948, which inaugurated the Stalinist era (1948–56). The congress of the Union of Polish Composers held in the vacation town of Łagów Lubuski in August 1949 is traditionally treated as a synecdoche for the broader pressures of Stalinism in Polish composition, most notably those placed on Polish composers to embrace the Soviet-derived style of socialist realism. Socialist realist compositions, the thinking went, should be accessible to non-elite listeners, engage with national and ideological themes, and be composed in a more tonal idiom using neo-traditional forms. "Formalism"—a catchall for Western modernism and avant-garde composition—was to be rejected as a decadent product of elitism and capitalism.[19]

172 | Chapter 6

The final two chapters of this book develop a contrasting narrative of the first postwar decade in Polish music, one that treats socialist realism as but one inflection point within a longer process of rebuilding Poland from the war. Ideas that have long been seen as essential elements of socialist realism—including a focus on accessibility, anti-internationalism, a concern for the "mass" audience, and a neoromantic aesthetics of expression—had roots in the mandate to rebuild Poland musically and to deploy music as part of the process of returning to normalcy that began as early as 1944. In drawing attention to such precedents for Polish socialist realism, I am not merely disputing the periodization or semantic extent of the term, but rather suggesting that the years 1944 to 1947 were themselves a defining period in Polish cultural politics. These years were not just a liberal prelude to Stalinism, but a time when the social contract binding musicians with the state was established, and during which core notions about music's broader cultural significance were being developed in response to the aftermath of war.

REBUILDING JEWISH POLAND?

The tragic, inescapable reality of the postwar period was that few of the Jewish musicians who had been central to Poland's classical music scene in the 1920s and 1930s had survived the Holocaust. The vast majority of the Jewish musical associations that had populated cities and towns prior to the war were never relaunched. Even among those Polish Jewish musicians who had survived—and the chances of survival were better among the acculturated members of the musical intelligentsia than among unacculturated Jews who were poor, nonurban, and Yiddish speaking—there were fundamental questions about the future. In this section I show that music was important to some of the key Jewish cultural organizations in early postwar Poland and consider how these efforts at Jewish cultural reconstruction unfolded at a distance from the main core of the musical intelligentsia, who had little evident investment in them.

In the immediate aftermath of the war, some Jewish survivors began to relaunch cultural life in Poland. Jonas Turkow, who had played a central role in the Warsaw Ghetto's musical life, was elected president of the newly relaunched Union of Yiddish Literati, Journalists, and Artists in Poland and oversaw Yiddish-language radio broadcasts.[20] Such enthusiasm was prompted in part by promises made by the new Polish state in 1944 that would extend formal equality for Jews and, it was hoped, rectify the prewar status of Jews as second-class citizens.[21] Some believed that the reestablishment of Jewish-identifying cultural organizations, such as Yiddish theater, newspapers (in Yiddish and Polish), and exhibitions of Jewish fine art, would honor those who had been murdered and demonstrate the continued vibrancy of Polish Jewry despite the Holocaust.[22] Others understood these activities as enacting a distinctly Jewish contribution to the broader mandate of reconstruction.[23] Individuals who shared such views often gathered under the Central Committee of Jews in Poland (Centralny Komitet Żydów w Polsce, CKŻP, 1944–50), the official organization representing the Jewish minority in Poland, which provided food, shelter, education, and cultural programming to survivors.[24] Under its Division of Culture and Propaganda, three major prewar Jewish artistic associations were resurrected: the Union of Yiddish Writers and Journalists (which briefly had been known in 1945 and early 1946 as the Union of Yiddish Literati, Journalists, and Artists in Poland before reverting to its old name), the Union for Artists of the Jewish Stage, and the Jewish Association for the Promotion of Fine Arts, each with memberships that had been decimated by the Holocaust.[25]

Music permeated the events of the Central Committee of Jews in Poland, even though it did not enjoy the same level of institutional support as did Jewish letters or fine art. The short-lived Association of Jewish Musicians and Composers in Poland was created in October 1946 by Shloyme Prizament (1889–1973), Leon Wajner (1898–1979), and a certain E. Halpern. Its mission was "to collect musical works and compositions of Jewish composers who had been killed during the German occupation."[26] Even though the activities of this group appear to have been limited (and its founders soon emigrated), the Central Committee's local branches organized numerous musical events, ensembles, and institutions during the early postwar period. A music school for Jewish students, named after the famed Polish Jewish violinist Bronisław Huberman, was opened in Wrocław, and a similar institution operated in the town of Wałbrzych.[27] Both of these were in Lower Silesia, part of the so-called reclaimed territories, the regions gained by Poland from Germany after the war, where many Jewish survivors were settling. The Central Committee called for the creation of choirs and other musical institutions.[28] In April 1945, the nascent Polish Radio in Lublin broadcast Jewish music each Sunday evening.[29] Local branches of the Central Committee routinely organized concerts.[30] "Jewish artistic brigades"

174 | Chapter 6

performed in Lower Silesia, in fall 1946 giving sixteen concerts for orphans, miners, and workers in the region.[31] Orphanages in Otwock, Zatrzebie, and elsewhere regularly organized concerts in which orphaned children performed.[32]

The members of the Central Committee of Jews in Poland had an abiding interest in documenting and commemorating Jewish loss during the Holocaust, as evinced by its members collecting thousands of testimonies from survivors.[33] Most notable from a musical perspective was the publication in 1947 of Shmerke Kaczerginski's *Undzer gezang* (Our song). The collection included sections devoted to both "partisan" and "ghetto" songs, which Kaczerginski had learned during the war or collected from witnesses afterward.[34] The Jewish wartime song repertoire was also popular in performances during the early postwar years. Singers who had performed in the ghettos toured Jewish communities and orphanages across Poland, where they performed music that had been sung in the ghettos.[35] So popular were Diana Blumenfeld's concerts of ghetto songs that tickets to one of her first postwar performance sold out a week in advance.[36] Turkow, her husband, recalled her first concerts in Lublin being met with audiences overflowing from the halls, in which "the distance between artists and audience had been erased" and whose "dry eyes began to redden, with tears flowing."[37] In March 1946 a concert in Łódź was dedicated to songs of the Wilno ghetto, performances of which were led by Kaczerginski.[38] A concert in Szczecin from December 1946, given by a traveling Jewish artistic brigade and titled "Jews in the Ghetto," was dedicated to their heroism and sacrifice.[39]

Survivors, however, had to contend with virulent anti-Jewish violence during the early postwar years, perpetrated by Poles against Jews. Between 1944 and late 1946, hundreds were killed in dozens of attacks.[40] Train travel was dangerous, and Jews returning to their homes were often greeted with disdain if not outright violence. Several factors contributed to this violence, including the resurgence in long-held anti-Jewish prejudices, the fact that thousands of Poles had expropriated Jewish property during the war (and did not wish to return it), and a conspiratorial belief that Jews were inherent supporters of communism (and thus, in this twisted logic, that an attack on Jews was also an attack on communist rule).[41] The most infamous of the early postwar pogroms was perpetrated in Kielce on July 4, 1946, when around forty Jews were murdered. The Union of Polish Composers denounced antisemitic violence at its initial congress, and some in the musical intelligentsia, such as Zygmunt Mycielski, wrote eloquently against it.[42]

Nonetheless, these attacks called into question the viability of Jewish life and cultural renewal in Poland. After the Kielce pogrom, more than a quarter of Poland's Jewish population emigrated. By the end of 1947, around 130,000 Jews, or somewhere between 40 and 50 percent of the Jewish community, had left.[43]

For Turkow, who had gone to remarkable lengths to organize musical and theatrical performances in the Warsaw Ghetto, this anti-Jewish violence spelled the end of Jewish cultural life in Poland. "I had believed at the beginning," he wrote in 1959, "that in the new Poland, in the democratic Poland, Jews would be able to finally breathe again."[44] Outright violence soon dissuaded him of this. He was advised to continue using his falsified "Aryan" identity from the occupation so as to avoid attacks.[45] A bomb was thrown at the radio station where he worked because of his Yiddish-language broadcasts, he believed.[46] It was too dangerous for him and his colleagues to travel on trains because Poles would pull Jews from the carriages and murder them.[47] When Turkow confronted the minister of public security, Stanisław Radkiewicz, about this anti-Jewish violence, the minister's cavalier reply seemed to underscore both the ubiquity of Polish antisemitism and the government's indifference to it: "What do you want me to do?" the minister reportedly replied. "Deport eighteen million Poles to Siberia?"[48] Turkow soon concluded "that to rebuild Jewish life in Poland was an impossible dream."[49] He left the country shortly thereafter.

The decision of Jewish musicians to emigrate often reflected multiple factors and considerations, not all of which have been preserved in the historical record. The musicologist Ewa Kowalska-Zając asserts, for instance, that the composer Roman Haubenstock-Ramati immigrated to Israel in 1950 due to his rejection of tightening socialist realist dogma in Poland.[50] But it is noteworthy that Haubenstock—who had survived the Holocaust in the Soviet Union and joined the Anders Army—had added the Hebrew "-Ramati" to his last name when the Anders Army moved through Palestine as a sign of his identification with his Jewish roots.[51] The composer Tadeusz Zygfryd Kassern likewise attributed his decision to defect from Poland to the United States in 1948 to Stalinist repression, but his defection also occurred shortly after the official antisemitism of the postwar state had become inescapably apparent to him.[52] Other Polish Jewish musicians did not return after the war. Aleksander Tansman, who had been naturalized as a French citizen in 1938 and spent the war in the United States, returned to Paris, which had been his home base for decades.[53] The young Mieczysław Weinberg,

176 | Chapter 6

who had fled east from Warsaw at the beginning of the war, had since become well established in the USSR, where he remained to his death.[54]

In rare cases Jewish musicians decided to return permanently to Poland from western Europe or North America. The conductor Grzegorz Fitelberg was motivated to return both because of his deep connections to the Polish musical establishment and because of the anti-Polish and anti-Jewish sentiments he had encountered in the United States, where he had spent much of the war. "Being a Jew is bad, being a Pole— also not good," he wrote in a letter of 1945. "But to be both a Pole and a Jew is very challenging. This is of course not my opinion of Jews and Poles, but rather that of nearly the entire world. I was in the States for *four* years. It was one great, hopeless disappointment."[55] Those of less prominence who remained in Poland often continued to use their Polonized names even after the war concluded. The violinist Witold Hugo Baruch, for instance, used the name Aleksander Laskowski until his death in 1946.[56] Others, such as the musicologist Zofia Lissa, downplayed their Jewishness during this time, a path was especially amenable to the highly acculturated.[57]

The still-fresh memory of prewar antisemitism could further cement ambivalence about the possibility of return among members of the musical intelligentsia, especially among those who had managed to establish themselves abroad during the war. Consider Mateusz Gliński, the founder and editor of *Muzyka*, a journal that advanced the nationalist aims of the musical intelligentsia but was subjected to thinly veiled antisemitic attacks in the 1930s (see chapters 1 and 2). In 1940 he was able to leave Poland on the basis of a fake invitation to conduct a cycle of Wagner operas in Brazil. Never intending to travel to South America, he instead lived in Rome and became the music critic for the Vatican's official paper.[58] In letters from 1941 sent to the musicologist Zdzisław Jachimecki, he described how he felt "enormous nostalgia" for his time in Poland, from which he is only rescued by "work—difficult, poorly paying work."[59] During the war he asked for news of all his friends and colleagues—and even his old enemies. "I am unable to tell you how important these matters are to me and how much I suffer from nostalgia (despite my entire resentment toward many of our dear colleagues from their attack on *Muzyka* and its editor)," he wrote in a letter in 1943.[60]

The ease with which he was able to establish himself in Rome as a critic, conductor, ensemble leader, and publisher during the war cast into relief the barriers his projects had faced in prewar Poland.[61] In 1946 he wrote to Jachimecki,

When I consider that I am now fifty-three years old and that in Poland, despite all my efforts, I was unable to conduct, my artistic project was crushed due to personal intrigue and the caprices of a few mediocre individuals, and others attempted to discredit me as an artist, I feel satisfaction: through my own work and diligence I obtained among foreigners all that was so difficult to achieve at home. But this also gives rise to a sad and bitter reflection: where did those twenty years of my life go, which, as I see it, could have yielded so much, much more for Poland than they did, if they yielded anything at all.[62]

What is particularly striking is how Gliński measures the shortcomings of his activities in the language of national service that was typical of the musical intelligentsia. He underscores his continued faith in such a project even as he bemoans his inability to realize his aims. In 1947 he reiterated this point. "If I had to return to my native realm, I would be attacked from all directions and, to be certain, I would not be able to accomplish even a small portion for Polish music of that which I do for the Italians."[63] Gliński reminds us that for the Jewish members of the musical intelligentsia, relationships to postwar Poland reflected not only the experiences of the Holocaust and postwar politics, but also longer histories of attack and exclusion that had coursed through the community for decades.

THE MUSICAL INTELLIGENTSIA AS POSTWAR FORCE

For members of the musical intelligentsia who did remain in Poland, the early postwar years spelled rapid changes in position, title, and daily work alike. Indicative of the musical intelligentsia's growing sway—especially of its younger, "progressive" branch—the underground networks it had created in occupied Warsaw often supplied the leaders of the new institutions of state. When the Union of Polish Composers, first created in Lublin, subsumed the prewar Association of Polish Composers in 1945, Piotr Perkowski, who had served on the board of association in the 1930s, became its president (and would remain so until 1948, when Mycielski took over).[64] In the same year he was elected head of the far larger Professional Union of Musicians, thereby ensuring that he was in charge of the unions in which *all* of Poland's musicians were members.[65] Perkowski's double role reflected the clout he had garnered as a leader of the musical underground during the occupation and as an organizer before the war. But his rapid transition from underground organizing to postwar officialdom was far from exceptional.

178 | Chapter 6

His colleagues from the underground musicians' group were also appointed to new positions. They became the director of the Poznań State Opera (Zygmunt Latoszewski), the rector of the State Higher Music School in Katowice (Bolesław Woytowicz), the head of the Baltic Philharmonic (Zbigniew Turski), rector of the Warsaw Conservatory (Stanisław Kazuro), and an on-the-ground organizer for the Ministry of Culture and Art (Mirosław Dąbrowski). The pianist Zbigniew Drzewiecki was appointed rector of the Cracow Conservatory and the progressive composer Roman Palester its vice-rector.[66] Stefan Kisielewski, another young progressive composer, was appointed a professor at the conservatory in part because Drzewiecki knew him and knew he needed work.[67] While there was widespread persecution of those who had held prominent positions in the Home Army, the musicians who had held lower-level positions in it (or who were only tangentially connected to it) largely evaded retaliation.[68]

That, within a few months of the war's conclusion, the musical intelligentsia was enmeshed with the institutions of the state is evinced by their own complaints about their new workload. For Palester, writing in 1946, this amounted a sea change in his colleagues' standing: "Our present-day composers [are] holding in their hands the entirety of our musical life and [are] having a decisive influence on its direction, heading unions, directing orchestras and conservatories."[69] Such remarks reflect a drastic reversal from the prewar stance of composers, in which crisis and relative powerlessness were the predominant themes. Others complained about how their new positions burdened them with administrative tasks that left less time to compose.[70] Bronisław Rutkowski, who had recently returned to Poland, complained that quality had taken a back seat to quantity because composers were too concerned with "organization, organization, organization"—this coming from an avid organizer who before the war had written about the obligations of musicians to better organize musical life.[71] The *Ruch Muzyczny* editorial board echoed his complaints, and Perkowski was compelled to address them in his 1947 speech at the annual congress of the Union of Polish Composers.[72]

The early years of reconstruction had also inaugurated a generational shift, in which the younger members of the musical intelligentsia, who tended to be aligned with progressive or modernist aesthetics, gained new levels of influence over musical institutions at the expense of older, generally more conservative ones. Indeed, nearly all the figures mentioned in the prior paragraphs were aligned with the progressive branch of the musical intelligentsia, including Perkowski, Palester,

Rutkowski, Kisielewski, Drzewiecki, Mycielski, Woytowicz, and Turski. The older generation, which was more aligned with the conservatives, did not disappear after the war. For instance, Piotr Rytel, the most extreme of the conservatives, continued to work as a music critic for a number of Warsaw papers and taught composition at the Warsaw Conservatory, as he had done before the war.[73] But the progressives were no longer the beleaguered newcomers that they had been in the 1920s. Rather, they now held influential positions guiding the key institutions of Polish musical life, including the Union of Polish Composers, the Polish Music Publishers, the journal *Ruch Muzyczny*, the Warsaw musicology institute, and the Warsaw and Cracow Philharmonics. This last institution, a retooled version of the Philharmonic of the General Government, was important to the progressive musical intelligentsia since its leadership was sympathetic to new music and its musicians were capable of performing complex modernist works.[74]

The Polish cultural bureaucracy turned to the progressive musical intelligentsia to run institutions because there were few other options. No doubt, many communist officials would have wished for more communists or at least socialists to occupy prominent positions in Polish musical life. A few musicians who had held leftist views, including Zofia Lissa, Stefania Łobaczewska, and Drobner, gained relevance after the war. But there were relatively few true believers in the musical intelligentsia who could act as devoted advocates for state socialism. After the war, membership in the Polish Workers' Party (PPR, after December 1948, PZPR) among professional musicians was weak, with only between 1 to 4 percent of members of the Professional Union of Musicians belonging to the PPR in 1947.[75] The party's subcommission on music, formed in May 1947, admitted that they had few allies in the two professional unions (the Union of Composers and the Professional Union of Musicians), at conservatories, and at the main music periodical, *Ruch Muzyczny*. These institutions were instead dominated, they claimed, by "right-wing elements."[76] Given the lack of alternatives, it was a straightforward matter for the tight-knit milieu of the musical intelligentsia to emerge at the forefront of state-sponsored musical life.[77] After all, its members had widespread authority among the creative community, deep interpersonal networks, experience running institutions, and an enduring commitment to social activism, even if not from within a communist framework. Many had endorsed visions of strong state involvement in the arts in the 1930s and continued to do so after the war.[78]

180 | Chapter 6

Core beliefs of the musical intelligentsia also found new resonance during reconstruction. There was a basic compatibility between the musical intelligentsia's long-standing self-conception as modernizing leaders before the war and the imperative to rebuild the country musically after it. Projects that had once been cast in terms of rectifying Poland's musical underdevelopment from a century of partition were now reframed as rectifying its destruction during the war. This tightening of the intelligentsia's commitment to the project of national reconstruction is well illustrated by the composer and critic Zygmunt Mycielski. At first he might seem an unlikely figure to sincerely support communist-led reconstruction. He was of gentry background (and nicknamed "the count"), he had celebrated the virtues of elite culture prior to the war, and he had spent a considerable portion of the decade prior to the war studying in Paris. Since we last encountered him, he had fled to France, joined the Polish army there, fought during the Battle of France in summer 1940, and was captured. For the remainder of the war he performed forced labor in POW camps in Germany. Throughout the period of captivity and after, he maintained an extensive correspondence with his one-time composition teacher, Nadia Boulanger.[79] He continued to write to her after the war, leaving behind an extensive archive that provides a rare instance of Polish musicians explaining conditions to an outsider who had few stakes in Polish politics of the day.

His letters bristle with a sense of social obligation toward nation, one that he believes can only be fulfilled by the labor of reconstruction. He chose to return to Poland, after a brief sojourn in France, even though he could have chosen a life abroad. "I should go over there [to Poland], where my mother, my brothers, my children, all my compatriots are," as he explained his decision to Boulanger. "What awaits them now; what is happening in central Europe?"[80] He departed for Poland despite his own doubts about what communism would spell for descendants of the aristocracy like himself. "If I am deported to Siberia or elsewhere as a 'lustful viper of capitalism,'" he assured his Parisian friends, "know that nothing physical affects me. . . . One must love life but not fear death—neither one's own nor that of others."[81] His decision also foreshadowed a long-lasting confirmation of his views about musicians' social responsibilities. Time and time again, he explained to his Parisian friends how Poland's decimation meant that he and his colleagues had to serve reconstruction. In 1947 he wrote, "You know that after I spent five years in the German camps, breathing open air was exhilarating. Every day I feel it more. I am happy to have returned here [to Poland]

and to be able to live and work here. And I believe that this is truly where I belong, where all of us belong who do not fear to reconstruct, and to construct, a country that has been devastated by too many cruelties."[82] Note here the slippage between "reconstruction" and "construction," of recovering from the war and building a different future, an imperative that he implies is best understood as a response to—and transcendence of—the war.

Reconstruction also led Mycielski to support the communist powers then ascendant in Poland. On the eve of parliamentary elections held in January 1947, he explained to Boulanger that he hoped that the Polish Workers' Party would prevail. His thinking is all the more remarkable because in this private letter, written in French, he was under no obligation to explain his politics, much less endorse the communists:

> Tomorrow morning our block will vote at 7 a.m., so I am spending this night writing letters before taking part in the election, which, I hope, will prove the government, the only one that gives guarantees of a loyal collaboration with our great Eastern ally. I've been thinking about this since 1939. It is necessary to live here to understand this even better. And I hope that my compatriots, despite their inclinations toward all that is madness, will be realistic enough after what has happened here, to admit—for once—that one cannot engage in sentimental politics but that only reason should dictate in this matter—a resistance like that of '39–'45 suffices for several centuries. If not—it's better not to think about it. The essential matter, the only one that counts, is to live. And this time, *at any cost*. And this *also demands courage.* . . . To live, to work, since we can reconstruct and construct also, and we can find the means of living in that which is given to us here.[83]

The letter courses with a politics of pragmatism that has been shaped by war. There is certainly an undercurrent of wry critique in phrases such as "our great Eastern ally" (the USSR) and "*collaboration loyale,*" which in the original French calls to mind a parallel between the Soviet Union and Vichy France. Yet he also rejects the Polish romantic tradition of hopeless yet brave resistance to foreign rule (the "inclinations toward all that is madness" is doubtless an allusion to the Warsaw Uprising of 1944) in exchange for the equal bravery, he believes, that is required to work within the system. The war is the at-once awesome and inexplicable force of gravity behind these beliefs, which he casts as only truly comprehensible to those on the ground in Poland. While it might seem an about-face for a "count" to endorse the communists, this letter also reveals a deeper level of continuity behind this seeming transformation, one in which notions of service and leadership remain intact even as the country's political leadership does not.

182 | Chapter 6

Mycielski's hopes were borne out. The elections did confirm the "loyal collaboration" with the USSR, but only because its results were forged to give an overwhelming victory to the communists. Over the following years Mycielski enacted the pragmatic compromise adumbrated in 1947: he served as the president of the Union of Polish Composers during the height of Stalinism (vice president 1947–48, president 1948–50) and became one of the main translators of socialist realist ideas into a form that would be palatable for Poland's composers.[84] He would by the 1960s become a staunch critic of state socialism, but in the early postwar period, he saw communist rule as the only viable path away from cataclysm.[85]

RECONSTRUCTION AS TRANSFORMATION

If work on behalf of reconstruction helped to define the postwar musical community, then, conversely, a failure to adequately serve the project of rebuilding could suggest a betrayal of the collective. Reconstruction helped to define the boundaries around the musical intelligentsia and the types of activities that its members viewed as valid. While, prior to the war, the musical intelligentsia endorsed a vision of musical modernization that included both international contact and the development of audiences in Poland, after the war, the focus fell on the latter at the expense of the former. Students and performers still traveled to western Europe during the first postwar years, if with less frequency than before the war.[86] However, the Association of Young Musician-Poles in Paris languished, reduced to handing out relief supplies to its members abroad while tussling with the Polish Embassy, its onetime patron.[87] The newfound ambivalence toward Paris is well captured by Mycielski, who had once been among the greatest advocates for Parisian studies. In 1945 he wrote of postwar Paris that "the rhythm of musical life flows along the old paths, depleted, rather than enriched, by the experiences that shocked that country."[88] But at around the same time, he also wrote to Boulanger that "it is useless to explain to you how much I wish to renew the bonds, already old, that connect almost all of us to French musical life."[89] This increased ambivalence about international exchange occurred prior to the tightening of Poland's borders and enactment of explicitly anti–western European musical policies in 1949 and the early 1950s.[90]

The fraying of the musical intelligentsia's internationalism is made clear by the fact that some Polish composers living abroad were now critiqued for failing to adequately support reconstruction. Composers who had spent the war abroad or moved there after its conclusion, such as Roman Palester, Antoni Szałowski, Konstanty Régamey, and Jerzy Fitelberg, were torn between maintaining their connections to the Polish musical community and returning to a Soviet-backed state.[91] Some were able to strike a balance of sorts. Régamey, for instance, contributed to several discussions about Polish musical aesthetics in the late 1940s despite having fled to Switzerland at the end of the war.[92] But others were met with scorn. In 1947 Tadeusz Ochlewski berated Palester, who had left for Paris, explaining, "That above 'music' there is something bigger: work. That the artist's active relation to the collective life is what matters. That I consider your departure," he wrote, "as betrayal."[93] That this collective work meant rebuilding the country is made even more apparent in a letter from the following year. "I hold it against you that you do not want to 'push yourself' to work on reconstruction."[94] While the idea that composers must contribute to the greater collective was a canonic belief of the musical intelligentsia, reconstruction forced a new focus on work within Poland's borders.

The new skepticism toward international activity is clearly sketched by Mycielski in a letter that reflects his own transformation from a committed Francophile to a Poland-based servant of the nation. In 1947 he unsuccessfully attempted to convince Szałowski to return from Paris to Poland, writing, "The single wise thing that I did was to return here—as a matter of fact, I never hesitated even for a moment. *There is work here*, and I knew that there would be when [the war began]. . . . And I don't know about how things are over there, where you are; I only know that we are not there, but rather we live here and will be here."[95] Mycielski here wields the equation of work for reconstruction with cultural citizenship to threaten Szałowski with losing a place in the musical community. Like with Ochlewski, the language of "work" assumes the central role.

If the internationalist strand of the interwar musical intelligentsia had begun to fray, then the second major focus from the interwar years—on building audiences at home—began to flourish. Cultural officials after 1945 had begun to define reconstruction as entailing the broadening and dissemination of musical culture, or its *upowszechnienie*, a word that is difficult to translate but that literally means "making universal or common." The musicologist Lisa Cooper Vest has illuminated the central role played by this concept in the 1950s, 1960s, and beyond in Poland, showing how it became the keyword for composers and cultural officials

FIGURE 16. Poland's composers had to balance renewing connections with western Europe against the imperative to rebuild their devastated country. Roman Palester chose to relocate to Paris in 1947, which led to increasing tensions with his colleagues who remained in Poland. He eventually broke off contacts with the country and lived the remainder of his life abroad. He is pictured here in the 1960s. Narodowe Archiwum Cyfrowe.

who sought a broader social relevancy for avant-garde compositional styles.[96] During the early postwar years, by comparison, it was often fused with discussions of reconstruction. For instance, in a statement likely dating from early 1945, the Ministry of Culture and Art declared that "the reconstruction of musical culture in Poland in the understanding of the Ministry of Culture and Art consists first and foremost of the dissemination [*upowszechnienie*] of music among the widest social classes, with special attention to the worker and peasant classes."[97] The Union of Polish Composers echoed this idea when, in their first postwar congress in 1945, they declared "their active contribution to the work of reconstruction and to the broadening [*upowszechnienie*] of Polish culture."[98] Several years later, in a widely disseminated essay titled "Music during the First Five Years of People's Poland" (that is, 1944–49), the musicologist Zofia Lissa listed off the physical destructions that faced Polish musical life at the war's conclusion (burnt halls, destroyed libraries, dead musicians) before claiming that "the reconstruction of Polish musical culture began, first and foremost, through its broadening [*upowszechnienie*]."[99] Centrally, the fusion of *upowszechnienie* with reconstruction implied that the rebuilding of the country's musical life was not a return to the oft-critiqued concert culture of the Second Republic, as the "re" in "reconstruction" might imply. Rather, reconstruction was to create a transformed musical culture, one that was to be more democratic, accessible, and perhaps vibrant than its prewar iteration.

The commitment to the project of disseminating musical culture could take root among the musical intelligentsia because the idea was familiar to them, even if the term *upowszechnienie* had gained new centrality after the war. Like the prewar discourse of "musicalization" and the work of the concert organization ORMUZ, postwar cultural dissemination efforts aimed to create a more "musical" populace by bringing performances of concert music to those who lived outside the major metropolises or did not belong to the educated, urban intelligentsia. Members of the musical intelligentsia could not have missed the centrality of class within these postwar discussions, an aspect that was soft-pedaled in ORMUZ's prewar discourse. But for those who had been invested in prewar musicalization, the new rhetoric was difficult to distinguish from the rhetoric they had long endorsed. For Stanisław Wiechowicz, who had spent years leading amateur choirs before the war, "today's slogans" seemed indistinguishable from those of the past. "All of the efforts of my life up to this point have been devoted to furthering the dissemination and broadening of musical culture [*upowszechnienie*] (only that earlier it was not called that)," he wrote to the musicologist Zofia Lissa in April 1948.[100] Even Chybiński—whose antipathy toward communism and Soviet rule I discussed earlier—wrote in his private, unpublished diary that "only under Sov.[iet] influence will the Polish proletariat learn to value scholarly work and the work of artists, and this will not occur immediately."[101]

186 | Chapter 6

Others constructed historical lineages for these postwar efforts and turned to ORMUZ as a model for engaging new audiences. In a 1945 article, the composer Roman Palester connected ORMUZ and the Polish Music Publishing Society to the ideas of Szymanowski and Fitelberg—whom he described as having done more for the popularization of Polish music than anyone else. The composers of his generation had "passed the exam of their social consciousness [uspołecznienia] and demonstrated a heartfelt care for the dissemination and deepening of the reach of musical culture in Poland," he asserted.[102] Such claims insisted on continuity in the creation of musical culture, giving familiar roots to new policies. References to interwar models were especially prominent during the two weeklong conferences held in 1947 and early 1948 that were devoted to music and the topic of cultural dissemination.[103] Here, key figures from the Polish Music Publishing Society and ORMUZ led discussions, including Bronisław Rutkowski and Tadeusz Ochlewski. Rutkowski noted, "This idea of broadening the dissemination of music [upowszechnienie] is not new" before mentioning that ORMUZ's thousands of prewar performances had attempted to accomplish similar goals.[104] Ochlewski chimed in to comment on his experiences with ORMUZ.[105] Another participant reiterated that "all the forms of the dissemination of musical culture [upowszechnienie] that we created before the war" are still current.[106] Others drew on their work leading choirs before the war or participating in other popularizing musical events.[107]

The postwar focus on the dissemination of musical culture demonstrates how the interests of the musical intelligentsia and those of communist officials became intertwined during reconstruction. For members of the musical intelligentsia, this focus appeared a realization of older aims. At last, they thought, the state was supporting musicalization, even if they were skeptical of the ideological rhetoric that accompanied this support. For communist officials, meanwhile, the new rhetoric offered a pathway for establishing Polish programs that resembled those in Soviet musical life, where bringing the classics to the masses had been an enduring project.[108] Even if these officials did not agree with the political stances of the musicians who would carry out such work, the shared emphasis on disseminating musical culture would help bring them into the fold of socialist action. Reconstruction helped to hold this fragile alliance together, bringing individuals with varied political and musical motivations into a shared project of unquestioned significance.

BECOMING THE STATE

So far I have discussed several forces of cultural continuity within Poland's musical community. Not only did many of the same people who had been active during the interwar years and the occupation reemerge to lead institutions during the period of reconstruction, but they also retrenched notions of elite leadership and musical modernization that had been developed earlier. The final source of continuity to be considered in this chapter lies in the reconfiguration of interwar musical associations into state-sponsored institutions. While it is often assumed that the postwar state wished to divorce itself from the "capitalist" Second Republic (1918–39), the rapid reconstruction in the postwar years also provided an opportunity for savvy members of the musical intelligentsia to relaunch their older projects under a new guise. No organization exemplifies this perdurance of interwar organizing as does the Polish Music Publishing Society (Towarzystwo Wydawnicze Muzyki Polskiej, TWMP), discussed in chapter 2, which would become the Polish Music Publishers in April 1945 (Polskie Wydawnictwo Muzyczne, typically known by its acronym, PWM). While it might seem that music publishing would be of peripheral relevance to postwar reconstruction, PWM was, much like its predecessor, a key patron of musical culture throughout the postwar years.

The main protagonist in the establishment of PWM was Tadeusz Ochlewski. As we saw in chapter 2, Ochlewski had been a central figure in the Polish Music Publishing Society, the umbrella association that ran the concert-touring group ORMUZ, published the journal *Muzyka Polska*, gave concerts of baroque music under the auspices of the Association of Enthusiasts for Early Music, and published early and modern Polish compositions. During the occupation he had continued this last branch of the society's activities by commissioning manuscripts from composers and musicologists, providing them with financial support, and, at the same time, laying the groundwork for the rapid reestablishment of postwar publishing. The opportunity to enact these plans arose in April 1945, when Mieczysław Drobner, then in charge of the nascent Music Department of the Ministry of Culture and Art, met Ochlewski in the hours before a piano recital and gave him a choice: he could direct either the new state-run concert bureau or the state music publisher. He had the duration of the concert to decide. After choosing the publishing house, Drobner drew up and stamped the papers while the two were still in the concert hall.[109] This anecdote suggests the rapidity

FIGURE 17. The founding of PWM and its journal *Ruch Muzyczny* was a watershed moment for the progressive musical intelligentsia, seen here gathered in the publisher's headquarters in 1945. Tadeusz Ochlewski, the founder of PWM, is third from the right, standing. At center is the cultural official Jerzy Borejsza. From the left: Jerzy Waldorff, Adam Chromiński, Stefan Kisielewski, Aniela Szlemińska, Artur Malawski, Andrzej Panufnik, Jan Ekier, Eugenia Umińska, Jerzy Borejsza, Roman Palester, Jadwiga Szamotulska, Zygmunt Mycielski, Jan Maklakiewicz (?), Walerian Bierdiajew, Tadeusz Ochlewski, Tadeusz Wilczak, Barbara Palester. AKP, I-XXVII/1.

with which positions in state-backed musical institutions were appointed in the aftermath of the war. It also reveals how prewar connections—the two had corresponded in relation to ORMUZ before the war—could be pivotal in securing postwar positions. Indeed, Ochlewski would lead PWM for nearly twenty years, underscoring the long-range consequences that a seemingly haphazard postwar appointment could portend. (The concert bureau, meanwhile, went to Gerard Gadejski, whom we last encountered as the go-between among musicians in Polish Warsaw and in the Warsaw Ghetto.)[110]

Ochlewski's understanding of the significance of music publishing was indelibly shaped by the destruction of the war and the widespread loss of musical manuscripts during it. Prior to the war, relatively few Polish compositions had been published, meaning that during the war, decades' worth of compositions existed as single (or a small number of) manuscript copies. If the manuscript was lost, so too was the work.

Ochlewski understood this issue firsthand. In 1944, as he fled the Warsaw Uprising, he bemoaned how his efforts to collect manuscripts for eventual publication after the war seemed to have come to naught. "The Society for Polish Music [i.e., Polish Music Publishing Society] no longer exists, the same with the Association of Enthusiasts for Early Music. I worry about the fate of your scores," he wrote to Palester.[111] Some composers had indeed lost works. Palester found the only copy of his violin concerto in a trash heap, thereby saving the work from oblivion.[112] Others, including Andrzej Panufnik, reconstructed lost works from memory.[113] So valuable were the material remains of musical culture that the Ministry of Culture and Art ran a special commission to dig out scores that may have survived from beneath the rubble of major institutions in Warsaw and to clean, reglue, and press the sheet music.[114] For those who had seen the systematic destruction following the pacification of the Warsaw Uprising, the failures of prewar and wartime publication were a crucial weak point in Polish musical culture.

Music publishing was thus a means not only of disseminating new works but also of preserving musical culture from the cataclysms the likes of which Polish composers had just survived. Explaining PWM's practice of making miniscule print runs of complex scores, a report noted that "the entire matter has an exclusively social aspect: it is first and foremost a preservation of the work, which could be lost or destroyed as a single copy."[115] Ochlewski also believed that the war underscored the imperative of its survivors to rebuild. "Our current situation imposes a special obligation on institutions such as the state Polish Music Publishers and charges it with exceptional responsibility. We are—as someone described it—the 'last Mohicans,'" he wrote in another otherwise circumspect document around the time he was founding PWM. "We must create momentum and energy that will propel our knowledge and our aspirations far in front of us. Everything that we can carry out now must be done completely since we cannot trust the future. We don't see heirs."[116] Ochlewski had long bemoaned the decline of Polish culture, but now, he suggested, the task of countering such decay lay with him and his colleagues uniquely.

Reflecting this desire to bridge historical chasms, Ochlewski believed that PWM would continue the objectives of the interwar Polish Music Publishing Society (TWMP). Echoing the idea that music publishing should be understood as a national good, as TWMP had advocated, he claimed in April 1945 that "[PWM's] goal is not material gain, but rather the good of musical culture. Its task is to fill the giant deficits in

Polish music publishing as well as to utilize all creative possibilities in this field to help with the emergence and accessibility of these goods to society."[117] PWM was aided by TWMP in more concrete ways as well. Despite Ochlewski's fears that the Warsaw Uprising had brought TWMP to an end, its publications and manuscripts had survived. PWM assumed responsibility for the manuscripts that TWMP had commissioned during the occupation, treating the manuscripts (some three quarters of which were complete) as a source of "valuable capital."[118] In addition, hundreds of already printed volumes published by TWMP before the war had survived in the basement of the Warsaw Philharmonic.[119] This cache of ready-for-market publications helped Ochlewski argue that PWM could begin operations immediately.[120] The members of the TWMP unanimously agreed for these holdings to be transferred to PWM and, at the same time, for the TWMP to be liquidated.[121] As a result, the majority of PWM's sales in the first postwar years came not from new publications but from sales of old volumes that had been published by TWMP prior to the war.[122] In this sense the interwar institution and Ochlewski's continuation of it during the occupation provided both an ideological and material basis for the rapid relaunching of music publishing. The continuities between the interwar organization, its wartime continuation, and PWM were explicitly noted in the publishers' founding documents and in evaluations of the publisher for the mid-1950s.[123]

PWM balanced its support for new music with the publication of works that served to popularize and disseminate musical culture. The bread and butter of its output during the first postwar years was pedagogical materials and music that fell squarely under the rubric of popularization. Scores for the stage or concert hall made up only about 18 percent of the volumes published from 1945 through the end of 1948.[124] Even so, PWM managed to support the compositional ambitions of the musical intelligentsia. For instance, in its catalog from 1945 through 1948 the categories of chamber music and orchestral music were dominated by works of Palester, Woytowicz, Szałowski, Bacewicz, Panufnik, and Lutosławski.[125] The contents of the rental parts library also tended heavily toward the same group of composers.[126] This may be attributed in part to the fact that the State Music Publishing Council (Państwowa muzyczna rada wydawnicza), which made decisions concerning publication, had numerous members who had long been sympathetic to such composers and were eager to see these works in print between 1945 and 1948.[127] Chybiński was the president of the council, a position that recapitulated his prewar role of an elder leader and an advocate within

TWMP. Its other members included progressive composers (Palester, Kassern, Perkowski, Woytowicz), the conservative composer Piotr Rytel, conductors (Latoszewski, Walerian Bierdiajew), instrumentalists (Drzewiecki, Eugenia Umińska), and musicologists (Stefania Łobaczewska and Hieronim Feicht, in addition to Chybiński).[128] In mid-1947 Ochlewski boasted that there had "never been an institution as useful to composers as PWM," a self-serving statement that nevertheless captures the sense that the early postwar years were a time in which institutions of historic scope could be erected.[129]

In addition to preserving and disseminating new works, PWM also published the main forum for discussion within the musical intelligentsia, *Ruch Muzyczny* (Musical currents; literally, "musical movement"), which began publication in October 1945. Its founding was a watershed event for the musical intelligentsia. Seeking to ground itself in the Polish musical past, the journal took its name from a periodical that had been published in Warsaw from 1857 to 1861. For its founding editor, Stefan Kisielewski, the postwar *Ruch Muzyczny* was more directly a continuation of the journal *Muzyka Polska*, which had been published by TWMP from 1934 to 1939.[130] Indeed, many of the same individuals who had been involved with *Muzyka Polska* and TWMP took up places with *Ruch Muzyczny*. Kisielewski (who served from October 1945 to April 1947) was joined in October 1946 by Mycielski as coeditor. Kisielewski had been the secretary of the prewar *Muzyka Polska* and Mycielski a contributor. After Kisielewski resigned, Bronisław Rutkowski, the editor of the prewar *Muzyka Polska*, joined the editorial board.[131] Just as important, the journal replicated the foci on bird's-eye views of musical life and modernist composition that had been central to *Muzyka Polska*. Underscoring the journal's allegiances to the progressive branch of the musical intelligentsia, the editorial board saw Karol Szymanowski and Chopin as their most important models for integrating Polish music into the "great chorus of universal human culture," an idea that would have been as at home in the 1920s as it was in 1945.[132]

The advent of Stalinism put new pressures on Ochlewski's leadership of PWM. Most consequentially, *Ruch Muzyczny* shut down in late 1949, after it had been criticized in the Soviet musical press for supporting "formalist" composition.[133] PWM's support of modernist composition also became an issue. In June 1948 Ochlewski claimed to Palester that "for its publishing of contemporary music, PWM is strongly attacked and must defend itself obstinately."[134] Despite these pressures, Ochlewski continued to publish new concert works. In fall 1948 he even managed to secure three million złoty to publish contemporary scores, "even in the face of the fight with 'formalism,'" he noted. He then proceeded to use the funds to publish Palester's String Quartet No. 3, a modernist-inspired (and thus arguably "formalist") work.[135] At the height of the Stalinist and socialist realist era in 1951—when PWM published dozens of ideologically tinged mass songs in enormous print runs of twenty thousand copies—it continued to publish concert works of Bacewicz, Lutosławski, and Panufnik in far smaller quantities.[136] Throughout the Stalinist era, Ochlewski maintained control of PWM; Lissa, a party member, complained in 1954 to the Central Committee of the Polish United Workers' Party that although PWM was placing too much emphasis on elite composition and not enough on popularization works, Ochlewski was an avid organizer who would be difficult to replace.[137] In a scathing report from a similar time period titled "The Ideological Situation among Polish Composers," she described PWM as dominated by "reactionaries" over whom the communist party had little influence.[138]

There were numerous ways in which PWM had departed from its prewar roots as TWMP. It was now a state-backed entity, with all the political pressures and bureaucratic maneuvering this entailed. It also had a near monopoly on music publishing in Poland, turning out tens of thousands of volumes that served a wide range of musical audiences.[139] At the same time, however, PWM maintained core aspects of TWMP's mission, including its dedication to the progressive musical intelligentsia. There thus arises the intriguing possibility that it was under state socialism that the prewar aims of TWMP were most effectively realized. It is certainly the case that PWM outstripped the wildest dreams of TWMP's organizers when it came to the volume and breadth of its publications, as by the early 1950s it issued approximately one new title *per day*.[140] Ochlewski even claimed that *Ruch Muzyczny*'s circulation surpassed that of all Polish music periodicals to date, although this perhaps says more about the precarious state of music periodicals prior to the war than it does about *Ruch Muzyczny*'s popularity.[141] And PWM did so all while continuing to publish the new music of Ochlewski's colleagues and—if the quips of communist cultural officials are to be believed—maintaining a measure of autonomy as well.

THE MUSICAL INTELLIGENTSIA BEYOND RUPTURE

The musical intelligentsia was simultaneously fractured and consolidated in the years immediately following the war. The divergent fates of

Tadeusz Ochlewski and Mateusz Gliński demonstrate that reconstruction could amplify the divisions long present within the musical intelligentsia. In the mid-1930s, the two men were engaged in similar projects of building a national public for classical music in Poland. Gliński contended with antisemitic attacks, denials of state funding for *Muzyka*, and emigration. Ochlewski's organization, by comparison, benefited from *Muzyka*'s crumbling in the 1930s, while he found amenable conditions for continuing his work during the occupation. The result was that when the opportunity of reconstruction arrived, Ochlewski was positioned to seize it, whereas Gliński was not. Ultimately, PWM became an institution that would support and shape Polish music for decades, while *Muzyka* remains little more than a footnote.

This comparison reveals the imperative of thinking beyond tidy chronological boundaries, such as prewar and postwar, when examining the institutions of Polish music and the experiences of Polish Jewish musicians. Indeed, prewar antisemitism and wartime anti-Jewish violence reinforced one another in shaping who could hold authority within the musical community. It is of course the case that, within a few short years after World War II, the patchwork of musical organizations that had defined musical life of the interwar years had been replaced by state institutions. But these institutions were not created ex nihilo. Rather, they reflected both the aims of the state and the ongoing dynamics of the Polish musical establishment at the moment of liberation and long before. To conceive of the postwar period as fundamentally defined by external impositions—of Stalinism, socialist realism, or even communism itself—is to overlook the power that the musicians of Poland held to build their visions of musical culture.

7

The Aesthetics of Loss

In September 1945 Poland's composers gathered in Cracow for the Festival of Contemporary Polish Music, a three-day retrospective of works, most of which had been composed during the war. That the progressive composers now held considerable sway over Polish musical institutions is confirmed by the festival's programming, which was sponsored by the Union of Polish Composers and featured exclusively works of modernist-aligned composers such as Roman Palester, Grażyna Bacewicz, and Piotr Perkowski, along with their mentor, Karol Szymanowski.[1] For those in attendance, the festival was an opportunity not only to hear large-scale pieces that had been difficult to premiere during the occupation, but also to reflect on the past and future of Polish composition. It was "the most important musical event since the regaining of independence," pronounced Stefan Kisielewski, a composer and founding editor of *Ruch Muzyczny*. The compositions heard those days, he believed, were nothing less than "a demonstration of an exceptional creative output, which could be the legitimization of our vitality, of our right to live."[2]

Kisielewski was not the only member of the musical intelligentsia to believe that concert music held a profound significance in the aftermath of the war. Defining how the war had shaped musical culture in Poland became a core concern of the musical intelligentsia during the early postwar years. Its members offered answers to questions such as how the violence of war had affected Polish musical development, why Polish composition had survived the war relatively intact, and which aesthetic

194

directions were appropriate in its aftermath. Reconstruction entailed not only relaunching musical institutions, as discussed in chapter 6, but also defining the past from which postwar Polish composition would grow. To do so, the musical intelligentsia retold the wartime past to highlight the resilience of Polish classical music and sketched a vision of postwar aesthetics that would underwrite the continuity of Polish culture across cataclysm. Emphasizing the productivity of Polish composers during the war, its members cast these years as a time of artistic growth. Not only that, but they saw the new audiences that turned to classical music during the occupation and who continued to flood concert halls in the early postwar years as proof that there was, finally, the broad social recognition of classical music for which they had long advocated. Leaders of the musical intelligentsia believed their task was to devise a musical style—emotional, communicative, yet modern—that would engage these new audiences, keep them attending concerts, and thereby guarantee the relevance of new music. These ideas, developed as early as 1945, were turbocharged by the advent of socialist realist aesthetics in 1948 and 1949, which both codified the centrality of emotion to postwar aesthetics and demanded that the war be treated as a heroic episode, thereby limiting more despondent musical reactions to its tragedies.

Over the last few chapters I have described several reasons why the experiences of Polish Jewish musicians slipped into the margins of Polish musical culture. Some of these are obvious, such as Nazi racial segregation, the prevalence of anti-Jewish violence after the war, Jewish emigration from Poland, and a general desire to move on from the terrible past. Others are less so, including the implicit ethnonationalist framing of Polish cultural survival, pressures on politically active Polish Jews to downplay their ethnic backgrounds, and still fresh memories of prewar anti-Jewish discrimination. In this chapter I will consider how this Polish-Jewish bifurcation within the musical community was further cemented through selective interpretations of the wartime past. Indeed, the idea that the war years were a time of musical growth was a perspective not easily embraced by Polish Jews. At the same time that Poles were asserting that long-standing deficiencies in Polish musical culture were being rectified during and after the war, Jewish commentators questioned the value of musical performances on the eve of the Holocaust. Thus, instances of music making that, at first glance, would appear similar among Poles and Jews, such as occupation-era café performances, were interpreted in diametrically opposed terms.

196 | Chapter 7

Even so, the experiences of Polish Jews were not absent from the postwar musical scene. Their stories circulated in the margins of official discourse, appearing in glancing mentions in Polish-language articles, rumors of survival and despair, court cases, and ambiguous acts of commemoration. These are reminders both of how the concert hall had been for decades an arena of Jewish acculturation and of what had been destroyed by the Holocaust. Sometimes Jewish musical commemoration emerged center stage, too, especially around the commemorations of the Warsaw Ghetto Uprising, the main locus for Holocaust memory in early postwar Poland. Yet even here the window for musical reflection on the Jewish past was narrow, and by the early 1950s it had largely been closed.

LISTENING TO THE AFTERMATH OF WAR

One of the most profound musical responses to the war in Poland is a set of three songs composed in 1945 by Tadeusz Zygfryd Kassern to honor his fallen friend, the violinist and composer Roman Padlewski. The cycle, titled *Tryptyk żałobny za śpiew solowy z fortepianem* (Mourning triptych for solo voice and piano), affords vivid insight into how individual loss became inscribed into a broader conception of national suffering and survival. To borrow the terminology of Jeffrey K. Olick, it shows how "collected memory"—the aggregated experiences of individuals—can become enmeshed in "collective memory," or the narratives shared by a group.[3] As an instance of a composer of Jewish background commemorating a friend through tropes of Polish Catholicism, the songs also reveal the messiness of identity categories and the inadequacy of assuming that postwar commemoration can be neatly sundered into ethnic or religious categories.

Kassern was born into a Jewish family but chose to be baptized at age sixteen.[4] He had worked as a lawyer in Poznań prior to the war, but he was also a significant composer, music critic, and organizer of Poznań's musical life.[5] He had evacuated to Lviv in 1939, spent about a year under Soviet rule, and then fled to Nazi-controlled Cracow. Near the end of 1942 he was denounced to the Gestapo, after which he fled Warsaw to avoid arrest. To mask his Jewish background he assumed the identity of his brother-in-law, a Polish forestry engineer who had been killed in the 1939 defense of Poland. It was thanks to this forged identity that Kassern avoided moving to the ghetto and ultimately survived the Holocaust.

Kassern is not, however, concerned with an expression of Jewish experience in the *Mourning Triptych*, although he would later write one of the earliest operas to memorialize the Holocaust.[6] Rather, his focus is the death of Roman Padlewski, a Polish composer and friend of his who had died fighting in the Warsaw Uprising a year prior, in 1944. The connections between the songs and Padlewski would have been inescapable for the audience at the premiere, not only because of the dedication, but also because the *Mourning Triptych* was performed immediately before Padlewski's String Quartet No. 2 during the Festival of Contemporary Polish Music.[7] While dedicated to a single fallen composer, the work opened a larger commemorative field by evoking the Warsaw Uprising in which Padlewski had died. For many in the audience, the uprising had been the defining tragedy of the war's conclusion, which scattered Warsaw's musicians, led to the death of 150,000 civilians, and saw the razing of the city's historic center. Yet public expression of memory of the uprising was sharply curtailed in postwar Poland: since it had been launched by the anti-communist Home Army and was brutally suppressed by the Germans while the Soviet army was stationed across the Vistula, the event fit poorly within the official narrative of Soviet-led "liberation" of Poland from German rule.[8]

Kassern based the *Triptych* on historical texts and musical sources, a decision that reflected his ongoing interest in early music as a source for contemporary composition.[9] The first song, "Stała pod krzyżem (Stabat Mater)" (Under the cross stood the grieving mother [Stabat mater]), is based on a text of the Stabat Mater by the counterreformation poet Stanisław Grochowski and quotes the well-known Stabat Mater sequence.[10] The melody and text of the second song, "Stała się jest rzecz dziwna" (A strange thing occurred), are derived from the *Cantional albo księgy chwal Boskych to jest Pieśni Duchowne* (Königsberg, 1554), a translation from Czech into Polish by Walenty z Brzozowa of a songbook of the Bohemian Brethren, a protestant Hussite sect who were expelled from Bohemia and secured refuge in Ducal Prussia.[11] Kassern attributes the final song, "Płaczy dzisiaj duszo wszelka" (Weep today, every soul), to the same songbook, although he in fact seems to have taken the text from an anonymous sixteenth-century passion. The melody is based with some modifications on a tune to the same text found in a well-known church songbook.[12]

What unites these source materials from disparate times and circumstances is their portrayal of the Virgin Mary's grief for her son, Jesus, during the crucifixion. In the first song, the text moves from describing

198 | Chapter 7

Mary's grief as she stands under cross to the final stanza where the speaker wishes to join the grieving:

> Pragnę stać pod krzyżem z Tobą
> dzielić się z Twoją osobą
> tak surowym płaczem

> I yearn to stand under the cross with You
> To share with You,
> Your raw lament

The second song recounts the joy of the Virgin birth and paints Jesus as forgiving man's sins, whereas the final song returns to the crucifixion and Mary's grief, now described as enveloping "every soul." Throughout, the song texts move between Mary's personal mourning for the loss of her child to the broader lament of the community, whether figured in terms of the speaker joining in the losses (in the first song) or as a universalized sense of grief (in the third). Thus, while Kassern had been inscribed as Jewish by the Nazi occupation, the symbolism he turned to in one of his first works to comment on the war was draw from, and reflects, his conversion to Catholicism and his interest in the expressive potentials of Polish Christianity across several centuries.

Kassern's use of Marian imagery in the *Triptych* partakes of a longer tradition that links Catholicism, gender, and selfless sacrifice for the Polish nation. The Virgin Mary had been the central figure in Polish Catholic devotion since 1655, when a military victory over the Swedes at Częstochowa was attributed to her prowess and she was crowned Queen of Poland. Her role as a militant protector of the nation only grew during the partitions (1795–1918), when she was associated with the struggle to regain Polish independence. From the late nineteenth century onward, she provided a model for how the female domestic space could sustain and reproduce the nation while men were absent, symbolism that often emphasized her ability to persevere through suffering.[13] Kassern's *Triptych* aligns with this latter sense of the Virgin's significance, as its calls attention to both Padlewski's absence and the female grief after his death. Thus, although the texts of the songs do not directly evoke the Polish nation, Kassern's decision to center the *Mourning Triptych* on Mary likely would have encouraged his listeners to interpret Padlewski's death in the Warsaw Uprising through a longer history of national sacrifice and survival. It also partook of a longer tradition of gendering the work of mourning, in which lament is defined as the work of the community's women.[14]

Kassern set these texts with music that probes the inescapable, repetitive process of grieving, an approach that is especially clear in the final song, "Weep today, every soul." As shown in figure 7, a series of fortissimo block chords begins the song. These can be parsed as an F-minor chord with an added major or minor sixth, although this chord often appears in second inversion with doubled Cs in the bass. The two inversions of this chord are, in fact, the only chordal harmonies heard throughout the song. The rest of the song is spun out of the soprano's line with one or two countermelodies in the piano to support her. Notice how the opening chord reemerges throughout the song, interrupting the soprano's contrapuntal lines like a stark reminder of the opening. The chords seem inescapable yet also oddly static—never really progressing, never really changing. Nor is this repetitiveness resolved by the song. Rather, the soprano melody expires over the same chords—now pianissimo. We might hear the constant return of this chord as a musical equivalent to the inescapability and repetitiveness of traumatic loss, in which grief continually reasserts itself into the speaker's consciousness.[15] Perhaps, in this sense, the songs imbue national imagery with a more immediate sense of grief.

At the same time that the *Triptych* seems to subsume Padlewski's death into a collective national narrative, it also calls attention to details of his life and death. Several of Padlewski's early works had focused on the Virgin Mary, including a large-scale a cappella Stabat Mater (1939), so Kassern no doubt was alluding to the significance she had for him as a composer.[16] The details of Padlewski's death are also alluded to in the songs. After Padlewski was wounded in battle, he spent two days dying at a makeshift hospital in Warsaw's historic center. As he lay in agony, he grasped a small portrait of the Virgin Mary, which his mother, Nadzieja Padlewska, had given him. He wished to hide his terminal state from her, fearing that she would be devastated to know that she would outlive him. For those aware of this backstory, the *Triptych*'s focus on Mary's grief could be heard as drawing a parallel between Mary and Padlewska, suggesting that much as Mary grieved the crucifixion, so too Padlewska grieved Padlewski's death. If this simile is taken to its logical conclusion, it also suggests that Padlewski's sacrifice for the nation in the Warsaw Uprising is a figure of Christ's sacrifice for humanity.

We know these details about Padlewski's death because of letters sent to his mother about his demise.[17] As a close friend of the Padlewski family, Kassern doubtless knew them as well. But so did many other

EXAMPLE 7. Tadeusz Zygfryd Kassern, *Tryptyk żałobny za śpiew solowy z fortepianem* (Mourning triptych for solo voice and piano), "Płaczy dzisiaj duszo wszelka," mm. 1–14. AKP, Mus CLXVIII rps 24. Used by permission of the estate of Tadeusz Zygfryd Kassern.

musicians. In fact, Padlewski's story had become so widely publicized that *Ruch Muzyczny* published the letters to his mother concerning his death in November 1945, about two months after the *Mourning Triptych* premiered.[18] For those in the musical intelligentsia who were familiar with Padlewski's story, the *Mourning Triptych* would have not only evoked general concerns with nation and sacrifice, but also cued up the grieving of his family and the rumors that circulated in the music community about his demise. In speaking both to individual and collective dimensions of Padlewski's death, the work exemplifies the transition between individual responses to trauma and the desire to give meaning to these losses by narrating them through national discourses.

FROM RUMOR TO WAR MEMORY

Kassern's *Triptych* points to a prominent modality through which the memory of wartime experience traveled among the musical intelligentsia: rumor. Unlike news or official discourse, rumors often circulate orally, their contents are unverified (or unverifiable), and they are transmitted outside of pathways of the official press or institutions of authority.[19] Listening carefully to the rumors that spread among the musical intelligentsia (and became enmeshed in the historical record) reveals the backdrop against which more defined narratives of the war were erected, suggesting the ways in which memories of wartime loss were at once ubiquitous and untamed in everyday life. Rumor would also offer one of the major ways that Jewish musical experience was discussed and documented during a time when few established conventions for memorializing the Holocaust existed, underscoring that this early postwar period was far from one defined by "silence" about the Holocaust.[20]

Rumors often concerned who had survived and how. In the first issue of *Ruch Muzyczny*, the editors published a list of those who had died, not all of whom in fact had. This and similar lists include the names of musicians who were identified as having perished in the Warsaw Ghetto (Marian Neuteich, Ignacy Rosenbaum, Stella Dobrzycka, J. Familier-Hepnerowa, and Dawid Lachs) and the Vilnius Ghetto (Cecylia and Fanny Krewer).[21] A brief note in the "Chronicle" section of the same journal described the existence of the Jewish Symphony Orchestra in the Warsaw Ghetto, saying that it had been under the direction of Neuteich and performed a repertoire of Beethoven, Dvořák, Mendelssohn, and Stravinsky.[22] A 1945 article titled "Chopin under the Occupation" likewise discusses not only performances in Polish Warsaw but also notable Chopin interpreters—Leon Boruński, Ryszard Werner, and Familier-Hepnerowa—who were "known to the author" to have lived and died in the Warsaw Ghetto.[23] Such brief mentions of Jewish musicians in the postwar Polish-language press suggest the cultural proximity of the Warsaw Ghetto and Polish Warsaw, as discussed in chapter 4, while leaving unanswered the question of how the authors learned of such information in the first place.

In other instances rumor played a pivotal role in the wave of retributive justice that swept postwar Poland, which sought accountability for acts of collaboration during the Nazi occupation.[24] A few musicians were caught up in the trials held for alleged collaborators in state courts. All musicians, however, had to have their wartime activities reviewed by the verification committees of the Professional Union of Musicians, which could suspend membership (and thus, in theory, prevent a musician from being employed) for "participating in propagandistic events, in German-language events, in events of low moral level (pornography, etc.), and those boycotted by the population."[25] Because of the haziness of evaluating claims of musical collaboration—musicians were to be excused for compromising performances if done under duress—wartime reputation and word-of-mouth information substantiated both accusations of, and defenses against, collaboration. For instance, when an article appeared insinuating that Kazimierz Sikorski had collaborated with the Germans by running the Warsaw Conservatory during the occupation, his students and colleagues—most aligned with the progressive branch of the musical intelligentsia—mobilized to his defense. They argued that he had taken the position with the blessing of the underground and that the conservatory had aided wartime resistance.[26] In this case, a well-established social network helped to counteract rumors of malfeasance.

One of the most striking incidents to put on display how Jewish experience was both inescapable and hidden in the rumors of the musical community was the trial of the violinist Helena Zarzycka. She was accused of threatening to expose Jewish musicians who were playing in the Philharmonic of the General Government, of which she had been a member.[27] A slate of witnesses confirmed that sometime in late 1942 or early 1943, the German conductor of the orchestra, Rudolf Hindemith (the brother of the composer Paul Hindemith) received an anonymous letter that claimed that a handful of musicians in the orchestra were of "non-Aryan" background. After Hindemith threated to report the matter to the Gestapo for investigation, Zarzycka claimed responsibility for the letter.[28] Hindemith asked her if she understood the magnitude of her accusations and allegedly told her that he "didn't care who played in the orchestra—a Pole, Jew, or negro, so long as they were professionals."[29] She and Hindemith agreed to keep the matter a secret. These revelations are striking because they suggest that an official propaganda instrument of the German occupation likely had Jewish members, that the conductor of said orchestra was indifferent to this fact, and that someone with knowledge of this fact had chosen to denounce these Jews, at what could have been great cost to the orchestra and its members.

The situation became murkier as the trial unfolded. In her defense, Zarzycka denied having written the denunciation. Rather, she said that she had lied to Hindemith, claiming credit for the letter because she was afraid that if no one did so, many of the musicians in the orchestra who were involved in the Polish underground would be exposed in the Gestapo investigation he had threatened. She further worried that her own "non-Aryan" background might be exposed in such an investigation (her grandmother was Jewish).[30] The court also heard testimony about how she had helped a Jewish colleague, Halina Kowalska-Trzonkowa, by providing her with "material and moral support," how she had treated Jews with "complete warmth" during the occupation, and how she had helped to hide other Jews during the occupation.[31] The court found this evidence convincing and exonerated her.[32] The trial records thus leave it unclear who, in fact, had written the denunciation. Nonetheless, they do provide a glimpse of how much is hidden behind the historical record of wartime and early postwar years. Actions that may at first glance appear as clear evidence of collaboration could in fact conceal a complex choreography of desperation and survival.

In other cases, traces of Jewish experience are discernable only on the level of subtext. Consider the case of Roman Palester, the composer then emerging as a leading figure in Polish contemporary music. He had (what the Nazis considered to be) a Jewish father, and his family had helped hide Jewish escapees. Although he does not appear to have had any investments in Jewish identity, Jewish topics emerged in several of the projects on which he worked. He had composed music for some of the most important war films of the 1940s, including *Zakazane piosenki* (Forbidden songs), about the songs of the occupation; *Ostatni etap* (The last stage), about Auschwitz; and *Ulica graniczna* (Border street), about Polish Jewish solidarity and the Warsaw Ghetto Uprising.[33] Was there an echo of the family's experiences in the film *Border Street*? In this film, an important character is a converted Jewish doctor, as was Palester's father, and the forgery of a name and blackmail in the

204 | Chapter 7

film are reminiscent of the Palesters' own wartime travails.[34] Or, is there buried in the suggestion put forth by the writer Jarosław Iwaszkiewicz that Roman ought to write an opera about Jews hiding during the occupation an echo of familiarity with Palester's family and circumstances? Iwaszkiewicz wrote to Palester in 1950:

> I have thought much about our last conversation and many issues and topics have occurred to me. . . . How do you feel about a Jewish topic? It would be about Jews in hiding. A young Jew would leave his hiding space for some reason (for what reason?) and would be killed. As was the norm in those times when burials were banned, his sister would go to bury him, knowing that this would expose her. The Germans kill her, leaving behind a young peasant, who was in love with the Jewish sister, whom he was hiding. In the end, he will be called to fight against Hitlerism and fascism in general.[35]

The details of this proposed libretto do not match identically with those of the Palesters, who were hiding in Warsaw rather than the countryside and who were both in hiding *and* hiding others. We do not know whether Iwaszkiewicz hoped Palester might have found this scenario appealing precisely because of its similarity to his real experiences, even as the story also foregrounds themes such as Polish Jewish solidarity that were contradicted by the Palesters' own stark experiences of Polish-led blackmail and betrayal.

Palester's reticence about explicitly linking his compositions to the war extended even to those works that are most connected to mourning. In the late 1980s he described his Requiem as "my due to the several people close to me who perished in the [Warsaw] Uprising," namely his stepbrother, who was killed in action, and his father, who was run over by a truck after its conclusion.[36] These intentions are not indicated in the work's paratext. The first version of the composition (from 1945) bore a French-language dedication "to the victims of the war," but Palester removed this already generalized message, which did not specify which victims he was commemorating, from the finished orchestral version in 1948. Nor did he specify commemorative intentions in private correspondence, writing cryptically that a Polish premier "is vital to me because of moral, extramusical considerations" without providing further details.[37] Nonetheless, at least one listener seemed to draw connections to the Jewish war experience. In a closed listening session held by the Union of Polish Composers of the piece in 1950, Jerzy Urbański commented, "This music, written in the face of the tragedy of the ghetto [*pisana w obliczu tragedii w getcie*], is an eloquent witness to the subjective reaction of the composer."[38]

The Aesthetics of Loss | 205

Scholars are often suspicious of such anecdotes, questioning whether fleeting allusions by contemporaries can undergird even the more speculative of historical interpretations.[39] When attending to twentieth-century compositions especially, we are accustomed to works of commemoration that announce their intentions overtly, inserting themselves explicitly and eloquently into the politics of memory.[40] Instead of succumbing to doubt about works whose commemorative politics are ambiguous, however, we might rather see the unclear linkages created by observers between compositions and wartime commemoration as a defining feature of the immediate postconflict period of "living memory," when narratives about the war and its meaning had yet to be fully formed.[41] Perhaps works that display an ambivalence about the possibility of commemoration in fact come closest to expressing the immediacy of wartime loss.

DEFINING THE PAST

Against this backdrop of rumor, many in the musical intelligentsia sought to impose a degree of conceptual clarity and coherence on the wartime past. These commentators focused almost exclusively on Polish Warsaw, ignoring musicians in both the ghettos and the Soviet Union. They reiterated the view that musical productivity was itself a form of resistance that proved the continuing vitality of the nation. The composer Witold Rudziński demonstrates this line of thinking when he wrote in 1945 that "for the majority of Polish composers, the war was not a vacation, an absolution from work. . . . Through his determined work, [the Polish musician] voiced a protest against how fate had stopped him from continuing the creative work he had begun before the war. He expressed the stubborn conviction that the ongoing revival of Polish culture [that had begun after WWI] could not be stifled."[42] For the musicologist Stefania Łobaczewska, meanwhile, the war had helped to rectify long-standing national deficiencies. Postwar premieres of wartime works had shown "how much our musicians had worked during the years of the occupation and what distance they traveled toward realizing these aims" of creating a "Polish School" of composition. Placing the war in a sweeping historical narrative, she noted that thanks to this wartime productivity, "our obligations to history have been fulfilled; the debts and deficiencies incurred during the eighteenth and nineteenth century have been settled."[43] Palester summarized this common interpretation when he wrote in 1946 that an "almost unanimous

206 | Chapter 7

chorus of reviewers, musicians, and musicologists has recognized and announced to our public that the current state of Polish composition should be seen as exceptionally successful. . . . We have not only caught up to Europe, but we are close to beginning to lead it!" Although he did not share this interpretation of Polish compositional parity with western Europe, he nonetheless cast the wartime generation (including, of course, himself) as possessing a remarkable crop of talents, whose stylistic development was unaffected by what he euphemistically termed the "dissonances" and "unexpected obstacles" of the occupation.[44]

Palester's 1943 *Ogiński Polonaises* seemed to demonstrate with particular clarity the perdurance of Polish culture across cataclysms. In this composition, Palester arranged polonaises by the early romantic composer Michał Kleofas Ogiński (1765–1833). The piece remains close to Ogiński's original harmonic language while expanding the polonaises through changes in the instrumentation, including a harpsichord that performs a quasi-continuo part. By basing the composition on Ogiński's polonaises, Palester evoked an earlier moment of persecution: Ogiński was a diplomat and advocate for Polish independence at the time of the partitions in the eighteenth century. He introduced a melancholy cast to the stately genre of the polonaise, thereby turning the genre into a symbol of nostalgia for national loss.[45] In turning to music that conjured this earlier history, Palester drew on established signifiers of nation, much like Kassern's *Triptych* had turned to Marian imagery.

Palester's compositional decisions further reinforced the connections between Ogiński's polonaises and national longing. As shown in example 8, near the end of the piece the orchestra fades into one of the thinnest and quietest textures yet. From this clearing we hear the harpsichord playing the first phrase of Ogiński's most famous polonaise, "Farewell to the Fatherland." Of all of Ogiński's polonaises, this one most clearly evoked a sense of both personal and national loss. Ogiński had composed it as he emigrated from Poland following the defeat of the Kościuszko Uprising in 1794. In Palester's arrangement, the harpsichord stands as a symbol for the sounds of a long-past era: it is as if a memory of this earlier time emerges as a frail and ghostlike melody from within the contemporary arrangement.

For Kisielewski the work was nothing short of living proof of Poland's national—and spiritual—continuity: "This work has its own symbolic significance: antique polonaises, transformed by a contemporary 'modernist,' are an ark of the covenant [*arka przymierza*] 'between the old and new years.' It is a manifestation of the continuity of our

EXAMPLE 8. The nostalgic polonaise "Farewell to the Fatherland" emerges ghostlike from Roman Palester's *Polonezy M. K. Ogińskiego* (Ogiński polonaises), rehearsal no. 39. Polskie Wydawnictwo Muzyczne.

208 | Chapter 7

culture, enduring above the wars and cataclysms that befall our country. Of a culture that was able to withstand all persecutions, endure and be for us that true, nonmaterial, yet no less real fatherland—the spiritual fatherland."[46] The phrase "ark of the covenant 'between the old and new years'" is an allusion to *Konrad Wallenrod* (1828), an epic in verse by Adam Mickiewicz, Poland's most canonized romantic poet.[47] The epic is set in the distant past and portrays Lithuanian treachery against the Teutonic Knights. But from its publication onward, it was seen as an allegory for Polish survival under partition.[48] Kisielewski's allusion to these lines is especially significant because the original passage discusses the power of song to awaken the hero to the defense of his nation. In his view, music could ground Polish culture in a foundation that remained stable despite both historical cataclysms and the recent trauma of World War II. Indeed, in December 1945 he returned to the same allusion, extrapolating it to national culture itself: "Artistic creation is an 'ark of the covenant between the old and new years'; it unfurls bridges over wars, coups, and revolutions; it determines the unity and identity of national culture."[49]

The musical intelligentsia also interpreted the venues in which music was performed in Polish Warsaw in a sympathetic light, casting these as the physical spaces that enabled national culture to endure. Looking back on the occupation from 1946, Konstanty Régamey claimed that "even people who, before the war, had never taken part in concerts considered it a point of honor to regularly attend all performances in the cafés," suggesting an expansion in audience prompted by the war.[50] For Kisielewski, such growth in listenership was evidence that the occupation had improved the social standing of music. "The lack of radios and musical events stimulated a hunger for music; the gloominess and hopelessness of the atmosphere led people to take a greater interest in art at home. . . . They began to value the importance of music."[51] These comments should be interpreted against the backdrop of the musical intelligentsia's long-standing frustration with the purportedly unmusical nature of Polish society and its lack of commitment to classical music in the 1930s. They suggest that the war had proved the relevance of their art.

Many believed that the positive transformation of musical culture, begun during the war, was continuing after it. Mycielski wrote that "in conditions that would frighten Amundsen, Byrd, and Francisco Pizarro"—thereby comparing ruined Warsaw to the harsh conditions encountered by polar explorers and conquistadors—"something essentially new is being created. The public attacks the box offices and

The Aesthetics of Loss | 209

entrances to halls, in which someone plays, sings, or directs."[52] The cellist Kazimierz Wiłkomirski recalled concerts with audiences spilling into the hallways, and in which each and every symphonic concert was an "artistic celebration."[53] Others remembered the early postwar years as a time when it was difficult to get tickets to concerts of pieces by Witold Lutosławski, Grażyna Bacewicz, and Bolesław Woytowicz because of high demand.[54] In 1945, Palester reported that the postwar audience is "full of deep interest in contemporary works." They are "a non-blasé audience, hungering for fresh and good music."[55] For musicians performing in front of such audiences, the desire for music seemed comprehensible only as an effect of the war. As the soprano Ewa Bandrowska-Turska remarked in a letter from 1948, "All that people lived through has left its imprint on everything. It simply deepened the feeling for life, as well as art, and it created another type of human. . . . I can't explain the completely exceptional reaction of audiences in any other way."[56]

A very different perspective, however, took root among those writing about the Warsaw Ghetto. The negative postwar view of the Warsaw Ghetto cafés is put on clear display in the discourse surrounding the café Sztuka (Art), the venue popular among the acculturated intelligentsia, where both Władysław Szpilman and Wiera Gran had performed. This café offers a useful point of comparison between Polish and Jewish reception of occupation-era music because it was similar in many ways to the cafés outside the ghetto: not only had some of its most famous performers survived, but its performances were in Polish and were based in the tradition of the interwar cabaret, whose tropes of popular, urban culture were readily legible to Jewish and non-Jewish audiences alike. Michał Borwicz, who was Jewish but had not been in the Warsaw Ghetto, spent a good portion of the introduction to his 1947 anthology of ghetto poems discussing the powerful satire and wit that characterized performances in ghetto cafés, especially Sztuka. But, he concluded, "There were many critiques of these open events in the ghetto. These didn't have to do with the programs, but rather with the very fact that such events occurred. They called to mind the concept of entertainment, and entertainment in such circumstances seemed at the very least tactless."[57] Szpilman's 1946 memoirs, *Śmierć miasta* (The death of a city), also painted a negative picture of the ghetto cafés in general. Tellingly, the memoirs spend more time describing the cafés Szpilman disliked, often using rather evocative imagery to do so, than Sztuka, where he found a receptive audience.[58] This distancing of Szpilman from the context of Sztuka is also evidenced in the reception of *Her First Ball*, the

210 | Chapter 7

fifteen-minute piece composed by Szpilman and premiered at Sztuka, which I discussed in chapter 4. In a review of an early postwar performance, Jerzy Waldorff, who was a close friend of Szpilman's and had helped author Szpilman's memoirs, described the piece as overcoming what he believed to be the tired tropes of prewar popular song. He does not mention that the piece was created in the Warsaw Ghetto or that its creators were Jewish.[59]

Wiera Gran, the star singer of Sztuka, became inextricably tied to the idea that the ghetto cafés were compromised. When she attempted to relaunch her performance career after the war, she was hounded by rumors that she had collaborated with the Gestapo. She was exonerated of these charges five times: by the Polish Special Courts in 1945, by the professional unions of both musicians and stage actors, by the Jewish Civic Court in a trial lasting from 1947 to 1949, and again by the Warsaw district court in 1949.[60] The courts called dozens of witnesses, yet no factual basis for the accusations against her was ever uncovered. The opinions against her were vague, secondhand hearsay. Even so, the rumor that she had collaborated with the Gestapo harmed her career in Poland and followed her to Israel and France after she emigrated in 1950.[61]

Her trial advanced a narrative that the ghetto cafés were, at best, a place of Jewish weakness and, at worst, collaborationist dens of evil. This unflattering view grew in part out of the gendered nature of her trial. As the historians Katarzyna Person and Ewa Koźmińska-Frejlak have both observed, men were generally charged by postwar courts with concrete acts of wartime collaboration, whereas women were instead charged with keeping the wrong company. Such charges were thinly cloaked euphemisms for sexual relations with the enemy, or "collaboration through the body."[62] The sexual tenor of Gran's trial was made clear when she was accused of being "the lover of a certain Szterenfeld from the Thirteen and also had relations with Gancwajch, also of the Thirteen."[63] She was accused of having participated in "orgies" held at the Hotel Britania, a notorious meeting point for Jewish Gestapo agents.[64] Reflective of this sexualized subtext, the trial focused on the minutiae of her behavior in the ghetto. Witnesses were interrogated about her interactions with patrons following performances (presumably to determine whether she had flirted with them), her living conditions (which could have ascertained if she had kept lovers), and even why her husband had remained outside the ghetto on the *aryjska strona*. There were no attempts to defend the social, artistic, or political function of the ghetto cafés, which were instead painted as seats of sexualized corruption.

The Aesthetics of Loss | 211

While the Jewish Civic Court ultimately exonerated Gran, it did so while condemning the ghetto cafés and Sztuka in the strongest possible terms. In their opinion, the judges wrote:

> The ghetto created a kind of surrogate artistic life in the form of café performances. Jewish cafés in the ghetto created the appearance that a certain tolerable level of life was being maintained, one in contradiction to the general, desperate situation of the Jewry that was crowded into the ghetto. The cafés strengthened the feeling of passivity toward encroaching and unavoidable events while distancing themselves from the resistance movement that with time matured into the heroic act of the uprising in the Warsaw Ghetto. A portion of the Jewish artistic world, searching to maintain itself through performances in cafés like Sztuka, encountered the café regulars who were recruited in large part from the tycoons who preyed on Jewish poverty or from those who served the Hitlerian regime.[65]

The opinion comes close to asserting that the Jews in the ghetto bore responsibility for their own deaths, misled into passivity by entertainments in the cafés. Needless to say, this view is anachronistic: for much of Sztuka's existence it was impossible for internees to know that the "unavoidable events" of mass murder were on the horizon, much less for them to conceive of the Holocaust as a possibility.[66] Nor was there widespread interest in armed resistance in the ghetto prior to the mass deportations in summer 1942 and thus after Sztuka closed its doors.[67] The opinion nonetheless demonstrates how the postwar focus on heroic struggle and armed resistance within the ghetto led Jews to rewrite the history of the cafés. Against this postwar backdrop there was little space to consider the multifaceted social functions of the ghetto café—in which shady dealings, escapism, and probing social commentary existed alongside one another—as Stanisław Różycki had done in 1941 for the Oyneg Shabes archive. Thus, while the cafés of Polish Warsaw were being recruited into a narrative of national continuity—their many shortcomings subsumed into a story of Polish music's unending development—the analogous spaces in the ghetto were condemned as detrimental not only to Jewish culture but to Jewish life itself.

CONTAINING WARTIME EMOTION

The notion that music itself was a source of cultural continuity across the war foretold a new aesthetic of composition. Consider in this regard the ideas of composer and critic Zygmunt Mycielski. In his public writings he suggested that the cataclysm of war had created as its byproduct an

212 | Chapter 7

aesthetic key to resolving the musical intelligentsia's long-standing concern for defining new music's social worth. In 1945 he wrote that, during war, "art is a gateway, as in the Middle Ages the monastery entrance was for individuals who were persecuted by physical or metaphysical violence."[68] The imperative facing composers, in his view, was to maintain their heightened social relevance that the war had created. "Under indifference or pressure our art, it turned out, will wither, but here in the heaviest moments music awakens truly mass reactions, which it is necessary to maintain at any price by supplying listeners with the highest artistic qualities."[69]

Mycielski's use of the term "mass" is significant because it suggests how he described the war in terms of the musical intelligentsia's long-standing concern with how a non-elite audience could be brought into musical culture, as well as the ongoing discussions about the popularization of musical culture in reconstruction. It also shows him endorsing the narrative of the war as a positive aesthetic transformation, one that had increased interest in classical music. His definition of the "highest artistic qualities" that he believed composers must endorse to maintain such broad, "mass" interest did not involve commemoration of the war or even an acknowledgment of its trauma. Rather, he focuses on an accessible, unifying style:

> We are not concerned with experimental trifles, but rather with good, honest, sincere Polish music. We are concerned with expression, which one must search for very deeply, and which must be imparted in a very straightforward manner. It is not about currying favor or quenching personal ambitions, or of gaining the title of "author," but rather about the fact that works exist and that they go into the world, without regard to whether some Johnny, Stan, or Frankie wrote them. It is like with the old sculptors who did not worry themselves with signing their works, but rather about the portal, the cathedral, about the entirety of the building.[70]

While Mycielski believed that "expression" is the key to sustaining audience interest in new music, it is not the expression of an individual composer's personal point of view that matters, but rather if a composer can mobilize a more general sense of music's elemental power. The word *expression* underwrites the contact between listener and composer, but the composer's own interior world and ambitions are irrelevant, for he must serve the collective as an anonymous craftsperson instead. The war mattered, but only indirectly, as that which had opened the renewed relevance of new music.

In private, Mycielski understood that the war's implications were far messier, more complicated, and darker than his published views on aesthetics suggested. In a letter to Nadia Boulanger from 1946, he attempted to convey both the incommensurability of life in Warsaw's ruins and the code of avoidance that adhered among its residents: "It is not easy to speak with you about life here. One must see it—see Warsaw first and foremost. The courage and the energy of the people who are literally hanging onto the ruins, and the entire country too. . . . It is impossible to make you understand over there what has taken place here; with every step, each person carries his years in such a natural manner and every being is a world that has endured a shipwreck."[71] These hastily written sentences suggest how immense trauma can exist alongside seeming normalcy, the "natural manner" of survivors obscuring the cataclysms each has survived. He here described what the sociologist Eviatar Zerubavel has termed a "conspiracy of silence," in which all in a group are aware of reality but choose not to speak it.[72] His aesthetics, too, argue for a conspiracy of silence, in which the war has been refigured primarily as an event that underscored the social mandate of the artist, whose personal experiences, individual losses, and countless traumas are to be left unsaid.

Mycielski's earliest postwar composition suggests the inescapability of the darkness of war and the degree to which his aesthetic pronouncements about music were a conscious attempt to shape a public narrative about the conflict. In spring 1946 he began a cycle of songs on texts from *Ocalenie* (Rescue), a collection of poems written by Czesław Miłosz during the war. In choosing Miłosz's poems, Mycielski ignored his own calls for a music that would evade the tangible legacy of wartime trauma. The poems' inextricable links to the war are signaled in the title of Miłosz's collection: "rescue" is a literal description of the contents of the volume, which were rescued from the Miłosz apartment by Czesław's wife, Janina, when the Warsaw Uprising began.[73] In addition, the poems in the collection confront the ethical dilemmas of war and the powerlessness of its victims. The best-known ones, including "Campo di Fiori" and "A Poor Christian Looks at the Ghetto," concern the witnessing of the Holocaust by non-Jewish, Catholic Poles who had failed to prevent the annihilation of the Warsaw Ghetto.

Nor do the texts that Mycielski chose to set from this collection paint an affirmative or resilient view of art, as his public statements called for. Instead, the text—drawn from "Przedmowa" (Dedication), the final poem of *Rescue*—grapples with the failure of artists to confront the noxious ideologies of interwar and wartime Europe. Mycielski set each stanza of the poem as a separate song, turning Miłosz's single poem into a cycle. The first song describes a mourner visiting the grave of a close

214 | Chapter 7

friend, the familiarity of their relationship underscored by the use of the informal second-person singular pronoun "*ty*" throughout:

> Ty, którego nie mogłem ocalić,
> Wysłuchaj mnie.
> Zrozum tę mowę prostą, bo wstydzę się innej.
> Przysięgam, nie ma we mnie czarodziejstwa słów.
> Mówię do ciebie milcząc, jak obłok czy drzewo.
>
> You whom I could not save,
> Listen to me.
> Try to understand this simple speech as I would be ashamed of another.
> I swear, there is in me no wizardry of words.
> I speak to you with silence like a cloud or a tree.[74]

It is an intimate address, one that is to cut through the artifice of poetry. The dead friend is not, however, a martyr or even a sympathetic victim of the war. Instead, the speaker mourns both the friend's death and his moral demise: he "mixed up farewell to an epoch with the beginning of a new one" (second song) and his poetry was "a connivance with official lies" (fourth song). In the fifth and final song, the speaker lays a book including the poem "Dedication"—presumably *Rescue*—on the grave "so that you should visit us no more," conjuring a desire for closure for the friend's ethical failures.

Mycielski set these poetic texts in a dissonant and austere musical language. In the first song, "You Whom I Could Not Save," there are only two consonant sonorities in the entire song, at the very beginning and end, as shown in example 9. The opening begins from three Cs, spaced an octave apart, and each line in the piano moves chromatically around this pitch. This relative independence of the lower voices in the piano is maintained throughout, in an accompaniment texture that features little rhythmic variety. While the voice moves largely by step or small leap, Mycielski underscores the words "I speak to you" with a striking octave leap across two Cs, calling back to mind the opening sonority, only to be outdone three measures later when the voice jumps a ninth on the words "like a cloud." Mycielski's focus on the pitch class C, as well as the narrow movements of the lines in the opening, can be heard as a return to the building blocks of musical language, an almost childlike simplicity in every line that evokes the speaker's desire for "simple speech" free from "wizardry of words."

While the contrapuntally naïve and austerely dissonant techniques seem to capture the disquiet of the text, it is unclear if Mycielski would

EXAMPLE 9. Zygmunt Mycielski, *Ocalenie, pięć pieśni do słów Czesława Miłosza*, I. "Ty, którego nie mogłem ocalić . . ." Polskie Wydawnictwo Muzyczne.

216 | Chapter 7

have understood them to be congruent with his public calls for an expressive musical style of broad appeal. Their evocative focus on subjectivity, friendship, and personal failure seems at odds with an aesthetics of anonymous craftsmanship. Indeed, he would never publish the composition and it would remain a private utterance until his death.[75] The songs of *Rescue* were dark and unabashedly tragic statements that focused on the limits of artistic agency during wartime at a moment when he declared the future of Polish music to lie in its ability to move beyond wartime despondency. They illustrate the distance between public and private expressions of the war among the musical intelligentsia, and that those shaping the discourse of postwar aesthetics were grappling with memories that were not easily incorporated into their aesthetic ideals.

BEYOND WARTIME REPRESENTATION

Mycielski was not the only composer to suggest that postwar music should be permeated with emotion but devoid of representational content about the war. Régamey described in 1946 "a turning away from overly radical experiments and even a certain return to romantic elements, accompanied by a tremendous reserve toward current themes, to the programmatic transformation of the surrounding events into sounds" among his colleagues. "The trace of these events could be discovered only in the newly pronounced seriousness and self-restraint of musical expression," he noted.[76] In this vein, Palester's works were routinely praised for their emotional content, with one critic writing that he had abandoned "matter-of-fact music" during the war and embraced a style he could only describe as romantic, even as he cautioned that "the word romanticism is an improvised label for indisputable newness, which could be the beginning of a new musical style of our era."[77] Similarly, when Witold Rudziński implored his colleagues in the Union of Polish Composers in 1947 to write more pieces about the war, he was met with a chilly response by the membership, which confirmed the rejection of such themes. The reply of Stanisław Wiechowicz was typical of those present: "The hardships that met the nation during the last war were so great and heavy that a certain amount of time is needed before they can be transformed into works of art."[78]

Perhaps the most vocal commentator to promulgate this position was the critic and composer Stefan Kisielewski. He had trained as a composer prior to World War II, but during and after the war he shifted to focus more of his attention on his literary output and criticism.[79] Although he continued to compose throughout his life, his greater cultural impact derived from his novels and essays, which demonstrated a deliberately contrarian and inflammatory style and, by the mid-1950s, often critiqued state socialism. During the early postwar years, however, his interests in literary and musical matters were more balanced, leading him to hold sway with both musical and literary circles: among musicians, he was known as the founder and head editor of *Ruch Muzyczny* and a professor at the Higher School of Music in Cracow, but he also worked at the illustrated cultural journal *Przekrój* (Cross section) and was a regular, if often controversy-provoking, contributor to *Tygodnik Powszechny* (The universal weekly), a periodical that pushed at the boundaries of Polish Catholicism.[80]

In an essay for *Tygodnik Powszechny* written in 1945, he condemned authors who grappled with wartime themes in their literary works.[81] In his essay "War Topics," he claimed that the reader "does not want to have Majdanek, Auschwitz, the murder of the Jews, and so forth described for him. The realism of these descriptions torments him. For several years, he has already seen more than enough of these things," he insisted.[82] It is noteworthy that he centers the murder of the Jews as the wartime event most in need of elision. Instead of dwelling on such themes, he thought, writers should follow the lead of the "masses," who, he believed, desired an escape from the aftermath of the war through art that would serve "the enrichment of the human psyche." In speaking of the "masses," Kisielewski, like Mycielski, sought to justify his aesthetics by evoking the purported desires of a non-elite audience, although whether the "masses" really wished to avoid representations of the war is less clear. "The social role of the writer is to free society from the nightmares of occupation and not to stubbornly cram those nightmares in front of our eyes," he concluded.[83] Thus, the focus ought to be on the redemptive and positive rather than the traumatic, a position more baldly stated but not dissimilar from Mycielski's public aesthetics.

This belief that art must serve the aim of liberating audiences from the war and leading them into a purportedly better future helps make sense of his views about music composition. Writing about the Festival of Contemporary Polish Music, he sought to divide Polish new music into "forward-looking" (*patrzące w przyszłość*) and "dated" (*przeszłościowe*) compositional styles. The overtures of Grażyna Bacewicz and Szałowski rehashed (dated) interwar neoclassicism, he believed, while Piotr

218 | Chapter 7

Perkowski's ballet *Swantewit* and Kassern's *Concerto for Voice* were too close to the (dated) style of Szymanowski. Panufnik's *Pięć polskich pieśni wiejskich* (Five Polish peasant songs) and Jan Ekier's piano compositions were neither dated nor forward looking but rather "pretty, pleasant, and subtle," but they lacked "greatness" and "struggle."[84] The compositions that he believed were forward looking included Palester's Symphony No. 2, Artur Malawski's Symphony No. 1, and Lutosławski's Trio for oboe, clarinet, and bassoon. All of their works shared a set of values: "There is a striving for a new monumentality, for a greatness of construction, encompassing a charge of emotionality. This expression, however, employs thoroughly contemporary means—the goal [of these works] is not experimentation exclusively, but rather they desire to rehabilitate themselves and justify their existence precisely by the creation of a new emotionality and a new greatness, not only through 'new shivers' like what the impressionists or even people of Stravinsky's time wanted."[85]

Like Mycielski and Régamey, Kisielewski rejects experimentation and is skeptical of France and western Europe. He turns to the language of emotion to fortify the significance of new composition to war-wearied audiences, seeking to justify and rehabilitate new music. While Kisielewski saw great potential in both Malawski and Lutosławski, he also believed that their works were still somewhat preliminary.[86] It was thus Palester and his Symphony No. 2, shown in example 10, that most clearly pointed toward the future: It is "a work that is without a doubt both monumental and emotional. . . . The path toward a 'new monumentality' has been clearly and confidently charted."[87] Perhaps Kisielewski was struck by the symphony's dense orchestration or its use of traditional forms—its sonata form first movement, passacaglia (movement 2), and double fugue in the final movement. Or perhaps the symphony's monumentality derives from how its serpentine and richly dissonant themes build across the work's oversized dimensions.

At first glance this description might seem to have nothing to do with the war. But on a closer read, we might hear the topical silence as the very heart of Kisielewski's point. Indeed, the wartime past was the festival's inescapable context: the works he discussed had (mostly) been composed during the war, and Kisielewski, as we saw earlier, had seen the festival as a vindication of Polish musical survival across cataclysm. The forward-looking aesthetic of the monumental and the emotional is perhaps the musical equivalent of the literary aesthetic that could "free people from the nightmares of the occupation." That Kisielewski turns

EXAMPLE 10. Roman Palester, Symphony No. 2, mm 1–5. Polskie Wydawnictwo Muzyczne.

220 | Chapter 7

here to the language of "monumentality" to make this claim is no accident. As Alexander Rehding has shown, musical monumentality was not only about the size or grandeur of works, but rather about a historical aura that seemed to solidify community against disruption. Monumental works offered a "petrified, sonic impulse that brings together this imagined [national] community and enables it to identify as a group" by offering a "compelling vision of stability."[88] In the case of postwar Poland, the musically monumental offered stability against the immediate destabilization of the war itself.

SOCIALIST REALIST WAR MEMORY

The idea that wartime memories could be shaped through music did not dissipate when the language of socialist realism came to dominate Polish musical discourse in 1948 and 1949. Rather, both proponents and skeptics of the new rhetoric shared the belief that music could help audiences relate to the war, even as they disagreed about the specific contours of wartime memorialization. To see how this occurred, we must recall that semantic pliability was a core feature of socialist realist musical discourse, both in Poland and the Soviet Union, where the terminology had originated. Because of the contradiction of applying the concept of realism (an aesthetic premised on representing "reality") to textless instrumental music (which struggles to represent anything, much less "reality"), discourse played a central role in "rendering works socialist realist," as Pauline Fairclough has shown in the Soviet context. Critics had to code works as "realist" through the "verbal tropes" and "standard terms" that they used to define the style.[89] If anything, such semantic coding took on even greater significance in postwar Poland, where the language of socialist realism was hastily introduced in the summer and fall of 1948. As Vest has observed, socialist realist rhetoric was often grafted onto more familiar ideas about cultural progress long endorsed by Poland's composers.[90]

The Stalinist period saw a continuation of the aesthetic slogans, ideas, and precepts developed by Mycielski, Kisielewski, and others that recruited art music into the project of reconstruction. Ideas about emotion and contact with the mass listener were reconstituted as the core values of "realist" composition. At the 1948 annual congress of the Union of Polish Composers, Zygmunt Mycielski, now the union's president, explained that in talking of realism, "We are concerned with what I would term intelligible art; this is art in which both emotion, and the means through which emotion is conveyed, can be easily felt by the lis tener without excessive preconditions."[91] Such views were reinforced when Włodzimierz Sokorski, the vice-minister of culture, gave a speech titled "Formalism and Realism in Music," which explained that "the only test [for realism] is the emotional reaction of the listener."[92] During the fifth annual congress of the union in June 1950, Mycielski further explained, "To cut ourselves off from formalist methods depends on simplifying musical language, on a deepening of emotional expression."[93] Theses for Woytowicz's speech at the same meeting, preserved in the archives of the Central Committee of the Communist Party, likewise defined the turn away from formalism through, first, "a simplification of the means of expression," and, second, "a deepening of emotional expression" before mentioning other factors such as works connected to contemporary topics or the use of folklore.[94] The linkage of emotion to realist aesthetics came to permeate the responses to the Festival of Polish Music in reviews by Lissa, Sokorski, and Aleksander Jackowski.[95] It offered a critical lens for praising works of Mycielski and Woytowicz, and for suggesting that Bacewicz was now on the path toward realism.[96]

On another level, the earlier assumption that expression, emotion, and mass contact were to be accompanied by topical silence about the war began to unravel during the Stalinist period. There was a shift toward heroic, triumphalist accounts of the wartime experience already at the very onset of the state's interventionist attitude toward cultural production, marked by the hardline communist president Bolesław Bierut's 1947 speech at the opening of a radio station in Wrocław.[97] "In the psyche of hundreds of thousands of people, the tragedy [of the war] is still taking place," he observed. "Does the poet, the artist, the creator whose consciousness is sensitized to human experiences have the right to reflect these tragic days in art? Yes." But, he cautioned,

> the nation did not only suffer and unearth itself from the ruins of the crematoria; the nation extracted itself from the abysses of tragedy through its struggle, through its unequalled heroism and deeds, deeds that were the loftiest experiences and passions, in which hundreds of thousands of the most active and noble people took part. Should these deeds, these passions, these experiences not serve as inspiration for the artist, should they not be incorporated into an eternal monument for the honor and pride of the nation, as a model for future generations? . . . Artistic work should not awake doubts when there is a need for enthusiasm and belief in victory; it should not glorify depression when the nation wishes to live and to act.[98]

What is noteworthy about Bierut's rhetoric is how it takes the language of action and work—keywords of reconstruction—and projects them

222 | Chapter 7

backward into the war itself. The claim that artistic representations of the war were a social ill certainly had precedents among the musical intelligentsia. Yet his speech differed in calling for art that explicitly celebrated heroism and action on the nation's behalf. Indeed, the aesthetics of avoidance endorsed by the likes of Mycielski and Kisielewski had been powerful among the musical intelligentsia because it refused to take a stance on tragedy and heroism alike.

When Bierut referred to the "nation's" struggle, he no doubt had in mind the Polish nation. Yet the push toward a heroic commemorative style generated works focused on both Polish and Jewish instances of heroic struggle. Polish and Polish Jewish commemorative discourse displayed a certain parallelism in the late 1940s, during which both Polish and Polish Jewish communities celebrated resistance over more ambiguous memories of loss, collaboration, and helplessness.[99] For Jewish commentators, the Warsaw Ghetto Uprising of 1943 had become the centerpiece of this narrative, and it was celebrated on a yearly basis.[100] The high point of these commemorations occurred in 1948, the five-year anniversary of the uprising, featuring the unveiling of Nathan Rapoport's Monument to the Ghetto Heroes, which was constructed on the ruins of the Warsaw Ghetto (see figure 18). A concert performed by Jewish orphans was part of the event, as was a cantata composed by Leon Wajner, who had survived the Holocaust in the Soviet Union and helped publish ghetto and camp songs with the Central Committee of Jews in Poland.[101]

Wajner's cantata exemplifies an aesthetics that merges an explicit politics of Jewish national identification with service to the socialist state.[102] Wajner set a Yiddish translation of the poem "Żydom polskim" (To the Polish Jews), by the left-wing Polish poet Władysław Broniewski. The poet, who was not Jewish, writes of witnessing the horror of the Holocaust from the distance of exile.[103] The poem opens by praising the fighters in the Warsaw Ghetto Uprising and it underscores the intertwined fates of Poles and Jews during the war, who are "bound together by the execution wall, by Dachau, by Auschwitz." The poem also evokes global inaction in the face of Holocaust through its dedication to Szmul Zygielbojm, a Bundist politician on the National Council of the Polish government-in-exile in London, who committed suicide in protest when the Allies failed to intervene against the liquidation of the Warsaw Ghetto. By setting a Yiddish translation of this poem, Wajner takes a message of Polish witnessing to the Holocaust and places it within the language of the vast majority of Jewish victims (and

FIGURE 18. Nathan Rapoport's Monument to the Ghetto Heroes (Pomnik Bohaterów Getta) was erected on the rubble of the Warsaw Ghetto for the fifth anniversary of the Warsaw Ghetto Uprising (1948). In this photograph, international participants in the World Congress of Intellectuals in Defense of Peace visit the monument in fall 1948. The eastern part of the monument, which is visible, depicts Jews being led to their deaths; the western side, not visible, depicts the heroism and resistance of the Jews. Narodowe Archiwum Cyfrowe.

survivors) in Poland. The poem and cantata ultimately suggest a positive future, in which from the destruction, "only one race will arise: the good, the noble." This message, of common triumph over racism and wartime brutality, fit well enough the official aesthetics of forward-directed transcendence, and Wajner builds the cantata towards a forte, major-key conclusion.[104]

Wajner's cantata reveals the public reach achieved by Jewish-centered musical commemorations in the postwar years and the narrow historical window in which such works could be created. The piece was premiered

224 | Chapter 7

by the city's most important classical music ensemble, the Warsaw Philharmonic, and a two-hundred-person choir, both conducted by Mieczysław Mierzejewski.[105] For the director of the Warsaw Philharmonic, Jan Maklakiewicz, Wajner's cantata was nothing less than an affirmation of Jewish national strength. "The fascist barbarians aimed for the complete annihilation of [the Jewish nation]. . . . The sum of this suffering, the sum of the victims of the Jewish nation, cannot be compared to those of any other nation. But while people perished, the soul of the Jewish nation could not be killed. And like a phoenix from the ashes, Jewish culture was reborn after the war."[106] The frank statement of the exceptional nature of Jewish suffering is noteworthy. Yet Wajner's composition was also a last gasp of such public memorializations: Not only were many Polish Jews leaving the country, but just months after the fifth anniversary of the Warsaw Ghetto Uprising in 1948, communists attacked the celebrations for their alleged Zionism.[107] From this point on, the ideologically diverse coalition that led the uprising was written out of the official history and, instead, the Warsaw Ghetto Uprising was portrayed as part of an international communist class struggle that had little to do with Jewishness.[108] Indicative of this transformation, when Kassern proposed a work similar in intent to Wajner's just a few months after the fifth anniversary celebrations, his proposal was rebuffed for supporting "Jewish 'nationalistic' tendencies."[109]

For many composers, the pressures for a new, heroic response to the war became inescapable during the discussion of Zbigniew Turski's Symphony No. 2 "Olimpica" at the Łagów Lubuski congress. During the congress his symphony was harshly attacked for "formalism."[110] The attendees at the congress were primed to hear the work as a response to the war because Turski introduced the symphony in these terms. He wished that "as if in the moment of the lighting of the Olympic flame at the stadium of the XIV Olympiad"—the work had won the gold medal at the games—"the smoke of the crematoria would rise up."[111] The transcript of the congress further summarizes him as saying that "the entire legacy of the occupation weighed on the composer as he began his first major work after the war. And precisely from this creative mindset there followed a certain psychological exhibitionism that can be noted in the symphony."[112] Although these are a summary of his remarks, they make clear that he understood the symphony's Olympic performance as a way of transmitting Polish wartime experience to an international audience. We also know that some of the chief proponents of socialist realist aesthetics at the conference were already familiar

EXAMPLE 11. Zbigniew Turski, Symphony No. 2 "Olimpica," mm. 721–39. Polskie Wydawnictwo Muzyczne.

(continued)

EXAMPLE 11. (*continued*)

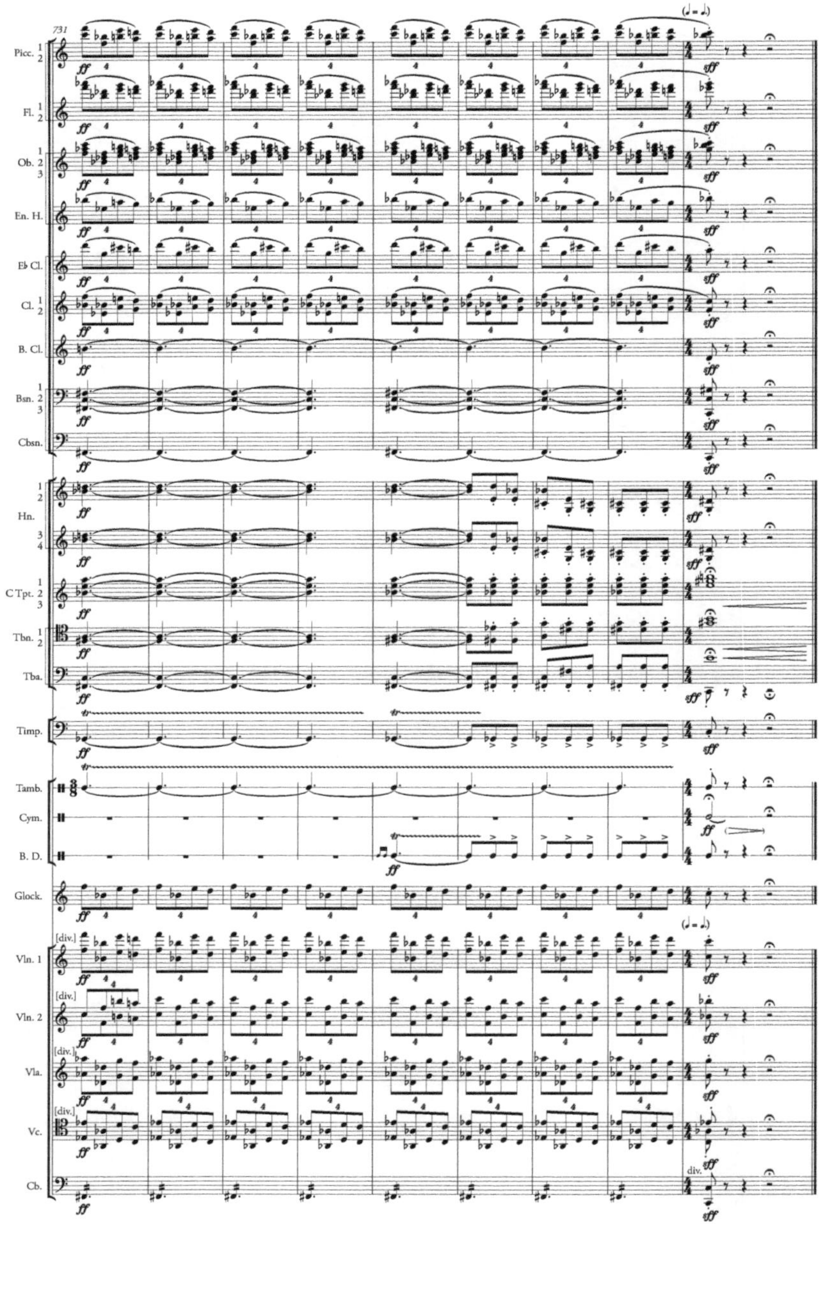

The Aesthetics of Loss | 227

with the backstory that the composer had given to the work: The musicologists Józef Chomiński and Zofia Lissa had read and discussed in February 1949 Turski's "auto-analysis" of the work, a now-lost document in which he described "his mindset while composing."[113] Thus, it was clear to all involved in the congress that the work had not only been created in the aftermath of the war but was also a response to its destruction.

Primed with this background, the first composers to react to the work at Łagów praised it because of its emotional content, defending it via the established paradigm in which emotionality was a key facet of "realist" composition. Piotr Perkowski explained that "the entirety [of the work] left an impression that was simply shocking—it is beautiful in its control of emotion and tension."[114] The conductor Stanisław Wisłocki, who had led the performance of the symphony during the congress, likewise remarked that it had been "a big pleasure to work on the performance, first and foremost because of its type of emotionality."[115] The tenor of the discussion changed when the vice-minister of culture, Sokorski, took the floor. Emotion, he asserted, was an insufficient criterion to consider a composition as "realist": "To be sure, one feels an emotional charge in the work, but it is the emotion of a lost man, in this case one lost in the nightmares of the occupation. The composer evidently did not have a sophisticated relationship to his experiences from that time and submissively yielded to them. . . . The work horrifies and disorients the listener. . . . If we are to speak of formalism, we certainly mean works that escape from any kind of content, but also those whose content is a denial of our values."[116] Sokorski shifted the definition of "formalism" from works that lacked any expressive content to ones whose expressive content did not align with a narrower set of "our" values—those of triumph and positive, forward direction.

The ensuing debate reveals how the attempts to promulgate a heroic, socialist realist view of the war were contested by composers. The composer Tadeusz Szeligowski implied that Sokorski had an overly elastic definition of formalism: "Since formalist music arises from games played with forms it should leave no impression on us. Such is not the case with the *Olympic Symphony*, whose emotional charge—even if nightmarish—is not, however, trivial to us."[117] Others—including Rudziński, Perkowski, and Ekier—defended the work by arguing that it was an important historical document. Perkowski believed that the work should be performed because "we must remember past evil in order to build a new, better life."[118] Rudziński encouraged all to remem-

228 | Chapter 7

ber that "the genesis of the work was the terrifying years of the occupation and the work could be treated as a historical document of those times."[119] Both Sokorski and Lissa replied to these points by arguing that this music was not able to fulfill a task of mobilization and that its emotionality was ultimately not directed toward relevant political goals. Turski eventually conceded this point, saying that he had intended to finish the work with optimistic accents but had failed to do so.[120] Indeed, the work's conclusion, as shown in example 11, is abrupt. The brief final movement gains in intensity, heading into a frenetic conclusion that gives way to a barely prepared ending on an E-major chord held in the trumpets, trombones, and tuba. The suddenness of this resolution undermines any sense of closure. This view of the work—in which tragedy had not been properly sublimated into victory—predominated in Rudziński and Sokorski's published reports on Łagów.[121]

SOCIALIST SOUNDS OF WAR

The Łagów congress marks the point at which Polish musical responses to the war were pulled into a transnational commemorative idiom, practiced across the Eastern Bloc. Heroism had been a keystone of socialist realist composition in the USSR for some years, and this aesthetic had been extended to the notion of rebuilding from the war in pieces such as Shostakovich's *Song of the Forests*, a brazen paean to Stalin celebrating postwar reforestation efforts.[122] Indeed, Shostakovich's composition was the subject of a listening session at the Union of Polish Composers in 1950, where it was compared to Palester's darker and more despondent Requiem.[123] Polish works that proffered narratives of positive transformation were composed in the years after Łagów, such as Andrzej Panufnik's *Symfonia Pokoju* (Symphony of peace), completed in 1951. The work's movements progress from portrayals of tragedy in the first movement (Lamentoso), to a scene of struggle in the second movement, before an apotheosis with choir in the final movement. It was, in short, what Sokorski and Lissa had wished Turski had done. By the early 1950s, socialist realism was not only defined by accessibility, communist ideology, and a growing rejection of Western aesthetics, but it was also shot through with attempts to shape the cultural meaning of the near-universal trauma that Polish citizens had experienced.

Ultimately, there were several forces at play that limited and defined the trajectory of musical responses to the aftermath of the war. The views of the musical intelligentsia, who sought a unifying and powerful style that would confirm the relevance of new music, dovetailed with those of communist officials who hoped to project heroism both backward into the war itself and forward into the building of state socialism. Although they disagreed about aesthetics and politics, both the musical intelligentsia and cultural officialdom rejected the diverse memories of the war that had circulated through rumor and intimate artistic utterance in favor of visions of music that would insist on a unified significance for the recent wartime past. Both the musical intelligentsia and its communist patrons agreed that music was to serve national continuity.

Conclusion

A Generation in the Shadow of the Cold War

The sociality of the musical intelligentsia was a source of continuity across the seemingly insurmountable ruptures of war, mass murder, and political transformation in midcentury Poland. Its leaders within the wartime generation maintained and grew their stature from the 1920s into the 1950s. We have seen how their ideas, ideals, and ideologies proved to be adaptable, pointing in the interwar years toward authoritarian centralization and education of the masses, and, after the war, toward reconstruction and the building of state socialism. Their concerns for nation, culture building, and the relation between "mass" and "elite" culture run like threads through these decades, connecting seemingly disparate moments of Polish musical history. Their ideas, too, subtended a hierarchical imagination of Polish musical culture, which reinforced the musical intelligentsia's authority to organize, lead, and define musical culture.

These continuities in culture across the war are not only evident in retrospect to historians and musicologists. Continuity was also a value cultivated by the musical intelligentsia itself, who portrayed Polish musical culture as having survived and grown across the midcentury. That resilience was itself a core belief of the community suggests how the musical intelligentsia was borrowing ideals from the Polish gentry and nobility. "The ability to adapt to different historical circumstances," the sociologist Longina Jakubowska has pointed out, "is the key to noble identity [in Poland], and nobility endures through a skillful

232 | Conclusion

conversion and reconversion of the capital they historically accumulated."[1] To act as if one is above the events of mere history is to possess an influence and staying power, she suggests. But unlike the nobility—whose boundaries were tightly drawn as a hereditary class and who once possessed actual political power—the musical intelligentsia operated in a more fluid space between received prestige, mutual action, and fears of irrelevance. For this milieu to assert that it had been relatively unharmed by war, that Polish music was on a path of continual growth and development, its members drew and redrew the boundaries around who—and whose experiences—mattered to the story of the country and its music.

Perhaps all continuity narratives rely on some measure of abstraction and simplification. But in the case of the Polish musical intelligentsia, the stakes of narrating the war years through the lens of continuity were especially high because of the scope of human suffering that this paradigm downplayed. Death was everywhere in wartime and postwar Poland, and no one in the musical community was unaffected by the war. But loss was also not evenly felt between Poles and Jews. To endorse a sense of forward-directed musical progress, the musical intelligentsia reinforced the lines of ethnonational belonging that had long coursed through the community. Whether intentionally or not, they placed Jewish loss in the margins of a story about Polish musical development, even when such suffering afflicted Polish Jews who had been their professional colleagues, friends, and lovers.

The early 1950s marked a generational caesura in the Polish musical intelligentsia, during which the wartime generation began to fade from prominence. At this time, more and more composers who had been born in the 1920s entered the musical intelligentsia. They were too young to have participated in interwar internationalism, institution building, and debates about the shape of musical culture of the 1920s and 1930s. For some, such as the composers of the "Grupa 49"—Jan Krenz, Kazimierz Serocki, and Tadeusz Baird—youth offered a way of creating distance from the politics of the pre-communist era, too. As Serocki (born in 1922) asserted in 1949, "The youngest generation does not lug behind it the baggage of the past, because the prior periods of their lives—their carefree childhood and the years of occupation, during which they wandered about in confusion—could not create habits that are difficult to overcome."[2] By 1958, Mycielski remarked with amazement at the distance between himself and the younger composers. "A generation has already arisen who doesn't remember the war! . . . This all is normal to them, just as the world was normal to us when we were twenty years old."[3] Such remarks are reminders that, while the wartime generation's strategies for responding to trauma would have long afterlives, the war- and Holocaust-themed works created by younger composers—from Penderecki's *Dies Irae* to Henryk Górecki *Symphony of Sorrowful Songs*—require grappling with these composers' temporal separation from the events they commemorate, as well as the vicissitudes of Holocaust memory in Poland in the 1960s, 1970s, and beyond.

In addition to the growing distance from the war, there were also major aesthetic changes afoot in Polish composition in the mid-1950s. After Stalin's death in 1953, the cultural discourse that had to that point been largely focused on music and reconstruction shifted. Western-oriented, avant-garde musical styles that had once been rejected now served as emblems of musical modernization under state socialism. The pivotal composer in this transition to the avant-garde was Witold Lutosławski. He was one of the youngest members of the wartime generation, with relatively little investment in interwar musical politics, yet he had also established a prominent reputation during the occupation and shortly thereafter. It was his Concerto for Orchestra in 1954 that inaugurated the shift toward a more avant-garde aesthetic. As Vest writes, the premiere and the extensive discussion of the composition in the press marked "a moment in which critics, composers, and political leaders seemed to recognize a new path forward," even though the work drew on established markers of socialist realism such as neo-traditional forms and folk sources.[4] Over the following decades he would become a leading proponent of the avant-garde, one of the few composers educated before the war to become a figurehead of this movement.[5]

While the wartime generation excelled at building narratives of cultural resilience, they were less successful at securing a place for themselves within canons of twentieth-century composition, despite possessing the elite positionality and cultural capital that generally aid canonization. Their work to rebuild from the destruction of war and to develop an account of Polish music as directed toward an ever-progressing future would, by the late 1950s, support a new music scene of fecundity that is widely acknowledged as a core part of the canon of twentieth-century concert music. But the works of Mycielski, Palester, Kassern, and Régamey are not much played, nor are their names well known. Their fading relevance was due in part to how the musical intelligentsia thought of itself in terms of generations, successive waves of youth whose difference from their elders was believed to propel Polish

234 | Conclusion

music forward. While in the 1920s this idea allowed the wartime generation to solidify itself against older, more conservative composers, by the 1950s they had become the established status quo against which younger composers now rebelled. Bronisław Rutkowski, a key figure of the wartime generation, grasped this irony when he asked in 1957, "And who today admonishes the musical youth? Precisely those who acted more or less the same way as today's youth when they were young. . . . Back in the day, they justified their actions on the basis of the eternal right of the young. Today, however, they deny this same right to others—precisely to the young."[6]

These generational dynamics were compounded by shifts in the allocation of musical prestige among Polish composers in response to the Cold War. As scholars such as Anne Shreffler, Danielle Fosler-Lussier, and Mark Carroll have discussed, Western observers during the Cold War placed great emphasis on abstract, avant-garde compositional styles practiced by the likes of Pierre Boulez, Karlheinz Stockhausen, and Milton Babbitt, which they saw as exemplifying values such as "freedom" and "autonomy" that they believed were absent in the Soviet Union and Eastern Bloc.[7] Because the Polish avant-garde embraced techniques including serialism and aleatoric composition that were prized in the West, their compositions appeared exceptional to West German and US critics especially, defying their expectations that music from behind the "Iron Curtain" would be conservative, drab, and socialist realist. Western observers could encounter these Polish compositions on a new scale, too, thanks to the Warsaw Autumn Festival of Contemporary Music (1956–), an annual state-sponsored music festival that Lisa Jakelski has described as "one of the most significant zones of cross-border cultural contact during the Cold War."[8]

In reality, the Polish avant-garde of the 1960s had much in common with the older wartime generation. Their embrace of values such as emotion, communication, and national tradition—which had deep roots in Polish musical aesthetics of the 1930 and 1940s—was part of what made Polish avant-garde composition compelling to listeners and observers.[9] Nor was the more experimental side of their aesthetics exceptional within the Eastern Bloc, whose composers were concerned with many of the same problems of modernity and experimentation as those outside it.[10] But for Western Cold War–era observers who were unaware of this broader context or of the historical roots of the Polish avant-garde, its "brand" became one of friction against the dismal musical aesthetics purportedly mandated by state socialism.

This was an interpretation its advocates in Poland were all too eager to support.[11]

Members of the wartime generation were often ambivalent about the rise of the avant-garde and not always able—or willing—to chase the international prestige it offered. Upon hearing Krzysztof Penderecki's *Threnody for the Victims of Hiroshima* (1961) at the Warsaw Autumn Festival in 1964, Mycielski wrote that the work—which he critiqued for its static formal blocks, unconventional orchestration, and a near absence of pulse—"should be bad, but it is good. It is music like oysters, snails, and vodka."[12] He expressed more frustration that the rise of the avant-garde seemed to marginalize his own compositional voice, which had been shaped by interwar neoclassicism and postwar socialist realism.[13] In 1958 he wrote to Roman Maciejewski about the first Warsaw Autumn Festival that "a tiny fragment of life in the West suddenly takes on the weight of dogma here. There is thus now a fashion among those youths [whose alpha and omega is Webern and his prophets], to assert that all of our music is sh*t, because Szeligowski and Grażyna [Bacewicz] don't write under the influence of Nono or Webern or even Messiaen."[14] Nonetheless, he supported the musical internationalism exemplified by the Warsaw Autumn Festival, acting as host for the numerous visits to the country of his celebrity composition teacher, Nadia Boulanger, one of which is illustrated in figure 6.[15]

The entanglements of the wartime generation with Stalinism also offered younger composers a foil to their new ambitions. In an influential speech at the Union of Polish Composers in 1957, Lutosławski cast the Thaw of 1956 as a new beginning for Polish composition while painting the previous decade as a time of communist oppression and restrained creativity, dominated by those to whom "the very concept of beauty is foreign."[16] This view was shared by many of his avant-garde colleagues, who fused Stalinism, socialist realism, and the wartime generation together into a vision of oppressive, communist hegemony against which their new compositional directions revolted.[17] Needless to say, this was a narrative that ignored the deep social investments that had driven early postwar and Stalinist-era musical aesthetics. It also overlooked the uncomfortable truth that the musical intelligentsia had gained much in the way of prestige, power, and material support from Stalinist reconstruction.

For some within the wartime generation, too, their alliances with the Polish state during reconstruction looked less sanguine in retrospect than they did when the country lay in ruins in 1945. Mycielski evolved

236 | Conclusion

from a devoted proponent of communist reconstruction to a critic of state socialism by the 1960s. Letters written by him that fell into the hands of the state Security Service (Służba Bezpieczeństwa) describe his growing dissatisfaction with the regime and its oppressive intellectual climate.[18] "In this country, no one writes, or even says, what they are truly thinking," he wrote to Jerzy Waldorff.[19] But he did say and write what he was thinking, both through signed letters of support against Soviet power in Poland and in his posthumously published diaries.[20] Perhaps most notably, he took a public stand against the Soviet invasion of Czechoslovakia in 1968 in the most influential Polish émigré publication in Paris, *Kultura*.[21]

The Cold War also created a new political environment that Poland's composers had to navigate, not always with success. The career of the composer Roman Palester makes the stakes of misjudging the trajectories of state socialism especially clear. As discussed in chapter 6, he had relocated to Paris in 1947, a decision that frustrated commentators in Poland. Critics in Poland also became dismayed that his music in the late 1940s was veering away from the expressive and monumental style of his wartime works, which, as we saw in chapter 7, had played the central role in defining early postwar responses to the war. Many still admired his earlier works for their "emotional charge."[22] But those hearing his newer compositions noted a troubling change. The musicologist Stefania Łobaczewska wrote to Lissa that his music seemed to show a greater "abstraction" in 1948 than it had earlier.[23] Lissa drew additional attention to this change in his oeuvre in 1949, commenting that his work, including the Requiem, "stuns with the strength of its emotional tension and testifies to the composer's emotional deepening." Yet, she believed, his other works pointed toward a "certain growth in the intellectual element that is taking from the composer the possibility of direct expression."[24] These were early warnings signs that Palester's use of techniques such as dodecaphony would not be welcomed in Poland at a time when these were being condemned as markers of "formalist" excess and abstraction.[25] His role as a leading voice of postwar aesthetics in Poland, one central to defining musical responses to the war, was fast fading.

At the same time, his contacts in the United States implored him to take a clearer position on his relation to the communist state in Poland, especially should he wish to emigrate to the United States.[26] He broke ties with Poland in 1951 by publishing two articles in the Paris-based Polish émigré journal *Kultura*. These were permeated with the language of the developing Cold War schism between East and West. A "moral crisis" is unfolding on "both sides of the 'Iron Curtain,'" he exclaimed while pointing to the "fight of the millions of people who, against their will, were given over to the captivity of a hostile system," of Soviet-dominated eastern Europe.[27] Palester's claims resemble those found in Czesław Miłosz's far more successful book published around the same time, *The Captive Mind*. (Tellingly, "Ketman," an excerpt from *The Captive Mind*, was published in the same issue of *Kultura* as Palester's "Konflikt Marsjasza.") Yet Palester lacked Miłosz's talent for crafting pithy metaphors that played into the expectations of Western readers about Soviet oppression in eastern Europe, such as the Murti-Bing pills (to describe indoctrination) or Ketman (the practice of dividing one's mind so as to better pay lip service to ideology).[28] He enjoyed none of Miłosz's subsequent fame.

Having chosen the West, Palester was propelled even further to serve its political aims. From 1952 he was employed by Radio Free Europe in Munich, a US-backed propaganda instrument that broadcast anti-communist programming into the Eastern Bloc.[29] He worked there for the next twenty years, where his duties included preparing and recording broadcasts on arts, literature, and music that were broadcast into Poland from the station's Munich headquarters. This employment amplified the fallout for Palester of breaking ties with Poland. He had already been expelled from the Union of Polish Composers (in 1951) and had broken off ties with PWM, his publisher, but likely due to his employment, his name was censored in Polish publications into the 1970s.[30] His associations with Radio Free Europe meant that risks of public discussion of him in Poland were high, as the musicologist Tadeusz Kaczyński learned when he published what he believed was a politically neutral interview with the composer in *Ruch Muzyczny* in 1964.[31] In retaliation for this publication, the Ministry of Internal Affairs prevented Kaczyński from traveling to the West until 1970.[32]

From the early 1950s onward, Palester was working in musical styles that were popular among the Polish avant-garde, but he received little of their recognition. He completed dozens of works that made use of serial, aleatoric, and sonoristic techniques.[33] Because such techniques were viewed as unexceptional outside the Eastern Bloc, however, his works were not afforded the oppositional tenor accorded to the Polish avant-garde in Poland. He wrote with despair in a letter that "we of the middle generation (also a euphemism) have proven, according to the critics here [in West Germany], that there is no one on the level of

238 | Conclusion

Stravinsky or Bartók. Therefore, it is not worth playing us much. And if one of us writes something in the style of Boulez or Stockhausen, no one wants to play it. Because that domain is reserved for the young."[34] At the same time, he was unable to benefit from the support in Poland provided to avant-garde composers by the Warsaw Autumn Festival, Union of Polish Composers, and the publisher, PWM.[35] His decisions early in the postwar years to break off ties with Poland, based on a misjudgment of how deeply Stalinism would affect musical circles, meant that the brand of the Polish avant-garde was formed in his absence. He reveals that, whether within Poland or beyond its borders, navigating the politics of the Cold War was vital to the professional viability of Polish composers.

Because the Cold War was essential to shaping the careers of Polish composers and to securing the international visibility of Polish composition, it can be easy to forget that it was not the only form of politics relevant to composers, especially to Polish Jewish members of the wartime generation. Put bluntly, the establishment of communist rule against the backdrop of a tightening Cold War schism was not the most significant trauma Polish Jews had recently survived. Their experiences do not always fit into the East-versus-West binary. Nor do they accord with what Katarzyna Chmielewska has described as a value-laden, "axiological" dichotomy through which communism is often understood in Polish collective memory and historiography, a stark division between those who were agents of the state and those who resisted it.[36] For instance, when Polish musicologists in the late 1980s began to rehabilitate the works of émigrés from the wartime generation, they emphasized communist repression as a major reason why these composers were absent from the Polish concert hall, while saying less about the relationship between emigration and Jewish survival that was embodied in the biographies of Tadeusz Zygfryd Kassern, Roman Haubenstock-Ramati, and Szymon Laks.[37] In reality, it is not always easy to disentangle whether a composer emigrated because they feared communism or antisemitism or for other inscrutable reasons.

Tadeusz Zygfryd Kassern, for instance, explained his decision to defect from his diplomatic post in New York City as a broader rejection of communist rule in Poland, which he had witnessed firsthand on a visit to the country in 1948. But this decision also occurred shortly after his proposal to compose an opera commemorating the Warsaw Ghetto Uprising and to organize the Polish premiere of Arnold Schoenberg's Holocaust cantata, *A Survivor from Warsaw*, had been firmly rejected by the Polish Ministry of Culture and Art, decisions reflective of a starkly anti-Jewish turn in the government in late 1948. Most likely we will never know how Kassern weighed the growing authoritarian nature of the communist government and its increasingly antisemitic heading in the late 1940s as he decided to defect. What is certain is that during the Red Scare in the United States, publicly underscoring his rejection of Polish communism was a matter of survival, while condemning antisemitism was not.[38] The historical record emphasizes the former at the expense of the latter.

Whatever his motivations for emigration, Kassern's distance from Stalinist Poland allowed him to create one of the earliest large-scale musical memorializations of the Holocaust. The work was a four-act opera titled *The Anointed*, which he completed in 1951, thanks to a commission from the Koussevitzky Foundation. As he explained in an English-language letter from 1950:

> "The Anointed" has been conceived as a dramatico-musical monument (the first in the history of opera) to the fight of the Jewish nation for freedom. The hero of my opera, the powerful, great cabbalist, Sabbatai Zwi, was the speaker for this fight in the 17th century. The idea of composing "The Anointed" (now being done to an English text) received a strong impetus during the war years when being in Poland under the Nazi occupation, I witnessed the most inhuman tragedy that befell the Jewish nation. Since that time the urge to contribute a musical monument to Jewish history never left me. After the war, in Poland, I was offered a large commission to write an opera. I suggested "The Anointed" as a ghetto-uprising memorial, but I was severely rebuked and forbidden to write this opera because the Communist Government considered it as favoring Jewish "nationalistic" tendencies and this the Communists strongly opposed. You will understand why I am so deeply attached to writing and doing this work here in this free country [the United States].[39]

In this letter Kassern frames his opera within a Cold War paradigm in which the United States is equated with freedom and communist Poland with oppression. Yet the composition itself fits poorly into such Cold War binaries. As I have discussed elsewhere, Kassern cloaked Sabbatai's story in the rhetoric of Polish romantic nationalism, whose equations of suffering with nationhood he turns into an idiom for commemorating Jewish resistance and loss. Despite these deep roots in the Polish intellectual world, however, the opera is in English, written for a US audience who would be unfamiliar with these traditions.[40] While fleeing from Stalinism enabled Kassern to engage with Polish and Jewish history in ways that had been foreclosed in Poland, he found little audience

240 | Conclusion

for his ideas in the United States either. It is another instance in which some of the most powerful responses to the Holocaust among the musical intelligentsia remain both present—in this case, sitting on library shelves waiting to be performed—yet also absent from the predominant narratives of postwar Polish composition.

Throughout this book I have sought to uncover what has been left out of Polish musical culture while also elucidating how and why these absences formed. I have rejected the simplistic claim that the Holocaust was greeted with silence among Poles and Polish Jews after the war, as well as the idea that a de-Judaized, ethnonationalist memory of the Holocaust was an inevitable byproduct of communist rule and national homogenization in postwar Poland. Rather, I have sought to restore some of the complex reality that was lived by the Polish-speaking musical community while its members were building a Polish musical identity that was seemingly unburdened by the genocide, political revolution, and ethnic homogenization that had inescapably transformed their country.

In doing so, I have shown that the fundamental drama unfolding within midcentury Polish concert music concerned the question of whose experiences of the twentieth century were taken as canonic by musicians and whose were not. Inclusion and exclusion formed a subcutaneous politics, unfolding on the level of interpersonal debates, friendship, and animosity within the Polish musical community, whose members were in conversation not only with each other, but also with ideologies that spanned from the far left to the far right. At times, this politics led to polemics about who should build the country's musical culture and who should not. But it also took on a more subtle, if no less powerful form: of asserting genealogies that would at once anchor the present in a selective understanding of the community's past and portend a future in which concert music finally mattered. Ultimately, the musical meanings of war, mass murder, and occupation were never straightforward or self-evident, but rather they were contested and defined by those who lived them as they pursued aims that were sometimes quotidian, sometimes monumental.

APPENDIX I

Cast of Characters

GRAŻYNA BACEWICZ (1909–1969). Composer and violinist. Studied in Paris (1932–33, 1934–35) with Nadia Boulanger (composition), Carl Flesch (violin), and André Touret (violin). From 1936 to 1938, she was principal violinist of the of the Polish Radio Orchestra. During WWII, she was active as a composer and violinist in occupied Warsaw. Her compositions exemplify the transition from neoclassical to avant-garde aesthetics across the midcentury.

NADIA BOULANGER (1887–1979). One of the most consequential composition teachers of the twentieth century. She instructed dozens of Polish composers who traveled to France to work with her. After the war she visited Poland several times as a highly feted guest during the Warsaw Autumn Festival of Contemporary Music. Confidant of Zygmunt Mycielski.

ADOLF CHYBIŃSKI (1880–1952). Founding figure of Polish musicology, who completed his doctoral studies in Munich under Adolf Sandberger and in 1912 was authorized to establish a chair of musicology at the Jan Kazimierz University in Lviv. His research focused on Polish renaissance and baroque music and folk music of the Tatra Mountains. Zofia Lissa, Stefania Łobaczewska, and Józef Chomiński were among his students. He held antisemitic views.

MIECZYSŁAW DROBNER (1912–1986). Organizer and composer. Founding member of Cracow's Association of Young Musicians and conductor at the Cracow opera from 1931 to 1939. Survived the Holocaust in the Soviet Union and, from 1944, assumed key positions in state-backed musical institutions, notably as head of the Department of Music in the Ministry of Culture and Art. From 1946 to 1958, professor and rector at the State Higher Music School in Łódź and from 1958 to 1982 at the State Higher Music School in Cracow.

GRZEGORZ FITELBERG (1879–1953). Conductor and major proponent of Polish new music, including a proponent of the Young Poland in Music

242 | Appendix 1

movement. He was the chief conductor of the Warsaw Philharmonic from 1908 to 1911 and 1924 to 1934. He then founded and led the Symphony Orchestra of the Polish Radio from 1934 until the outbreak of the war. He spent the war in North and South America and returned to Poland in 1946, where he resumed his distinguished conducting career, and in 1947 he took leadership of the Great Symphony Orchestra of the Polish Radio. Father of the composer Jerzy Fitelberg.

MATEUSZ GLIŃSKI (1892–1976). Critic, publisher, conductor, and violinist. Trained in Warsaw in music and law before continuing his musical training in Leipzig with Max Reger and Arthur Nikisch and in Russia with Alexander Glazunov. Returned to Warsaw in 1918 and ran a law practice until WWII. Founding member of the Polish Section of the International Society for Contemporary Music and founder of the periodical *Muzyka*, which sought to both develop audiences in Poland and connect Polish composition to broader European currents. Spent the war in Rome, where he was the music critic for the Vatican's *L'Osservatore Romano*. After the war he emigrated to Canada, where he lived until his death.

WIERA GRAN (1914 or 1916–2007). Singer and cabaret artist. From 1934, performer in Warsaw cabarets and cafés. Spent much of the occupation in the Warsaw Ghetto, where she became the star performer of the café Sztuka. Escaped the ghetto in 1942 and lived in hiding on the outskirts of Warsaw. After the war she was dogged by accusations that she had collaborated with the Gestapo and its agents in the Warsaw Ghetto. Despite repeated exonerations, the rumors followed her into emigration, first to Israel in 1950 and later to Paris.

ZDZISŁAW JACHIMECKI (1882–1953). Founding figure of Polish musicology. Student of Guido Adler. In 1911 he was authorized to establish the Seminar in Music Theory and History at the Jagiellonian University. Published notable works on Chopin and Polish music history.

TADEUSZ ZYGFRYD KASSERN (1904–1957). Composer, music critic, and lawyer. Survived the Holocaust in Lviv, Cracow, and Warsaw. From 1945 he worked in the Polish consulate general in New York, and he defected from Poland in 1948. As an émigré in New York, he completed in 1951 his most significant work, an opera titled *The Anointed*, which he intended as a musical monument to the Warsaw Ghetto Uprising of 1943.

STEFAN KISIELEWSKI (1911–1991). Composer, critic, and writer. Trained in composition in Warsaw and Paris and, in the late 1930s, active with *Muzyka Polska* and the Polish Music Publishing Society. In 1945 he founded the consequential music periodical *Ruch Muzyczny*. From 1945 to 1989 he contributed to the *Tygodnik Powszechny*, a periodical that pushed as the boundaries of Polish Catholicism. Notable for his contrarian essays and political commentary, including his critiques of state socialism.

JÓZEF KOFFLER (1896–1943). First Polish composer to use twelve-tone technique. Active in both the International Society for Contemporary Music and with Jewish-identified musical organizations in Lviv. Under Soviet rule from 1939 to 1941, he was a professor of composition in the Lviv State Conservatory. After the German invasion he fled to Wieliczka and survived the

Cast of Characters | 243

liquidation of the ghetto there only to be murdered along with his family near Krosno.

ZOFIA LISSA (1905–1980). One of Poland's most consequential musicologists. Studied with Adolf Chybiński. She published more than four hundred works on topics including twelve-tone music, film music, music psychology and ontology, nationalism, and race. She survived the war in Lviv, Uzbekistan, and Moscow. A true believer in communism, she became one of the main translators of Soviet aesthetics to Polish audiences in the 1940s and 1950s. Founder of the musicology institute at the University of Warsaw.

WITOLD LUTOSŁAWSKI (1913–1994). Graduated in composition from the Warsaw Conservatory in 1937, but his hopes of studying in Paris were dashed by the war. Concertized in occupied Warsaw's cafés in a piano duo with Andrzej Panufnik. By the mid 1950s he had emerged as a leading proponent of avant-garde compositional techniques.

STEFANIA ŁOBACZEWSKA (1888–1963). Musicologist who studied with Adolf Chybiński and Guido Adler. Her interwar writings reveal an interest in both Poland's feminist and socialist movements. From 1945, she was professor at the State Higher Music School in Cracow and rector from 1952 to 1955. Appointed to the musicology department of the Jagiellonian University in 1951, which she led from 1954 until her death.

ZYGMUNT MYCIELSKI (1907–1987). Composer, critic, and diarist of gentry background. Throughout the 1920s and 1930s he was frequently based in Paris, where he studied with Nadia Boulanger, with whom he maintained a lifelong friendship. After fighting in the 1939 defense of Poland, he escaped the country and joined the Polish army in France. Captured by the Germans in 1940, he was held captive in a forced labor camp until liberation. He returned to Poland and was active in organizing postwar Polish musical life. One of the most respected commentators on Polish musical culture after the war, he was a staunch critic of state socialism by the 1960s.

TADEUSZ OCHLEWSKI (1894–1975). Violinist and organizer. Founding member of the Association of Enthusiasts for Early Music, an association dedicated to early music, which was expanded in 1928 to become the Polish Music Publishing Society. Under the auspices of the Publishing Society, from 1934 to 1939 he led ORMUZ, an effort to disseminate classical music through thousands of concerts for students and for audiences in remote towns. He continued these projects in various forms during the occupation and in April 1945 founded PWM, the Polish Music Publishers, which he directed until his retirement in 1965.

ROMAN PALESTER (1907–1989). Composer of concert and film music. His early works were distinguished at interwar festivals of the International Society of Contemporary Music. During the occupation his family, themselves of Jewish background, hid Jews in their apartment and were involved in Żegota, the Polish underground's efforts to save Jews. After the war he was celebrated as the leading light of Polish new music and composed scores for numerous films about the war, including *Ulica graniczna* and *Ostatni etap*. He lost this standing

244 | Appendix 1

after relocating to Paris in 1947 and breaking ties with the country in 1951. From 1952 he worked for Radio Free Europe in Munich.

PIOTR PERKOWSKI (1901–1990). Composer and organizer. Founder of the Association of Young Musician-Poles in Paris and active in the Polish Music Publishing Society and in the Polish ISCM section. He played a key role in organizing musicians in occupied Warsaw. One of the most active organizers of the early postwar period, he served as head of the Union of Polish Composers and of the Professional Union of Musicians, among many other commitments. From 1945 to 1971 (excepting four years spent in Wrocław), he was professor at the Warsaw Higher School of Music.

KONSTANTY RÉGAMEY (1907–1982). Critic and composer. Prior to the war, a major theorist of music and musical meaning. He was active in the Polish ISCM section and as an editor of *Muzyka Polska*. He began composing during the occupation, while based in Warsaw. Active in the underground and Home Army, he used his (neutral) Swiss passport to evade capture. After the Warsaw Uprising he fled to Switzerland and became a professor of Slavic and Oriental languages at the University of Lausanne. He remained in contact with the Polish new music community.

BRONISŁAW RUTKOWSKI (1898–1964). Organist and organizer. Born in a tiny village in the Polish borderlands, the region where he would dedicate much of his efforts at improving musical life, he was a main instigator of the Polish Music Publishing Society, the journal *Muzyka Polska*, and ORMUZ. A member of the Home Army who fought in the Warsaw Uprising (1944), he was imprisoned in the Gross Born and Sandbostel POW camps. He taught at the Cracow Higher School of Music after the war, serving as its rector from 1955 to his death.

KAZIMIERZ SIKORSKI (1895–1986). Composer and organizer who studied with Nadia Boulanger in the 1920s. His appointment to the Warsaw Conservatory (1927–39) was a victory for Poland's modernist-aligned composers, who appreciated his aesthetic and theoretical openness. He served in leadership positions of numerous interwar organizations, including the Polish ISCM section and the Polish Music Publishing Society. During the occupation he led the Warsaw Conservatory, and afterward was a professor in Łódź and Warsaw.

WŁADYSŁAW SZPILMAN (1911–2000). Pianist and composer who trained in Warsaw and Berlin with Franz Schreker. His survival in the Warsaw Ghetto and in the ruins of the city were conveyed in his memoirs, published in 1946 as *The Death of a City*, which formed the basis of the 2002 film *The Pianist*. From 1945 until 1962 he led the popular music section of the Polish Radio and composed hundreds of songs. In 1961 he founded the International Festival of Song. In 1963 his focus turned to performing classical repertoire with the Warsaw Quintet, which toured to dozens of countries over the following decades.

KAROL SZYMANOWSKI (1882–1937). Composer, writer, and teacher who led the modernist-aligned revitalization of Polish composition. He influentially encouraged the generation of composers younger than him to study in Paris and devote themselves more fully to building musical culture in Poland from the ground up.

ALEKSANDER TANSMAN (1897–1986). One of the most famous Polish composers of the interwar years, based in Paris from 1919. He saw his compositions, especially his mazurkas, as synthesizing French and Polish music, much as he believed Chopin had done a century prior. After gaining French citizenship in 1938, he left occupied Paris in 1941 thanks to financial support from Charlie Chaplin and spent the war in Los Angeles. He returned to Paris in 1946.

JONAS TURKOW (1898–1988). Actor, director, and impresario. Committed to Yiddish as an artistic theatrical language, he toured as an actor and directed at several theaters in interwar Poland, where he produced classic Yiddish plays as well as translations from the European repertoire. He spent most of the war in the Warsaw Ghetto with his wife, the actress and singer Diana Blumenfeld. He was a main organizer of artistic and musical life in the ghetto. He was involved in Jewish organizations after the war but soon emigrated, settling in New York in 1947 and in Israel in 1966.

JERZY WALDORFF (1910–1999). Music critic and essayist notable for his many books on classical music. Prior to the war, he was a leading translator of fascist ideas into Polish musical discourse and authored antisemitic screeds. In 1946 he played a central role in editing and publishing Władysław Szpilman's memoirs about surviving the Warsaw Ghetto.

BOLESŁAW WOYTOWICZ (1899–1980). Pianist and composer who studied in Warsaw and with Nadia Boulanger. During the war he ran a musical café in Warsaw that functioned as a de facto concert hall, offering hundreds of classical performances. After the war he was professor at the state conservatory in Katowice until his retirement in 1975.

APPENDIX 2

Key Institutions

Presented in alphabetical order by the name or abbreviation primarily used in the body text.

Association of Young Musician-Poles in Paris | Stowarzyszenie Młodych Muzyków-Polaków w Paryżu | SMMP
Main mutual aid organization for Polish musicians studying and living in Paris, founded in late 1926 by Piotr Perkowski. By 1935 had over one hundred members, many of whom would go on to prominent careers in Poland. Helped create community abroad, organize recitals for its members, financially support members, and facilitate their contacts with the Parisian musical world. Relaunched in 1945 with a more limited scope, but increasingly tussled with the Polish state and disbanded in 1950.
Key people: Piotr Perkowski, Zygmunt Mycielski, Stanisław Wiechowicz, Tadeusz Zygfryd Kassern, Bolesław Woytowicz, Eugenia Umińska, Irena Dubiska, Antoni Szałowski, Grażyna Bacewicz, Tadeusz Szeligowski.

Central Committee of Jews in Poland | Centralny Komitet Żydów w Polsce | CKŻP
After the war, the official organization representing the Jewish minority in Poland, which provided food, shelter, education, and cultural programming to survivors. It collected thousands of testimonies from survivors, organized concerts, and published collections of Holocaust-era songs.
Key people: Jonas Turkow, Leon Wajner, Shmerke Kaczerginski.

CKI | Centralna Komisja Imprezowa | Central Commission for Entertainments
Major effort to organize artistic and musical life in the Warsaw Ghetto. The CKI was headed by Jonas Turkow and was intended to regulate the

performances organized in the ghetto houses. It also organized performances in the extensive network of soup kitchens and orphanages run by the Jewish self-help organizations in the ghetto.

Key people: Jonas Turkow, Diana Blumenfeld.

International Society for Contemporary Music | ISCM | Polskie Towarzystwo Muzyki Współczesnej

Founded in 1922 to promote international exchange through music and to showcase the modernist compositions of its members. Its main task was the organizing of a peripatetic annual festival, to which each member nation would submit works. The Polish section was founded in 1924 during the Prague ISCM festival. It sent compositions to the festival throughout the interwar years and hosted the 1939 festival in Warsaw and Cracow. After the war the Polish ISCM section renewed its activities, but it had to cease operations at the behest of official decree in 1951. It was reinstituted in 1957 and remains in operation.

Key people: Karol Szymanowski, Mateusz Gliński, Adolf Chybiński, Zbigniew Drzewiecki, Grzegorz Fitelberg, Józef Koffler, Roman Palester, Konstanty Régamey. A branch of the Polish ISCM section was established in Lviv in 1930, in which Zofia Lissa, Stefania Łobaczewska, and Koffler were active.

Ministry of Culture and Art | Ministerstwo Kultury i Sztuki | MKiS

Branch of the postwar Polish state. The Music Department of MKiS created and funded musical institutions and oversaw their activities. In the early postwar years it was largely staffed by those belonging to or sympathetic to the musical intelligentsia, although after 1948 communist officials played a greater role in its activities.

Key people: Mieczysław Drobner, Zofia Lissa, Włodzimierz Sokorski.

Muzyka | Music

One of interwar Poland's main music periodicals, published from 1924 to 1938 by Mateusz Gliński. Initially intended as an unofficial mouthpiece of the Polish section of the ISCM, it was modeled on western European periodicals. Gliński believed that the periodical could help develop audiences in Poland by publishing accessible yet well-informed articles primarily about classical music.

Key people: Mateusz Gliński.

Muzyka Polska | Polish Music

Published from 1934 to 1939 by the Polish Music Publishing Society. Major forum for discussion of modernist composition and issues of musical culture in the 1930s. Was the main model for *Ruch Muzyczny*.

Key people: Adolf Chybiński, Kazimierz Sikorski, Teodor Zalewski, Bronisław Rutkowski, Konstanty Régamey, Stefan Kisielewski.

ORMUZ | Organizacja Ruchu Muzycznego | Organization for Musical Culture

From 1934 to 1939, organized hundreds of tours of musicians who performed for schoolchildren and audiences in small towns throughout

248 | Appendix 2

the Polish borderlands. Committed to "musicalizing" Poland through such work, the group also provided much-needed employment to musicians during the Depression. Operated under the auspices of the Polish Music Publishing Society.

Key people: Tadeusz Ochlewski and, as performers, Grażyna Bacewicz, Witold Lutosławski, Bolesław Woytowicz, and Eugenia Umińska.

Polish Music Publishing Society | Towarzystwo Wydawnicze Muzyki Polskiej | TWMP
Umbrella organization founded in 1928 that successfully gained state support for the promotion of Polish music. Its mission included the performance and publication of both early music (under the auspices of one of its branches, the Association of Enthusiasts for Early Music) and contemporary Polish music. It published *Muzyka Polska,* a main forum for the musical intelligentsia. It also published the musicology journals *Kwartalnik Muzyczny* (from 1928) and *Rocznik Muzykologiczny* (1935–36). The concert tour organization ORMUZ also operated under its auspices. Renamed the Polish Music Society on the eve of the war and continued limited operations during the occupation. Dissolved in 1945 when it was folded into PWM.

Key people: Bronisław Rutkowski, Tadeusz Ochlewski, Teodor Zalewski, Stefan Kisielewski, Adolf Chybiński.

PWM | Polskie Wydawnictwo Muzyczne | Polish Music Publishers
Founded in 1945 by Tadeusz Ochlewski as a successor to the Polish Music Publishing Society. Played a key role in supporting modernist composition, all while publishing a high volume of works aimed at students and amateurs. Remains to this day the most significant Polish music publishing house.

Key people: Tadeusz Ochlewski.

Ruch Muzyczny | Musical Currents (lit. musical movement)
Main forum of the postwar musical intelligentsia, founded in 1945 and published by PWM. Conceived of by Stefan Kisielewski as a successor to *Muzyka Polska.* It published articles on musical modernism and the state of musical culture in Poland. Forced to stop publishing in 1949 presumably due to its overt support for modernist ("formalist") composition. Reopened in 1957 and continued publishing, with various closures and changes in mission to the present.

Key people: Stefan Kisielewski, Zygmunt Mycielski, Bronisław Rutkowski, Jerzy Broszkiewicz, Stefania Łobaczewska, Roman Haubenstock (-Ramati).

Union of Polish Composers | Związek Kompozytorów Polskich | ZKP
From 1945, the main professional organization of Polish composers and musicologists, through which state funding and performance opportunities were channeled. It was formed from the Association of Polish Composers, an interwar association. Yearly congresses of the ZKP were major events that figure heavily in the historiography of

postwar Polish composition. Notable for its considerable autonomy from the state and the indifference of many of its members to state socialism. A relatively elite group, its membership of about 170 during the period of this book was dwarfed by the thousands of musicians who belonged to the Professional Union of Musicians (Związek Zawodowy Muzyków), which included performers and composers of "light" music.

The presidents of the ZKP during the early postwar period were Piotr Perkowski (1945–48), Zygmunt Mycielski (1948–50), Witold Rudziński (1950–51), and Tadeusz Szeligowski (1951–54).

Warsaw Conservatory | Państwowe Konserwatorium Muzyczne, Państwowa Wyższa Szkoła Muzyczna w Warszawie

The interwar years in Poland saw a great diversity of music schools that catered to both professional and amateur students, many of which were private or run by local music associations. Of these, the Warsaw Conservatory (State Music Conservatory) was the premiere institution for advanced music education in Poland. Nationalized in 1918, it was closed during the first year of the occupation. It was reopened under official German control in September 1940 but continued to teach a prewar curriculum. After the war, music education in Poland was standardized and institutions devoted to professional music training were renamed State Higher Schools of Music. The Warsaw Conservatory thus became the State Higher School of Music in Warsaw. (It should not be confused with the Fryderyk Chopin Higher School of Music, also in Warsaw, which was a distinct institution operated by the Warsaw Music Society and had used that name since 1919.) Today the Warsaw Conservatory is known as the Chopin University of Music.

As faculty: Karol Szymanowski, Kazimierz Sikorski, Piotr Rytel, Bolesław Woytowicz. *As students*: Grażyna Bacewicz, Mateusz Gliński, Stefan Kisielewski, Witold Lutosławski, Tadeusz Ochlewski, Roman Palester, Andrzej Panufnik, Piotr Perkowski, Bronisław Rutkowski.

Warsaw Philharmonic | Filharmonia Warszawska

Founded in 1901, the concert hall and its orchestra would become the most significant venue for classical music in Poland. Jewish musicians were prominent in the ensemble and in its audiences. The hall was heavily damaged in 1939, and the institution was shuttered by official decree during the occupation. Jewish members of the orchestra who had been imprisoned in the Warsaw Ghetto founded the Jewish Symphony Orchestra, while many Polish members joined the Philharmonic of the General Government in Cracow. After the war there were contentious fights over the future of the institution, and it was eventually nationalized and transformed into the National Philharmonic in Warsaw.

Key people: Leopold Julian Kronenberg, Aleksander Rajchman, Grzegorz Fitelberg, Witold Hugo Baruch, Jan Maklakiewicz.

Notes

INTRODUCTION

1. See Porter-Szűcs, *Poland in the Modern World*, 146, for a summary of war deaths.

2. Interwar census data such as these, although essential for understanding the demographics of the country, are also problematic because they assume that ethnic categories are clearly definable and mutually exclusive. See Zubrzycki, *The Crosses of Auschwitz*, 55–56, note 32.

3. Nidecka, *Żydzi w kulturze muzycznej Galicji*; Guesnet, Matis, and Polonsky, *Jews and Music-Making in the Polish Lands*; Jakubczyk-Ślęczka, "Musical Life of the Jewish Community in Interwar Galicia"; Błaszczyk, *Żydzi w kulturze muzycznej ziem polskich*; Fater, *Muzyka żydowska w Polsce*; Fuks, *Muzyka ocalona*.

4. The historiography of concert music in Poland has focused on processes of aesthetic development that span from the 1930s to the 1960s rather than on (Polish Jewish) trauma. See Thomas, *Polish Music since Szymanowski*; Bylander, *Engaging Cultural Ideologies*; Jagiełło-Skupińska, Zymer, and Grzywacz, *Warsaw Autumn as a Realisation of Karol Szymanowski's Vision*. For a theorization of this phenomenon that focuses on ideologies of modernization and center-periphery dynamics, see Vest, *Awangarda*. An important exception is Naliwajek, *Sounds of Apocalypse*.

5. Alexander, "Toward a Theory of Cultural Trauma," 10.

6. Lorenz and Bevernage, *Breaking Up Time*; Jordheim, "Against Periodization."

7. See Jakubowska, *Patrons of History*, ch. 2; Walicki, "Polish Conceptions of the Intelligentsia"; Żarnowski, "Inteligencja polska"; Bauer, "The Ideological Roots of the Polish Jewish Intelligentsia."

252 | Notes to Pages 4–9

8. On eastern Europe as a foil to western European modernity, see Wolff, *Inventing Eastern Europe,* and Karnes, "Inventing Eastern Europe." On interwar Poland specifically, see Ciancia, *On Civilization's Edge.*

9. Khan, "The Sociology of Elites," 362.

10. For a synthesis of this wide literature, see Weber, "Art Music and Social Class."

11. "Od Redakcji," *Muzyka* 1, no. 2 (1924): n.p.

12. For a discussion of social circles as a defining aspect of Polish social resilience, albeit in a much later period, see Wedel, "The Ties That Bind in Polish Society."

13. Vest, *Awangarda.*

14. For overviews of culture, politics, religion, and daily life among Polish Jewry of this time, see Polonsky, *The Jews in Poland and Russia,* 3: chs. 1–5; Biale, "A Journey between Worlds"; and Mendelsohn, *The Jews of East Central Europe,* ch. 1.

15. Endelman, "Assimilation"; Weeks, "The Best of Both Worlds."

16. HaCohen, *The Music Libel,* 5.

17. Mendelsohn, "On the Jewish Presence in Nineteenth-Century European Musical Life"; Conway, *Jewry in Music.* The foundational scholarship on musical assimilation and nationalism has focused on the German context; see Botstein, "The Aesthetics of Assimilation and Affirmation;" Steinberg, "Mendelssohn's Music and German-Jewish Culture."

18. Goldberg, "On the Wings of Aesthetic Beauty," esp. 414–16.

19. Goldberg, "On the Wings of Aesthetic Beauty," 416.

20. Dubrowska, "Leopold Julian Kronenberg"; Dziadek, "Powstanie i pierwszy okres działalności Filharmonii (1901–1908)."

21. Landau-Czajka, *Syn będzie Lech,* ch. 1; Polonsky, *The Jews in Poland and Russia,* 3:131–34; Mendelsohn, *The Jews of East Central Europe,* 67; Lichten, "Notes on the Assimilation and Acculturation of Jews in Poland"; Kijek, "Was It Possible to Avoid 'Hebrew Assimilation'?"

22. Polonsky, *The Jews in Poland and Russia,* 3:61. See also Bauer, "The Ideological Roots of the Polish Jewish Intelligentsia."

23. Shore, *Caviar and Ashes*; Skaff, *Law of the Looking Glass,* esp. 167–84; Holmgren, "Cabaret Nation."

24. I underscore here the broadness of "Jewishness" and the challenges of reducing it to the narrower categories of religion, race, ethnicity, or nation. See Batnitzky, *How Judaism Became a Religion*; Gonzalez-Lesser, "Jewishness as *Sui Generis.*"

25. Mendelsohn, *The Jews of East Central Europe,* 30–31.

26. Polonsky, *The Jews in Poland and Russia,* 3:136–37.

27. Prokop-Janiec, *Polish-Jewish Literature.*

28. On the methodological challenges of studying Jews on the edges of Jewishness, see Miller and Ury, "Cosmopolitanism: The End of Jewishness?"; Endelman, *Leaving the Jewish Fold.*

29. In adopting this historically and culturally bounded definition of antisemitism, I am influenced by David Engel's critique of the term's use as an ahistorical catchall for a wide variety of anti-Jewish prejudices and actions, and

Notes to Pages 9–14 | 253

by the blossoming of scholarship about the historiography and conceptual undercarriage of the term in response to him. See Engel, "Away from a Definition of Antisemitism"; Judaken, "AHR Roundtable: Rethinking Anti-Semitism"; Goldberg, Ury, and Weiser, *Key Concepts in the Study of Antisemitism*; and Ury and Miron, *Antisemitism and the Politics of History*.

30. Porter, *When Nationalism Began to Hate*, 16.

31. Ury, *Barricades and Banners*; Michlic, *Poland's Threatening Other*; Blobaum, *Antisemitism and Its Opponents*; Krzywiec, *Chauvinism, Polish Style*.

32. For an overview, see Porter-Szűcs, *Poland in the Modern World*, ch. 2 and 6.

33. Michlic, *Poland's Threatening Other*.

34. Polonsky, "Why Did They Hate Tuwim and Boy So Much?"

35. Snyder, *The Reconstruction of Nations*, 59.

36. Volkov, "Antisemitism as a Cultural Code."

37. HaCohen, *The Music Libel*.

38. Hanebrink, *A Specter Haunting Europe*.

39. Mendelsohn, *The Jews of East Central Europe*, 42–43.

40. Moss, *An Unchosen People*, 18.

41. Polonsky, *The Jews in Poland and Russia*, 3:87.

42. Polonsky, *The Jews in Poland and Russia*, 3:79–91.

43. Moss, *An Unchosen People*.

44. Filar and Patterson, *From Buchenwald to Carnegie Hall*, 36–37.

45. Weeks, "The Best of Both Worlds."

46. I prefer "Pole" over more cumbersome phrases, such as "Polish-Polish" or "ethnic/Catholic Polish," because it conveys the unmarked, hegemonic status of ethnic Polishness at this time. On these alternatives, see Underhill, "Bruno Schulz's Galician Diasporism," 28, note 19, and Aleksiun, "Regards from My 'Shtetl,'" 60.

47. Gilbert, *Music in the Holocaust*; Flam, *Singing for Survival*; Wlodarski, "Musical Testimonies of Terezín"; Karas, *Music in Terezín*; and Beckerman, "Postcard from New York—Trio from Terezín."

48. Calico, *Arnold Schoenberg's "A Survivor from Warsaw"*; Wlodarski, *Musical Witness*, chs. 1–2; and, more broadly, Potter, *Art of Suppression*.

49. The stark differences for musicians between the German occupation of eastern and western Europe is evinced in the essays collected in Fanning and Levi, *The Routledge Handbook to Music under German Occupation*.

50. For examples of such scholarship, see Loeffler, "In Memory of Our Murdered (Jewish) Children"; Karnes, "Recollecting Jewish Musics from the Baltic Bloodlands"; and Milewski, "Hidden in Plain View."

51. Steinlauf, *Bondage to the Dead*, ch. 2.

52. In addition to the research of Jan T. Gross, discussed in greater detail below, studies that examine this more complicated Polish positionality include Grabowski, *Hunt for the Jews*; Zimmerman, *The Polish Underground and the Jews*; Kornbluth, *The August Trials*, chs. 1–2; Biskupska, *Survivors*.

53. Zubrzycki, *The Crosses of Auschwitz*; Steinlauf, *Bondage to the Dead*; Huener, *Auschwitz, Poland, and the Politics of Commemoration*; and Glowacka and Zylinska, *Imaginary Neighbors*.

254 | Notes to Pages 14–27

54. Gross, *Neighbors*; Zubrzycki, "Narrative Shock and Polish Memory Remaking"; Polonsky and Michlic, *The Neighbors Respond*.

55. Gross, *Upiorna dekada*, 58–59. Examples of such work include Brown, *A Biography of No Place*; Underhill, "Re-Judaizing the Polish (Studies) Landscape"; Shore, *Caviar and Ashes*; Meng, *Shattered Spaces*.

56. Gross, *Upiorna dekada*, 58–59.

57. For critiques of "silence" as a paradigm in Holocaust studies, see Cesarani and Sundquist, *After the Holocaust*; Diner, *We Remember with Reverence and Love*.

58. Wlodarski, *Musical Witness*, 1.

59. Gordon, *Ghostly Matters*, esp. 19.

60. See Bothe and Nesselrodt, "Survivor: Towards a Conceptual History"; Judt, *Postwar*, 803–31.

61. Biess, "Feelings in the Aftermath," 43.

62. In *The Era of the Witness*, Wieviorka interprets the 1961 trial of Adolf Eichmann, a key architect of the Final Solution, as inaugurating this shift. See also Felman, *The Juridical Unconscious*, ch. 3; Dean, *The Moral Witness*, ch. 3.

63. Haltof, *Polish Film and the Holocaust*; Milewski, "Hidden in Plain View."

64. Brenner, *Polish Literature and the Holocaust*.

65. Shore, *Caviar and Ashes*, 6.

66. Cizmic, *Performing Pain*; Sprigge, *Socialist Laments*; Rogers, *Resonant Recoveries*.

67. The topic of representation and its limits was a main concern of trauma studies as it entered humanities disciplines in the 1990s. See Bond and Craps, *Trauma*, chs. 2–3.

68. There is a rich discourse about generations in Polish musicology, indicative of the weight this concept held for many twentieth-century composers and their interpreters. See, for example, Lindstedt, "Pokolenia kompozytorskie"; Ciesielski, "Pokolenie kompozytorskie 'debiut 1930.'"

69. See Abosede George's comments in Lichtenstein, "AHR Conversation: Each Generation Writes Its Own History of Generations," 1522.

70. Thomas, *Polish Music since Szymanowski*, 93–97.

71. For a discussion of this historiography, see Vest, *Awangarda*, 176–79. On the institutions and aesthetics of the Polish avant-garde, see Vest, *Awangarda*; Jakelski, *Making New Music in Cold War Poland*; Reyland, "The Spaces of Dream"; Thomas, *Polish Music since Szymanowski*.

CHAPTER 1

1. Wightman, *Karol Szymanowski*, 234–44.

2. Downes, *Szymanowski, Eroticism and the Voices of Mythology*; Blobaum, *A Minor Apocalypse*, 233–40.

3. Quoted in Wightman, *Karol Szymanowski*, 238.

4. Cohen, *Stefan Wolpe*, 12; Sonevytsky, *Wild Music*, 23–24.

5. Drzewiecki, *Wspomnienia muzyka*, 83.

6. Vest, *Awangarda*, ch. 1.

Notes to Pages 27–32 | 255

7. Chylińska, *Karol Szymanowski*; Samson, *The Music of Szymanowski*.

8. Thomas, *Polish Music since Szymanowski*, ch. 1.

9. Shore, *Caviar and Ashes*, ch. 1; Makowiecki, *Warszawskie kawiarnie literackie*; Pinsker, *A Rich Brew*, ch. 2.

10. On Polish class distribution, see Żarnowski, *State, Society and Intelligentsia*, ch. 9.

11. Jedlicki, *A Suburb of Europe*, 221; Walicki, "Polish Conceptions of the Intelligentsia"; and Żarnowski, "Inteligencja polska."

12. Charle, *Birth of the Intellectuals*; Fulcher, *The Composer as Intellectual*, 3–4.

13. Jedlicki, *A Suburb of Europe*; Porter, *When Nationalism Began to Hate*, ch. 2; Blejwas, *Realism in Polish Politics*.

14. Gella, "The Life and Death of the Old Polish Intelligentsia."

15. Jakubowska, *Patrons of History*, 45. The Polish intelligentsia's inheritance of the gentry ethos also differentiates it from the Russian intelligentsia, for whom radicalism and social revolution were more important. See Walicki, "Polish Conceptions of the Intelligentsia."

16. Bauer, "The Ideological Roots of the Polish Jewish Intelligentsia."

17. Porter-Szűcs, *Poland in the Modern World*, 70. My understanding of cultural politics in interwar Poland also draws on Plach, *The Clash of Moral Nations*, and Ciancia, *On Civilization's Edge*.

18. Davies, *God's Playground*, 2:290–308.

19. Żarnowski, *State, Society and Intelligentsia*, ch. 9.

20. Micińska, *At the Crossroads, 1865–1918*, ch. 2.

21. BN, Mycielski papers, III 14360, "Pamiętnik," 7.

22. BnF, N.L.a. 89, Mycielski to Nadia Boulanger, 19 October 1931.

23. Karczewski, "Transnational Flows of Knowledge"; Karczewski, "Call Me by My Name."

24. Karczewski, "For a Pole, It All Was a Great Abomination," 1999.

25. Zygmunt Mycielski, reply to "Zasadnicze zagadnienia współczesnej kultury muzycznej w Polsce: Ankieta," *Muzyka Polska* 1, no. 2 (1934): 87.

26. Indicative of this shift, surveys in 1933 and 1934 by two major music periodicals, *Muzyka* and *Muzyka Polska*, asked about the "reasons for the collapse of musical culture [*ruch muzyczny*] in Poland." "Ankieta," *Muzyka* 10, no. 1 (1933): 18; "Zasadnicze zagadnienia współczesnej kultury muzycznej w Polsce: Ankieta," *Muzyka Polska* 1, no. 2 (1934): 85–86.

27. Teodor Zalewski, [reply to "Zasadnicze zagadnienia"], *Muzyka Polska* 1, no. 2 (1934): 106; Bronisław Rutkowski, [reply to "Zasadnicze zagadnienia"], *Muzyka Polska* 1, no. 2 (1934): 113.

28. Michał Kondracki, "ORMUZ," *Prosto z Mostu* 1, no. 12 (1935): 1; Przerembska, *Ideały wychowania w edukacji muzycznej*, 100–110.

29. Roman Palester, [reply to "Zasadnicze zagadnienia"], *Muzyka Polska* 1, no. 2 (1934): 124; Kondracki, "ORMUZ," 1.

30. Mrygoń, *Stanisław Wiechowicz* 1:14–55.

31. Stanisław Wiechowicz, [reply to "Zasadnicze zagadnienia"], *Muzyka Polska* 1, no. 2 (1934): 111; Tadeusz Szeligowski, [reply to "Zasadnicze zagadnienia"], *Muzyka Polska* 1, no. 2 (1934): 99.

256 | Notes to Pages 33–38

32. On the intelligentsia's earlier commitment to social hierarchy through projects aimed at "improving" the lower classes, see Porter, *When Nationalism Began to Hate*, 55–57.

33. Chowrimootoo and Guthrie, "Colloquy: Musicology and the Middlebrow," 328.

34. Wood, *Becoming Metropolitan*.

35. Holmgren, "Cabaret Nation," 279.

36. Sztyma, "On the Dance Floor, on the Screen, on the Stage"; Rothstein, "The Polish Tin Pan Alley, a Jewish Street"; Holmgren, "The Polish-Language Cabaret Song."

37. Holmgren, "Acting Out."

38. Tadeusz Ochlewski, [response to "Zasadnicze zagadnienia"], *Muzyka Polska* 1, no. 2 (1934): 88. See also Stanisław Szpinalski, "Ormuz czy radio?," *Prosto z Mostu* 5, no. 7 (1939): 5; Bronisław Rutkowski, [response to "Zasadnicze zagadnienia"], *Muzyka Polska* 1, no. 2 (1934): 112–13. The journal *Muzyka* did, however, publish translations of several more sympathetic articles about jazz. César Saerchinger, "Co to jest jazz-band?," *Muzyka* 2, no. 6 (1925): 240–43; Jack Hylton, "Narodziny i życie Jazz'u," *Muzyka* 10, no. 1 (1933): 12–14.

39. Konstanty Régamey, "Z muzyki: Ormuz," *Prosto z Mostu* 2, no. 28 (1936): 7 (emphasis in the original).

40. Quoted in "Muzyka polska w niebezpieczeństwie! (Pierwsze wyniki ankiety 'Muzyki')," *Muzyka* 10, nos. 4–6 (1933): 137.

41. Helman, *Roman Palester*, 27–35; BJ, SMM, Teczka 1, "Okólnik 2," 10 March 1935.

42. BJ, 289–11, Palester to Zdzisław Jachimecki, 3 January 1939.

43. Roman Palester, "Kryzys modernizmu muzycznego," *Kwartalnik Muzyczny*, nos. 14–15 (1932): 489–503, here 489.

44. Palester, "Kryzys modernizmu muzycznego," 502–3.

45. Palester, [reply to "Zasadnicze zagadnienia"], *Muzyka Polska* 1, no. 2 (1934): 119–25, here 122.

46. Palester, [reply to "Zasadnicze zagadnienia"], 124.

47. Michalski, *Powróćmy jak za dawnych lat*, 712.

48. Holmgren, "Acting Out."

49. Helman, *Roman Palester*, 42–43.

50. Michał Kondracki, "O kierunkach współczesnej muzyki polskiej," *Muzyka Polska* 4, no. 6 (1937): 267–73, here 271.

51. Konstanty Régamey, "Z ruchu muzycznego w Polsce: Warszawa," *Muzyka Polska* 3, no. 6 (1936): 409.

52. Sieradz, *The Beginnings of Polish Musicology*, and "100 Years of Polish Musicology," special issue of *Musicology Today* 9 (2012).

53. Adolf Chybiński, "O zadaniach historycznej muzykologii w Polsce," *Muzyka* 7, no. 10 (1930): 587–95; Adolf Chybiński, "Dookoła dawnej muzyki," *Pion* 3, no. 8 (1935): 2.

54. Blobaum, "The 'Woman Question' in Russian Poland."

55. Kałwa, *Kobieta aktywna w Polsce międzywojennej*.

56. Ryta Gnus, "Muzyczki polskie w okresie XX-lecia niepodległości," *Bluszcz* 74, no. 46 (1938): 57–59; S. Jagodzińska-Niekraszowa, "Zarys

twórczości polskich kompozytorek XIX i XX stulecia," *Muzyka Polska* 2, no. 8 (1935): 247–54.

57. Lindstedt, "Why Are Our Women-Composers So Little Known?"; Dziadek, "'Female' Music Criticism in Poland 1890–1939."

58. Suchmiel, *Działalność naukowa kobiet w uniwersytecie we Lwowie*, 131–35. For an overview of women's political and social activism in Poland during this period, see Żarnowska, "Women's Political Participation in Inter-War Poland," and Żarnowska and Szwarc, eds., *Równe prawa i nierówne szanse.*

59. Piekarski, *Przerwany kontrapunkt*, 222–24.

60. For a discussion of postwar gender representation in Polish musicology, see Beszterda, "Female Composers, Gender and Politics in Communist Poland."

61. AKP, Lissa Papers, "Życiorys"; Szalsza, "Nieznane fakty z życia Zofii Lissy."

62. Zofja Lissa, "Moje najgłębsze wzruszenie muzyczne," *Muzyka* 12, nos. 3–4 (1935): 76–77.

63. Her findings were published as Zofja Lissa, "O harmonice Aleksandra Skrjabina," *Kwartalnik Muzyczny*, no. 8 (1930): 320–55, and Zofja Lissa, "Geschichtliche Vorform der Zwölftontechnik," *Acta Musicologica* 7 (1935): 15–21.

64. For instance, Zofja Lissa, "Politonalność i atonalność w świetle najnowszych badań," *Kwartalnik Muzyczny*, nos. 6–7 (1930): 192–237.

65. Drzewiecki, *Wspomnienia*, 85–86; Vest, "Discursive Foundations," 306. Major contributions to the 1936 polemics about twelve-tone music among the musical intelligentsia include: Józef Koffler and Stefania Łobaczewska, "Dwugłos polemiczny: O muzyce dwunastotonowej," *Muzyka* 13, nos. 1–6 (1936): 20–22; Konstanty Régamey, "Czy atonalizm jest naprawdę atonalny?," *Muzyka Polska* 3, no. 1 (1936): 32–39; Stefan Kisielewski, [Review of] "Józef Koffler: *Variations sur une valse de Johann Strauss*," *Muzyka Polska* 3, no. 6 (1936): 401–4.

66. Kałwa, *Kobieta aktywna*, ch. 4; Plach, *The Clash of Moral Nations*, ch. 4.

67. Zofja Lissa, "Radjo we współczesnej kulturze muzycznej (Psychologiczne, artystyczne, społeczne i pedagogiczne problematy radja)," *Kwartalnik Muzyczny*, no. 16 (1932): 643–59. Prior to 1926 the number of registered radio receivers in the territory of the Second Republic was in the low hundreds; by 1932, there were over 310,000. See Kaszuba, "The Development of Radio Services in the Second Polish Republic."

68. Lissa, *Muzyka i film.*

69. Skaff, *The Law of the Looking Glass*, chs. 5 and 7.

70. Lissa, "Muzyka dla Karola"; Lissa, "Muzïka v sovetskom L'vove," 91. See also the Russian-language certificate signed by Julia Bristiger on 3 August 1944, which is held in Lissa's papers in AKP, which claims that Lissa helped the leadership of the Communist Party of Western Ukraine.

71. Zofja Lissa, "Muzyka dla mas," *Sygnały*, no. 17 (1936): 2.

72. Jazowska, "Helena Dorabialska."

73. Dziadek, "Twórczość krytycznomuzyczna Stefanii Łobaczewskiej."

74. Łobaczewska, "Kobieta w muzyce," 176.

75. Kondracka, "Kobiety na Uniwersytetach," 280–82. During the 1930s only about 3 percent of lecturers and professors at Polish universities were women.

258 | Notes to Pages 41–47

76. Adolf Chybiński, "O siedmiu pieczęciach dawnej muzyki," *Lwowskie Wiadomości Muzyczne i Literackie* 8, no. 74 (1933): 2–3; Muszkalska, "Bronisława Wójcik-Keuprulian," 62.

77. Wójcik-Keuprulian, *Korespondencja do Szwajcarii,* 154–55 (letter to Ludwik Bronarski, 30 July 1935).

78. Fuks, *Żydzi w Warszawie,* 246, 342.

79. Kronenberg, *Wspomnienia,* 164. The details of the incident are described in Dziadek, "Zdzisław Birnbaum."

80. Kronenberg, *Wspomnienia,* 166.

81. Jan Maklakiewicz, "Zagadnienia współczesnej twórczości muzycznej w Polsce," *Muzyka Polska* 1, no. 1 (1934): 33–37, here 36.

82. Długońska, "Piotr Rytel."

83. Karol Szymanowski, "Kwestia żydostwa," in *Pisma,* 2:238–40 (emphasis in the original). For a discussion, see Tuchowski, *Nationalism, Chauvinism and Racism,* 113–16.

84. Jerzy Waldorff, "Z batalistyki muzycznej," *Kurier Poranny,* 15 December 1938; Urbanek, *Waldorff,* 71–73.

85. B.R., "Z ruchu muzycznego w Polsce: Warszawa," *Muzyka Polska* 2, no. 6 (1935): 143–45, here 144.

86. HaCohen, *The Music Libel against the Jews.*

87. Prokop-Janiec, *Polish-Jewish Literature in the Interwar Years,* especially ch. 1.

88. Polonsky, "The New Jewish Politics and Its Discontents."

89. "Od redakcji," *Muzyka* 1, no. 2 (1924), copyright page; BJ, PWM, pudło no. 4 G-5/1–126, 3, 28, Gliński to Chybiński, 24 September 1924 and 28 December 1924.

90. Gliński and Glińska, *Testament,* 59; "Międzynarodowe Tow. Muzyki Współczesnej," *Muzyka* 1, no. 1 (1924): 46–47; BJ, PWM, G-5/3, 24 September 1924.

91. Replies from Aleksander Tansman and Józef Koffler to "Muzyka polska w niebezpieczeństwie," *Muzyka* 11, nos. 10–11 (1934): 369–70.

92. Plohn, "Muzyka we Lwowie a Żydzi" (the article is dated September 1936). Similar articles include Zofja Lissa, "Rola Żydów w rozwoju muzyki europejskiej," *Chwila,* 15 December 1929, 10–11; Apte, "Udział Żydów w muzyce."

93. For a similar point in the German context, see Loeffler, "Richard Wagner's 'Jewish Music,'" 10.

94. Artur Mehrer, "Jacques Halevy," *Nasza Opinja,* no. 86 (1937): 8; Artur Mehrer, "W stulecie urodzin G. Bizet," *Nasza Opinja,* no. 167 (1938): 11.

95. Serialized as Józef Reiss, "Dusza żydostwa w muzyce," *Muzyk Wojskowy* 3 (1928), no. 9, 1–4; no. 10, 1–2; no. 11, 2–3; no. 13, 1–2; no. 14, 1–2.

96. Loeffler, *The Most Musical Nation,* 127; Móricz, *Jewish Identities.*

97. Nemtsov, "Neue jüdische Musik in Polen."

98. Nemtsov, "Neue jüdische Musik in Polen," 92.

99. Ury, "Strange Bedfellows?"

100. Loeffler, "Richard Wagner's 'Jewish Music,'" 4; Bohlman, *Jewish Music and Modernity,* 190–91.

Notes to Pages 47–54 | 259

101. Reiss, "Dusza żydostwa," no. 10, 2.

102. Reiss, "Dusza żydostwa," no. 13, 2.

103. Sperlich, "'S' is nito kein Nechten': Notizen zu Juliusz Wolfsohn."

104. "Jüdische Musik: Ein Verein zur Förderung jüdischer Musik in Wien," *Die Stimme*, 22 March 1928, 11; Nemtsov and Schröder-Nauenburg, "Zwischen Zionismus und Antisemitismus."

105. "Professor Julius Wolfsohn (zu seinem 50. Geburtstage)," *Die Stimme*, 2 January 1930, 10; "Konzertabend Prof. Juliusz Wolfsohn," *Die Stimme*, 13 April 1934, 7; Juliusz Wolfsohn, "Wie steht es mit der neuen jüdischen Musik?," *Die Stimme*, 28 September 1933, 9.

106. T. Lot, "Prof. Wolfsohn in Krakau," *Die Stimme*, 6 March 1930, 10.

107. "Juliusz Wolfsohn," *Die Stimme*, 9 February 1933, 8.

108. Gliński and Glińska, *Testament*, 64.

109. N. Landau, "Koncert Żyd. Tow. Art. Lit., a szerzenie kultury muzycznej," *Chwila*, 5 November 1936, 9.

110. Bohlman, *The World Centre for Jewish Music in Palestine*, 57.

111. Józef Koffler, "O żydowską kulturę muzyczną," *Nasza Opinja*, no. 66 (1936): 12.

CHAPTER 2

1. Jakubczyk-Ślęczka, "Jewish Music Organizations in Interwar Galicia."

2. For instance, the Jewish Music Society (Żydowskie Towarzystwo Muzyczne) had monthly dues of 1 złoty (or 50 grosze, if one was a professional musician). BN XIXA, 1a, "Statut Żydowskiego Towarzystwa Muzycznego" (1933).

3. Pekacz, *Music in the Culture of Polish Galicia*, 124–37; Jaworski, "Towarzystwa muzyczne w Królestwie Polskim"; Sargeant, *Harmony and Discord*, ch. 2.

4. For discussions and critiques of this idea, see Nowak, "System wartości społeczeństwa polskiego"; Wedel, *The Unplanned Society*; Kennedy, *Professionals, Power, and Solidarity*, ch. 5; Bohlman, *Musical Solidarities*, 41–49.

5. Mannheim, "The Problem of Generations," 304.

6. Vest, *Awangarda*, ch. 1.

7. Bohlman and Pierce, "Friend and Force"; Helman, *Neoklasycyzm w muzyce polskiej*.

8. For a discussion of Polish Jewish musicians who studied in Germany in the pre-Nazi era, see Sacks, "Ostbahnhof Berlin."

9. AKP, SMMP, Dokumenty główne, "Członkowie Stowarzyszenia Młodych Muzyków Polaków w Paryżu."

10. Bohlman and Pierce, "Friend and Force."

11. Quoted in Jasiński, *Koniec epoki*, 313–14.

12. Helman, *Neoklasycyzm w muzyce polskiej*.

13. Czesław Marek, "Kilka słów o mej 'Sinfonia brevis,'" *Muzyka* 5, no. 11 (1928): 521.

14. Quoted in Gąsiorowska, *Bacewicz*, 102–3.

15. Konstanty Régamey, "Muzyka polska na tle współczesnych prądów," *Muzyka Polska* 4, nos. 7–8 (1937): 341–52, here 351.

260 | Notes to Pages 54–62

16. Jakelski, "Górecki's *Scontri*"; Jakelski, "Witold Lutosławski and the Ethics of Abstraction."

17. Taruskin, "Back to Whom?," 293.

18. Szymanowski, "Uwagi w sprawie współczesnej opinii muzycznej w Polsce," in *Pisma* 1:33–47, here 44–45.

19. McMahon, *The Races of Europe*. On race science in Poland, see Stauter-Halsted, "Bio-Politics between Nation and Empire"; Gawin, *Race and Modernity*, 131–32.

20. Trochimczyk, "Chopin and the 'Polish Race'"; Helman, "The Dilemma of Twentieth-Century Polish Music."

21. Mosse, *Toward the Final Solution*, ch. 7; Balibar, "Racism and Nationalism"; McMahon, *The Races of Europe*; Hudson, "From 'Nation' to 'Race,'" 257.

22. Karol Szymanowski, "Karol Szymanowski o muzyce współczesnej: Wywiad specjalny *Kuriera Polskiego*," in *Pisma* 1:58–66, here 60.

23. Karol Szymanowski, "Fryderyk Chopin," in *Pisma* 1:89–102, here 98.

24. Z.[ygmunt] M.[ycielski], "Paryż: Stowarzyszenie Młodych Muzyków Polaków w Paryżu," *Muzyka Polska* 2, no. 6 (1935): 156.

25. *Stowarzyszenie Młodych Muzyków Polaków w Paryżu*, 4.

26. AKP, SMMP, correspondence received, K-LV/102, speech by Łabuński from 1931.

27. Mgl, "Impresje muzyczne," *Muzyka* 8, no. 2 (1931): 86–87, here 86.

28. Fulcher, *The Composer as Intellectual*, 20–22.

29. Cała, *Żyd—wróg odwieczny?*, 335–37. On the rapprochement between the radical right and the Catholic Church in Poland during the late 1920s, see Porter-Szűcs, *Faith and Fatherland*, 179–86 and chs. 6–9.

30. Junyk, *Foreign Modernism*, 16.

31. Camiscioli, *Reproducing the French Race*, 34–48.

32. *Stowarzyszenie Młodych Muzyków Polaków w Paryżu*, 28.

33. Zahra, *The Great Departure*, 130; Móricz, *In Stravinsky's Orbit*.

34. "Konkurs Stowarzyszenia Młodych Muzyków Polaków w Paryżu," *Przegląd Muzyczny* 4, no. 6 (1928): 14.

35. Letter to Édouard Ganche, 11 February 1927, quoted in Poniatowska, "Le 'credo musical,'" 46. On his mazurkas, see Milewski, "The Mazurka and National Imaginings," ch. 4.

36. Suchowiejko, "Recepcja muzyki polskiej w Paryżu."

37. Régamey, "Muzyka polska na tle współczesnych prądów," 342.

38. Tansman, *Regards en arrière*, 141–43.

39. Stefania Łobaczewska, "U źródeł współczesnej muzyki polskiej," *Życie Sztuki* 3 (1938): 48–94, here 87–91.

40. Jachimecki, "Muzyka polska od roku 1915 do roku 1930," 934.

41. Bronisław Rutkowski, "Dziesięciolecie pracy Stowarzyszenia Miłośników Dawnej Muzyki w Warszawie," *Muzyka Polska* 3, no. 6 (1936): 375–79; Zalewski, *Pół wieku*, 87.

42. T. Z., "Towarzystwo Wydawnicze Muzyki Polskiej," *Muzyka Polska* 1, no. 3 (1934): 240–43; Zalewski, *Pół wieku*, 97–114.

Notes to Pages 62–65 | 261

43. See, for instance, the declaration from the society's congress, held in July 1935. Reprinted in Bronisław Rutkowski, "Muzyka w roku 1935," *Życie Sztuki* 3 (1938): 307–8; Applegate, *Bach in Berlin*, ch. 3.

44. Bronisław Rutkowski, "10-lecie Stowarzyszenia Miłośników Dawnej Muzyki," *Gazeta Muzyczna* 2, no. 1 (1937): 1.

45. *Towarzystwo Muzyki Polskiej: Katalog wydawnictw (1939).* Many contemporary scores were also available on a rental basis from the Polish Music Publishing Society; see AAN, Konsulat RP w Marsylii, 486, "Towarzystwo Wydawnicze Muzyki Polskiej: Muzyka Polska Współczesna."

46. Konstanty Régamey, "Czy atonalizm jest naprawdę atonalny?," *Muzyka Polska* 3, no. 1 (1936): 32–39; Michał Kondracki, "O kierunkach współczesnej muzyki polskiej," *Muzyka Polska* 4, no. 6 (1937): 267–80.

47. BJ, SMM, Teczka 1, "Okólnik 2" (10 March 1935).

48. "Z Towarzystwa Muzyki Polskiej," *Muzyka Polska* 6, no. 5 (1939): 282–83.

49. Marciniec, "Ministerstwo Sztuki i Kultury," 104.

50. Marciniec, "Ministerstwo Sztuki i Kultury," 99.

51. Rogoyska, "Z dziejów mecenatu artystycznego w Polsce w latach 1918–1930," 139. For musicians' opinions on the matter, see "Notatki," *Gazetka Muzyczna* 2, no. 3 (1937): 2.

52. Wojciechowski, "Próby integracji kultury plastycznej."

53. Wojciechowski, "Próby integracji kultury plastycznej," 562.

54. Pollakówna, "Ministerstwo Sztuki i Kultury."

55. BJ, PWM, P-28/125, Pulikowski to Chybiński, 17 May 1936.

56. See the tabulations in Pierce, "Life and Death for Music," 73, table 1.

57. As described in BJ, PWM, P-28/68, Pulikowski to Chybiński, 8 September 1934.

58. BUP, 805 III, Chybiński to Bronarski, 26 December 1930. See also Sieradz, "*Kwartalnik Muzyczny*," 70.

59. Zalewski, *Pół wieku*, 183; Jerzy Walldorf [Waldorff], writing in *Prosto z Mostu*, cited in *Muzyka Polska* 4, no. 6 (1937): 297; BUP, 805 III, Chybiński to Bronarski, 24 January 1930.

60. Gliński and Glińska, *Testament Mateusza Glińskiego*, 64.

61. See the discussion in BJ, PWM, M-19/18, Miketta to Chybiński, 17 November 1930; Piskurewicz, *W służbie nauki i oświaty*, 131.

62. BJ, PWM, P-28/68, Pulikowski to Chybiński, 8 September 1934; [Mateusz Gliński], "Klika czy nie klika?," *Muzyka* 14, no. 3 (1937): 84–86.

63. Zalewski, *Pół wieku*, 183.

64. BJ, PWM, S-10, Sikorski to Chybiński, 17 January 1936, 8 February 1936.

65. BJ, PWM, R-19/1–65, Rutkowski to Chybiński, 15 December 1936.

66. Polish nouns that refer to ethnic groups or nationalities are capitalized, while those of religious groups are not. While sometimes the capitalization of "Jew" (*Żyd*) is used to reflect a distinction between thinking of Jews as a national or ethnic group (*Żyd*) and a religious one (*żyd*), Chybiński's lowercase use of *żyd* is best understood as reinforcing the antisemitism of the passages in

262 | Notes to Pages 65–70

which the term appears. The capitalized *Żyd* is neutral and does not have the pejorative connotations of its Russian-language cognate.

67. BUP, 805 III, 154, Chybiński to Bronarski, 14 January 1937.

68. Cited in Sieradz, "*Kwartalnik Muzyczny*," 97 (Pulikowski to Chybiński, 1935).

69. Cited in Sieradz, "*Kwartalnik Muzyczny*," 377.

70. BUP, 805 III, 156, Chybiński to Bronarski, 29 January 1937.

71. Examples include B.[ronisław] R.[utkowski], "Z ruchu muzycznego w Polsce: Warszawa," *Muzyka Polska* 2, no. 6 (1935): 143–45; Tadeusz Szeligowski, "Wolność i kneble," *Muzyka Polska* 5, no. 11 (1938): 500–503; Jerzy Walldorf [Waldorff], "Totalistyczne finezje," *Muzyka Polska* 6, no. 2 (1939): 74–77.

72. AAN, Konsulat RP w Marsylii, 486, "Towarzystwo Wydawnicze Muzyki Polskiej: Muzyka Polska Współczesna."

73. Sieradz, "*Kwartalnik Muzyczny*," 384–85.

74. "Ormuz i Szarmuz," *Echo* 1, no. 5 (1937): 7–8.

75. "ORMUZ: IV rok działalności," *Muzyka Polska* 5, no. 6 (1938): 301–7.

76. Soviet influence is mentioned in A., "Muzyka przechodzi do natarcia," *Tygodnik Illustrowany*, no. 49 (1934): 971. On the Soviet projects, see Fairclough, *Classics for the Masses*; Edmunds, *The Soviet Proletarian Music Movement*, ch. 4.

77. Bronisław Rutkowski, "Organizacja ruchu muzycznego w Polsce," *Muzyka Polska* 1, no. 3 (1934): 180–83, here 183.

78. T.[adeusz] O.[chlewski], "Drugi rok działalności 'Ormuzu,'" *Muzyka Polska* 3, no. 3 (1936): 226–29; "ORMUZ: Pierwsze półrocze drugiego sezonu koncertowego," *Muzyka Polska* 2, no. 8 (1935): 309–10.

79. [Mateusz Gliński], "Impresje muzyczne: Tragedja bezrobocia i niemocy organizacyjnej naszych muzyków," *Muzyka* 11, no. 4 (1934): 163–64.

80. BN, Rps akc. 17260, Eugenia Umińska, "Wspomnienia warszawskie," 33.

81. Karol Szymanowski, "The Educational Role of Musical Culture in Society," in *Szymanowski on Music*, 281–317, here 284.

82. Szymanowski, "The Educational Role of Musical Culture in Society," 292.

83. Blejwas, *Realism in Polish Politics*; Jedlicki, *A Suburb of Europe*, ch. 5.

84. Leczyk, *Druga Rzeczpospolita*, 145; Ciancia, *On Civilization's Edge*, 8.

85. Ciancia, *On Civilization's Edge*, chs. 4 and 5.

86. Ciancia, *On Civilization's Edge*.

87. Michał Kondracki, "Rycerze Ormuzu," *Pion*, no. 38 (1937): 4.

88. Michał Kondracki, "ORMUZ," *Prosto z Mostu* 1, no. 12 (1935): 1

89. BN, Rps akc. 17260, Eugenia Umińska, "Wspomnienia warszawskie," 32.

90. BN, Rps akc. 17260, Eugenia Umińska, "Wspomnienia warszawskie," 31.

91. See, for instance, "Z Ormuzu," *Muzyka Polska* 5, no. 2 (1938): 85; Jan Gipski, "Krzemieniec," *Muzyka Polska* 3, no. 2 (1936): 140–41.

92. "ORMUZ na wołyńskim błocie," *Gazetka Muzyczna* 2, no. 5 (1937): 4.

93. Zdzisław Broncel, "Nieznany kraj muzyki: Rozmowa z H. Sztompką o polskiej zapadłej prowincji," *Prosto z Mostu* 1, no. 1 (1935): 9.

94. The one exception I have located describes the reactions of an "eleven-year-old Ukrainian peasant." Tadeusz Ochlewski, "Po pierwszym roku 'Ormuz'u,'" *Muzyka Polska* 2, no. 6 (1935): 157–60, here 159.

95. BJ, SMM, Teczka 1, Zarząd Okręgowy to SMM, 24 September 1935.

96. BJ, SMM, Teczka 1, Stanisław Lachman [?] to SMM, 25 September 1935.

97. BJ, SMM, Teczka 7. Surveys are preserved from the towns of Żywiec and Mielec.

98. Rutkowski, "Organizacja ruchu muzycznego w Polsce," *Muzyka Polska* 1, no. 3 (1934): 180–83, here 181.

99. Plach, *Clash of Moral Nations*, ch. 3.

100. T.[adeusz] O.[chlewski], "Drugi rok działalności 'Ormuzu,'" *Muzyka Polska* 3, no. 3 (1936): 226–29; Tadeusz Ochlewski, "Po pierwszym roku 'Ormuz'u,'" *Muzyka Polska* 2, no. 6 (1935): 157–60, here 157. On the Women's Union for Citizenship Work, see Plach, *Clash of Moral Nations*, 106.

101. BN, Rps akc. 17260, Eugenia Umińska, "Wspomnienia warszawskie," 33.

102. Rutkowski, "Organizacja ruchu muzycznego w Polsce," *Muzyka Polska* 1, no. 3 (1934): 180–83, here 181.

103. Tadeusz Ochlewski, response to the survey concerning "Zasadnicze zagadnienia współczesnej kultury muzycznej w Polsce," *Muzyka Polska* 1, no. 2 (1934): 88–92, here 88.

104. Stanisław Szpinalski, "ORMUZ czy radio?," *Prosto z Mostu* 5, no. 7 (1939): 5.

105. Zalewski, *Pół wieku*, 160.

106. BN, XIX A5, 1982 K 1026/37.

107. Tadeusz Ochlewski, "O.R. Muz.," *Muzyka Polska* 1, no. 4 (1934): 332–34, here 332.

108. ORMUZ wrote to the Association of Young Musicians in Cracow implying that it knew of these requirements before they appeared. See BJ, SMM, Teczka 1, ORMUZ to SMM, 20 August 1935. The regulations appear as "Okólnik nr. 80 z dnia 11 września 1935 w sprawie organizacji audycyj muzycznych na rok szkolny 1935/36 w państwowych gimnazjach ogólnokształcących," *Dziennik Urzędowy Ministerstwa Wyznań Religijnych i Oświecenia Publicznego Rzeczypospolitej Polskiej*, no. 8 (1935): 168–70; "Komunikat o organizowaniu audycyj muzycznych przy współudziale 'ORMUZU,'" *Dziennik Urzędowy Ministerstwa Wyznań Religijnych i Oświecenia Publicznego Rzeczypospolitej Polskiej*, no. 11 (1935): 236–37.

109. BJ, SMM, Teczka 7, "Projekt audycyj szkolnych" (likely from 1936).

110. BJ, SMM, Teczka 7.

111. Porter-Szűcs, *Poland in the Modern World*, 100–101; Rudnicki, "Anti-Jewish Legislation," 160–66. Kenneth B. Moss locates the turn toward Jewish despair already in the late 1920s in *An Unchosen People*.

112. Polonsky, *Politics in Independent Poland*, 419–35.

113. A major Polish-language source about the Reichsmusikkammer was Otto Graf, "Organizacja życia muzycznego w Niemczech," *Muzyka Polska* 2, no. 6 (1935): 113–26.

264 | Notes to Pages 73–79

114. Teodor Zalewski, "Problem organizacji zawodu muzycznego," *Muzyka Polska* 2, no. 6 (1935): 104–12; Piotr Perkowski, "Dookoła projektu Izby Muzyczej," *Muzyka* 12, nos. 3–4 (1935): 75; Marjan Neuteich, "Na marginesie projektu utworzenia Izby Muzycznej," *Pion* 3, no. 20 (1935): 3–4.

115. Steinweis, *Art, Ideology & Economics in Nazi Germany*, 17–20.

116. "Ankieta 'Muzyki Polskiej,'" *Muzyka Polska* 4, no. 1 (1937): 12–13. Responses were published across several issues from Witold Maliszewski, Stanisław Szpinalski, Jerzy Braun, Stanisław Wiechowicz, Stanisław Piasecki, Tadeusz Szeligowski, Ludomir Rogowski, and Zygmunt Mycielski.

117. Zygmunt Mycielski, "W odpowiedzi na ankietę," *Muzyka Polska* 4, no. 11 (1937): 503–5.

118. Stanisław Szpinalski, "Czy potrzebna jest planowość w organizacji życia muzycznego w Polsce?," *Muzyka Polska* 4, no. 2 (1937): 63–65.

119. Tadeusz Szeligowski, "Conditio sine qua non," *Muzyka Polska* 4, no. 9 (1937): 394–97.

120. Taruskin, *The Oxford History of Western Music* 4:476–79; Móricz, *Jewish Identities*, 214–15.

121. Jerzy Walldorf [Waldorff], "Totalistyczne finezje," *Muzyka Polska* 6, no. 2 (1939): 74–77; Walldorf [Waldorff], *Sztuka pod dyktaturą*.

122. J. Walldorf [Waldorff], "Obsesja osesków: Judeofobia," *Kurier Poranny*, 18 June 1939, 12.

123. Tadeusz Szeligowski, "Wolność i kneble," *Muzyka Polska* 5, no. 11 (1938): 500–503.

124. Tadeusz Szeligowski, "Dwie odpowiedzi," *Muzyka Polska* 6, no. 3 (1939): 141–45.

125. Reittererová and Reitterer, "Musik und Politik," 231.

126. Point 7 of the statute, as given in BJ, SMM, Teczka 1, SMM to Stanisław Potempki, 5 March 1937.

127. BJ, SMM, Teczka 2, "Statutowe sprawy"; BJ, SMM, Teczka 2, Włodzimierz Poźniak to Dyrekcji Gimnazjum Prywatnego P. P. Benedyktynek w Staniątkach, 15 November 1938.

128. BJ, SMM, Teczka 2, Mieczysław Drobner to SMM, 20 December 1938, and other resignation letters in the same file.

129. J. Ernicz-Homańska, "Z ruchu muzycznego w Warszawie," *Nasza Opinja*, no. 185 (1939): 4.

CHAPTER 3

1. "XVII Festiwal Muzyki Współczesnej," *Muzyka Współczesna* 4, nos. 1–2 (1939): 1–8.

2. "XVII Festiwal Międzynarodowego Towarzystwa Muzyki Współczesnej w Warszawie i Krakowie," *Muzyka Polska* 6, no. 4 (1939): 171–80, here 171.

3. On the fraught attempts by the ISCM to maintain neutrality during a time of tightening political pressures prior to the Poland festival, see Shreffler, "The International Society for Contemporary Music"; Collins, Kelly, and Tunbridge, "Round Table."

Notes to Pages 79–84 | 265

4. AAN, 322, 12246, Józef Targowski to Ministerstwo Spraw Zagranicznych, 1 April 1939.

5. BL, Add MS 52256–52257, vol. 1, Alfredo Casella to Edward Clark, 29 March 1939; Michał Kondracki, "Po Festiwalu," *Tygodnik Illustrowany*, 7 May 1939, 372–73.

6. BL, Add MS 52256–52257, vol. 1, Edward Dent to Edward Clark, 5 April 1939.

7. Michał Kondracki, "Po Festiwalu," *Tygodnik Illustrowany*, 7 May 1939, 372–73.

8. Konstanty Régamey, "Po festiwalu warszawskim," *Muzyka Polska* 6, no. 5 (1939): 253–69, here 254 and 257.

9. "Głosy prasy zagranicznej po festiwalu warszawskim: Węgry," *Muzyka Polska* 6, nos. 6–7 (1939): 336.

10. Régamey, "Po festiwalu warszawskim," 255–56.

11. Szpilman, *Śmierć miasta*, 9.

12. Quoted in Mazower, *Hitler's Empire*, 64.

13. Szpilman, *Śmierć miasta*, 21.

14. AAN, 366/1, 265, "Sprawozdanie Zarządu Filharmonii Warszawskiej Sp. Akc." (28 January 1947).

15. *OLM*, 1:118. The two volumes of memoirs and other primary sources edited by Katarzyna Naliwajek with various co-editors are an invaluable source for understanding the musical culture of occupied Warsaw. See Naliwajek, Markowska, and Spóz, *Okupacyjne losy muzyków*. Subsequent references to these volumes appear as *OLM*.

16. On the bombing of Warsaw, see Snyder, *Bloodlands*, 119–21.

17. BUP, 800/1, "Pamiętnik Adolfa Chybińskiego (autograf)," 107.

18. ZKP, Mycielski personal file (239A), "Życiorys" (24 October 1946).

19. BnF, N.L.a 89, Mycielski to Boulanger, 22 September 1939.

20. BnF, N.L.a 89, Mycielski to Boulanger, 2 December 1939.

21. BnF, N.L.a 89, Mycielski to Boulanger, 18 February 1940.

22. Snyder, *Bloodlands*, 126–27; Mazower, *Hitler's Empire*, 66–68.

23. These figures should be treated as approximate. Michlic, *Poland's Threatening Other*, 196.

24. Wyka, "The Excluded Economy," 26. Translation modified.

25. Naliwajek, "Nazi Musical Imperialism," 56–71.

26. PISM, A.9.III.1/1, "Działalność władz okupacyjnych na terytorium rzeczypospolitej za okres od 1.IX.39–1.XI.40," 137; Konstanty Régamey, "Muzyka polska pod okupacją niemiecką [1946]," in *OLM*, 2:62–65, here 62.

27. Majer, *"Non-Germans" under the Third Reich*, 286.

28. Biskupska, *Survivors*, 52.

29. Biskupska, *Survivors*, ch. 2.

30. Biskupska, *Survivors*, 56–57.

31. Connelly, "Nazis and Slavs."

32. See Friedrich, "Collaboration in a 'Land without a Quisling'"; Connelly, "Why the Poles Collaborated So Little"; Kornbluth, *The August Trials*, chs. 1–2.

266 | Notes to Pages 84–88

33. Gliński and Glińska, *Testament Mateusza Glińskiego*, 51–55.

34. Nikodemowicz, "Moje lwowskie lata."

35. Kostka, *Tadeusz Zygfryd Kassern*, 132.

36. Filar and Patterson, *From Buchenwald to Carnegie Hall*; Gran, *Sztafeta oszczerców*.

37. Engelking and Leociak, *The Warsaw Ghetto*, 36–51.

38. Szarota, *Okupowanej Warszawy*, 41.

39. PISM, A.9.III.2C/14, "Muzyka na ziemiach Polski podczas wojny"; PISM, A.9.III.1/2, "Raport sytuacyjny za okres 10.XI.40–1.II.41."

40. PISM, A.9.III.2C/14, "Muzyka na ziemiach Polski podczas wojny"; AAN, 202/VII, 3, "Sytuacja na odcinku kulturalnym" (23 June 1941).

41. Piotr Perkowski as cited in Lorentz, *Walka o dobra kultury*, 1:39.

42. PISM, A.9.III.2C/14, "Muzyka na ziemiach Polski podczas wojny."

43. PISM, A.9.III.2C/14, "Muzyka na ziemiach Polski podczas wojny."

44. Sprout, *Musical Legacy of Wartime France*, 13; Locke, "Swing in the Protectorate."

45. Szarota, *Okupowanej Warszawy*, 265–69.

46. Piotrowski, *Dziennik Hansa Franka*, 254 (31 October 1939).

47. PISM, A.9.III.2C/14, "Muzyka na ziemiach Polski podczas wojny."

48. *The Nazi Kultur in Poland*, 184.

49. PISM, A.9.III.1/1, "Działalność władz okupacyjnych na terytorium rzeczypospolitej za okres od 1.IX.39 do 1.XI.40."

50. PISM, A.9.III.1/3, "Raport sytuacyjny okupacji niemieckiej za czas od 1.I do 1.VII. 1941 r."

51. Naliwajek-Mazurek, "The Use of Polish Musical Tradition."

52. "Muzyka pod okupacją," *Kultura Jutra* 1, no. 3 (1943): 18–20. See also "Wystawa Chopinowska w Krakowie—'pomnik wielkoduszności niemieckiej,'" *Przegląd Spraw Kultury* 1, no. 10 (1943): 7.

53. Milewski, "Chopin's Mazurkas"; Porter, *When Nationalism Began to Hate*.

54. Applegate and Potter, "Germans as the 'People of Music.'"

55. PISM, A.9.III.2C/14, "Muzyka na ziemiach Polski podczas wojny."

56. Naliwajek-Mazurek, "Nazi Censorship in Music."

57. Janina Godlewska-Bogucka in *OLM*, 2:146.

58. PISM, A.9.III.2C/14, "Muzyka na ziemiach Polski podczas wojny."

59. Lehnstaedt, *Occupation in the East*, 96–99; Naliwajek, "Nazi Musical Imperialism."

60. *Philharmonie des Generalgouvernements*; Lachowicz, *Muzyka w okupowanym Krakowie*, 24–50.

61. Wiłkomirski, *Wspomnienia*, 550; Lachowicz, *Muzyka w okupowanym Krakowie*, 52. Musicians were to be paid five hundred złoty a month; see ANK, SMKr, 220, "Auszug aus dem Protokoll über die Besprechung des Herrn Generalgouverneurs mit dem Kapellmeister Herrn Dr. Hanns Rohr am Mittwoch, den 17. Juli 1940."

62. Lachowicz, *Muzyka w okupowanym Krakowie*, 28–44.

63. ANK, SMKr, 220, "Auszug aus dem Protokoll über die Besprechung des Herrn Generalgouverneurs mit dem Kapellmeister Herrn Dr. Hanns Rohr am

Mittwoch, den 17. Juli 1940." See also Naliwajek, "Nazi Musical Imperialism," 72–75.

64. "Muzyka pod okupacją," *Kultura Jutra* 1, no. 3 (1943): 18–20, here 20.

65. "Od wydawców," *Przegląd Spraw Kultury* 1, no. 1 (1943): 1–4; "Rok okupacji niemieckiej w Polsce," *Biuletyn Informacyjny*, 9 January 1941; "Rok okupacji niemieckiej w Polsce: Próba zestawienia ogólnego," *Biuletyn Informacyjny*, 27 February 1941; "Pełny front walki," *Biuletyn Informacyjny*, 5 March 1942.

66. "Muzyka na przełomie," *Kultura Jutra* 1, no. 1 (1943): 14–17.

67. "Konkurs," *Biuletyn Informacyjny*, 15 November 1942; Panufnik, *Composing Myself*, 115; Fauser, *Sounds of War*, especially ch. 5.

68. PISM, A.9.III.1/4, "Raport sytuacyjny okupacji niemieckiej za czas od 29 VII-30 VIII 1941: Instrukcja dla pracowników kulturalnych."

69. BJ, PWM, O-1/101, Tadeusz Ochlewski to Adolf Chybiński, 1 May 1942 and 1 March 1943; BUP, 803 III/5, Ochlewski to Chybiński, 26 November 1943.

70. PISM, A.9.III.1/20, "Sprawozdanie ze stanu oświaty i kultury na ziemiach polskich za okres od 1. IV do 30. VI. 1942."

71. PISM, A.9.III.2C/32–36.

72. Palester, "Fragmenty wspomnień z lat 1939–1945," 286.

73. Grabowski, *Delegatura Rządu*.

74. Biskupska, *Survivors*, especially 291–94.

75. *OLM*, 2:49.

76. Lorentz, *Walka o dobra kultury*, 1:26–31.

77. Lorentz, *Walka o dobra kultury*, 1:31; Palester and Jędrychowska, "Rozmowa z Romanem Palestrem," 76–77; BnF, N.L.a 78, Feliks Łabuński to Nadia Boulanger, 12 March 1942.

78. Described in Roman Palester to Zofia Makomaska, 18 November 1943, in Palester, *Słuch absolutny*, 242.

79. Ochlewski, "Muzyka w Warszawie podczas okupacji." For an example of this commissioning and funding work see, BJ, PWM, O-1, 10 May 1943.

80. BJ, PWM, O-1/110, Ochlewski to Chybiński, 9 September 1943.

81. BUP, 803 III/5, Ochlewski to Chybiński, 13 December 1943; BJ, PWM, O-1, Ochlewski to Chybiński, 1 October 1943, 8 October 1943, 1 November 1943.

82. PISM, A.9.III.1/20, "Sprawozdanie ze stanu oświaty i kultury na ziemiach polskich za okres od 1. IV. do 30. VI. 1942"; PISM, A.9.III.2C/14, "Muzyka na ziemiach Polski podczas wojny"; PISM, B. 1791, "Straty kulturalne: Muzyka."

83. BJ, PWM, O-1/98, postscript by Bronisław Rutkowski on a letter from Tadeusz Ochlewski to Adolf Chybiński, 29 January 1942.

84. Lorentz, *Walka o dobra kultury*, 1:37.

85. Jerzy Waldorff, "Dawna i przyszła opera," *Radio i Świat*, 21 October 1945, 5.

86. AAN, 366/1, 265, "Sprawozdanie Zarządu Filharmonii Warszawskiej Sp. Akc." (28 January 1947).

268 | Notes to Pages 93–100

87. Gross, *Polish Society*, 264–66; Porter-Szűcs, *Poland in the Modern World*, ch. 7.

88. Straszewska, "Biuletyn Informacyjny," 147.

89. "Pan Dołżycki," *Biuletyn Informacyjny*, 30 August 1940; Fuks, "Filharmonia Warszawska w latach okupacji niemieckiej," 127.

90. Perkowski as cited in Lorentz, *Walka o dobra kultury*, 1:38.

91. Perkowski as cited in Lorentz, *Walka o dobra kultury*, 1:38.

92. *OLM*, 1:201.

93. AAN, 202/VII, 2, "Raport sytuacyjny za okres od 15 VIII do 15 XI 1941." See also Kazimierz Sikorski [1977] in *OLM*, 2:96–99.

94. PISM, A.9.III.1/20, "Sprawozdanie ze stanu oświaty i kultury na ziemiach polskich za okres od 1. IV. do 30. VI. 1942."

95. Janusz Miketta, "Ze statystyki szkolnictwa muzycznego," *Kwartalnik Muzyczny*, nos. 10–11 (1931): 156–69.

96. PISM, A.9.III.1/18, "Sprawozdanie za okres od 15. XII.1942–15.V.1943 z terenu nauki, sztuki i kultury."

97. For instance, during the three-month period from April 1 to June 30, 1942, twenty-five concerts were organized. PISM, A.9.III.1/20, "Sprawozdanie ze stanu oświaty i kultury na ziemiach polskich za okres od 1. IV. do 30. VI. 1942."

98. PISM, A.9.III.1/20, "Sprawozdanie ze stanu oświaty i kultury na ziemiach polskich za okres od 1. IV. do 30. VI. 1942"; PISM, A.9.III.2C/14, "Muzyka na ziemiach Polski podczas wojny."

99. Olszewski, "Moje wspomnienia," 171.

100. Panufnik, *Composing Myself*, 115.

101. Olszewski, "Moje wspomnienia," 171; BJ, PWM, O-1/102, Ochlewski to Chybiński (no date); Régamey, "Muzyka polska pod okupacją niemiecką [1946]," 63; A.[dam] Rieger, "Życie muzyczne pod okupacją: Kraków," *Ruch Muzyczny* 1, no. 2 (1945): 11–12; Lorentz, *Walka o dobra kultury*, 1:31.

102. Iwaszkiewicz in *OLM*, 1:149 (diary entry from 30 May 1942).

103. For an analysis, see Milewski, "Hidden in Plain View."

104. These were initiated by Rudnicki and organized by Ochlewski, with help from Perkowski and Rutkowski; see "Polska twórczość muzyczna pod okupacją," *Ruch Muzyczny* 1, no. 1 (1945): 14–16.

105. Régamey, "Muzyka polska pod okupacją niemiecką [1946]," 63.

106. Régamey, "Muzyka polska pod okupacją niemiecką [1946]," 63–64.

107. Jan Krenz [1981], in *OLM*, 2:88.

108. AKP, K-XLIV/108, Régamey to Wiechowicz, 18 February 1944.

109. Jarzębska, "Syntez neoklasycznego i dodekafonicznego idiomu," 120–22.

110. AKP, K-XLIV/109, Régamey to Wiechowicz, 5 March 1944.

111. PISM, A.9.III.2C/14, "Muzyka na ziemiach Polski podczas wojny."

112. Quoted in Loutan-Charbon, *Constantin Regamey*, 23–24.

113. Piotr Perkowski quoted in Lorentz, *Walka o dobra kultury*, 1:36.

114. Kuraś, "Kawiarnia 'U Aktorek.'"

115. Domański [Erhardt], "Sztuka i Moda," 10–11.

116. PISM, A.9.III.2C/14, "Muzyka na ziemiach Polski podczas wojny."

117. Szarota, *Okupowanej Warszawy*, 181 and 91.

Notes to Pages 100–109 | 269

118. Szarota, *Okupowanej Warszawy*, 195. These costs are for goods on the black market, which were necessary to supplement starvation-level rations.

119. Jasiński, *Zmierzch starego świata*, 694–95.

120. Szarota, *Okupowanej Warszawy*, 32–34.

121. Bolesław Woytowicz, "W okupowanej Warszawie [1969]," *OLM*, 1:94–111, here 96.

122. Lindorfówna, "Wojna—okupacja niemiecka."

123. Arciszewska, *Po obu stronach oceanu*, 10–11.

124. Domański [Erhardt], "Sztuka i Moda."

125. Domański [Erhardt], "Sztuka i Moda," 11. On his pseudonym, see *OLM*, 2:113.

126. Partial programs for the years 1941–44 are published in *Pamiętnik Teatralny* 46 (1997): 540–51.

127. Witold Lutosławski in *OLM*, 2:31–35.

128. Witold Lutosławski in *OLM*, 2:31.

129. PISM, A.9.III.2C/14, "Muzyka na ziemiach Polski podczas wojny." The other cafés permitted to perform classical repertoire, according to this report, were Lardello, which featured an orchestra, and Zachęta.

130. Woytowicz, "W okupowanej Warszawie," 94–98.

131. Diary of Zofia Nałkowska (23 March 1943) in *OLM*, 1:230. Eugenia Umińska [1968], in *OLM*, 1:204; BUP, 803 III/2, Jan Dunicz to Adolf Chybiński, 11 December 1942.

132. Woytowicz, "W okupowanej Warszawie," 98.

133. PISM, A.9.III.2C/14, "Muzyka na ziemiach Polski podczas wojny."

134. "Muzyka pod okupacją," *Kultura Jutra* 1, no. 3 (1943): 19.

135. "Muzyka na przełomie," *Kultura Jutra* 1, no. 1 (1943): 14.

136. *OLM*, 2:36.

137. Woytowicz, "W okupowanej Warszawie," 98–101.

138. Naliwajek, *Sounds of Apocalypse*, 96.

139. Kochanski, *The Eagle Unbowed*, 114.

140. Lutosławski, in *OLM*, 2:36; Panufnik, *Composing Myself*, 110–14.

141. Jasiński, *Zmierzch starego świata*, 694.

142. AKP, Palester papers, "Eidesstattliche Versicherung (1966)"; VHA, Palester-Chlebowczyk, tape 4, 10:00–12:00.

143. Waldorff, *Moje cienie*, 104–6.

144. Palester, "Fragmenty wspomnień z lat 1939–1945," 288.

145. Jasiński, *Zmierzch starego świata*, 705.

CHAPTER 4

1. Engelking, *Holocaust and Memory*, 81–83; Paulsson, *Secret City*, 61–66.

2. For prior discussions of music in the Warsaw Ghetto, see Fuks, "Muzyka w gettach"; Fuks, "Życie muzycznego w gettach"; Gilbert, *Music in the Holocaust*, ch. 1.

3. Goldberg, "The History of the Jews in the Ghettos," 95.

4. Hirsch, "Righting and Remembering the Nazi Past"; Loeffler, "Why the New 'Holocaust Music' Is an Insult to Music."

270 | Notes to Pages 110–116

5. The definitive account of the archive is Kassow, *Who Will Write Our History?*

6. The content of the archive has been published by the Jewish Historical Institute in Warsaw as *Archiwum Ringelbluma.*

7. See Engelking and Leociak, *The Warsaw Ghetto,* 36–72.

8. Polonsky, "Warsaw."

9. Paulsson, *Secret City,* 58–59.

10. VHA, Palester-Chlebowczyk, tape 4, 5:00–10:00; tape 2, 4:00–4:30.

11. VHA, Palester-Chlebowczyk, tape 2, 4:45.

12. VHA, Palester-Chlebowczyk, tape 2.

13. *OLM,* 2:143.

14. USHMM, RG-15.084M, file 301–7290 (Marcel Reich, "Opracowanie o życiu muzycznym w getcie warszawskim").

15. Tuszyńska, *Vera Gran,* 69–70.

16. USHMM, RG-15.189M, file 313/36, "Protokół rozprawy sądowej z dnia 4 grudnia 1948 r.," 254.

17. USHMM, RG-15.189M, file 313/36, "Protokół rozprawy sądowej z dnia 10 stycznia 1948 r.," 170; Jonas Turkow, "Warszawa się bawi . . .," trans. Aleksandra Geller, in *Archiwum Ringelbluma,* 26:4–28, here 17–18.

18. Hirsch, *Jewish Orchestra in Nazi Germany.*

19. Engelking and Leociak, *The Warsaw Ghetto,* 536; USHMM, RG-15.189M, file 313/36, "Protokół dnia 1 grudnia 1948 r.," 238; AŻIH 211, Aneks 252, pp. 4–60.

20. Engelking and Leociak, *The Warsaw Ghetto,* 577–80, 626–33.

21. USHMM, RG-15.084M, file 301–7290 (Reich, "Opracowanie o życiu muzycznym w getcie warszawskim," 7).

22. Stanisław Różycki, "To jest getto! (Reportaż z inferna XX wieku)," in *Archiwum Ringelbluma,* 33:42–76, here 56. He makes a similar point in Stanisław Różycki, "Obrazki uliczne z getta," in *Archiwum Ringelbluma,* 5:19–36, here 25–26. Ringelblum also observed that censorship was relatively lax in the ghetto; see Naliwajek, *Sounds of Apocalypse,* 117.

23. Gombiński [Mawult], *Wspomnienia,* 47.

24. Gombiński [Mawult], *Wspomnienia,* 47.

25. Sara W., "Sztuka na bruku," *Gazeta Żydowska,* 8 November 1940.

26. Janczewska, "*Gazeta Żydowska.*"

27. A list of the Jewish Symphony Orchestra's known concerts, including repertoire and excerpts from press reviews, is provided in Engelking and Leociak, *The Warsaw Ghetto,* 627–33.

28. "Żydowska Orkiestra Symfoniczna w Warszawie," *Gazeta Żydowska,* 28 January 1941; H. Cz., "Koncert żydowskiej Orkiestry Symfonicznej," *Gazeta Żydowska,* 4 August 1941; "Pomóżmy naszym muzykom!," *Gazeta Żydowska,* 15 August 1941.

29. "Żydowska Orkiestra Symfoniczna w Warszawie," *Gazeta Żydowska,* 28 January 1941; "Cycl koncertów symfonicznych," *Gazeta Żydowska,* 6 December 1940; "Pomóżmy naszym muzykom!," *Gazeta Żydowska,* 15 August 1941.

30. See, for example, H. Cz., "Koncert żydowskiej Orkiestry Symfonicznej," *Gazeta Żydowska,* 4 August 1941; A.R., "Wrażenia muzyczne," *Gazeta*

Żydowska, 22 August 1941; Wiktor Hart [Marcel Reich], "Szymon Pullman na estradzie 'Feminy,'" *Gazeta Żydowska*, 27 March 1942.

31. Witold Hugo Baruch papers (private collection), Witold Baruch to Zofia Dutkiewicz, 14 March 1941.

32. USHMM, RG-15.084M, file 301–7290 (Reich, "Opracowanie o życiu muzycznym w getcie warszawskim").

33. Reich-Ranicki, *The Author of Himself*, 113–76. He adopted the name "Ranicki" following the war.

34. USHMM, RG-15.084M, file 301–7290 (Reich, "Opracowanie o życiu muzycznym w getcie warszawskim").

35. USHMM, RG-15.084M, file 301–7290 (Reich, "Opracowanie o życiu muzycznym w getcie warszawskim").

36. USHMM, RG-15.084M, file 301–7290 (Reich, "Opracowanie o życiu muzycznym w getcie warszawskim").

37. Michman, "Jewish Leadership in Extremis."

38. Engelking and Leociak, *The Warsaw Ghetto*, 136–56; Gutman, "The Judenrat as a Leadership."

39. Person, *Assimilated Jews in the Warsaw Ghetto*, 69.

40. "Żydowska Orkiestra Symfoniczna w Warszawie," *Gazeta Żydowska*, 28 January 1941.

41. Fuks, "Filharmonia warszawska w latach okupacji niemieckiej," 132. These included the bassist Józef Łabuszyński, cellists Józef Bakman and Izydor Lewak, violists Wacław Baruch, Czesław Bem, and Kazimierz Szpilman, violinists Adam Dobrzyniec, Henryk Fiszman, Artur Flatau, Jakub Szulc, Józef Waghalter, and Ignacy Mitelman—as well as the concertmaster of the Warsaw Philharmonic, Ludwik Holcman.

42. Reich-Ranicki, *The Author of Himself*, 154; Aleksander Rozetsztejn, "Inter arma musae non silent: Na marginesie 35-lecia pracy artystycznej Adama Furmańskiego," *Gazeta Żydowska*, 27 June 1941.

43. Witold Baruch and Hugo Baruch are the same person. See Baruch papers (private collection), "Testimonium ortus et baptismi."

44. See press clippings and documents in Baruch papers (private collection): Henryk Opieński, "Popis warszawskiego Instytutu Muzycznego," *Nowa Gazeta*, 17 June 1907; "Z sali koncertowej," *Ilustrowany Kuryer Codzienny*, 14 April 1921; Polskie Radjo S.A. to Witold Baruch, 26 May 1933.

45. Baruch papers (private collection), "Testimonium ortus et baptismi," "Akt notarialny—ślub."

46. POLIN, DZB.413.12.2019, Witold Baruch to Zofia Dutkiewicz, 9 October 1941, 21 December 1941.

47. POLIN, DZB.413.12.2019, Witold Baruch to Zofia Dutkiewicz, 21 December 1941.

48. Rachel Auerbach, "Z ludem pospołu: O losie pisarzy i artystów żydowskich w getcie warszawskim," *Nasze Słowo*, no. 19 (1947): 10.

49. Rachel Auerbach, "Z ludem pospołu: O losie pisarzy i artystów żydowskich w getcie warszawskim," *Nasze Słowo*, no. 12 (1948): 12.

50. USHMM, RG-15.084M, file 301–7290 (Reich, "Opracowanie o życiu muzycznym w getcie warszawskim").

272 | Notes to Pages 119–123

51. Reich-Ranicki, *The Author of Himself*, 3–112.

52. Jonas Turkow, "Warszawa się bawi . . .," 16.

53. Kassow, *Who Will Write Our History?*, 119–24; Sakowska, "Komitety domowe."

54. Turkow, "Warszawa się bawi . . .," 16.

55. Turkow, "Warszawa się bawi . . .," 9. See also Reich-Ranicki, *The Author of Himself*, 153.

56. See the entry of 26 April 1941 in Ringelblum, *Notes from the Warsaw Ghetto*, 158; and Jurandot, *City of the Damned*, 75.

57. Turkow, "Warszawa się bawi . . .," 9.

58. Turkow, "Warszawa się bawi . . .," 20.

59. Turkow, "Warszawa się bawi . . .," 12.

60. Fishman, *The Rise of Modern Yiddish Culture*, chs. 6 and 7.

61. See Caplan, *Yiddish Empire*; and Bułat, "Turkow Family."

62. See Kassow, *Who Will Write Our History?*, 123.

63. Turkow, "Warszawa się bawi . . .," 16.

64. Turkow, "Warszawa się bawi . . .," 17.

65. Turkow, *C'était ainsi*, 169–71.

66. Turkow, "Warszawa się bawi . . .," 18.

67. Copies of performance schedules were sent to the Abteilung für Volksaufklärung und Propaganda by the CKI. AŻIH 211, Aneks 252, 4–60.

68. AŻIH 211, Aneks 252, CKI to Abteilung für Volksaufklärung und Propaganda, 30 April 1941.

69. AŻIH 211, Aneks 252, Dina Turkow to Abteilung für Volksaufklärung und Propaganda.

70. Gran, *Sztafeta oszczerców*, 73. Gran's memoirs must be approached with a great deal of caution: they are an extended polemic in which Gran seeks to exonerate herself from what she sees as the "relay of slanders" (the book's title), which she believes destroyed her postwar career and life. Although much of the book is devoted to quotations from her postwar trials, other claims are, at best, impossible to substantiate and, at worst, libelous. Nonetheless, she provides an important counterpoint to the more canonized voices of Szpilman and Turkow. For further discussion of this issue, see Tuszyńska, *Vera Gran*; Wróbel Best, "The Other Heroine Is Memory."

71. Turkow, "Warszawa się bawi . . .," 8.

72. Turkow, "Warszawa się bawi . . .," 16.

73. Turkow, "Warszawa się bawi . . .," 19.

74. Kassow, *Who Will Write Our History?*, 128.

75. [Stanisław Różycki], "Kawiarnie," in *Archiwum Ringelbluma*, 5:67–76, here 68.

76. Engelking and Leociak find evidence of ninety-five ghetto cafés or similar establishments; see *The Warsaw Ghetto*, 634–40.

77. [Różycki], "Kawiarnie," 68.

78. Turkow, *C'était ainsi*, 169.

79. Turkow, *C'était ainsi*, 168; Ringelblum, *Notes from the Warsaw Ghetto*, 125.

Notes to Pages 123–128 | 273

80. The prices are provided in [Różycki], "Kawiarnie," 68.

81. Kaplan, *Scroll of Agony*, 291.

82. See Gilbert, *Music in the Holocaust*, 28–30.

83. Kassow, *Who Will Write Our History?*, 253.

84. [Różycki], "Kawiarnie," 67.

85. [Różycki], "Kawiarnie," 76.

86. See Kassow, *Who Will Write Our History?*, 251–55.

87. See Stanisław Różycki, "Obrazki uliczne z getta," in *Archiwum Ringelbluma*, 5:19–36; [Stanisław Różycki?], "Moralność ulicy," in *Archiwum Ringelbluma*, 5: 37–51.

88. [Różycki], "Kawiarnie," 76.

89. [Różycki], "Kawiarnie," 67.

90. [Różycki], "Kawiarnie," 69.

91. [Różycki], "Kawiarnie," 70.

92. [Różycki], "Kawiarnie," 71.

93. [Różycki], "Kawiarnie," 71.

94. [Różycki], "Kawiarnie," 74.

95. [Różycki], "Kawiarnie," 74.

96. Person, *Assimilated Jews*, 21–23; Majewska, "Czym wytłumaczy Pan . . .?"; Kassow, *Who Will Write Our History?*, chs. 1–4.

97. Turkow, *C'était ainsi*, 168.

98. [Różycki], "Kawiarnie," 73.

99. USHMM, RG-15.189M, file 313/36, "Protokół rozprawy sądowej z dnia 4 grudnia 1948 r." (testimony of Zygmunt Jankowski, a.k.a. Maciej Czarnecki).

100. USHMM, RG-15.189M, file 313/36, "Protokół rozprawy sądowej z dnia 29 listopada 1947," 134.

101. USHMM, RG-15.189M, file 313/36, "Protokół dnia 1 grudnia 1948 r.," 238.

102. Person, *Warsaw Ghetto Police*, 27–32.

103. USHMM, RG-15.189M, file 313/36, "Protokół rozprawy sądowej z dnia 4 grudnia 1948 r.," 259.

104. USHMM, RG-15.189M, file 313/36, "Protokół dnia 1 grudnia 1948 r.," 238. Her view was shared by the testimony of Aleksander Jasielski, Leon Piotrowski, and Maciej Czarnecki.

105. USHMM, RG-15.189M, file 313/36, "Protokół rozprawy sądowej z dnia 4 grudnia 1948 r.," 266 (Zygmunt Jankowski, a.k.a. Maciej Czarnecki).

106. Person, "Sexual Violence during the Holocaust."

107. USHMM, RG-15.189M, file 313/36, "Protokół rozprawy sądowej z dnia 4 grudnia 1948 r.," 256. For Gran's description of the incident, see USHMM, RG-15.189M, file 313/36, "Protokół rozprawy jawnej w sprawie Wiery Gran w drugim terminie odbytej w dni 15 stycznia 1949 roku."

108. USHMM, RG-15.189M, file 313/36, "Protokół rozprawy sądowej z dnia 4 grudnia 1948 r.," (testimony of Jerzy Jurandot) and "Protokół rozprawy sądowej z dnia 29 listopada 1947 r." (testimony of Jemiołkowski).

109. USHMM, RG-15.189M, file 313/36, "Protokół dnia 1 grudnia 1948 r.," 238.

274 | Notes to Pages 128–134

110. USHMM, RG-15.189M, file 313/36, "Protokół rozprawy sądowej z dnia 29 listopada 1947," 137, and "Protokół rozprawy sądowej z dnia 4 grudnia 1948 r.," 255.

111. USHMM, RG-15.189M, file 313/36, "Protokół rozprawy sądowej z dnia 10 stycznia 1948 r."

112. USHMM, RG-15.691, IPN GK 453/739, "Życiorys" (written by Gran).

113. Holmgren, "Cabaret Nation."

114. Berg, *The Diary of Mary Berg*, 104.

115. Borwicz, *Pieśń ujdzie cało*, 20–24; Gran, *Sztafeta oszczerców*, 62. Borwicz had not been interned in the Warsaw Ghetto.

116. Engelking and Leociak, *The Warsaw Ghetto*, 588.

117. Mazurczak, "Władysław Szpilman's Post-War Career in Poland."

118. Tuszyńska, *Vera Gran*, 69–71.

119. USHMM, RG-15.189M, file 313/36, "Protokół przesłuchania świadka Gadejskiego Gerarda," 59.

120. Lerski, *Syrena Record*, 377.

121. *OLM*, 2:143–46.

122. Holmgren, "Cabaret Nation," 288.

123. Milewski, "Chopin's Mazurkas."

124. Naliwajek-Mazurek, "The Use of Polish Musical Tradition."

125. Tuszyńska, *Vera Gran*, 87–88.

126. Reich-Ranicki, *The Author of Himself*, 144.

127. Gutman, *Resistance*.

128. Paulsson, *Secret City*.

129. *OLM*, 2:145.

130. Perkowski as cited in Lorentz, *Walka o dobra kultury*, 1:38.

131. Lissa, "O Sewerynie Barbagu"; AAN, 366/1, 292, Departament Muzyki Ministerstwa Kultury i Sztuki to Zarząd Związku Zawodowego Muzyków R.P., Koło "Warszawa," 9 April 1945.

132. Wiłkomirski, *Wspomnienia*, 571–73.

133. Tuszyńska, *Vera Gran*, 92–114.

134. POLIN, DZB.413.12.2019, Baruch to Dutkiewicz, 28 July 1942.

135. Baruch papers (private collection), "Życiorys Jana Ignaczaka."

136. Baruch papers (private collection), "Metryka Urodzenia"; "Polizeiliche Abmeldung"; "Umowa pomiędzy Towarzystwem krzewienia Polskiej Muzyki Ludowej . . . a ob. Laskowski Aleksander" (1 October 1945); copy of a notarized statement by Stanisław Ulankiewicz and Aleksander Rowiński (22 May 1946).

137. Gross, "A Tangled Web"; Biskupska, *Survivors*, ch. 4 and 290–92; Connelly, "Why the Poles Collaborated So Little"; Zimmerman, *The Polish Underground and the Jews*, chs. 6–7; Kornbluth, *The August Trials*, chs. 1–2.

138. Grabowski, *Szantażowanie Żydów w Warszawie*.

139. VHA, Palester-Chlebowczyk, tape 4; Zimmerman, *The Polish Underground and the Jews*, 303–17.

140. Prekerowa, *Konspiracyjna Rada*, 215–17.

141. Prekerowa, *Konspiracyjna Rada*, 216; "Maria Palester," *Polish Righteous*.

Notes to Pages 134–142 | 275

142. Palester, *Słuch absolutny*, 137–38. The *Kennkarte* is held in the AKP Palester papers.

143. Palester, "Fragmenty wspomnień z lat 1939–1945," 289.

144. Helman, *Roman Palester*, 82–87.

145. Palester, "Fragmenty wspomnień z lat 1939–1945," 286.

146. Palester, "Twórczość muzyczna w nowej Polsce," *Ruch Muzyczny* 2, nos. 11–12 (1946): 13–19, here 14.

147. AKP, Palester papers, Przypkowski to Palester, 10 July 1959.

CHAPTER 5

1. Adler, *Survival on the Margins*, 21.

2. Snyder, *Bloodlands*, 189–96; Hanebrink, *A Specter Haunting Europe*, 138–45; Gross, *Neighbors*.

3. Warsaw emerged as the central site for memoirs of music under occupation in the 1970s, as discussed in Naliwajek-Mazurek, "Muzyka w okupowanej Warszawie," 17.

4. Piekarski, "Poza granicami kraju."

5. Stefania Łobaczewska, "Z opery i sal koncertowych: Lwów," *Muzyka* 7, no. 4 (1930): 243–44.

6. Shore, *Caviar and Ashes*, ch. 6

7. Michalski, *Powróćmy jak za dawnych lat*, 334–37.

8. Mick, *Lemberg, Lwów, L'viv*, 263.

9. Amar, *The Paradox of Ukrainian Lviv*, 50; Hryciuk, *Polacy we Lwowie*, 63–80.

10. Plokhy, *Gates of Europe*, 262.

11. Gross, *Revolution from Abroad*, 197–200.

12. For a discussion of these estimates, see Jolluck, *Exile and Identity*, 9–11. These numbers do not refer to Lviv alone.

13. Mick, *Lemberg, Lwów, L'viv*, 262; Amar, *The Paradox of Ukrainian Lviv*, 66–67.

14. For an overview of this general theme, see Hryciuk, *Polacy we Lwowie*, 112. Examples include Zofia Lissa, "Muzïka v sovetskom L'vove"; "Koncerty radzieckich artystów," *Czerwony Sztandar*, 8 December 1939; "Ognisko nowej kultury," *Czerwony Sztandar*, 29 December 1939.

15. "Lwowska rozgłośnia organizuje orkiestrę symfoniczną," *Czerwony Sztandar*, 5 November 1939; "Przed otwarciem Filharmonii we Lwowie," *Czerwony Sztandar*, 12 January 1940; Gross, *Revolution from Abroad*, 136–37.

16. Nikodemowicz, "Moje lwowskie lata," 191. On visits of Soviet performers, see "Koncerty radzieckich artystów," *Czerwony Sztandar*, 8 December 1939.

17. PISM, A.9.III.2C/14, "Muzyka na ziemiach Polski podczas wojny," 11.

18. Gross, *Revolution from Abroad*, 75–113; Hryciuk, *Polacy we Lwowie*, 101.

19. Gran, *Sztafeta oszczerców*, 9–11.

20. W. Łuk, "Muzyka na ulicy: Nowy występ orkiestry jazzowej Warsa," *Czerwony Sztandar*, 26 February 1941.

276 | Notes to Pages 142–145

21. Wnuk, "The Polish Underground under Soviet Occupation."

22. Hrab, *Muzykolohiia iak universytets'ka dystsyplina*, 75–76; Mazepa and Mazepa, *Shliakh do muzychnoï akademiï u L'vovi*, 2:36; BUP 800/1, Pamiętnik Adolfa Chybińskiego, p. 108.

23. DALO, R-2056, op. 1, s. 2, a. 1.

24. Mazepa and Mazepa, *Shliakh do muzychnoï akademiï u L'vovi*, 2:41; Sołtys, *Tylko we Lwowie*, 151–52.

25. BUP, 800/1, Pamiętnik Adolfa Chybińskiego, p. 108.

26. Stefania Łobaczewska, "Ze zjazdu kompozytorów i muzykologów," *Czerwony Sztandar*, 29 May 1941, p. 4.

27. BUP, 800/1, Pamiętnik Adolfa Chybińskiego, p. 108.

28. DALO, R-2056, op. 1, s. 4, a. 1.

29. DALO, R-2056, op.1, s. 3, a. 3.

30. Mazepa and Mazepa, *Shliakh do muzychnoï akademiï u L'vovi*, 2:40.

31. BUP, 800/1, Pamiętnik Adolfa Chybińskiego, p. 109.

32. Connelly, *Captive University*, 91.

33. AKP, Wiechowicz papers, Chybiński to Wiechowicz, 14 December 1942.

34. Mick, *Lemberg, Lwów, L'viv*, 211. The 1921 Polish census used the term *Ruthenian* instead of *Ukrainian*, terminology that downplayed the national identity and aspirations of Ukrainians in the Second Republic. See Ciancia, *On Civilization's Edge*, 203–4.

35. Plokhy, *Gates of Europe*, 195

36. Plokhy, *Gates of Europe*, 212–13.

37. Mick, *Lemberg, Lwów, L'viv*, 158–62.

38. Plokhy, *Gates of Europe*, 235–37.

39. Mick, "Lviv under Soviet Rule," 144–45.

40. Amar, *The Paradox of Ukrainian Lviv*, 39–42.

41. Mick, "Incompatible Experiences," 340.

42. Plokhy, *Gates of Europe*, chs. 20–23.

43. M.O. Hrinchenko, "Muzykal'na tvorchist' i muzykal'nyĭ fol'klor Zakhidnoï Ukraïny," *Radians'ka Muzyka*, no. 6 (1939): 22–32.

44. Vasyl' Barvins'kyĭ, "Shcho prynesla Radians'ka vlada muzykal'niĭ kul'turi L'vova," *Radians'ka Muzyka*, no. 5 (1940): 5–7.

45. DALO, R-2056, op. 1, s. 3, a. 9.

46. Roman Savyts'kyĭ, "Khronika: Muzykal'ne zhyttia L'vova," *Radians'ka Muzyka*, no. 5 (1940): 60–61.

47. "Otwarcie sezonu koncertowego," *Czerwony Sztandar*, 19 December 1939; J. Burski, "Koncert Beethovenowski," *Czerwony Sztandar*, 21 January 1941; J. Burski, "Z sali koncertowej," *Czerwony Sztandar*, 12 February 1941; Stefania Łobaczewska, "Z Filharmonii lwowskiej," *Czerwony Sztandar*, 10 May 1941.

48. "Otwarcie sezonu koncertowego," *Czerwony Sztandar*, 19 December 1939.

49. Amar, *The Paradox of Ukrainian Lviv*, 69–72; Hryciuk, *Polacy we Lwowie*, 44–48.

50. J. Burski, "Z sali koncertowej i przed mikrofonem," *Czerwony Sztandar*, 16 January 1941.

Notes to Pages 146–152 | 277

51. Milewski, "Chopin's Mazurkas," 129–30.

52. Tadeusz Boy-Żeleński, "'Krakowiacy i górale' w Teatrze Polskim," *Czerwony Sztandar*, 21 June 1941; Stefania Łobaczewska, "Muzyka i tańce w widowisku," *Czerwony Sztandar*, 21 June 1941.

53. Mick, *Lemberg, Lwów, L'viv*, 267; Hryciuk, *Polacy we Lwowie*, 128–33.

54. Janusz Miketta, "Ze statystyki szkolnictwa muzycznego," *Kwartalnik Muzyczny*, nos. 10–11 (1931): 156–69. The data are broken into "Roman Catholic," "Jewish" (*wyznanie mojżeszowe*), and "other."

55. AAN, 541, 107, "Staatskonservatorium im Lemberg (Studentenstatistik)." This information is dated 3 July 1941, after the German invasion, and therefore likely represents levels near the end of the Soviet period.

56. Mazepa and Mazepa, *Shliakh do muzychnoï akademiï u L'vovi*, 2:37–39.

57. Nikodemowicz, "Moje lwowskie lata," 191.

58. Lissa, "Muzïka v sovetskom L'vove," 92–93.

59. Juer Weiler, "Polityka Polskiego Radia wobec Żydów," *Nasza Opinja*, no. 75 (1937): 8.

60. Pinchuk, "Sovietisation and the Jewish Response."

61. Quoted in Gołąb, *Józef Koffler*, 232–33.

62. Reittererová and Reitterer, "Musik und Politik," 231.

63. Gołąb, *Józef Koffler*, 179–80.

64. Masters, "New-Music Internationalism," 162–76; Bohlman, *The World Centre for Jewish Music in Palestine*, 57.

65. Gołąb, "Garść informacji o Józefie Kofflerze."

66. Gołąb, *Józef Koffler*, 230–31.

67. BUP, 800/1, Pamiętnik Adolfa Chybińskiego, 107.

68. Mick, "Incompatible Experiences," 342–46.

69. Michlic, "The Soviet Occupation of Poland, 1939–41"; Gross, *Upiorna dekada*, 76–89; Hanebrink, *A Specter Haunting Europe*.

70. AKP, Wiechowicz papers, Chybiński to Wiechowicz, 14 December 1942.

71. See chapter 2, note 66, on the lowercase use of "jew." Chybiński's use of "red army" and "ukrainian" is likely a similar dismissal through letter case, since these words should be capitalized in Polish.

72. It was published by the Derzhavne Vydavnytstvo Mystetstvo (State Publishing House "Art").

73. Mazepa, "Okres radziecki." On calls for composers in Western Ukraine to embrace folk music, see the unsigned editorial in *Radians'ka Muzyka*, no. 5 (1939): 1; M.O. Hrinchenko, "Muzykal'na tvorchist' i muzykal'nyĭ fol'klor Zakhidnoï Ukraïny," *Radians'ka Muzyka*, no. 6 (1939): 22–32.

74. Gołąb, *Józef Koffler*, 223.

75. Gołąb, *Józef Koffler*, 121–22.

76. Tomoff, *Creative Union*, chs. 1 and 3.

77. "Do pidsumkiv plenumu Orhkomitetu spilky kompozytoriv SRSR," *Radians'ka Muzyka*, no. 3 (1940): 13–18, here 16.

78. I wish to thank Peter J. Schmelz for bringing these compositions to my attention.

278 | Notes to Pages 152–156

79. Mick, *Lemberg, Lwów, L'viv*, 289.

80. Mick, *Lemberg, Lwów, L'viv*, 288–95.

81. Amar, *The Paradox of Ukrainian Lviv*, 94–115.

82. Mazepa and Mazepa, *Shliakh do muzychnoï akademiï u L'vovi*, 2:45.

83. AAN, 541, 107, "Bericht der kommissarischer Verwaltung des Musikhochschule (Staats Konservatorium) im Lemberg," May 1942; AKP, Wiechowicz papers, Chybiński to Wiechowicz, 14 December 1942.

84. Sołtys, *Tylko we Lwowie*, 156–57.

85. BUP, 804/III, pp. 4–6, Chybiński to Dr. L. Krüger, 21 February 1942. The university was not reopened, and only a series of technical courses for Ukrainian students was allowed. See Hryciuk, *Polacy we Lwowie*, 350.

86. AKP, Wiechowicz papers, Chybiński to Wiechowicz, 14 December 1942.

87. AKP, Wiechowicz papers, Chybiński to Wiechowicz, 14 December 1942.

88. AKP, Wiechowicz papers, Chybiński to Wiechowicz, 24 April 1943. This dearth of activities is further confirmed in a 1943 report sent to the London government-in-exile. PISM, A.9.III.1/18, "Ministerstwo Spraw Wew. Sprawozdanie nr. 5/1943," pp. 14, 24, 45.

89. On antisemitism in Lviv's press during the German occupation, see Hryciuk, *"Gazeta Lwowska,"* 135.

90. Scherzo, "Poemat o muzyce," *Gazeta Lwowska* 1, no. 5 (14 August 1941): 3.

91. USHMM, RM-15.084M, File 301/5398, Jan Gorbaty (1945).

92. Gołąb, *Józef Koffler*, 234–38.

93. Błaszczyk, *Żydzi w kulturze muzycznej ziem polskich*, 181; Friedman, *Zagłada Żydów lwowskich*, 37.

94. "Wiadomości ze Lwowa: Z życia muzycznego," *Gazeta Żydowska*, 22 February 1942, 2; Salmon, "The Polish Pianist Artur Hermelin."

95. USHMM, RM-15.084M, File 301/5398, Jan Gorbaty (1945).

96. Edele and Warlik, "Saved by Stalin?," table 2.

97. Jolluck, *Exile and Identity*, xiv.

98. Kochanski, *The Eagle Unbowed*, 163–91.

99. Gutman, "Jews in General Anders' Army."

100. Holmgren, "The Jews in the Band."

101. Kochanski, *The Eagle Unbowed*, 371.

102. Kersten, *The Establishment of Communist Rule in Poland*, 9–10.

103. Babiracki, *Soviet Soft Power*, 18–20.

104. Sword, *Deportation and Exile*, 132–39.

105. L.L., "Praca kulturalno-oświatowa Związku Patriotów Polskich," *Wolna Polska*, nos. 21–22 (1946): 6.

106. AAN, 130, 707, "Wykaz polskich placówek kult-oświatowych w ZSRR"; AAN, 130, 747 (entire file).

107. AAN, 130, 715, "Radio na usługach ZPP."

108. AAN, 130, 715, "Zjazd Kulturalno Oświatowy Delegatów ZPP w Pawłodarze."

109. AAN, 130, 715, "Tezy do referatu w związku z 'Tygodniem polskiego słowa, pieśni, tańca i muzyki.'"

Notes to Pages 156–161 | 279

110. His dissertation, completed in Tel Aviv in 1977, has recently been translated into Polish as Nussbaum, *Historia złudzeń*.

111. Nussbaum, "Jews in the Kosciuszko Division and First Polish Army," 192–96.

112. Nussbaum, *Historia złudzeń*, 129–30.

113. Babiracki, *Soviet Soft Power*, 19–29.

114. Pierce, "Zofia Lissa."

115. Zymer, "Zofia Lissa i Włodzimierz Iwannikow," 55.

116. Lissa, "Muzyka polska w ZSRR," 446.

117. AAN, 366/12, 201, "Protokół z posiedzeń I Konferencji w sprawie propagandy Sztuki i Nauki polskiej w ZSRR" (15 September 1945).

118. AKP, Lissa papers, certificate in connection with official travel (21 June 1943). The initial trip was extended from six days to run until early August.

119. Bohlman, *Musical Solidarities*, ch. 6.

120. Naszkowski, *Lata próby*, 291–92; Sokorski, *Polacy pod Lenino*, 20.

121. Janina Broniewska, "W dywizji," *Nowe Widnokręgi*, no. 14 (1943): 8–9; U., "Teatrzyk Żołnierza," *Nowe Widnokręgi*, no. 13 (1943): 5; Pasternak, *W marszu i na biwaku*, 195.

122. Lissa, "Muzyka Polska w ZSRR," 452.

123. Lissa, *Śpiewnik żołnierza polskiego*.

124. Pasternak, *W marszu i na biwaku*, 184–85.

125. Wieczorek, *Na froncie muzyki*, ch. 4; Zaremba, *Komunizm, legitymizacja, nacjonalizm*.

126. Babiracki, *Soviet Soft Power*, 17.

127. Kersten, *Polski Komitet Wyzwolenia Narodowego*, 98.

128. Fijałkowska, *Polityka i twórcy*, 23.

129. Kersten, *The Establishment of Communist Rule*, 39–41, 62–65.

130. Drobner, *Bezustanna walka*, 3:118, 132.

131. Drobner, *Wspomnienia*, 6.

132. Drobner, *Wspomnienia*, 6–10.

133. Fijałkowska, *Polityka i twórcy*, 23; AAN, 185, XV/2 (entire file); AAN, 185, XV/2, "Pismo okólne nr. 1," 26 November 1944.

134. AAN, 185, XV/2, "Pismo okólne nr. 1," 26 November 1944.

135. AAN, 185, XV/2, "Pismo okólne nr. 3," 29 November 1944.

136. AAN, 185, XV/6 (entire file).

137. AAN, 185, XV/2, memo from Urząd Wojewódzki Rzeszowski to Resort Kultury i Sztuki (23 October 1944); "Sprawozdania Wydział Kultury i Sztuki" (Rzeszów, 13 October to 15 November 1944); memos from Urząd Wojewódzki Białostocki to Ob. Kierownik Resortu Kultury i Sztuki (13 November 1944, 4 December 1944, 30 December 1944).

138. AAN, 366/1, 173, "Sprawozdanie na grudzień 1944"; Drobner, *Wspomnienia*, 18.

139. Drobner, *Wspomnienia*, 17.

140. AAN, 185, XV/2, Sprawozdania Wydział Kultury i Sztuki (Rzeszów, 13 October to 15 November 1944).

280 | Notes to Pages 161–171

141. AAN, 185, XV/2, 15, memo from Urząd Wojewódzki Białostocki to Ob. Kierownik Resortu Kultury i Sztuki (30 December 1944); AAN, 366/1, 173, "Osiągnięcia Ministerstwa Kultury i Sztuki w dziedzinie muzyki."

142. See Adler, *Survival on the Margins*, 293–98; Mick, "Lviv under Soviet Rule," 156–57; Levin, *The Lesser of Two Evils*.

143. Drobner, *Wspomnienia*.

144. See Pierce, "Zofia Lissa."

145. See, for instance, Lissa, "Muzyka polska w ZSRR w latach 1941–1945."

146. Lissa, "Rola tradycji w muzyce polskiej, 1945–1969."

147. Shore, "Children of the Revolution," 40.

148. Mycielski, *Dziennik 1950–1959*, 206. The history of Lissa's experiences after the Thaw (1956), during which the Stalinist system was unwound, and during the anti-Zionist campaign of 1968 still needs to be written, but see Lissa to Zygmunt Mycielski, 10 February 1958, in Klubiński, "Zygmunt Mycielski i Zofia Lissa"; Józef Chomiński, "Perspektywy muzykologii w Polsce," *Kierunki*, 2 June 1968, 6–7.

CHAPTER 6

1. Borodziej, *The Warsaw Uprising of 1944*, 74–92.

2. Majewski, *Wojna i kultura*, 294–99.

3. Crowley, *Warsaw*, 24–26.

4. VHA, Palester-Chlebowczyk, tape 5, 15:40–23:15.

5. Szpilman, *Śmierć miasta*.

6. Piotr Perkowski in Drozdowski, Maniakówna, and Strzembosz, *Ludność cywilna w Powstaniu Warszawskim*, vol. 1, part 2, 251–55, here 255.

7. BUP, 800/1, Pamiętnik Adolfa Chybińskiego, p. 110.

8. BUP, 800/1, Pamiętnik Adolfa Chybińskiego, p. 119, 24 November 1944.

9. BUP, 800/1, Pamiętnik Adolfa Chybińskiego, p. 136, 16 January 1945.

10. BUP, 800/1, Pamiętnik Adolfa Chybińskiego, p. 122, 7 December 1944.

11. Zofia Lissa, "Trzy rozmowy z Woytowiczem," *Kuźnica*, no. 3 (1949): 6–7.

12. Jerzy Waldorff, "Dawna i przyszła opera," *Odrodzenie*, 23–30 December 1945, 8.

13. Iwaszkiewicz in *OLM*, 1:282.

14. AKP, Palester recordings, "Filharmonia Krakowska" (Radio Free Europe broadcast from 15 September 1965); Stefan Kisielewski, "Kraków stolicą muzyki (nieco wspomnień)" [1960], in *Pisma*, 2:245–52.

15. Gross, "Social Consequences of War"; Kunakhovich, *Communism's Public Sphere*, ch. 1.

16. Zaremba, *Komunizm, legitymizacja, nacjonalizm*, 144; Crowley, *Warsaw*, 30; and, more broadly, Kenney, *Rebuilding Poland*.

17. Lebow, "We Are Building a Common Home," 216 and 220.

18. Lebow, "'We Are Building a Common Home," 220.

19. On socialist realism in Polish music, see Helman, *Neoklasycyzm*, 71–80; Thomas, *Polish Music since Szymanowski*, chs. 4 and 5; Tompkins, *Composing*

the Party Line, ch. 1; Wieczorek, *Na froncie muzyki*; Vest, *Awangarda*, 26–50; Bylander, "Clichés Revisited."

20. Turkov, *En Pologne*, 36–51.

21. Żółkiewska, *Zerwana przeszłość*, 55.

22. Żółkiewska, *Zerwana przeszłość*, 51–57.

23. Żółkiewska, *Zerwana przeszłość*, 62–64.

24. Engel, "The Reconstruction of Jewish Communal Institutions"; Żółkiewska, *Zerwana przeszłość*, 60–62.

25. Żółkiewska, *Zerwana przeszłość*, 26, 62–107.

26. USHMM, RG-15.153, bulletin of 9 October 1946.

27. USHMM, RG-15.106M, Reel 7, 308/117, Szkoła Muzyczna im. Br. Hubermana to Przewodniczący Wydz. Kultury CKŻP, 28 February 1949; USHMM, RG-15.106M, Reel 7, 308/118, Szkoła Muzyczna Żydowskiego Towarzystwa Kultury i Sztuki w Wałbrzychu to Centralny Komitet Żydów w Polsce, 13 June 1949.

28. USHMM, RG-15.153, "Komunikat CKŻP Wydział Kultury," 21 February 1946.

29. USHMM, RG-15.153, bulletin of 18 April 1945.

30. USHMM, RG-15.106M, Reel 7, 308/121, and Reel 9, 308/135.

31. USHMM, RG-15.153, "Żydowska brygada artystyczna na Dolnym Śląsku," 5 November 1946.

32. USHMM, RG-15.153, bulletin of 12 September 1945.

33. Jockusch, *Collect and Record!*, ch. 3.

34. Werb, "Shmerke Kaczerginski," 404–5; Werb, "Fourteen Shoah Songbooks," 64–68.

35. USHMM, RG-15.153, bulletins of 23 May 1945, 20 June 1945, 3 August 1945, 12 September 1945, 29 March 1946, 5 November 1946, 28 December 1946; "Koncerty Loli Folman," *Nasze Słowo*, no. 4 (1946): 12.

36. USHMM, RG-15.153, bulletin of 1 December 1944.

37. Turkow, *La lutte pour la vie*, 240.

38. USHMM, RG-15.153, bulletin of 29 March 1946.

39. USHMM, RG-15.153, bulletin of 28 December 1946.

40. Engel, "Patterns of Anti-Jewish Violence."

41. Engel, "Patterns of Anti-Jewish Violence"; Gross, *Fear*, ch. 4; Engel, "On Continuity and Discontinuity"; Cichopek-Gajraj, *Beyond Violence*.

42. Palester, "Zjazd kompozytorów," *Twórczość* 1, no. 3 (1945): 187–92, here 188; Zygmunt Mycielski, "Na kieleckiej drodze," in Mycielski, *Ucieczki z pięciolinii*, 492–94 (originally published in 1946).

43. Stola, "Jewish Emigration from Communist Poland," 171–73.

44. Turkov, *En Pologne*, 246.

45. Turkov, *En Pologne*, 16.

46. Turkov, *En Pologne*, 43–44.

47. Turkov, *En Pologne*, 30–31.

48. Turkov, *En Pologne*, 84.

49. Turkov, *En Pologne*, 247.

50. Kowalska-Zając, *Oblicza Awangardy*, 15–16.

51. Wojciechowski, "Wiedeński świat Romana Haubenstocka-Ramatiego."

282 | Notes to Pages 175–179

52. Pierce, "Messianism Refigured."

53. Cegiełła, *Dziecko szczęścia* 2, chs. 5–7.

54. Fanning, *Mieczysław Weinberg*, 1–46.

55. Fitelberg, *Korespondencja Grzegorza Fitelberga*, 76 (Fitelberg to Stefan Spiess, 6 November 1945).

56. Baruch papers (private collection), copy of a notarized statement by Stanisław Ulankiewicz and Aleksander Rowiński (22 May 1946).

57. On this phenomenon more generally, see Koźmińska-Frejlak, "Asymilacja do polskości."

58. Gliński and Glińska, *Testament*, 51–55.

59. BJ, 280–11, Gliński to Jachimecki, 19 October 1941.

60. BJ, 280–11, Gliński to Jachimecki, 6 July 1943.

61. Activities are detailed in BJ, 280–11, Gliński to Jachimecki, 6 July 1943.

62. BJ, 280–11, Gliński to Jachimecki, 4 March 1946.

63. BJ, 280–11, Gliński to Jachimecki, 28 October 1947.

64. The Association of Polish Composers was formed in 1927, out of the Section of Contemporary Composers of the Warsaw Music Society, itself conceived as an aesthetically conservative alternative to the ISCM. Perkowski and other progressive composers staged a takeover of it in 1931. See Pierce, "Life and Death," 67, note 42.

65. AAN, 366/1, 292, "Protokół zebrania informacyjnego" (22 February 1945).

66. AAN, 366/1, 214, "Sprawozdania Rektora Zbigniewa Drzewieckiego" (12 April 1946); Helman, *Roman Palester*, 118.

67. Kisielewski, "Kraków stolicą muzyki (nieco wspomnień)," 245.

68. Micgiel, "Bandits and Reactionaries"; Waśkiewicz, "The Polish Home Army." One who did not avoid retaliation was Edmund Rudnicki, the director of the radio before the war and during the occupation. In November 1947 the music subcommission of the PPR opposed him as a candidate for the Music Council of the Polish Radio, noting that he was "one of the leading activists of the London group among Polish musicians." See AAN, 1400, 295/XVII-19, p. 83, F. Kulczycki to Wydział Kulturalno-Oświatowy Komitetu Centralnego PPR, 27 November 1947.

69. Palester, "Twórczość muzyczna w nowej Polsce," *Ruch Muzyczny* 2, nos. 11–12 (1946): 13–19, here 16.

70. ZKP, 12/2, II Walny Zjazd, 1–3 October 1946, p. 4; Palester, "Twórczość muzyczna w nowej Polsce," *Ruch Muzyczny* 2, nos. 11–12 (1946): 13–21, here 18.

71. Bronisław Rutkowski, "Zamiast fachowych rozważań noworocznych," *Ruch Muzyczny* 3, no. 1 (1947): 1–2, here 1.

72. Unsigned editorial, *Ruch Muzyczny* 3, no. 22 (1947): 1; Piotr Perkowski, "Droga kompozytorów polskich: Przemówienie wygłoszone na Walnym Zjeździe Zw. Zaw. Komp. Polskich w dn. 21 i 22 X 1947 r.," *Ruch Muzyczny* 3, no. 22 (1947): 8.

73. Długońska, "Piotr Rytel," 132–38.

74. Woźniakowska, *60 lat Filharmonii*, 42, 250; Waldorff, "Działalność Państwowej Filharmonii w Krakowie"; Zbigniew Drzewiecki, "W Sprawie Centralnej Rady Muzycznej," *Ruch Muzyczny* 1, no. 5 (1945): 2–5, here 2.

75. AAN, 1400, 295/XVII-19, 78–82 ("Ankieta sprawozdawcza"). The data were recorded by city. In Warsaw, 3.8 percent of members belonged to the PPR; in Katowice, 1.2 percent; in Sopot, 1 percent; in Łódź, 1.3 percent.

76. See several documents in AAN, 1400, 295/XVII-19: Koło muzyków P.P.R. to Wydział Kulturalno-Oświatowy Komitetu Centralnego P.P.R., April 1947; letter of 27 May 1947 to Komitet Miejski P.P.R. w Łodzi; "Memoriał Partyjnych Kół Muzycznych w sprawach muzycznych," 12 March 1948; "Protokół z posiedzenia podkomisji muzycznej" (13 August 1947).

77. The durability of the musical intelligentsia resembled that displayed by Polish academia. See Connelly, *Captive University*, chs. 8 and 9; Zysiak, "Hysteresis, Academic Biography, and Political Field."

78. See, for instance, "Memoriał w sprawie potrzeb muzyki polskiej," *Ruch Muzyczny* 2, nos. 11–12 (1946): 2–6. Much of the issue was devoted to articles arguing in favor of stronger state involvement in music.

79. Bohlman and Pierce, "Friend and Force."

80. BnF, Mus. N.L.a. 89 (fin), Mycielski to Annette Dieudonné, Nadia Boulanger, and Mademoiselle M. de Manziazly, 4 May 1945.

81. BnF, Mus. N.L.a. 89 (fin), Mycielski to Annette Dieudonné, Nadia Boulanger, and Mademoiselle M. de Manziazly, 4 May 1945.

82. BnF, N.L.a 89, Mycielski to Annette Dieudonné, 16 November 1947.

83. BnF, Mus. N.L.a. 89 (fin), Mycielski to Boulanger, 17 January 1947.

84. Vest, *Awangarda*, 29–33.

85. Bohlman and Pierce, "Friend and Force," 234–35.

86. Both Andrzej Panufnik and Witold Lutosławski made trips to Paris during the early postwar period for several months. Panufnik, *Composing Myself*, 156; Nikolska, *Conversations with Witold Lutosławski*, 35.

87. Tadeusz Kaczyński, "Ostatnia rozmowa z Antonim Szałowskim," *Ruch Muzyczny*, no. 10 (1973): 4; AAN, 1450, 354/IV/161, "Protokół Zebrania Muzyków Polskich z dnia 23 lipca 1945 roku w lokalu P.K.W.N."

88. Zygmunt Mycielski, "O naszej pracy uwag kilka," *Ruch Muzyczny* 1, no. 5 (1945): 5–8, here 5.

89. BnF, N.L.a. 89, Mycielski to Boulanger, 9 April 1946.

90. Stola, *Kraj bez wyjścia?*, 34–41; AAN, 366/1, 728, "Sprawozdanie Wydziału Muzyki Departamentu Twórczości Artystycznej za I kwartał 1950 roku."

91. Boczkowska, "O Jerzy Fitelbergu w Nowym Jorku."

92. See Vest, *Awangarda*, 28–32; Naliwajek-Mazurek, "Konstanty Regamey."

93. AKP, Palester papers, Ochlewski to Palester, 26 November 1947.

94. AKP, Palester papers, Ochlewski to Palester, 16 November 1948.

95. BN, Szałowski papers, Rps 10300 III, Mycielski to Szałowski, 2 August 1947.

96. Vest, *Awangarda*, ch. 3; Vest, "Educating Audiences."

97. AAN, 366/1, 310, untitled document about reconstruction (likely April 1945 or earlier).

98. "Deklaracja Zjazdu Kompozytorów Polskich w Krakowie," *Ruch Muzyczny* 1, no. 1 (1945): 11–12, here 11.

284 | Notes to Pages 185–190

99. AAN, 366/12, 233, Zofia Lissa, "Muzyka polska w okresie 5-lecia Polski Ludowej."

100. AKP, Lissa papers, Wiechowicz to Lissa, 28 April 1948.

101. BUP, 800/1, Pamiętnik Adolfa Chybińskiego, 132 (7 January 1945).

102. Palester, "Zjazd kompozytorów," *Twórczość* 1, no. 3 (1945): 187–92, here 188.

103. AAN, 366/18, 14, Conference from 18 to 25 September 1947, organized by the Centralny Instytut Kultury (Central Institute of Culture) in Szklarska Poręba; AAN, 366/18, 12, Conference from 29 December 1947 to 10 January 1948, organized by the Centralny Instytut Kultury in Szklarska Poręba. The Central Institute of Culture was tasked with coordinating nonprofessional artistic activities across cultural domains, with a focus on disseminating culture. See AAN, 366/3, 69, "Protokół z Konferencji Naczelników Wydziałów" (27–28 September 1946), p. 15.

104. AAN, 366/18, 12, Stenographic transcription of the "Konferencja Muzyczna w Szklarskiej Porębie."

105. AAN, 366/18, 14, "Dyskusja nad referatami prof. Rutkowskiego i prezesa Swatonia," 8.

106. AAN, 366/18, 14, stenographic transcription of day three of the conference.

107. AAN, 366/18, 14, remarks by Szczepański and Kozietulski in "Dyskusja nad referatami prof. Rutkowskiego i prezesa Swatonia."

108. See Fairclough, *Classics for the Masses*.

109. Drobner, *Wspomnienia*, 37–38.

110. Untitled announcement, *Ruch Muzyczny* 2, no. 3 (1946): 21.

111. AKP, Palester papers, Ochlewski to Palester, 11 November 1944.

112. Palester and Jędrychowska, "Rozmowa z Romanem Palestrem," 78.

113. Panufnik, *Composing Myself*, 148.

114. AAN, 366/1, 174, p. 18, "Sprawozdanie rzeczowe z działalności Komisji Zabezpieczenia Zbiorów i Bibliotek Muzycznych."

115. ANK, 2334, 45, "Związek Kompozytorów Polskich: Materiał informacyjny," p. 381 [1949].

116. AAN, 366/1, 312, "Sprawozdanie," 30 April 1945.

117. AAN, 366/1, 312, "Sprawozdanie," 30 April 1945.

118. AAN, 366/1, 312, "Sprawozdanie," 18 June 1945.

119. ANK, 2334, 593, "Bilans za 1945 i 1946."

120. AAN, 366/1, 312, "Memoriał w sprawie utworzenia państwowej instytucji muzycznej wydawniczej." The asset transfer to PWM is described in AAN, 366/1, 312, "Sprawozdanie Dyrektora Polskiego Wydawnictwa Muzycznego dla Państwowej Muzycznej Rady Wydawniczej" (30 April 1945), 112.

121. AAN, 366/1, 312. "Sprawozdanie PWM."

122. See AAN, 366/1, 312, "Sprawozdanie budżetowe" (November and December 1945), "Sprawozdanie budżetowe" (March 1946), "Sprawozdanie budżetowe" (May 1946).

123. AAN, 366/1, 312, "Materiał informacyjny o Polskim Wydawnictwie Muzycznym," 46–47; AKP, Lissa papers, Lissa to Komitet Centralny PZPR, Wydział Kultury, 10 March 1956.

Notes to Pages 190–198 | 285

124. ANK, 2334, 562, "Zestawienie produkcji i zbytu Polskiego Wydawnictwa Muzycznego od i.IV.1945–31.XII.1948."

125. ANK, 2334, 562, "Zalecenia Państwowej Muzycznej Rady Wydawniczej" (1 April 1945 to 1 April 1948).

126. ANK, 2334, 593, "Katalog muzyki symfonicznej."

127. ANK, 2334, 562, "Uchwały Prezydium Państwowej Muzycznej Rady Wydawniczej."

128. AAN, 366/1, 288, "Skład Państwowej Muzycznej Rady Wydawniczej."

129. AKP, Palester papers, Ochlewski to Palester, 21 June 1947.

130. Kisielewski, "Kraków stolicą muzyki," 249.

131. Michałowska, *"Ruch Muzyczny" 1945–1949*, xxxii–xxxiii.

132. Editorial, *Ruch Muzyczny* 1, no. 1 (1945): 1.

133. Kulakovskiy, "Pol'skiy muzïkal'nïy zhurnal 'Ruch Muzyczny.'" See also Gwizdalanka and Meyer, *Witold Lutosławski*, 191–94.

134. AKP, Palester papers, Ochlewski to Palester, 23 June 1948.

135. AKP, Palester papers, Ochlewski to Palester, 28 October 1948.

136. ANK, 2334, 562, "Plan wydawniczy Polskiego Wydawnictwa Muzycznego na rok 1951."

137. AKP, Lissa papers, Lissa to Wydział Kultury KC PZPR, 13 November 1954.

138. AAN, 237-XVIII, 120, "Sytuacja ideologiczna w środowisku kompozytorów polskich."

139. Sitarz, "In the Shadow of PWM."

140. ANK, 2334, 38, "O Polskim Wydawnictwie Muzycznym"; Stefan Jarociński, "O działalności Polskiego Wydawnictwa Muzycznego," *Przegląd Kulturalny* 1, no. 16 (1952): 4.

141. AAN 366/1, 312, "Rok pracy" (1946). The report states that *Ruch Muzyczny* was published in runs of 3,000 copies per issue. In 1947 *Ruch Muzyczny* had 500 subscribers and was printed in runs of 2,500 copies. AAN, 366/1, 312, "Sprawozdanie za I kwartał 1947 r."

CHAPTER 7

1. AAN, 366/1, 288, "Program Festiwalu Współczesnej Muzyki Polskiej."

2. Kisielewski, "Pierwsze Boże Narodzenie," *Ruch Muzyczny* 1, no. 6 (1945): 2–4, here 3.

3. Olick, "Collective Memory."

4. Kostka, *Tadeusz Zygfryd Kassern*, 18–21.

5. Kostka, *Tadeusz Zygfryd Kassern*, 66–79.

6. See Pierce, "Messianism Refigured."

7. AAN, 366/1, 288, "Program Festiwalu Współczesnej Muzyki Polskiej."

8. Sawicki, *Bitwa o prawdę*, ch. 2.

9. AKP, Kassern papers, "Sylwetka Kompozytora."

10. Mazurkiewicz, *Z dawnej literatury maryjnej*, 100–108.

11. Witkowski, "Kancjonał polski Walentego z Brzozowa," 33.

12. Mioduszewski, *Śpiewnik kościelny*, 449.

13. Porter, "Hetmanka and Mother."

286 | Notes to Pages 198–204

14. See Sprigge, *Socialist Laments*, 61.

15. Wlodarski, *Musical Witness*, 7.

16. These include the 1933 song "The Gorget" (Throat armor), which depicts prayer to Mary in a quasi-liturgical manner. I wish to thank Katarzyna Naliwajek for bringing these works to my attention.

17. AKP, Padlewski papers, "Z listu p. dr. Piotrowskiej do p. Padlewskiej," "Z listu p. Moniki Żeromskiej do p. Padlewskiej."

18. "Śmierć Romana Padlewskiego," *Ruch Muzyczny* 1, no. 4 (1945): 14–15.

19. See especially Kapferer, *Rumor*, ch. 1; Neubauer, *The Rumour*, 3–4.

20. Cesarani and Sundquist, *After the Holocaust*; Diner, *We Remember with Reverence and Love*.

21. "Ci, co odeszli . . .," *Ruch Muzyczny* 1, no. 1 (1945): 3–5; "Kronika," *Ruch Muzyczny* 1, no. 6 (1945): 22; "Muzycy wileńscy zmarli w czasie wojny," *Ruch Muzyczny* 1, no. 5 (1945): 22.

22. "Kronika," *Ruch Muzyczny* 1, no. 6 (1945): 22.

23. Zbigniew Wielicki, "Chopin pod okupacją," *Odrodzenie* 2, nos. 10–12 (1945): 12.

24. Finder and Prusin, "Jewish Collaborators on Trial in Poland"; Kornbluth, *The August Trials*.

25. A copy of the guidelines written by Drobner and distributed to the creative unions is reprinted in "Pierwsza dyskusja o weryfikacji."

26. The accusations appeared as Legato, "Profesor Kazuro zakasał rękawy," *Express Wieczorny* 1, no. 121 (20 August 1946): 3. Examples of defense include Bronisław Rutkowski, "Konserwatorium muzyczne w Warszawie w latach okupacji," *Ruch Muzyczny* 2, no. 24 (1946): 2–7; "Rezolucja Związku Kompozytorów Polskich" and "Oświadczenie prof. Stanisława Kazuro," *Ruch Muzyczny* 2, no. 24 (1946): 60–61.

27. IPN, Kr 502/1237, Michał Śliwiński, Otto Teusch, Zdzisław Roesner, Jerzy Strzemieński, and Józef Stojko to Pan Prokurator przy Sądzie Okręgowym Karnym w Warszawie (18 April 1947).

28. IPN, Kr 502/1237, "Wyrok w Imieniu Rzeczypospolitej Polskiej" (13 May 1948).

29. IPN, Kr 502/1237, "Protokół przesłuchania świadka [Józef Stojko]" (31 May 1947).

30. IPN, Kr 502/1237, "Protokół przesłuchania oskarżanego-podejrzanego" (18 December 1947).

31. IPN, Kr 502/1237, "Wniosek oskarżonej Heleny Zarzyckiej" (24 March 1948).

32. IPN, Kr 502/1237, "Wyrok w Imieniu Rzeczypospolitej Polskiej" (13 May 1948).

33. Milewski, "Hidden in Plain View"; Haltof, *Screening Auschwitz*, 72–73.

34. For an analogous discussion of Jewish traces in the film *Forbidden Songs*, see Milewski, "Hidden in Plain View."

35. Quoted in Helman, *Roman Palester*, 167.

36. Palester and Jędrychowska, "Rozmowa z Romanem Palestrem," 79.

37. Fitelberg, *Korespondencja Grzegorza Fitelberga*, 196 (no date).

38. ZKP, 12/92, "Protokół z konferencji kompozytorskiej Warszawa 4. II. 1950 r.," p. 13.

39. On the dialectic between anecdote and narrative as a founding tension of musical-historical writing, see Richards, "Carl Philipp Emanuel Bach."

40. Fauser, "Ensounding Trauma, Performing Commemoration."

41. Traba, "Symbole pamięci."

42. Witold Rudziński, "Kompozytor polski pod okupacją," *Odrodzenie* 2, no. 22 (1945): 10.

43. AAN, 366/1, 311, Stefania Łobaczewska, "Współczesna muzyka polska."

44. Roman Palester, "Twórczość muzyczna w nowej Polsce," *Ruch Muzyczny* 2, nos. 11–12 (1946): 13–19, here 13–14.

45. McKee, "Dance and the Music of Chopin," 212–15.

46. Stefan Kisielewski, "Życie muzyczne Krakowa," *Tygodnik Powszechny*, 29 April 1945, 4.

47. Mickiewicz, *Konrad Wallenrod*, lines 835–38.

48. Miłosz, *The History of Polish Literature*, 220–21.

49. Stefan Kisielewski, "Pierwsze Boże Narodzenie," *Ruch Muzyczny* 1, no. 6 (1945): 2–4, here 3.

50. Régamey, "Muzyka polska pod okupacją niemiecką [1946]," *OLM*, 2:63.

51. S. K., "Życie muzyczne pod okupacją," *Ruch Muzyczny* 1, no. 1 (1945): 12–13.

52. Mycielski, "O naszej pracy uwag kilka," *Ruch Muzyczny* 1, no. 5 (1945): 5–8, here 6.

53. Wiłkomirski, *Wspomnień ciąg dalszy*, 52–57.

54. Włodzimierz Sokorski, "Notatki muzyczne," *Ruch Muzyczny*, no. 15 (1974): 3; Bohdan Wodiczko in "1945: Wspomnienia muzyków," *Ruch Muzyczny*, no. 10 (1975): 8.

55. Palester, "Zjazd kompozytorów," *Twórczość* 1, no. 3 (1945): 187–92, here 192.

56. AKP, Kassern papers, Bandrowska-Turska to Kassern, 23 April 1948.

57. Borwicz, *Pieśń ujdzie cało*, 25.

58. Szpilman, *Śmierć miasta*, 71–73.

59. Jerzy Waldorff, "Życie muzyczne w kraju: Warszawa," *Ruch Muzyczny* 1, no. 5 (1945): 12–13. On the authorship of *Death of a City*, see Pierce "Sonic Transformations."

60. USHMM, RG-15.189M, file 313/36; USHMM, RG-15.691, IPN GK 453/739.

61. Tuszyńska, *Vera Gran*.

62. Koźmińska-Frejlak, "I'm Going to the Oven"; Person, "Sexual Violence during the Holocaust."

63. USHMM, RG-15.189M, file 313/36, "Protokół przesłuchania świadka Dawida Sznajera" (20 February 1947), p. 46.

64. USHMM, RG-15.189M, file 313/36, "Protokół, 6 listopada 1946" (testimony of Dawid Sznajer).

65. USHMM, RG-15.189M, file 313/36, "Uzasadnienie."

288 | Notes to Pages 211–221

66. Reports of mass deportations to death camps from Lublin and Łódź had begun to reach the Warsaw Ghetto in spring 1942; however, such rumors of the unimaginable were rarely interpreted as clear evidence of impending death. See Goldberg, "Rumor Culture," 109.

67. Gutman, *Resistance*.

68. Mycielski, "O naszej pracy uwag kilka," *Ruch Muzyczny* 1, no. 5 (1945): 5–8, here 6.

69. Mycielski, "O naszej pracy uwag kilka," 6.

70. Mycielski, "O naszej pracy uwag kilka," 6.

71. BnF, Mus. N.L.a. 89 (fin), Mycielski to Boulanger, 13 January 1946.

72. Zerubavel, *The Elephant in the Room*.

73. Shallcross, *The Holocaust Object*, 72–75.

74. Miłosz, *The Collected Poems*.

75. Helman, ". . . Tylko to jest ocalenie." Mycielski's *Ocalenie* was published by PWM in 1989.

76. Régamey, "Muzyka polska pod okupacją niemiecką [1946]," *OLM*, 2:65.

77. Jerzy Broszkiewicz, "Pierwszy sezon muzyczny w Krakowie," *Twórczość* 1, no. 5 (1945): 145–52, here 151.

78. ZKP, 12/3, III Walny Zjazd, 20–21 October 1947, pp. 7–8.

79. Wiszniowska, *Stańczyk Polski Ludowej*, 29–34. On his compositions, see Gąsiorowska, *Kisielewski*.

80. Szyszka, *Droga klerka*, 102–18.

81. One book marked by its blunt recounting of wartime fates is the series of stories published by Zofia Nałkowska in 1946 as *Medaliony*, translated as *Medallions*.

82. Stefan Kisielewski, "Tematy wojenne," *Tygodnik Powszechny* 1, no. 9 (1945): 3.

83. Kisielewski, "Tematy wojenne."

84. Kisielewski, "Festival [*sic*] Polskiej Muzyki Współczesnej w Krakowie," *Ruch Muzyczny* 1, no. 1 (1945): 24–25, here 25.

85. Kisielewski, "Festival [*sic*] Polskiej Muzyki Współczesnej w Krakowie."

86. He described Malawski's symphony as "thicket, a symphony—a jungle" and Lutosławski's trio as "a laboratory work, an artistic study."

87. Kisielewski, "Festival [*sic*] Polskiej Muzyki Współczesnej w Krakowie."

88. Rehding, *Music and Monumentality*, 42–43.

89. Fairclough, "Was Soviet Music Middlebrow?," 364–65.

90. Vest, *Awangarda*, 31.

91. Zygmunt Mycielski, "Przemówienie na walnym zjeździe kompozytorów polskich," *Ruch Muzyczny* 5, no. 1 (1949): 2–6, here 3.

92. Włodzimierz Sokorski, "Formalizm i realizm w muzyce," *Ruch Muzyczny* 4, nos. 23–24 (1948): 2–5, here 4.

93. Zygmunt Mycielski, "Przemówienie prezesa Zygmunta Mycielskiego," *Muzyka* 1, nos. 3–4 (1950): 17–23, here 22.

94. AAN, 237/XVIII, 74, "Tezy do referatu prof. Bolesława Woytowicza na Walnym Zjeździe Kompozytorów Polskich w dniach 16–18. VI. [1950]."

Notes to Pages 221–228 | 289

95. Aleksander Jackowski, "Po pierwszym etapie Festiwalu Muzyki Polskiej," *Muzyka* 2, no. 7 (1951): 3; Zofia Lissa, "Z perspektywy Festiwalu Muzyki Polskiej," *Muzyka* 2, no. 12 (1951): 3; Włodzimierz Sokorski, "Festiwal Muzyki Polskiej: Cele i zadania," *Muzyka* 2, nos. 3–4 (1951): 3.

96. Witold Rudziński, "W sprawie 'Symfonii polskiej' Z. Mycielskiego," *Muzyka* 2, no. 10 (1951): 45; Lissa, "Próba podsumowania Festiwalu i wyników Zjazdu," *Muzyka* 3, nos. 1–2 (1952): 21–33, here 27; Stefania Łobaczewska, "IV Sonata na fortepian i skrzypce Grażyny Bacewiczówny," *Muzyka* 2, no. 11 (1951): 22; AAN, 366/1, 723, "Protokół z II posiedzenia Centralnej Komisji Ocen Festiwalu Muzyki Polskiej" (21 April 1951).

97. Fijałkowska, *Polityka i twórcy*, 52–53; Tompkins, *Composing the Party Line*, 25.

98. Bierut, *O upowszechnienie kultury*, 17–19.

99. Cała, "Kształtowanie się polskiej i żydowskiej wizji martyrologicznej."

100. Shore, "Język, pamięć i rewolucyjna awangarda."

101. Wajner, *Cantos de lucha y resurgimiento*, 245–47.

102. On this phenomenon more broadly, see Shore, "Children of the Revolution," 24.

103. Shore, *Caviar and Ashes*, 261–62.

104. The score is published in Wajner, *Cantos de lucha y resurgimiento*, 211–20.

105. Jan Maklakiewicz, "Twórczość muzyczna Leona Wajnera," *Nasze Słowo*, no. 8 (1948): 12.

106. Maklakiewicz, "Twórczość muzyczna Leona Wajnera."

107. Shore, "Children of the Revolution," 27.

108. Steinlauf, *Bondage to the Dead*, 71; Shore, "Język, pamięć i rewolucyjna awangarda"; Szaynok, "Mémoire de l'insurrection du ghetto de Varsovie (1944–1989)."

109. Quoted in Pierce, "Messianism Refigured," 246.

110. Thomas, *Polish Music since Szymanowski*, 46–51; Jakelski, "Witold Lutosławski and the Ethics of Abstraction," 172–77.

111. "Konferencja Kompozytorów w Łagowie Lubuskim, 5–8 VIII 1949, Protokoł," *Ruch Muzyczny* 5, no. 14 (1949): 12–31, here 18.

112. "Konferencja Kompozytorów w Łagowie Lubuskim," 18.

113. AKP, Lissa Papers, Chomiński to Lissa, 5 February 1949.

114. "Konferencja Kompozytorów w Łagowie Lubuskim," 18.

115. "Konferencja Kompozytorów w Łagowie Lubuskim," 18.

116. "Konferencja Kompozytorów w Łagowie Lubuskim," 19.

117. "Konferencja Kompozytorów w Łagowie Lubuskim," 19.

118. "Konferencja Kompozytorów w Łagowie Lubuskim," 19.

119. "Konferencja Kompozytorów w Łagowie Lubuskim," 19.

120. "Konferencja Kompozytorów w Łagowie Lubuskim," 27.

121. Witold Rudziński, "Zjazd kompozytorów w Łagowie," *Odrodzenie*, no. 25 (1949): 4; Włodzimierz Sokorski, "Ku realizmowi socjalistycznemu w muzyce," *Kuźnica*, no. 36 (1949): 1.

122. Fay, *Shostakovich: A Life*, ch. 6; Frolova-Walker, "A Birthday Present for Stalin"; Sprigge, *Socialist Laments*.

290 | Notes to Pages 228–236

123. ZKP, 12/92, "Protokół z konferencji kompozytorskiej Warszawa, 4. II. 1950 r.," p. 13.

CONCLUSION

1. Jakubowska, *Patrons of History*, 2.
2. "Konferencja Kompozytorów w Łagowie Lubuskim, 5–8 VIII 1949, Protokoł," *Ruch Muzyczny* 5, no. 14 (1949): 12–31, here 28.
3. BN, Mycielski papers, III 14394, Mycielski to Roman Maciejewski, 18 May 1958.
4. See Vest, *Awangarda*, 53–56.
5. Jakelski and Reyland, *Lutosławski's Worlds*.
6. Bronisław Rutkowski, "Kłopoty z młodymi," *Ruch Muzyczny*, no. 8 (1957): 10–12.
7. Shreffler, "Ideologies of Serialism"; Fosler-Lussier, *Music Divided*; Carroll, *Music and Ideology*.
8. Jakelski, *Making New Music*, 1.
9. Vest, *Awangarda*; Jakelski, "Witold Lutosławski and the Ethics of Abstraction," 174–77; Jakelski, "Górecki's *Scontri*," 221–22; Reyland, "Lutosławski, 'Akcja', and the Poetics of Musical Plot."
10. See, for example, Schmelz, *Such Freedom, If Only Musical*; Karnes, *Sounds Beyond*; and Cornish, "Synthesized Socialism."
11. Vest, *Awangarda*, intro, chs. 5–6; and Lindstedt, "The Polish School of Composition."
12. Zygmunt Mycielski, "Przeżyłem VII Warszawską Jesień," *Ruch Muzyczny*, no. 19 (1964): 5.
13. Vest, *Awangarda*, 103, 166.
14. BN, Mycielski papers, III 14394, Mycielski to Maciejewski, 18 May 1958.
15. On his advocacy behind the scenes at the Warsaw Autumn Festival, see Jakelski, *Making New Music*, 19–21; Vest, *Awangarda*, 50–53, 166; and, more broadly, Bohlman and Pierce, "Friend and Force."
16. Witold Lutosławski, "W atmosferze wolności," in Erhardt, *50 lat*, 77–79.
17. For an analysis, see Vest, *Awangarda*, 60–62.
18. Gwizdalanka, "Głosy i dygresje," 13.
19. IPN, BU 0246/998/1, p. 16.
20. Morska, "Zygmunt Mycielski's Blues."
21. Bolesławska-Lewandowska, "Zygmunt Mycielski na łamach paryskiej 'Kultury.'"
22. Henryk Swolkień, "Życie muzyczne w kraju: Warszawa," *Ruch Muzyczny* 5, no. 15 (1949): 40–41, here 41.
23. AKP, Lissa papers, Łobaczewska to Lissa, 9 September 1948.
24. AAN, 366/12, 233, p. 360, Zofia Lissa, "Muzyka polska w okresie 5-lecia Polski Ludowej."
25. Helman, *Roman Palester*, 134–60.
26. AKP, Palester papers, Jerzy Fitelberg to Palester, 14 March 1949, 25 June 1950, 27 September 1950.

27. Palester, "Konflikt Marsjasza," 8.

28. Miłosz, *The Captive Mind*, 3–24, 54–81. On the reception of *The Captive Mind*, see Franaszek, *Milosz*, 285–305.

29. He had secured this position thanks to the help of the Polish conductor Artur Rodziński and his wife, Halina. They were friends with Allen Dulles, the head of the National Committee for a Free Europe, which had been formed in June 1949 under the patronage of the State Department and CIA and worked closely with anti-communist émigrés with the aim of preparing anti-communist resistance within the countries of eastern Europe. AKP, Palester papers, Halina Rodzińska to Palester, 7 September 1950, 30 October 1950, 17 February 1951, 20 May 1952; Machcewicz, *Poland's War on Radio Free Europe*, 22–24.

30. AKP, K-XLV/35 Palester to Wiechowicz, 3 September 1959; ZKP, Palester file, ZKP to Palester, 19 April 1951; Helman, *Roman Palester*, 335.

31. Tadeusz Kaczyński, "Trzydzieści pięć lat muzyki: Rozmowa z Romanem Palestrem," *Ruch Muzyczny*, no. 20 (1964): 5–7.

32. IPN, BU 0204/369 t.1, "Sprawa operacyjna dot. Tadeusz Wacław Kaczyński."

33. Helman, *Roman Palester*, 185–258.

34. AKP, Wiechowicz papers, K-XLV/35, Palester to Wiechowicz, 3 September 1959.

35. Four of Palester's works were performed at the Warsaw Autumn during his lifetime: Symphony No. 4 (in 1958), Concerto for viola and orchestra (in 1979), *Metamorfozy* (in 1981), and Symphony No. 5 (in 1988). See Helman, *Roman Palester*, 334–46.

36. Chmielewska, "Współczesny dyskurs historyczny," 44. For a thoughtful discussion of recent scholarship on Polish music in dialogue with Chmielewska's ideas, see Beszterda van Vliet, "On *Awangarda*."

37. Tarnawska-Kaczorowska, "Na rozpoczęcie," 12–13 and 22, note 6.

38. See Pierce, "Messianism Refigured."

39. AKP, Kassern papers, Outgoing correspondence, Kassern to Julius Rudel, 22 October 1950.

40. Pierce, "Messianism Refigured."

Bibliography

ARCHIVAL COLLECTIONS

Archiwum Akt Nowych (AAN)—Archive of Modern Records, Warsaw
  Central Committee of the Polish United Workers' Party, Culture Division
    (237/XVIII)
  Central Committee of the Polish Workers' Party (1400)
  Delegate's Bureau of the Polish Government-in-Exile (202/VII)
  Higher Vocational Courses and Schools in Lviv (541)
  Ministry of Culture and Art, Bureau for International Cooperation
    (366/12)
  Ministry of Culture and Art, Central Institute of Culture (366/18)
  Ministry of Culture and Art, Department of Music (366/1)
  Ministry of Culture and Art, Office of the Minister (366/3)
  Ministry of Foreign Affairs of the Second Republic (322)
  National Council of Poles in France (1450)
  Polish Committee of National Liberation (185)
  Union of Polish Patriots (130)
Archiwum Kompozytorów Polskich (AKP)—Archive of Polish Composers,
    University of Warsaw Library
  Association of Young Musician-Poles in Paris (SMMP)
  Tadeusz Zygfryd Kassern papers
  Zofia Lissa papers
  Roman Padlewski papers
  Roman Palester papers
  Stanisław Wiechowicz papers
Archiwum Ministerstwa Spraw Zagranicznych (AMSZ)—Archive of the
    Ministry of Foreign Affairs, Warsaw

294 | Bibliography

Department of Information and Propaganda (Z. 21)
Archiwum Narodowe w Krakowie (ANK)—The National Archive in Cracow
    City of Cracow: Office for Culture and Propaganda (SMKr)
    Polish Music Publishers (2334)
Archiwum Żydowskiego Instytutu Historycznego (AŻIH)—Archive of the
    Jewish Historical Institute, Warsaw
    The Jewish Society for Public Welfare: Central Commission for
        Entertainments
Witold Hugo Baruch papers, Warsaw, private collection
Biblioteka Jagiellońska (BJ)—Jagiellonian Library, Cracow
    Association of Young Musicians in Cracow (SMM)
    Zdzisław Jachimecki papers (280-11, 289-11)
    PWM Deposit, pre-1944 papers of Adolf Chybiński (PWM)
Biblioteka Narodowa (BN)—The National Library of Poland, Warsaw
    Zygmunt Mycielski papers
    Antoni Szałowski papers
    Social life documents (XIX)
    Eugenia Umińska memoir (Rps akc. 17260)
Biblioteka Uniwersytecka w Poznaniu (BUP)—The University Library in
    Poznań
    Adolf Chybiński papers
Bibliothèque nationale de France (BnF)—National Library of France, Paris
    Nadia Boulanger correspondence
The British Library, London (BL)
    Letters to Edward Clark
Derzhavnyĭ Arkhiv L'vivs'koï Oblasti (DALO)—State Archive of the Lviv
    Oblast, Lviv
    Jan Kazimierz University (F-26)
    State Conservatory in Lviv (R-2056)
Instytut Pamięci Narodowej (IPN)—The Institute for National Memory,
    Warsaw
    Zygmunt Mycielski files (BU 0246/998)
    Roman Palester files (BU 0204/369)
    Records of the criminal case of Helena Zarzycka (Kr 502/1237)
New York Public Library, Music Division
    Jerzy Fitelberg papers
POLIN Museum of the History of Polish Jews, Warsaw (POLIN)
    Witold Hugo Baruch papers
    Józef Kamiński papers
The Polish Institute and Sikorski Museum, London (PISM)
    Polish Government-in-Exile, Ministry of Internal Affairs
United States Holocaust Memorial Museum, Washington D.C. (USHMM)
    Bulletin of the Jewish Press Agency, Warsaw (RG-15.153)
    Central Committee of Jews in Poland, Culture and Propaganda Division
        (RG-15.106M)
    Holocaust survivor testimonies collected by the Central Jewish Historical
        Commission in Warsaw, 1945–46 (RG-15.084M)

Records of the District Court of Warsaw in the case of Wiera Gran-Jezierska (RG-15.691, IPN GK 453/739)
Trial of Wiera Gran-Jezierska by the Civic Court of the Central Committee of Jews in Poland (RG-15.189M, file 313/36)
Visual History Archive, USC Shoah Foundation (VHA)
Małgorzata Palester-Chlebowczyk, interview 46508, 30 July 1998
Związek Kompozytorów Polskich (ZKP)—Union of Polish Composers, Warsaw
Early postwar documents
Personnel files

PERIODICALS

Acta Musicologica

Biuletyn Informacyjny

Bluszcz

Chwila

Czerwony Sztandar

Echo

Express Wieczorny

Gazeta Lwowska

Gazeta Muzyczna

Gazeta Żydowska

Kierunki

Kultura Jutra

Kurier Poranny

Kuźnica

Kwartalnik Muzyczny

Lwowskie Wiadomości Muzyczne i Literackie

Lyra

Muzyka [1924–1938]

Muzyka [1950–1956]

Muzyka Polska

Muzyka Współczesna

Nasza Opinja

Nasze Słowo

Nowe Widnokręgi

Odrodzenie

Orkiestra

Pamiętnik Teatralny

Pion

Prosto z Mostu

Przegląd Kultury

Przegląd Spraw Kulturalnych

Radians'ka Muzyka

Radio i Świat

Revue musicale

Ruch Muzyczny

Die Stimme

Sygnały

Twórczość

Tygodnik Illustrowany

Tygodnik Powszechny

Wolna Polska

Życie Sztuki

OTHER PUBLISHED SOURCES

"100 Years of Polish Musicology," special issue of *Musicology Today* 9 (2012).

Adler, Eliyana R. *Survival on the Margins: Polish Jewish Refugees in the Wartime Soviet Union.* Cambridge, MA: Harvard University Press, 2020.

296 | Bibliography

Aleksiun, Natalia. "Regards from My 'Shtetl': Polish Jews Write to Piłsudski, 1933–1935." *Polish Review* 56, no. 1/2 (2011): 57–71.

Alexander, Jeffrey C. "Toward a Theory of Cultural Trauma." In *Cultural Trauma and Collective Identity*, edited by Jeffrey C. Alexander, Ron Eyerman, Bernhard Giesen, Neil J. Smelser, and Piotr Sztompka, 1–30. Berkeley: University of California Press, 2004.

Amar, Tarik Cyril. *The Paradox of Ukrainian Lviv: A Borderland City between Stalinists, Nazis, and Nationalists*. Ithaca, NY: Cornell University Press, 2015.

Applegate, Celia. *Bach in Berlin: Nation and Culture in Mendelssohn's Revival of the "St. Matthew Passion."* Ithaca, NY: Cornell University Press, 2005.

Applegate, Celia, and Pamela Potter. "Germans as the 'People of Music': Genealogy of an Identity." In *Music and German National Identity*, edited by Celia Applegate and Pamela Potter, 1–35. Chicago: University of Chicago Press, 2002.

Apte, Henryk. "Udział Żydów w muzyce." In *Udział Żydów w kulturze*, vol. 1, 68–71. Cracow: Nakładem Związku Zawodowego Nauczycieli Szkół Żydowskich, 1938.

Archiwum Ringelbluma: Konspiracyjne archiwum Getta Warszawy, 35 vol. Warsaw: Żydowski Instytut Historyczny, 1997–2018.

Arciszewska, Zofia. *Po obu stronach oceanu: Wspomnienia*. London: Polska Fundacja Kulturalna, 1976.

Babiracki, Patryk. *Soviet Soft Power in Poland: Culture and the Making of Stalin's New Empire, 1943–1957*. Chapel Hill: University of North Carolina Press, 2015.

Balibar, Étienne. "Racism and Nationalism." In *Race, Nation, Class: Ambiguous Identities*, edited by Étienne Balibar and Immanuel Maurice Wallerstein, translated by Chris Turner, 37–68. London: Verso, 1991.

Batnitzky, Leora. *How Judaism Became a Religion: An Introduction to Modern Jewish Thought*. Princeton, NJ: Princeton University Press, 2011.

Bauer, Ela. "The Ideological Roots of the Polish Jewish Intelligentsia." *Polin Studies in Polish Jewry* 24 (2012): 95–109.

Beckerman, Michael. "Postcard from New York—Trio from Terezín." *Music and Politics* 1, no. 1 (2007). http://dx.doi.org/10.3998/mp.9460447.0001.101.

Berg, Mary. *The Diary of Mary Berg: Growing up in the Warsaw Ghetto*. Edited by Susan Lee Pentlin. London: Oneworld Publications, 2006.

Beszterda, Marta. "Female Composers, Gender and Politics in Communist Poland." Master's thesis, University of Amsterdam, 2016.

Beszterda van Vliet, Marta. "On *Awangarda: Tradition and Modernity in Postwar Polish Music* by Lisa Cooper Vest." *Res Facta Nova* 23 (2022). http://dx.doi.org/10.14746/rfn.2022.23.11.

Biale, David. "A Journey between Worlds: East European Jewish Culture from the Partitions of Poland to the Holocaust." In *Cultures of the Jews: A New History*, edited by David Biale, 799–860. New York: Schocken, 2002.

Bierut, Bolesław. *O upowszechnienie kultury: Przemówienie Prezydenta Rzeczypospolitej Bolesława Bieruta na otwarciu radiostacji we Wrocławiu 16 listopada 1947*. Warsaw: Radiowy Instytut Wydawniczy, 1948.

Biess, Frank. "Feelings in the Aftermath: Toward a History of Postwar Emotions." In *Histories of the Aftermath: The Legacies of the Second World War in Europe*, edited by Frank Biess and Robert G. Moeller, 30–48. New York: Berghahn Books, 2010.

Biskupska, Jadwiga. *Survivors: Warsaw under Nazi Occupation*. Cambridge: Cambridge University Press, 2022.

Blejwas, Stanislaus A. *Realism in Polish Politics: Warsaw Positivism and National Survival in Nineteenth Century Poland*. New Haven, CT: Yale Concilium on International and Area Studies, 1984.

Blobaum, Robert, ed. *Antisemitism and Its Opponents in Modern Poland*. Ithaca, NY: Cornell University Press, 2005.

———. *A Minor Apocalypse: Warsaw during the First World War*. Ithaca, NY: Cornell University Press, 2017.

———. "The 'Woman Question' in Russian Poland, 1900–1914." *Journal of Social History* 35, no. 4 (2002): 799–824.

Błaszczyk, Leon Tadeusz. *Żydzi w kulturze muzycznej ziem polskich w XIX i XX wieku: Słownik biograficzny*. Warsaw: Stowarzyszenie Żydowski Instytut Historyczny w Polsce, 2014.

Boczkowska, Ewelina. "O Jerzym Fitelbergu w Nowym Jorku na podstawie źródeł archiwalnych." In *"American Dream": Polscy twórcy za oceanem*, edited by Beata Bolesławska-Lewandowska and Jolanta Guzy-Pasiak, 33–50. Warsaw: ISPAN, 2020.

Bohlman, Andrea F. *Musical Solidarities: Political Action and Music in Late Twentieth-Century Poland*. New York: Oxford University Press, 2020.

Bohlman, Andrea F., and J. Mackenzie Pierce. "Friend and Force: Nadia Boulanger in Polish Musical Culture." In *Nadia Boulanger and Her World*, edited by Jeanice Brooks, 229–53. Chicago: University of Chicago Press, 2020.

Bohlman, Philip V. *Jewish Music and Modernity*. New York: Oxford University Press, 2008.

———. *The World Centre for Jewish Music in Palestine, 1936–1940: Jewish Musical Life on the Eve of World War II*. Oxford: Oxford University Press, 1992.

Bolesławska-Lewandowska, Beata. "Zygmunt Mycielski na łamach paryskiej 'Kultury.'" *Polski Rocznik Muzykologiczny* 15 (2017): 78–98.

Bond, Lucy, and Stef Craps. *Trauma*. New York: Routledge, 2020.

Borkowski, Marian, Alicja Gronau-Osińska, and Aleksander Kościów, eds. *Piotr Perkowski: Życie i dzieło*. Warsaw: Wydawnictwo Akademii Muzycznej im. F. Chopina, 2003.

Borodziej, Włodzimierz. *The Warsaw Uprising of 1944*. Translated by Barbara Harshav. Madison: University of Wisconsin Press, 2006.

Borwicz, Michał. *Pieśń ujdzie cało: Antologia wierszy o Żydach pod okupacją niemiecką*. Warsaw: Centralna Żydowska Komisja Historyczna w Polsce, 1947.

Bothe, Alina, and Markus Nesselrodt. "Survivor: Towards a Conceptual History." *Leo Baeck Institute Yearbook* 61, no. 1 (2016): 57–82.

Botstein, Leon. "The Aesthetics of Assimilation and Affirmation: Reconsidering the Career of Felix Mendelssohn." In *Mendelssohn and His World*, edited by Larry Todd, 5–42. Princeton, NJ: Princeton University Press, 1991.

298 | Bibliography

Brenner, Rachel Feldhay. *Polish Literature and the Holocaust: Eyewitness Testimonies, 1942–1947*. Evanston, IL: Northwestern University Press, 2019.

Brown, Kate. *A Biography of No Place: From Ethnic Borderland to Soviet Heartland*. Cambridge, MA: Harvard University Press, 2004.

Bułat, Mirosława M. "Turkow Family." In *The YIVO Encyclopedia of Jews in Eastern Europe*. https://encyclopedia.yivo.org/article/1287.

Bychawska, Maria, and Henryk Schiller, eds. *100 lat Filharmonii w Warszawie 1901–2001*. Warsaw: Fundacja Bankowa im. Leopolda Kronenberga, 2001.

Bylander, Cindy. "Clichés Revisited: Poland's 1949 Łagów Composers' Conference." *Polski Rocznik Muzykologiczny* 2015: 15–34.

———. *Engaging Cultural Ideologies: Classical Composers and Musical Life in Poland 1918–1956*. Boston: Academic Studies Press, 2022.

Calico, Joy H. *Arnold Schoenberg's "A Survivor from Warsaw" in Postwar Europe*. Berkeley: University of California Press, 2014.

Cała, Alina. "Kształtowanie się polskiej i żydowskiej wizji martyrologicznej po II wojnie światowej." *Przegląd Socjologiczny* 49, no. 2 (2000): 167–80.

———. *Żyd—wróg odwieczny? Antysemityzm w Polsce i jego źródła*. Warsaw: Nisza, 2012.

Camiscioli, Elisa. *Reproducing the French Race: Immigration, Intimacy, and Embodiment in the Early Twentieth Century*. Durham, NC: Duke University Press, 2009.

Caplan, Debra. *Yiddish Empire: The Vilna Troupe, Jewish Theater, and the Art of Itinerancy*. Ann Arbor: University of Michigan Press, 2018.

Carroll, Mark. *Music and Ideology in Cold War Europe*. Cambridge: Cambridge University Press, 2003.

Cegiełła, Janusz. *Dziecko szczęścia: Aleksander Tansman i jego czasy*, vols. 1–2. Łódź: 86 Press, 1996.

Cesarani, David, and Eric J. Sundquist, eds. *After the Holocaust: Challenging the Myth of Silence*. London: Routledge, 2011.

Charle, Christophe. *Birth of the Intellectuals: 1880–1900*. Translated by David Fernbach and G. M. Goshgarian. Malden, MA: Polity, 2015.

Chmielewska, Katarzyna. "Współczesny dyskurs historyczny o polskim komunizmie w perspektywie narratologii." *Teksty Drugie*, no. 3 (2013): 36–51.

Chowrimootoo, Christopher, and Kate Guthrie, eds. "Colloquy: Musicology and the Middlebrow." *Journal of the American Musicological Society* 73, no. 2 (2020): 327–95.

Chybiński, Adolf, and Józef M. Chomiński. *Korespondencja 1945–1952*. Edited by Małgorzata Sieradz. Warsaw: PAN, 2016.

Chylińska, Teresa. *Karol Szymanowski: His Life and Works*. Translated by John Glowacki. Los Angeles: Polish Music History Series, 1993.

Ciancia, Kathryn. *On Civilization's Edge: A Polish Borderland in the Interwar World*. New York: Oxford University Press, 2020.

Cichopek-Gajraj, Anna. *Beyond Violence: Jewish Survivors in Poland and Slovakia, 1944–48*. New York: Cambridge University Press, 2014.

Ciesielski, Rafał. "Pokolenie kompozytorskie 'debiut 1930' (przyczynek do diachronii muzyki polskiej XX wieku)." *Res Facta Nova*, no. 18 (2017): 147–71.

Bibliography | 299

Cizmic, Maria. *Performing Pain: Music and Trauma in Eastern Europe*. New York: Oxford University Press, 2012.

Cohen, Brigid Maureen. *Stefan Wolpe and the Avant-Garde Diaspora*. Cambridge: Cambridge University Press, 2012.

Collins, Sarah, Barbara L. Kelly, and Laura Tunbridge, eds. "Round Table: A 'Musical League of Nations'? Music Institutions and the Politics of Internationalism between the Wars." *Journal of the Royal Musical Association* 147, no. 2 (2022): 1–72.

Connelly, John. *Captive University: The Sovietization of East German, Czech, and Polish Higher Education, 1945–1956*. Chapel Hill: University of North Carolina Press, 2000.

———. "Nazis and Slavs: From Racial Theory to Racist Practice." *Central European History* 32, no. 1 (1999): 1–33.

———. "Why the Poles Collaborated So Little: And Why That Is No Reason for Nationalist Hubris." *Slavic Review* 64, no. 4 (2005): 771–81.

Conway, David. *Jewry in Music: Entry to the Profession from the Enlightenment to Richard Wagner*. Cambridge: Cambridge University Press, 2012.

Cornish, Gabrielle. "Synthesized Socialism: Soviet Modernity and the Politics of Timbre in the Cold War." *Journal of the American Musicological Society* 75, no. 3 (2022): 547–98.

Crowley, David. *Warsaw*. London: Reaktion Books, 2003.

Davies, Norman. *God's Playground: A History of Poland*, vol. 2, rev. ed. New York: Columbia University Press, 2005.

Dean, Carolyn J. *The Moral Witness: Trials and Testimony after Genocide*. Ithaca, NY: Cornell University Press, 2019.

Diner, Hasia R. *We Remember with Reverence and Love: American Jews and the Myth of Silence after the Holocaust, 1945–1962*. New York: New York University Press, 2009.

Długońska, Barbara. "Piotr Rytel." *Zeszyty naukowe Akademia Muzyczna im. Stanisława Moniuszki w Gdańsku* 23 (1984): 113–41.

Domański, Alfred Jerzy [Mieczysław Jerzy Erhardt]. "Sztuka i Moda." *Ruch Muzyczny*, no. 8 (1960): 10–11.

Downes, Stephen C. *Szymanowski, Eroticism and the Voices of Mythology*. Burlington, VT: Ashgate, 2003.

Drobner, Bolesław. *Bezustanna walka*, vol. 3. Warsaw: PIW, 1967.

Drobner, Mieczysław. *Wspomnienia o początkach życia muzycznego w Polsce Ludowej, 1944–1946*. Cracow: PWM, 1985.

Drozdowski, Marian Marek, Maria Maniakówna, and Tomasz Strzembosz, eds. *Ludność cywilna w Powstaniu Warszawskim*, vol. 1. Warsaw: PIW, 1974.

Drzewiecki, Zbigniew. *Wspomnienia muzyka*. 2nd ed. Cracow: PWM, 2010 [1971].

Dubrowska, Małgorzata. "Leopold Julian Kronenberg: Współzałożyciel i opiekun Filharmonii Warszawskiej." In *100 lat Filharmonii w Warszawie, 1901–2001*, edited by Maria Bychawska and Henryk Schiller, 10–17. Warsaw: Fundacja Bankowa im. Leopolda Kronenberga, 2001.

Dziadek, Magdalena. "'Female' Music Criticism in Poland 1890–1939." *Interdisciplinary Studies in Musicology* 6 (2007): 155–68.

300 | Bibliography

———. *Od Szkoły Dramatycznej do Uniwersytetu: Dzieje wyższej uczelni muzycznej w Warszawie 1810–1944*. Warsaw: Uniwersytet Muzyczny Fryderyka Chopina, 2011.

———. "Powstanie i pierwszy okres działalności Filharmonii (1901–1908)." In *100 lat Filharmonii w Warszawie, 1901–2001*, edited by Maria Bychawska and Henryk Schiller, 40–65. Warsaw: Fundacja Bankowa im. Leopolda Kronenberga, 2001.

———. "Twórczość krytycznomuzyczna Stefanii Łobaczewskiej." *Muzyka* 49, no. 4 (2004): 87–112.

———. "Zdzisław Birnbaum: Zapomniany kapelmistrz filharmonii." *Ruch Muzyczny* 45, no. 22 (2001): 13–17

Dziębowska, Elżbieta ed. *Studia musicologica, aesthetica, theoretica, historica*. Cracow: PWM, 1979.

Edele, Mark, and Wanda Warlik. "Saved by Stalin? Trajectories and Numbers of Polish Jews in the Soviet Second World War." In *Shelter from the Holocaust: Rethinking Jewish Survival in the Soviet Union*, edited by Mark Edele, Sheila Fitzpatrick, and Atina Grossmann, 95–131. Detroit: Wayne State University Press, 2017.

Edmunds, Neil. *The Soviet Proletarian Music Movement*. Oxford: Peter Lang, 2000.

Elphick, Daniel. *Music Behind the Iron Curtain: Weinberg and His Polish Contemporaries*. Cambridge: Cambridge University Press, 2020.

Endelman, Todd M. "Assimilation." *The YIVO Encyclopedia of Jews in Eastern Europe*. https://encyclopedia.yivo.org/article/2008.

———. *Leaving the Jewish Fold: Conversion and Radical Assimilation in Modern Jewish History*. Princeton, NJ: Princeton University Press, 2015.

Engel, David. "Away from a Definition of Antisemitism: An Essay in the Semantics of Historical Description." In *Rethinking European Jewish History*, edited by Jeremy Cohen and Moshe Rosman, 30–53. Oxford: Littman Library of Jewish Civilization, 2009.

———. "On Continuity and Discontinuity in Polish-Jewish Relations: Observations on *Fear*." *East European Politics and Societies* 21, no. 3 (2007): 534–48.

———. "Patterns of Anti-Jewish Violence in Postwar Poland, 1944–1946." *Yad Vashem Studies* 26 (1998): 43–85.

———. "The Reconstruction of Jewish Communal Institutions in Postwar Poland: The Origins of the Central Committee of Polish Jews, 1944–1945." *East European Politics and Societies* 10, no. 1 (1996): 85–107.

Engelking, Barbara. *Holocaust and Memory*. Edited by Gunnar S. Paulsson and translated by Emma Harris. London: Leicester University Press, 2001.

Engelking, Barbara, and Jacek Leociak. *The Warsaw Ghetto: A Guide to the Perished City*. Translated by Emma Harris. New Haven, CT: Yale University Press, 2009.

Erhardt, Ludwik, ed. *50 lat Związku Kompozytorów Polskich*. Warsaw: ZKP, 1995.

Fairclough, Pauline. *Classics for the Masses: Shaping Soviet Musical Identity under Lenin and Stalin*. New Haven, CT: Yale University Press, 2016.

————. "Was Soviet Music Middlebrow? Shostakovich's Fifth Symphony, Socialist Realism, and the Mass Listener in the 1930s." *Journal of Musicology* 35, no. 3 (2018): 336–67.

Fanning, David. *Mieczysław Weinberg: In Search of Freedom.* Hofheim: Wolke, 2010.

Fanning, David, and Erik Levi, eds. *The Routledge Handbook to Music under German Occupation, 1938–1945: Propaganda, Myth and Reality.* London: Routledge, 2019.

Fater, Isaschar. *Muzyka żydowska w Polsce w okresie międzywojennym.* Translated by Ewa Świderska. Warsaw: Oficyna Wydawnicza, 1997.

Fauser, Annegret. "Ensounding Trauma, Performing Commemoration: Western Music in Times of War and Tumults." In *Performing Commemoration: Musical Reenactment and the Politics of Trauma,* edited by Annegret Fauser and Michael A. Figueroa, 19–40. Ann Arbor: University of Michigan Press, 2020.

————. *Sounds of War: Music in the United States during World War II.* New York: Oxford University Press, 2013.

Fauser, Annegret, and Michael A. Figueroa, eds. *Performing Commemoration: Musical Reenactment and the Politics of Trauma.* Ann Arbor: University of Michigan Press, 2020.

Fay, Laurel E. *Shostakovich: A Life.* New York: Oxford University Press, 2000.

Felman, Shoshana. *The Juridical Unconscious: Trials and Traumas in the Twentieth Century.* Cambridge, MA: Harvard University Press, 2002.

Fijałkowska, Barbara. *Polityka i twórcy: 1948–1959.* Warsaw: PWN, 1985.

Filar, Marian, and Charles Patterson. *From Buchenwald to Carnegie Hall.* Jackson: University Press of Mississippi, 2002.

Finder, Gabriel N., and Alexander V. Prusin. "Jewish Collaborators on Trial in Poland, 1944–1956." *Polin Studies in Polish Jewry* 20 (2008): 122–48.

Fishman, David E. *The Rise of Modern Yiddish Culture.* Pittsburgh, PA: University of Pittsburgh Press, 2005.

Fitelberg, Grzegorz. *Korespondencja Grzegorza Fitelberga z lat 1941–1953.* Edited by Adam Labus, Sylwia Polek, and Leon Markiewicz. Katowice: Fundacja Muzyczna Międzynarodowego Konkursu Dyrygentów im. Grzegorza Fitelberga, 2003.

Flam, Gila. *Singing for Survival: Songs of the Lodz Ghetto, 1940–45.* Urbana: University of Illinois Press, 1992.

Fosler-Lussier, Danielle. *Music Divided: Bartók's Legacy in Cold War Culture.* Berkeley: University of California Press, 2007.

Franaszek, Andrzej. *Milosz: A Biography.* Translated by Aleksandra Parker and Michael Parker. Cambridge, MA: Harvard University Press, 2017.

Friedman, Philip. *Zagłada Żydów lwowskich w okresie okupacji niemieckiej.* Munich: n.p., 1947.

Friedrich, Klaus-Peter. "Collaboration in a 'Land without a Quisling': Patterns of Cooperation with the Nazi German Occupation Regime in Poland during World War II." *Slavic Review* 64, no. 4 (2005): 711–46.

Frolova-Walker, Marina. "A Birthday Present for Stalin: Shostakovich's *Song of the Forests* (1949)." In *Composing for the State: Music in Twentieth-*

302 | Bibliography

Century Dictatorships, edited by Esteban Buch, Igor Contreras Zubillaga, and Manuel Deniz Silva, 96–120. Abingdon, UK: Routledge, 2016.

Frühauf, Tina. *Transcending Dystopia: Music, Mobility, and the Jewish Community in Germany, 1945–1989*. New York: Oxford University Press, 2021.

Fuks, Marian. "Filharmonia Warszawska w latach okupacji niemieckiej (1939–1945). In *100 lat Filharmonii w Warszawie 1901–2001*, edited by Maria Bychawska and Henryk Schiller, 119–41. Warsaw: Fundacja Bankowa im. Leopolda Kronenberga, 2001.

———. *Muzyka ocalona: Judaica polskie*. Warsaw: Wydawnictwa Radia i Telewizji, 1989.

———. "Muzyka w gettach." *Muzyka* 16, no. 1 (1971): 64–76.

———. "Życie muzycznego w gettach." *Biuletyn Żydowskiego Instytutu Historycznego* 82, no. 2 (1972): 41–56.

———. *Żydzi w Warszawie: Życie codzienne, wydarzenia, ludzie*. Poznań: Sorus, 1992.

Fulcher, Jane F. *The Composer as Intellectual: Music and Ideology in France, 1914–1940*. New York: Oxford University Press, 2005.

Gawin, Magdalena. *Race and Modernity: A History of the Polish Eugenics Movement*. Translated by Agnieszka Waśkiewicz. Warsaw: Instytut Historii PAN, 2018.

Gąsiorowska, Małgorzata. *Bacewicz*. Cracow: PWM, 1999.

———. *Kisielewski*. Cracow: PWM, 2011.

Gella, Aleksander. "The Life and Death of the Old Polish Intelligentsia." *Slavic Review* 30, no. 1 (1971): 1–27.

Gilbert, Shirli. *Music in the Holocaust: Confronting Life in the Nazi Ghettos and Camps*. Oxford: Oxford University Press, 2005.

Gliński, Mateusz, and Zofia Glińska. *Testament Mateusza Glińskiego*. London: Oficyna Poetów i Malarzy, 1982.

Glowacka, Dorota, and Joanna Zylinska, eds. *Imaginary Neighbors: Mediating Polish-Jewish Relations after the Holocaust*. Lincoln: University of Nebraska Press, 2007.

Goldberg, Amos. "The History of the Jews in the Ghettos: A Cultural Perspective." In *The Holocaust and Historical Methodology*, edited by Dan Stone, 79–100. New York: Berghahn Books, 2012.

———. "Rumor Culture among Warsaw Jews under Nazi Occupation: A World of Catastrophe Reenchanted." *Jewish Social Studies* 21, no. 3 (2016): 91–125.

Goldberg, Halina. "'On the Wings of Aesthetic Beauty Toward the Radiant Spheres of the Infinite': Music and Jewish Reformers in Nineteenth-Century Warsaw." *Musical Quarterly* 101, no. 4 (2019): 407–54.

Goldberg, Halina, Nancy Sinkoff, and Natalia Aleksiun, eds. *Polish Jewish Culture beyond the Capital: Centering the Periphery*. New Brunswick, NJ: Rutgers University Press, 2023.

Goldberg, Sol, Scott Ury, and Keith Ian Weiser, eds. *Key Concepts in the Study of Antisemitism*. Cham, Switzerland: Palgrave Macmillan, 2021.

Gołąb, Maciej. "Garść informacji o Józefie Kofflerze i jego rodzinie z ksiąg metrykalnych Gminy Żydowskiej w Stryju." *Muzyka* 52, no. 2 (2007): 61–73.

————. *Józef Koffler: Compositional Style and Source Documents*. Translated by Maksymilian Kapelański, Marek Żebrowski, and Linda Schubert. Los Angeles: Polish Music Center at USC, 2004.

Gombiński, Stanisław. [Jan Mawult]. *Wspomnienia policjanta z warszawskiego getta*. Edited by Marta Janczewska. Warsaw: Stowarzyszenie Centrum Badań nad Zagładą Żydów, 2010.

Gonzalez-Lesser, Emma. "Jewishness as *Sui Generis*: Extending Theorizations beyond the Debate of 'Race, Ethnicity, or Religion.'" *Ethnic and Racial Studies* 43, no. 3 (2020): 479–500.

Gordon, Avery F. *Ghostly Matters: Haunting and the Sociological Imagination*. 2nd ed. Minneapolis: University of Minnesota Press, 2008.

Grabowski, Jan. *Hunt for the Jews: Betrayal and Murder in German-Occupied Poland*. Bloomington: Indiana University Press, 2013.

————. *Szantażowanie Żydów w Warszawie, 1939–1943: "Ja tego Żyda znam!"* Warsaw: Centrum Badań nad Zagładą Żydów, 2004.

Grabowski, Waldemar. *Delegatura Rządu Rzeczypospolitej Polskiej na Kraj*. Warsaw: Pax, 1995.

Gran, Wiera. *Sztafeta oszczerców: Autobiografia śpiewaczki*. Paris: W. Gran, 1980.

Gross, Jan Tomasz. *Fear: Anti-Semitism in Poland after Auschwitz*. New York: Random House, 2006.

————. *Neighbors: The Destruction of the Jewish Community in Jedwabne, Poland*. Princeton, NJ: Princeton University Press, 2001.

————. *Polish Society under German Occupation: The Generalgouvernement, 1939–1944*. Princeton, NJ: Princeton University Press, 1979.

————. *Revolution from Abroad: The Soviet Conquest of Poland's Western Ukraine and Western Belorussia*. Princeton, NJ: Princeton University Press, 1988.

————. "Social Consequences of War: Preliminaries to the Study of Imposition of Communist Regimes in East Central Europe." *East European Politics & Societies* 3, no. 2 (1989): 198–214.

————. "A Tangled Web: Confronting Stereotypes Concerning Relations between Poles, Germans, Jews, and Communists." In *The Politics of Retribution in Europe: World War II and Its Aftermath*, edited by István Deák, Jan T. Gross, and Tony Judt, 74–129. Princeton, NJ: Princeton University Press, 2000.

————. *Upiorna dekada: Trzy eseje o stereotypach na temat Żydów, Polaków, Niemców i Komunistów, 1939–1948*. Cracow: TAiWPN Universitas, 1998.

Guesnet, François, Benjamin Matis, and Antony Polonsky, eds. *Jews and Music-Making in the Polish Lands*, vol. 32 of *Polin: Studies in Polish Jewry*. London: Littman Library of Jewish Civilization, 2020.

Gutman, Israel. "Jews in General Anders' Army in the Soviet Union." *Yad Vashem Studies* 12 (1977): 231–96.

————. "The Judenrat as a Leadership." In *On Germans and Jews under the Nazi Regime: Essays by Three Generations of Historians*, edited by Moshe Zimmermann, 313–35. Jerusalem: The Hebrew University Magnes Press, 2006.

Bibliography

———. *Resistance: The Warsaw Ghetto Uprising*. Boston: Houghton Mifflin, 1994

Gwizdalanka, Danuta. "Głosy i dygresje do 'teczek' i *Dzienników* Zygmunta Mycielskiego." *Ruch Muzyczny* 57, no. 3 (2013): 13.

Gwizdalanka, Danuta, and Krzysztof Meyer. *Witold Lutosławski: Droga do dojrzałości*. Cracow: PWM, 2003.

Haas, Michael. *Forbidden Music: The Jewish Composers Banned by the Nazis*. New Haven, CT: Yale University Press, 2013.

HaCohen, Ruth. *The Music Libel against the Jews*. New Haven, CT: Yale University Press, 2011.

Haefeli, Anton. *Die Internationale Gesellschaft für Neue Musik (IGNM): Ihre Geschichte von 1922 biss zur Gegenwart*. Zurich: Atlantis Musikbuch, 1982.

Haltof, Marek. *Polish Film and the Holocaust: Politics and Memory*. New York: Berghahn Books, 2012.

———. *Screening Auschwitz: Wanda Jakubowska's "The Last Stage" and the Politics of Commemoration*. Evanston, IL: Northwestern University Press, 2018.

Hanebrink, Paul. *A Specter Haunting Europe: The Myth of Judeo-Bolshevism*. Cambridge, MA: Belknap Press, 2018.

Helman, Zofia. "The Dilemma of Twentieth-Century Polish Music: National Style or Universal Values." In *After Chopin: Essays in Polish Music*, translated by Joanna Niżyńska and Peter Schertz, 205–42. Los Angeles: University of Southern California (Polish Music Center), 2000.

———. *Neoklasycyzm w muzyce polskiej XX wieku*. Cracow: PWM, 1985.

———. *Roman Palester: Twórca i dzieło*. Cracow: Musica Iagellonica, 1999.

———. "'. . . Tylko to jest ocalenie': Zygmunt Mycielski—pięć pieśni do słów Czesława Miłosza." In *Melos, logos, etos: Materiały sympozjum poświęconego twórczości Floriana Dąbrowskiego, Stefana Kisielewskiego, Zygmunta Mycielskiego*, edited by Krystyna Tarnawska-Kaczorowska, 141–58. Warsaw: ZKP, 1987.

Hirsch, Lily E. *Jewish Orchestra in Nazi Germany: Musical Politics and the Berlin Jewish Culture League*. Ann Arbor: University of Michigan Press, 2010.

———. "Righting and Remembering the Nazi Past: 'Suppressed Music' in American Concert Performance." *Music and Politics* 10, no. 1 (2016). https://doi.org/10.3998/mp.9460447.0010.102.

Holmgren, Beth. "Acting Out: Qui pro Quo in the Context of Interwar Warsaw." *East European Politics & Societies* 27, no. 2 (2013): 205–23.

———. "Cabaret Nation: The Jewish Foundations of Kabaret Literacki, 1920–1939." *Polin Studies in Polish Jewry* 31 (2019): 273–88.

———. "The Jews in the Band: The Anders Army's Special Troupes." *Polin Studies in Polish Jewry* 32 (2020): 177–91.

———. "The Polish-Language Cabaret Song: Its Multi-Ethnic Pedigree and Transnational Adventures, 1919–1968." In *Being Poland: A New History of Polish Literature and Culture since 1918*, edited by Przemysław Czapliński, Joanna Niżyńska, Agnieszka Polakowska, and Tamara Trojanowska, 258–72. Toronto: University of Toronto Press, 2019.

Hrab, Uliana. *Muzykolohiia iak universytets'ka dystsyplina: L'vivs'ka muzykolohichna shkola Adolfa Khybins'koho (1912–1941)*. Lviv: Ukrainian Catholic University, 2009.

Hryciuk, Grzegorz. *"Gazeta Lwowska": 1941–1944*. Wrocław: Wydawnictwo Uniwersytetu Wrocławskiego, 1992.

———. *Polacy we Lwowie 1939–1944: Życie codzienne*. Warsaw: Książka i Wiedza, 2000.

Hudson, Nicholas. "From 'Nation' to 'Race': The Origin of Racial Classification in Eighteenth-Century Thought." *Eighteenth-Century Studies* 29, no. 3 (1996): 247–64.

Huener, Jonathan. *Auschwitz, Poland, and the Politics of Commemoration, 1945–1979*. Athens: Ohio University Press, 2003.

Jachimecki, Zdzisław. "Muzyka polska od roku 1915 do roku 1930." In *Polska: Jej dzieje i kultura* 3: 925–38. Warsaw: Trzaski, Everta i Michalskiego, 1932.

Jagiełło-Skupińska, Aleksandra, Tomasz Zymer, and Anna Grzywacz, eds. *Warsaw Autumn as a Realisation of Karol Szymanowski's Vision of Modern Polish Music*. Warsaw: Polish Music Information Centre, 2007.

Jakelski, Lisa. "Górecki's *Scontri* and Avant-Garde Music in Cold War Poland." *Journal of Musicology* 26, no. 2 (2009): 205–39.

———. *Making New Music in Cold War Poland: The Warsaw Autumn Festival, 1956–1968*. Oakland: University of California Press, 2017.

———. "Witold Lutosławski and the Ethics of Abstraction." *Twentieth-Century Music* 10, no. 2 (2013): 169–202.

Jakelski, Lisa, and Nicholas W. Reyland, eds. *Lutosławski's Worlds*. Woodbridge, UK: Boydell Press, 2018.

Jakubczyk-Ślęczka, Sylwia. "Jewish Music Organizations in Interwar Galicia." *Polin Studies in Polish Jewry* 32, no. 1 (2020): 343–70.

———. "Musical Life of the Jewish Community in Interwar Galicia: The Problem of Identity of Jewish Musicians." *Kwartalnik Młodych Muzykologów UJ* 3 (2017): 135–57.

Jakubowska, Longina. *Patrons of History: Nobility, Capital and Political Transitions in Poland*. Farnham, UK: Routledge, 2012.

Janczewska, Marta. "*Gazeta Żydowska* (1940–1942)." In *Studia z dziejów trójjęzycznej prasy żydowskiej na ziemiach polskich (XIX–XX w)*, edited by Joanna Nalewajko-Kulikov, 167–79. Warsaw: Neriton, 2012.

Jarzębska, Alicja. "Syntez neoklasycznego i dodekafonicznego idiomu kompozytorskiego w 'Kwintecie' Konstantego Regameya." In *Oblicza polistylizmu: Materiały sympozjum poświęconego twórczości Konstantego Regameya*, edited by Krystyna Tarnawska-Kaczorowska, 112–36. Warsaw: Sekcja Muzykologów Związku Kompozytorów Polskich, 1988.

Jasiński, Roman, ed. *Koniec epoki: Muzyka w Warszawie, 1927–1939*. Warsaw: PIW, 1986.

———. *Zmierzch starego świata: Wspomnienia 1900–1945*. Cracow: Wydawnictwo Literackie, 2006.

Jaworski, Wojciech. "Towarzystwa muzyczne w Królestwie Polskim (1870–1914)." *Acta Universitatis Lodziensis* 94 (2015): 91–107.

Bibliography

Jazowska, Klaudia. "Helena Dorabialska: Krytyk muzyczny *Robotnika*." Thesis, Jagiellonian University, 2013.

Jedlicki, Jerzy. *A Suburb of Europe: Nineteenth-Century Polish Approaches to Western Civilization*. Budapest: Central European University Press, 1999.

Jockusch, Laura. *Collect and Record! Jewish Holocaust Documentation in Early Postwar Europe*. Oxford: Oxford University Press, 2012.

Jolluck, Katherine R. *Exile and Identity: Polish Women in the Soviet Union during World War II*. Pittsburgh, PA: University of Pittsburgh Press, 2002.

Jordheim, Helge. "Against Periodization: Koselleck's Theory of Multiple Temporalities." *History and Theory* 51, no. 2 (2012): 151–71.

Judaken, Jonathan, ed. "AHR Roundtable: Rethinking Anti-Semitism." *American Historical Review* 123, no. 4 (2018): 1122–1245.

Judt, Tony. *Postwar: A History of Europe since 1945*. New York: Penguin Press, 2005.

Junyk, Ihor. *Foreign Modernism: Cosmopolitanism, Identity, and Style in Paris*. Toronto: University of Toronto Press, 2013.

Jurandot, Jerzy. *City of the Damned: Two Years in the Warsaw Ghetto*. Translated by Jolanta Scicińska. Warsaw: Museum of the History of Polish Jews, 2015.

Kałwa, Dobrochna. *Kobieta aktywna w Polsce międzywojennej: Dylematy środowisk kobiecych*. Cracow: Historia Iagellonica, 2001.

Kapferer, Jean-Noël. *Rumor: Uses, Interpretations, and Images*. New Brunswick, NJ: Transaction Publishers, 1990.

Kaplan, Chaim Aron. *Scroll of Agony: The Warsaw Diary of Chaim A. Kaplan*. Translated by Abraham Isaac Katsh. Rev. ed. New York: Collier Books, 1981.

Karas, Joža. *Music in Terezín, 1941–1945*. 2nd ed. Hillsdale, NY: Pendragon Press, 2002.

Karczewski, Kamil. "'Call Me by My Name:' A 'Strange and Incomprehensible' Passion in the Polish Kresy of the 1920s." *Slavic Review* 81, no. 3 (2022): 631–52.

———. "'For a Pole, It All Was a Great Abomination': Grassroots Homonationalism and State Homophobia à La Polonaise—A History Lesson from a Place Between East and West." *Sexuality & Culture* 27, no. 6 (2023): 1996–2015.

———. "Transnational Flows of Knowledge and the Legalisation of Homosexuality in Interwar Poland." *Contemporary European History* (2022). https://doi.org/10.1017/S0960777322000108.

Karnes, Kevin C. "Inventing Eastern Europe in the Ear of the Enlightenment." *Journal of the American Musicological Society* 71, no. 1 (2018): 75–108.

———. "Recollecting Jewish Musics from the Baltic Bloodlands." *Acta Musicologica* 84 (2012): 253–88.

———. *Sounds Beyond: Arvo Pärt and the 1970s Soviet Underground*. Chicago: University of Chicago Press, 2021.

Kassow, Samuel D. *Who Will Write Our History? Emanuel Ringelblum, the Warsaw Ghetto, and the Oyneg Shabes Archive*. Bloomington: Indiana University Press, 2007.

Kaszuba, Elżbieta. "The Development of Radio Services in the Second Polish Republic: Social, Strategic and Political Rationale." *Społeczeństwo i Ekonomia* 1, no. 1 (2014): 117–32.

Kennedy, Michael D. *Professionals, Power, and Solidarity in Poland: A Critical Sociology of Soviet-Type Society*. Cambridge: Cambridge University Press, 1991.

Kenney, Padraic. *Rebuilding Poland: Workers and Communists, 1945–1950*. Ithaca, NY: Cornell University Press, 1997.

Kersten, Krystyna. *The Establishment of Communist Rule in Poland, 1943–1948*. Translated by John Micgiel and Michael H. Bernhard. Berkeley: University of California Press, 1991.

———. *Polski Komitet Wyzwolenia Narodowego*. Lublin: Wydawnictwo Lubelskie, 1965.

Khan, Shamus Rahman. "The Sociology of Elites." *Annual Review of Sociology* 38 (2012): 361–77.

Kijek, Kamil. "Was It Possible to Avoid 'Hebrew Assimilation'? Hebraism, Polonization, and Tarbut Schools in the Last Decade of Interwar Poland." *Jewish Social Studies* 21, no. 2 (2016): 105–41.

Kisielewski, Stefan. *Dzienniki*. Warsaw: Iskry, 1996.

———. "Kraków stolicą muzyki (nieco wspomnień)." In *Pisma i felietony muzyczne*, vol. 2, 245–52.

———. "O Bronisławie Rutkowskim (1898–1964)." In *Pisma i felietony muzyczne*, vol. 2, 234–40.

———. *Pisma i felietony muzyczne*, vols. 1–2. Warsaw: Prószyński i S-ka, 2012.

Klubiński, Michał, ed. "Zygmunt Mycielski i Zofia Lissa: Listy Cz. 1." *Ruch Muzyczny*, no. 11 (2014): 9–14.

Kochanski, Halik. *The Eagle Unbowed: Poland and the Poles in the Second World War*. Cambridge, MA: Harvard University Press, 2014.

Kondracka, Mariola. "Kobiety na Uniwersytetach." In *Równe prawa i nierówne szanse*, edited by Anna Żarnowska and Andrzej Szwarc, 271–84. Warsaw: Wydawnictwo DiG, 2000.

Kornbluth, Andrew. *The August Trials: The Holocaust and Postwar Justice in Poland*. Cambridge, MA: Harvard University Press, 2021.

Kostka, Violetta. "An Artist as the Conscience of Humanity: Life in Emigration and the Artistic Output of Tadeusz Zygfryd Kassern." *Musicology Today* 8 (2011): 134–59.

———. *Tadeusz Zygfryd Kassern: Indywidualne odmiany stylów muzycznych XX wieku*. Poznań: Rhytmos, 2011.

Kowalczyk, Henryka, and Krystyna Jaraczewska-Mockałło, eds. *Kazimierz Sikorski: Życie i twórczość w 100-lecie urodzin Profesora*. Warsaw: Akademia Muzyczna im. Fryderyka Chopina, 1995.

Kowalska-Zając, Ewa. *Oblicza Awangardy: Roman Haubenstock-Ramati*. Łódź: Akademia Muzyczna im. Grażyny i Kiejstuta Bacewiczów, 2000.

Koźmińska-Frejlak, Ewa. "Asymilacja do polskości jako strategia adaptacyjna ocalałych z Zagłady polskich Żydów." *Kwartalnik Historii Żydów*, no. 2 (2013): 236–47.

———. "'I'm Going to the Oven Because I Wouldn't Give Myself to Him': The Role of Gender in the Polish Jewish Civic Court." In *Jewish Honor Courts: Revenge, Retribution, and Reconciliation in Europe and Israel after the*

308 | Bibliography

Holocaust, edited by Laura Jockusch and Gabriel N. Finder, 247–78. Detroit, MI: Wayne State University Press, 2015.

Kronenberg, Leopold Juljan. *Wspomnienia*. Warsaw: F. Hoesick, 1933.

Krzywiec, Grzegorz. *Chauvinism, Polish Style: The Case of Roman Dmowski*. Translated by Jarosław Garliński. Frankfurt am Main: Peter Lang, 2016.

Kulakovskiy, L. "Pol'skiy muzïkal'nïy zhurnal 'Ruch Muzyczny' (1947–1948 gg.)." *Sovetskaya Muzïka*, no. 9 (1948): 96–100.

Kunakhovich, Kyrill. *Communism's Public Sphere: Culture as Politics in Cold War Poland and East Germany*. Ithaca, NY: Cornell University Press, 2022.

Kuraś, Marzena. "Kawiarnia 'U Aktorek.'" *Pamiętnik Teatralny* 46, nos. 1–4 (1997): 520–22.

Lachowicz, Stanisław. *Muzyka w okupowanym Krakowie 1939–1945*. Cracow: Wydawnictwo Literackie, 1988.

Landau-Czajka, Anna. *Syn będzie Lech: Asymilacja Żydów w Polsce międzywojennej*. Warsaw: Neriton, 2006.

Lebow, Katherine. "'We Are Building a Common Home': The Moral Economy of Citizenship in Postwar Poland." In *Histories of the Aftermath: The Legacies of the Second World War in Europe*, edited by Frank Biess and Robert G. Moeller, 215–30. New York: Berghahn Books, 2010.

Leczyk, Marian. *Druga Rzeczpospolita 1918–1939: Społeczeństwo, gospodarka, kultura, polityka*. Warsaw: Książka i Wiedza, 2006.

Lehnstaedt, Stephan. *Occupation in the East: The Daily Lives of German Occupiers in Warsaw and Minsk, 1939–1944*. New York: Berghahn Books, 2016.

Lerski, Tomasz. *Syrena Record: Pierwsza polska wytwórnia fonograficzna*. New York: Karin, 2004.

Levin, Dov. *The Lesser of Two Evils: Eastern European Jewry under Soviet Rule, 1939–1941*. Translated by Naftali Greenwood. Philadelphia, PA: Jewish Publication Society, 1995.

Lichten, Joseph. "Notes on the Assimilation and Acculturation of Jews in Poland, 1863–1943." In *The Jews in Poland*, edited by Chimen Abramsky, Maciej Jachimczyk, and Antony Polonsky, 106–29. Oxford: B. Blackwell, 1986.

Lichtenstein, Alex, ed. "AHR Conversation: Each Generation Writes Its Own History of Generations." *American Historical Review* 123, no. 5 (2018): 1505–46.

Lindorfówna, Zofia. "Wojna—okupacja niemiecka (Fragment wspomnień)." *Pamiętnik Teatralny* 46 (1997): 522–37.

Lindstedt, Iwona. "Pokolenia kompozytorskie: Prawda czy mit?" *Ruch Muzyczny* 23 (2021). https://ruchmuzyczny.pl/article/1612-pokolenia-kompozytorskie-prawda-czy-mit.

———. "The Polish School of Composition in 20th-Century Music: A Recapitulation." *Musicology Today* 15 (2018): 32–40.

———. "'Why Are Our Women-Composers So Little Known?': Concerning Women's Musical Output in Poland between the Two World Wars." *Musicology Today* 16 (2019): 44–64.

Lissa, Zofia. "Muzïka v sovetskom L'vove." *Sovetskaya Muzïka*, no. 9 (1940): 91–94.

———. "Muzyka dla Karola." In *Książka dla Karola*, edited by Kazimierz Koźniewski, 75–80. Warsaw: Czytelnik, 1983.

———. *Muzyka i film: Studium z pogranicza ontologii, estetyki i psychologii muzyki filmowej*. Lviv: Księgarnia Lwowska, 1937.

———. "Muzyka polska w ZSRR w latach 1941–1945." In *Polsko-rosyjskie miscellanea muzyczne*, edited by Zofia Lissa, 443–55. Cracow: PWM, 1967.

———. "O Sewerynie Barbagu: W dwudziestą rocznicę śmierci." *Ruch Muzyczny*, no. 20 (1964): 10–11.

———. "Rola tradycji w muzyce polskiej, 1945–1969." In *Tradycja i współczesność: O kulturze artystycznej Polski Ludowej*, edited by Juliusz Starzyński, 47–87. Warsaw: PIW, 1970.

———. *Śpiewnik żołnierza polskiego*. Moscow: Związek Patriotów Polskich w ZSRR, 1944.

Locke, Brian S. "Swing in the Protectorate: Czech Popular Music under Nazi Occupation, 1938–1945." In *Music in World War II*, edited by Pamela M. Potter, Christina L. Baade, and Roberta Montemorra Marvin, 199–225. Bloomington: Indiana University Press, 2020.

Loeffler, James. "'In Memory of Our Murdered (Jewish) Children': Hearing the Holocaust in Soviet Jewish Culture." *Slavic Review* 73, no. 3 (2014): 585–611.

———. *The Most Musical Nation: Jews and Culture in the Late Russian Empire*. New Haven, CT: Yale University Press, 2010.

———. "Richard Wagner's 'Jewish Music': Antisemitism and Aesthetics in Modern Jewish Culture." *Jewish Social Studies* 15, no. 2 (2009): 2–36.

———. "Why the New 'Holocaust Music' Is an Insult to Music—and to the Victims of the Shoah." *Tablet Magazine*, July 11, 2013.

Lorentz, Stanisław, ed. *Walka o dobra kultury, Warszawa 1939–1945*. Warsaw: PIW, 1970.

Lorenz, Chris, and Berber Bevernage, eds. *Breaking Up Time: Negotiating the Borders between Present, Past and Future*. Göttingen: Vandenhoeck & Ruprecht, 2013.

Loutan-Charbon, Nicole. *Constantin Regamey, compositeur*. Yverdon: Éditions de la Thièle, 1978.

Łobaczewska, Stefania. "Kobieta w muzyce." In *Almanach spraw kobiecych: Informacje, postulaty, zagadnienia*, edited by Herminja Naglerowa, 174–78. Warsaw: Nakładem Wydziału Prasowego Z.P.O.K., 1933.

Machcewicz, Paweł. *Poland's War on Radio Free Europe, 1950–1989*. Washington, DC: Woodrow Wilson Center Press, 2014.

Majer, Diemut. *"Non-Germans" under the Third Reich: The Nazi Judicial and Administrative System in Germany and Occupied Eastern Europe with Special Regard to Occupied Poland, 1939–1945*. Translated by Peter Thomas Hill, Edward Vance Humphrey, and Brian Levin. Baltimore, MD: John Hopkins University Press, 2003.

Majewska, Justyna. "'Czym wytłumaczy Pan . . .?': Inteligencja żydowska o polonizacji i asymilacji w getcie warszawskim." *Zagłada Żydów: Studia i Materiały* 11 (2015): 325–46.

Majewski, Piotr. *Wojna i kultura: Instytucje kultury polskiej w okupacyjnych realiach Generalnego Gubernatorstwa, 1939–1945*. Warsaw: TRIO, 2005.

Bibliography

Makowiecki, Andrzej Z. *Warszawskie kawiarnie literackie.* Warsaw: Wydawnictwo Iskry, 2013.

Mannheim, Karl. "The Problem of Generations." In Karl Mannheim, *Essays on the Sociology of Knowledge*, edited by Paul Kecskemeti, 276–322. London: Routledge, 1952.

Marciniec, Dariusz. "Ministerstwo Sztuki i Kultury Rzeczypospolitej Polskiej w latach 1918–1922." *Rocznik Łódzki* 63 (2015): 91–106.

"Maria Palester." *Polish Righteous.* https://sprawiedliwi.org.pl/en/stories-of-rescue/story-maria-palester

Masters, Giles. "New-Music Internationalism: The ISCM Festival, 1922–1939." PhD thesis, King's College London, 2021.

Mazepa, Leshek, and Teresa Mazepa. *Shliakh do muzychnoï akademiï u L'vovi.* Lviv: Spolom, 2003.

Mazepa, Leszek. "Okres radziecki w życiu i twórczości Józefa Kofflera." *Muzyka* 28, no. 1 (1983): 67–100.

Mazierska, Ewa. *Polish Estrada Music: Organisation, Stars and Representation.* Abingdon, UK: Routledge, 2023.

Mazower, Mark. *Hitler's Empire: How the Nazis Ruled Europe.* New York: Penguin Press, 2008.

Mazurczak, Filip. "Władysław Szpilman's Post-War Career in Poland." *Polin Studies in Polish Jewry* 32 (2020): 219–34.

Mazurkiewicz, Roman. *Z dawnej literatury maryjnej: Zarysy i zbliżenia.* Cracow: Wydawnictwo Naukowe Uniwersytetu Pedagogicznego, 2011.

McKee, Eric. "Dance and the Music of Chopin: The Polonaise." In *Chopin and his World*, edited by Jonathan D. Bellman and Halina Goldberg, 187–230. Princeton, NJ: Princeton University Press, 2017.

McMahon, Richard. *The Races of Europe: Construction of National Identities in the Social Sciences, 1839–1939.* London: Palgrave Macmillan, 2016.

Mendelsohn, Ezra. *The Jews of East Central Europe between the World Wars.* Bloomington: Indiana University Press, 1983.

———. "On the Jewish Presence in Nineteenth-Century European Musical Life." *Studies in Contemporary Jewry* 9 (1993): 3–16.

Meng, Michael. *Shattered Spaces: Encountering Jewish Ruins in Postwar Germany and Poland.* Cambridge, MA: Harvard University Press, 2011.

Micgiel, John. "Bandits and Reactionaries: The Suppression of the Opposition in Poland, 1944–1946." In *The Establishment of Communist Regimes in Eastern Europe, 1944–1949*, edited by Norman Naimark and Leonid Gibianskii, 93–110. Boulder, CO: Westview Press, 1997.

Michalski, Andrzej. *Wyższe szkolnictwo muzyczne w Polsce w latach 1945–1964.* Bydgoszcz: Wydawnictwo Uniwersytetu Kazimierza Wielkiego, 2009.

Michalski, Dariusz. *Powróćmy jak za dawnych lat: Czyli historia polskiej muzyki rozrywkowej (lata 1900–1939).* Warsaw: Iskry, 2007.

Michałowska, Maria. *"Ruch Muzyczny" 1945–1949, 1957–1959.* Cracow: PWM, 1981.

Michlic, Joanna B. *Poland's Threatening Other: The Image of the Jew from 1880 to the Present.* Lincoln: University of Nebraska Press, 2006.

———. "The Soviet Occupation of Poland, 1939–41, and the Stereotype of the Anti-Polish and Pro-Soviet Jew." *Jewish Social Studies* 13, no. 3 (2007): 135–76.

Michman, Dan. "Jewish Leadership in Extremis." In *The Historiography of the Holocaust*, edited by Dan Stone, 319–40. New York: Palgrave Macmillan, 2004.

Micińska, Magdalena. *At the Crossroads, 1865–1918: A History of the Polish Intelligentsia, Part 3*. Translated by Tristan Korecki. Frankfurt am Main: Peter Lang, 2014.

Mick, Christoph. "Incompatible Experiences: Poles, Ukrainians and Jews in Lviv under Soviet and German Occupation, 1939–44." *Journal of Contemporary History* 46, no. 2 (2011): 336–63.

———. *Lemberg, Lwów, L'viv, 1914–1947: Violence and Ethnicity in a Contested City*. West Lafayette, IN: Purdue University Press, 2016.

———. "Lviv under Soviet Rule, 1939–1941." In *Stalin and Europe: Imitation and Domination, 1928–1953*, edited by Timothy Snyder and Ray Brandon, 138–62. New York: Oxford University Press, 2014.

Mickiewicz, Adam. *Konrad Wallenrod: Powieść historyczna z dziejów litewskich i pruskich*. Warsaw: Biblioteka Polska, 1922 [1828].

Milewski, Barbara. "Chopin's Mazurkas and the Myth of the Folk." *19th-Century Music* 23, no. 2 (1999): 113–35.

———. "Hidden in Plain View: The Music of Holocaust Survival in Poland's First Post-War Feature Film." In *Music, Collective Memory, Trauma, and Nostalgia in European Cinema after the Second World War*, edited by Michael Baumgartner and Ewelina Boczkowska, 111–37. New York: Routledge, 2020.

———. "The Mazurka and National Imaginings." PhD diss., Princeton University, 2002.

Miller, Michael L., and Scott Ury. "Cosmopolitanism: The End of Jewishness?" *European Review of History: Revue européenne d'histoire* 17, no. 3 (2010): 337–59.

Miłosz, Czesław. *The Captive Mind*. Translated by Jane Zielonko. New York: Vintage International, 1990 [1953].

———. *The Collected Poems: 1931–1987*. New York: Ecco Press, 1988.

———. *The History of Polish Literature*. 2nd ed. Berkeley: University of California Press, 1983.

Mioduszewski, Michał. *Śpiewnik kościelny: Czyli pieśni nabożne z melodyjami w kościele katolickim używane*. Cracow: Drukarnia Stanisława Gieszkowskiego, 1838.

Morska, Izabela. "Zygmunt Mycielski's Blues, or How Some Testimonies Related to Queer History Simply Vanish into Thin Air." In *Go East! LGBTQ+ Literature in Eastern Europe*, edited by Gregory Woods, 93–100. Ljubljana: Založba Univerze v Ljubljani, 2020.

Moss, Kenneth B. *An Unchosen People: Jewish Political Reckoning in Interwar Poland*. Cambridge, MA: Harvard University Press, 2021.

Mosse, George L. *Toward the Final Solution: A History of European Racism*. Madison: University of Wisconsin Press, 1985.

312 | Bibliography

Móricz, Klára. *In Stravinsky's Orbit: Responses to Modernism in Russian Paris.* Oakland: University of California Press, 2020.

———. *Jewish Identities: Nationalism, Racism, and Utopianism in Twentieth-Century Music.* Berkeley: University of California Press, 2008.

Mrygoń, Adam. *Stanisław Wiechowicz*, vols. 1–2. Cracow: PWM, 1982.

Muszkalska, Bożena. "Bronisława Wójcik-Keuprulian: Niepokorna uczennica profesora." *Muzyka* 57, no. 4 (2012): 47–70.

Mycielski, Zygmunt. *Dziennik 1950–1959.* Warsaw: Iskry, 1999.

———. *Niby-dziennik ostatni, 1981–1987.* Warsaw: Iskry, 2012.

———. *Ucieczki z pięciolinii.* Warsaw: PIW, 1957.

Naliwajek, Katarzyna. "Nazi Musical Imperialism in Occupied Poland." In *The Routledge Handbook to Music under German Occupation*, edited by David Fanning and Erik Levi, 56–71. Abingdon, UK: Routledge, 2019.

———. *Sounds of Apocalypse: Music in Poland under German Occupation.* Bern: Peter Lang, 2022.

Naliwajek-Mazurek, Katarzyna. "Konstanty Regamey: Muzyka na rozdrożach historii i polityki." In *Twórcy, źródła, archiwa*, edited by Beata Bolesławska-Lewandowska and Jolanta Guzy-Pasiak, 65–92. Warsaw: ISPAN, 2017.

———. "Muzyka w okupowanej Warszawie." In *Okupacyjne losy muzyków: Warszawa 1939–1945*, vol. 1, edited by Naliwajek-Mazurek, 10–38. Warsaw: Towarzystwo imienia Witolda Lutosławskiego, 2014.

———. "Nazi Censorship in Music: Warsaw 1941." In *The Impact of Nazism on Twentieth-Century Music*, edited by Erik Levi, 153–76. Vienna: Böhlau, 2014.

———. "The Use of Polish Musical Tradition in the Nazi Propaganda." *Musicology Today* 7 (2010): 243–59.

Naliwajek-Mazurek, Katarzyna, Elżbieta Markowska, and Andrzej Spóz, eds. *Okupacyjne losy muzyków: Warszawa 1939–1945*, vols. 1–2. Warsaw: Towarzystwo imienia Witolda Lutosławskiego, 2014–15.

Nałkowska, Zofia. *Medallions.* Translated by Diana Kuprel. Evanston, IL: Northwestern University Press, 2000.

Naszkowski, Marian. *Lata próby.* Warsaw: Książka i Wiedza, 1967.

The Nazi Kultur in Poland. London: The Polish Ministry of Information, 1945.

Nelson, Amy. *Music for the Revolution: Musicians and Power in Early Soviet Russia.* University Park: Pennsylvania State University Press, 2004.

Nemtsov, Jascha. "Neue jüdische Musik in Polen in den 1920er-30er Jahren." In *Jüdische Kunstmusik im 20. Jahrhundert: Quellenlage, Entstehungsgeschichte, Stilanalysen*, edited by Jascha Nemtsov, 91–106. Wiesbaden: Harrassowitz, 2006.

Nemtsov, Jascha, and Beate Schröder-Nauenburg. "Zwischen Zionismus und Antisemitismus: Der Wiener Verein zur Förderung jüdischer Musik." In *Klesmer, Klassik, jiddisches Lied: Jüdische Musikkultur in Osteuropa*, edited by Karl Erich Grözinger, 49–59. Wiesbaden: Harrassowitz Verlag, 2004.

Neubauer, Hans-Joachim. *The Rumour: A Cultural History.* London: Free Association Books, 1999.

Nidecka, Ewa. *Twórczość polskich kompozytorów Lwowa a ukraińska szkoła kompozytorska: 1792–1939.* Rzeszów: Wydawnictwo Uniwersytetu Rzeszowskiego, 2005.

———, ed. *Żydzi w kulturze muzycznej Galicji*. Rzeszów: Wydawnictwo Uniwersytetu Rzeszowskiego, 2021.

Nikodemowicz, Andrzej. "Moje lwowskie lata." *Annales Universitatis Marie Curie-Skłodowska* 2 (2004): 189–98.

Nikolska, Irina. *Conversations with Witold Lutosławski, 1987–92*. Stockholm: Melos, 1994.

Nowak, Stefan. "System wartości społeczeństwa polskiego." *Studia Socjologiczne* 19, no. 4 (1979): 155–73.

Nussbaum, Klemens. *Historia złudzeń: Żydzi w Armii Polskiej w ZSRR 1943–1945*. Warsaw: Tetragon, 2016.

———. "Jews in the Kosciuszko Division and First Polish Army." In *Jews in Eastern Poland and the USSR, 1939–46*, edited by Antony Polonsky and Norman Davies, 183–218. New York: St. Martin's Press, 1991.

Ochlewski, Tadeusz. "Muzyka w Warszawie podczas okupacji." *Ruch Muzyczny*, no. 11 (1970): 16–17.

Olick, Jeffrey K. "Collective Memory: The Two Cultures." *Sociological Theory* 17, no. 3 (1999): 333–48.

Olszewski, Andrzej K. "Moje wspomnienia z życia muzycznego podczas okupacji niemieckiej." *Saeculum Christianum* 9, no. 2 (2002): 171–74.

Palester, Roman. "Fragmenty wspomnień z lat 1939–1945." In *Słuch absolutny: Niedokończona autobiografia i listy z lat wojny*, edited by Zofia Helman, 283–301. Warsaw: PWM, 2017.

———. "Konflikt Marsjasza." *Kultura*, July 1951: 3–16.

———. *Słuch absolutny: Niedokończona autobiografia i listy z lat wojny*. Edited by Zofia Helman. Warsaw: PWM, 2017.

———. "Uwagi o muzyce, czyli 'Pazylogia' i 'współczesny Apollo'." *Kultura*, December 1951: 4–22.

Palester, Roman, and Jagoda Jędrychowska [Kazimiera Kijowska]. "Rozmowa z Romanem Palestrem." In *Widzieć Polskę z oddalenia*, edited by Jagoda Jędrychowska [Kazimiera Kijowska], 75–97. Paris: Editions Spotkania, 1988.

Panufnik, Andrzej. *Composing Myself*. London: Methuen London, 1987.

Pasternak, Leon. *W marszu i na biwaku*. Warsaw: Wydawnictwo Ministerstwa Obrony Narodowej, 1958.

Paulsson, Gunnar S. *Secret City: The Hidden Jews of Warsaw, 1940–1945*. New Haven, CT: Yale University Press, 2002.

Pekacz, Jolanta T. *Music in the Culture of Polish Galicia, 1772–1914*. Rochester, NY: University of Rochester Press, 2002.

Person, Katarzyna. *Assimilated Jews in the Warsaw Ghetto, 1940–1943*. Syracuse, NY: Syracuse University Press, 2014.

———. "Sexual Violence during the Holocaust: The Case of Forced Prostitution in the Warsaw Ghetto." *Shofar* 33, no. 2 (2015): 103–21.

———. *Warsaw Ghetto Police: The Jewish Order Service during the Nazi Occupation*. Translated by Zygmunt Nowak-Soliński. Ithaca, NY: Cornell University Press, 2021.

Philharmonie des Generalgouvernements. Cracow: ZKW-Druck, Heinsohn, 1940.

314 | Bibliography

Piekarski, Michał. "Poza granicami kraju, lecz nie na emigracji. Polscy muzycy i kompozytorzy we Lwowie po 1945 roku." In *Muzyka polska za granicą* 4, edited by Beata Bolesławska-Lewandowska and Jolanta Guzy-Pasiak, 9–42. Warsaw: Instytut Sztuki PAN.

——. *Przerwany kontrapunkt: Adolf Chybiński i początki polskiej muzykologii we Lwowie 1912–1944*. Warsaw: Instytut Historii Nauki Polskiej Akademii Nauk, 2017.

Pierce, J. Mackenzie. "Life and Death for Music: A Polish Generation's Journey across War and Reconstruction, 1926–53." PhD diss., Cornell University, 2019.

——. "Messianism Refigured: Tadeusz Zygfryd Kassern's Musical Monument to the Warsaw Ghetto Uprising." *Holocaust and Genocide Studies* 36, no. 2 (2022): 242–65.

——. "Sonic Transformations: Urban Musical Culture in the Warsaw Ghetto, 1940–1942." In *The Oxford Handbook of Jewish Music Studies*, edited by Tina Frühauf, 240–60. New York: Oxford University Press, 2023.

——. "Zofia Lissa, Wartime Trauma, and the Evolution of the Polish 'Mass Song.'" *Journal of Musicology* 37, no. 2 (2020): 231–66.

"Pierwsza dyskusja o weryfikacji: Protokół Walnego Zgromadzenia Gniazda Warszawskiego ZASP, 26–27 IV 1945." *Pamiętnik Teatralny* 46, no. 1–4 (1997): 113–26.

Pinchuk, Ben-Cion. "Sovietisation and the Jewish Response to the Nazi Policies of Mass Murder." In *Jews in Eastern Poland and the USSR, 1939–46*, edited by Antony Polonsky and Norman Davies, 124–37. New York: St. Martin's Press, 1991.

Pinsker, Shachar. *A Rich Brew: How Cafés Created Modern Jewish Culture*. New York: NYU Press, 2018.

Piotrowski, Stanisław, ed. *Dziennik Hansa Franka*. Warsaw: Wydawnictwo Prawnicze, 1956.

Piskurewicz, Jan. *W służbie nauki i oświaty: Stanisław Michalski, 1865–1949*. Warsaw: PAN, Instytut Historii Nauki, Oświaty i Techniki, 1993.

Plach, Eva. *The Clash of Moral Nations: Cultural Politics in Piłsudski's Poland, 1926–1935*. Athens, OH: Ohio University Press, 2006.

Plohn, Alfred. "Muzyka we Lwowie a Żydzi." In *Almanach Żydowski*, edited by Herman Stachel, 40–57. Lviv: Wydawnictwo Kultury i Sztuki, 1937.

Plokhy, Serhii. *The Gates of Europe: A History of Ukraine*. Rev. ed. New York: Basic Books, 2021.

Pollakówna, Joanna. "Ministerstwo Sztuki i Kultury." In *Polskie życie artystyczne w latach 1915–1939*, edited by Aleksander Wojciechowski, 546–49. Wrocław: Zakład Narodowy im. Ossolińskich, 1974.

Polonsky, Antony. *The Jews in Poland and Russia*, vol. 3. Oxford: Littman Library of Jewish Civilization, 2010.

——. "The New Jewish Politics and Its Discontents." In *The Emergence of Modern Jewish Politics: Bundism and Zionism in Eastern Europe*, edited by Zvi Y. Gitelman, 35–53. Pittsburgh, PA: University of Pittsburgh Press, 2003.

———. *Politics in Independent Poland 1921–1939: The Crisis of Constitutional Government*. Oxford: Clarendon Press, 1972.

———. "Warsaw." *The YIVO Encyclopedia of Jews in Eastern Europe*. https:// encyclopedia.yivo.org/article/487.

———. "'Why Did They Hate Tuwim and Boy So Much?': Jews and 'Artificial Jews' in the Literary Polemics of the Second Polish Republic." In *Antisemitism and Its Opponents in Modern Poland*, edited by Robert Blobaum, 189–209. Ithaca, NY: Cornell University Press, 2005.

Polonsky, Antony, and Joanna B. Michlic, eds. *The Neighbors Respond: The Controversy over the Jedwabne Massacre in Poland*. Princeton, NJ: Princeton University Press, 2004.

Poniatowska, Irena. "Le 'credo musical' d'Alexandre Tansman à travers sa correspondance avec Edouard Ganche et Halina Szymulska." In *Hommage au compositeur Alexandre Tansman (1897–1986)*, edited by Pierre Guillot, 41–52. Paris: Presses de l'Université de Paris-Sorbonne, 2000.

Porter, Brian. "Hetmanka and Mother: Representing the Virgin Mary in Modern Poland." *Contemporary European History* 14, no. 2 (2005): 151–70.

———. *When Nationalism Began to Hate: Imagining Modern Politics in Nineteenth-Century Poland*. New York: Oxford University Press, 2000.

Porter-Szűcs, Brian. *Faith and Fatherland: Catholicism, Modernity, and Poland*. New York: Oxford University Press, 2011.

———. *Poland in the Modern World: Beyond Martyrdom*. Chichester, UK: Wiley-Blackwell, 2014.

Potter, Pamela M. *Art of Suppression: Confronting the Nazi Past in Histories of the Visual and Performing Arts*. Oakland: University of California Press, 2016.

Potter, Pamela M., Christina L. Baade, and Roberta Montemorra Marvin, eds. *Music in World War II: Coping with Wartime in Europe and the United States*. Bloomington: Indiana University Press, 2020.

Prekerowa, Teresa. *Konspiracyjna Rada Pomocy Żydom w Warszawie, 1942–1945*. Warsaw: PIW, 1982.

Prokop-Janiec, Eugenia. *Polish-Jewish Literature in the Interwar Years*. Translated by Abe Shenitzer. Syracuse, NY: Syracuse University Press, 2003.

Przerembska, Violetta. *Ideały wychowania w edukacji muzycznej w II Rzeczypospolitej*. Łódź: Wydawnictwo Uniwersytetu Łódzkiego, 2008.

Régamey, Konstanty. "Muzyka polska pod okupacją niemiecką." In *Okupacyjne losy muzyków: Warszawa 1939–1945*, edited by Katarzyna Naliwajek-Mazurek, Elżbieta Markowska, and Andrzej Spóz, vol. 2, 62–65. Warsaw: Towarzystwo imienia Witolda Lutosławskiego, 2014–15 [1946].

Rehding, Alexander. *Music and Monumentality: Commemoration and Wonderment in Nineteenth-Century Germany*. New York: Oxford University Press, 2009.

Reich-Ranicki, Marcel. *The Author of Himself: The Life of Marcel Reich-Ranicki*. Translated by Ewald Oser. Princeton, NJ: Princeton University Press, 2001.

316 | Bibliography

Reiss, Józef. "Dusza żydostwa w muzyce." *Muzyk Wojskowy* 3 (1928): no. 9, 1–4; no. 10, 1–2; no. 11, 2–3; no. 13, 1–2; no. 14, 1–2.

Reittererová, Vlasta, and Hubert Reitterer. "Musik und Politik—Musikpolitik: Die Internationale Gesellschaft für Neue Musik im Spiegel des brieflichen Nachlasses von Alois Hába 1931–1938." *Miscellanea Musicologica* 36 (1999): 129–310.

Reyland, Nicholas. "Lutosławski, 'Akcja,' and the Poetics of Musical Plot." *Music and Letters* 88, no. 4 (2007): 604–31.

———. "Personal Loss, Cultural Grief, and Lutosławski's Music of Mourning." In *Lutosławski's Worlds*, edited by Nicholas Reyland and Lisa Jakelski, 39–70. Woodbridge, UK: Boydell & Brewer, 2018.

———. "The Spaces of Dream: Lutosławski's Modernist Heterotopias." *Twentieth-Century Music* 12, no. 1 (2015): 37–70.

Richards, Annette. "Carl Philipp Emanuel Bach, Portraits, and the Physiognomy of Music History." *Journal of the American Musicological Society* 66, no. 2 (2013): 337–96.

Ringelblum, Emanuel. *Notes from the Warsaw Ghetto: The Journal of Emmanuel Ringelblum*. Translated and edited by Jacob Sloan. New York: McGraw-Hill, 1958.

Rogers, Jillian C. *Resonant Recoveries: French Music and Trauma between the World Wars*. New York: Oxford University Press, 2021.

Rogoyska, Maria. "Z dziejów mecenatu artystycznego w Polsce w latach 1918–1930." *Materiały do Studiów i Dyskusji* 5, no. 3–4 (1954): 128–200.

Rothstein, Robert A. "The Polish Tin Pan Alley, a Jewish Street." *Polin Studies in Polish Jewry* 32 (2020): 147–63.

[Różycki, Stanisław]. "Kawiarnie." In *Archiwum Ringelbluma: Konspiracyjne archiwum Getta Warszawy*, 5:67–76. Warsaw: Żydowski Instytut Historyczny, 2011.

Rudnicki, Szymon. "Anti-Jewish Legislation in Interwar Poland." Translated by Robert Blobaum. In *Antisemitism and Its Opponents in Modern Poland*, edited by Robert Blobaum, 148–70. Ithaca, NY: Cornell University Press, 2005.

Ryziński, Remigiusz. *Foucault in Warsaw*. Translated by Sean Gasper Bye. Rochester, NY: Open Letter, 2021.

Sacks, Adam J. "Ostbahnhof Berlin: Jewish Music Students of East European Origin at the Berlin Conservatory, 1918–1933." *Polin Studies in Polish Jewry* 32 (2020): 321–42.

Sakowska, Ruta. "Komitety domowe w getcie warszawskim." *Biuletyn Żydowskiego Instytutu Historycznego*, no. 61 (1967): 59–86.

Salmon, Hanna. "The Polish Pianist Artur Hermelin." *De musica* 13 (2019): 1–15.

Samson, Jim. *The Music of Szymanowski*. London: Kahn & Averill, 1980.

Sargeant, Lynn M. *Harmony and Discord: Music and the Transformation of Russian Cultural Life*. New York: Oxford University Press, 2011.

Sawicki, Jacek Zygmunt. *Bitwa o prawdę: Historia zmagań o pamięć Powstania Warszawskiego 1944–1989*. Warsaw: DiG, 2005.

Schmelz, Peter J. *Such Freedom, If Only Musical: Unofficial Soviet Music during the Thaw*. New York: Oxford University Press, 2009.

Shallcross, Bożena. *The Holocaust Object in Polish and Polish-Jewish Culture.* Bloomington: Indiana University Press, 2011.

Shore, Marci. *Caviar and Ashes: A Warsaw Generation's Life and Death in Marxism, 1918–1968.* New Haven, CT: Yale University Press, 2006.

———. "Children of the Revolution: Communism, Zionism, and the Berman Brothers." *Jewish Social Studies* 10, no. 3 (2004): 23–86.

———. "Język, pamięć i rewolucyjna awangarda: Kształtowanie historii powstania w getcie warszawskim w latach 1944–1950." *Biuletyn Żydowskiego Instytutu Historycznego* 48, no. 4 (1998): 44–61.

Shreffler, Anne C. "Ideologies of Serialism: Stravinsky's *Threni* and the Congress for Cultural Freedom." In *Music and the Aesthetics of Modernity: Essays,* edited by Karol Berger and Anthony Newcomb, 217–45. Cambridge, MA: Harvard University Press, 2005.

———. "The International Society for Contemporary Music and Its Political Context (Prague, 1935)." In *Music and International History in the Twentieth Century,* edited by Jessica C. E. Gienow-Hecht, 58–90. New York: Berghahn, 2015.

Sieradz, Małgorzata. *The Beginnings of Polish Musicology.* Translated by Lindsay Davidson. Berlin: Peter Lang, 2020.

———. *"Kwartalnik Muzyczny" (1928–1950) a początki muzykologii polskiej.* Warsaw: Instytut Sztuki PAN, 2015.

Sitarz, Andrzej. "In the Shadow of PWM: On Some Private Music Publishing Houses in Poland in the First Decade after the Second World War." *Music Iagellonica* 6 (2012): 225–46.

Skaff, Sheila. *The Law of the Looking Glass: Cinema in Poland, 1896–1939.* Athens, OH: Ohio University Press, 2008.

Snyder, Timothy. *Bloodlands: Europe between Hitler and Stalin.* New York: Basic Books, 2010.

———. *The Reconstruction of Nations: Poland, Ukraine, Lithuania, Belarus, 1569–1999.* New Haven, CT: Yale University Press, 2003.

Sokorski, Włodzimierz. *Polacy pod Lenino.* Warsaw: Książka i Wiedza, 1971.

Sołtys, Maria Ewa. *Tylko we Lwowie: dzieje życia i działalności Mieczysława i Adama Sołtysów.* Wrocław: Zakład Narodowy im. Ossolińskich, 2008.

Sonevytsky, Maria. *Wild Music: Sound and Sovereignty in Ukraine.* Middletown, CT: Wesleyan University Press, 2019.

Sperlich, Andreas. "'S' is nito kein Nechten': Notizen zu Juliusz Wolfsohn." In *Jüdische Kunstmusik im 20. Jahrhundert,* edited by Jascha Nemtsov, 137–48. Wiesbaden: Harrassowitz, 2006.

Sprigge, Martha. *Socialist Laments: Musical Mourning in the German Democratic Republic.* New York: Oxford University Press, 2021.

Sprout, Leslie A. *Musical Legacy of Wartime France.* Berkeley: University of California Press, 2013.

Stauter-Halsted, Keely. "Bio-Politics between Nation and Empire: Venereal Disease, Eugenics, and Race Science in the Creation of Modern Poland." *East Central Europe* 43, no. 1/2 (2016): 134–60.

Steinberg, Michael P. "Mendelssohn's Music and German-Jewish Culture: An Intervention." *Musical Quarterly* 83, no. 1 (1999): 31–44.

318 | Bibliography

Steinlauf, Michael C. *Bondage to the Dead: Poland and the Memory of the Holocaust*. Syracuse, NY: Syracuse University Press, 1997.

Steinweis, Alan. *Art, Ideology & Economics in Nazi Germany: The Reich Chambers of Music, Theater, and the Visual Arts*. Chapel Hill: University of North Carolina Press, 1993.

Stola, Dariusz. "Fighting against the Shadows: The *Anti-Zionist* Campaign of 1968." In *Antisemitism and Its Opponents in Modern Poland*, edited by Robert Blobaum, 284–300. Ithaca, NY: Cornell University Press, 2005.

———. "Jewish Emigration from Communist Poland: The Decline of Polish Jewry in the Aftermath of the Holocaust." *East European Jewish Affairs* 47, nos. 2–3 (2017): 169–88.

———. *Kraj bez wyjścia? Migracje z Polski, 1949–1989*. Warsaw: Instytut Pamięci Narodowej, 2010.

Stowarzyszenie Młodych Muzyków Polaków w Paryżu: Dotychczasowa działalność, cele i dążenia. Warsaw: Wyszyński, 1930.

Straszewska, Maria. "*Biuletyn Informacyjny, 1939–1941*." *Najnowsze Dzieje Polski* 11 (1967): 127–64.

Suchmiel, Jadwiga. *Działalność naukowa kobiet w uniwersytecie we Lwowie do roku 1939*. Częstochowa: Wydawnictwo WSP, 2000.

Suchowiejko, Renata. "Recepcja muzyki polskiej w Paryżu w latach 1919–1939: Analiza krytyczna źródeł prasowych." In *Muzyka polska za granicą: Między Warszawą a Paryżem (1918–1939)*, edited by Beata Bolesławska-Lewandowska and Jolanta Guzy-Pasiak, 9–29. Warsaw: Instytut Sztuki PAN.

Sword, Keith. *Deportation and Exile: Poles in the Soviet Union, 1939–48*. New York: St. Martin's Press, 1994.

Szalsza, Piotr. "Nieznane fakty z życia Zofii Lissy i jej najbliższej rodziny." *Muzyka* 65, no. 4 (2020): 171–81.

Szarota, Tomasz. *Okupowanej Warszawy dzień powszedni*. 4th ed. Warsaw: Czytelnik, 2010.

Szaynok, Bozena. "Mémoire de l'insurrection du ghetto de Varsovie (1944–1989)." In *Juifs et polonais, 1939–2008*, edited by Jean-Charles Szurek and Annette Wieviorka, 413–33. Paris: Albin Michel, 2009.

Szpilman, Władysław. *Śmierć miasta: Pamiętniki Władysława Szpilmana, 1939–1945*. Edited by Jerzy Waldorff. Warsaw: Wiedza, 1946.

Szymanowski, Karol. *Pisma*, vols. 1–2. Edited by Kornel Michałowski, Stefan Kisielewski, and Teresa Chylińska. Cracow: PWM, 1984–89.

———. *Szymanowski on Music: Selected Writings of Karol Szymanowski*. Edited and translated by Alistair Wightman. London: Toccata, 1999.

Szyszka, Michał. *Droga klerka: Filozofia sztuki Stefana Kisielewskiego*. Cracow: Universitas, 2010.

Sztyma, Tamara. "On the Dance Floor, on the Screen, on the Stage: Popular Music in the Interwar Period: Polish, Jewish, Shared." *Polin Studies in Polish Jewry* 32 (2020): 165–75.

Tansman, Alexandre. *Regards en arrière: Itinéraire d'un musicien cosmopolite au XXe siècle*. Edited by Cédric Segond-Genovesi and Mireille Zanuttini-Tansman. Paris: Éditions Aedam Musicae, 2013.

Tarnawska-Kaczorowska, Krystyna, ed. *Muzyka źle obecna*. Warsaw: Sekcja Muzykologów Związku Kompozytorów Polskich, 1989.

———. "Na rozpoczęcie." In *Muzyka źle obecna*, edited by Krystyna Tarnawska-Kaczorowska, 7–25. Warsaw: Sekcja Muzykologów Związku Kompozytorów Polskich, 1989.

Taruskin, Richard. "Back to Whom? Neoclassicism as Ideology." *19th-Century Music* 16, no. 3 (1993): 286–302.

———. *The Oxford History of Western Music*, 5 vols. New York: Oxford University Press, 2005.

Thomas, Adrian. *Polish Music since Szymanowski*. Cambridge: Cambridge University Press, 2005.

Tomasik, Krzysztof. *Homobiografie: Pisarki i pisarze polscy XIX i XX wieku*. Warsaw: Krytyka Polityczna, 2008.

Tomoff, Kiril. *Creative Union: The Professional Organization of Soviet Composers, 1939–1953*. Ithaca, NY: Cornell University Press, 2006.

Tompkins, David G. *Composing the Party Line: Music and Politics in Early Cold War Poland and East Germany*. West Lafayette, IN: Purdue University Press, 2013.

Towarzystwo Muzyki Polskiej: Katalog wydawnictw (1939). Warsaw: Towarzystwo Muzyki Polskiej, 1939.

Traba, Robert. "Symbole pamięci: II Wojna Światowa w świadomości zbiorowej Polaków." *Przegląd Zachodni* 55, no. 1 (2000): 52–67.

Trochimczyk, Maja. "Chopin and the 'Polish Race': On National Ideologies and the Chopin Reception." In *The Age of Chopin: Interdisciplinary Inquires*, edited by Halina Goldberg, 278–313. Bloomington: Indiana University Press, 2004.

Tuchowski, Andrzej. *Nationalism, Chauvinism and Racism as Reflected in European Musical Thought and in Compositions from the Interwar Period*. Translated by Tomasz Zymer. Berlin: Peter Lang, 2019.

Turkov, Ionas [Jonas Turkow]. *En Pologne, après la libération: L'impossible survie des rescapés juifs*. Translated by Maurice Pfeffer. Paris: Calmann-Lévy, 2008.

Turkow, Jonas. *C'était ainsi: 1939–1943, la vie dans le ghetto de Varsovie*. Translated by Maurice Pfeffer. Paris: Austral, 1995.

———. *La lutte pour la vie*. Translated by Maurice Pfeffer. Paris: Champion, 2005.

———. "Warszawa się bawi . . . ." In *Archiwum Ringelbluma: Konspiracyjne archiwum Getta Warszawy*, 26:4–28. Translated by Aleksandra Geller. Warsaw: Żydowski Instytut Historyczny, 2017.

Tuszyńska, Agata. *Vera Gran: The Accused*. Translated by Charles Ruas. New York: Alfred A. Knopf, 2013.

Underhill, Karen. "Bruno Schulz's Galician Diasporism: On the 1937 Essay 'E. M. Lilien' and Rokhl Korn's Review of *Cinnamon Shops*." *Jewish Social Studies* 24, no. 1 (2018): 1–33.

———. "Re-Judaizing the Polish (Studies) Landscape: The Doikeyt Model." *East European Politics & Societies* 28, no. 4 (2014): 693–703.

320 | Bibliography

Urbanek, Mariusz. *Waldorff: Ostatni baron Peerelu.* Warsaw: Iskry, 2008.
Ury, Scott. *Barricades and Banners: The Revolution of 1905 and the Transformation of Warsaw Jewry.* Palo Alto, CA: Stanford University Press, 2012.
———. "Strange Bedfellows? Anti-Semitism, Zionism, and the Fate of 'the Jews.'" *American Historical Review* 123, no. 4 (2018): 1151–71.
Ury, Scott, and Gai Miron, eds. *Antisemitism and the Politics of History.* Waltham, MA: Brandeis University Press, 2024.
Vest, Lisa Cooper. *Awangarda: Tradition and Modernity in Postwar Polish Music.* Oakland: University of California Press, 2021.
———. "The Discursive Foundations of the Polish Musical Avant-Garde at Midcentury: Aesthetics of Progress, Meaning, and National Identity." PhD diss., Indiana University, 2014.
———. "Educating Audiences, Educating Composers: The Polish Composers' Union and *Upowszechnienie.*" *Musicology Today* 7 (2010): 226–42.
Volkov, Shulamit. "Antisemitism as a Cultural Code: Reflections on the History and Historiography of Antisemitism in Imperial Germany." *The Leo Baeck Institute Year Book* 23, no. 1 (1978): 25–46.
Wajner, León. *Cantos de lucha y resurgimiento, 1939–1962.* Buenos Aires: Kium, 1962.
Waldorff, Jerzy. "Działalność Państwowej Filharmonii w Krakowie w sezonie 1945/46." In "Święto muzyki polskiej: program, Kraków, 23–29 czerwca 1946 r.," no pagination. Cracow: Państwowa Filharmonia, 1946.
———. *Moje cienie.* Warsaw: Czytelnik, 1979.
Walldorf [Waldorff], Jerzy. *Sztuka pod dyktaturą.* Warsaw: Biblioteka Polska, 1939.
Walicki, Andrzej. "Polish Conceptions of the Intelligentsia and Its Calling." *Slavica Lundensia* 22 (2005): 1–22.
Waśkiewicz, Andrzej. "The Polish Home Army and the Politics of Memory." *East European Politics and Societies* 24, no. 1 (2010): 44–58.
Weber, William. "Art Music and Social Class." In *The Routledge Reader on the Sociology of Music,* edited by John Shepherd and Kyle Devine, 221–29. New York: Routledge, 2015.
Wedel, Janine. "The Ties That Bind in Polish Society." In *Polish Paradoxes,* edited by Stanisław Gomułka and Antony Polonsky, 237–60. London: Routledge, 1990.
———, ed. *The Unplanned Society: Poland during and after Communism.* New York: Columbia University Press, 1992.
Weeks, Theodore R. "The Best of Both Worlds: Creating the *Żyd–Polak.*" *East European Jewish Affairs* 34, no. 2 (2004): 1–20.
Werb, Bret. "Fourteen Shoah Songbooks." *Musica Judaica* 20 (2013–14): 39–116.
———. "Shmerke Kaczerginski: The Partisan-Troubadour." *Polin Studies in Polish Jewry* 20 (2008): 392–411.
Wieczorek, Sławomir. *Na froncie muzyki: Socrealistyczny dyskurs o muzyce w Polsce w latach 1948–1955.* Wrocław: Wydawnictwo Uniwersytetu Wrocławskiego, 2014.

Wieviorka, Annette. *The Era of the Witness*. Translated by Jared Stark. Ithaca, NY: Cornell University Press, 2006.

Wightman, Alistair. *Karol Szymanowski: His Life and Work*. Aldershot, UK: Ashgate, 1999.

Wiłkomirski, Kazimierz. *Wspomnienia*. Cracow: PWM, 1971.

———. *Wspomnień ciąg dalszy*. Cracow: PWM, 1980.

Witkowski, Leon. "Kancjonał polski Walentego z Brzozowa wobec kancjanału czeskiego Jana Roha: Przyczynek do badań nad wpływami czeskimi w polskiej pieśni religijnej XVI wieku." *Zeszyty Naukowe Uniwersytetu Mikołaja Kopernika w Toruniu* 1 (1957): 19–56.

Wiszniowska, Monika. *Stańczyk Polski Ludowej: Rzecz o Stefanie Kisielewskim*. Katowice: Wydawnictwo Śląsk, 2004.

Wlodarski, Amy Lynn. "Musical Testimonies of Terezín and the Possibilities of Contrapuntal Listening." *Music & Politics* 16, no. 2 (2022). https://doi.org/10.3998/mp.3108.

———. *Musical Witness and Holocaust Representation*. Cambridge: Cambridge University Press, 2015.

Wnuk, Rafał. "The Polish Underground under Soviet Occupation, 1939–1941." In *Stalin and Europe: Imitation and Domination, 1928–1953*, edited by Timothy Snyder and Ray Brandon, 92–113. New York: Oxford University Press, 2014.

Wojciechowski, Aleksander. "Próby integracji kultury plastycznej." In *Polska odrodzona, 1918–1939: Państwo, społeczeństwo, kultura*, 2nd ed., edited by Jan Tomicki, 550–84. Warsaw: Wiedza Powszechna, 1988.

Wojciechowski, Piotr. "Wiedeński świat Romana Haubenstocka-Ramatiego: Fascynacje dziełami scenicznymi na przykładzie opery 'Ameryka.'" *Kwartalnik Młodych Muzykologów UJ* 7 (2010): 34–40.

Wolff, Larry. *Inventing Eastern Europe: The Map of Civilization on the Mind of the Enlightenment*. Stanford, CA: Stanford University Press, 1994.

Wood, Nathaniel D. *Becoming Metropolitan: Urban Selfhood and the Making of Modern Cracow*. DeKalb: Northern Illinois University Press, 2010.

Woytowicz, Bolesław. "W okupowanej Warszawie." In *Okupacyjne losy muzyków: Warszawa 1939–1945*, edited by Katarzyna Naliwajek-Mazurek, Elżbieta Markowska, and Andrzej Spóz, vol. 1, 94–111. Warsaw: Towarzystwo imienia Witolda Lutosławskiego, 2014–15 [1969].

Woźniakowska, Anna. *60 lat Filharmonii im. Karola Szymanowskiego w Krakowie: 1945–2005*. Cracow: Filharmonia im. Karola Szymanowskiego, 2004.

Wójcik-Keuprulian, Bronisława. *Korespondencja do Szwajcarii: Listy do Henryka Opieńskiego (1925–37) i Ludwika Bronarskiego (1929–38)*. Edited by Małgorzata Sieradz. Warsaw: ISPAN, 2018.

Wróbel Best, Jolanta. "The Other Heroine Is Memory (A Conversation with Agata Tuszyńska)." *Polish Review* 60, no. 1 (2015): 85–95.

Wyka, Kazimierz. "The Excluded Economy." In *The Unplanned Society*, edited by Janine Wedel, 23–61. New York: Columbia University Press, 1992.

Zahra, Tara. *The Great Departure: Mass Migration from Eastern Europe and the Making of the Free World*. New York: W. W. Norton, 2016.

322 | Bibliography

Zalewski, Teodor. *Pół wieku wśród muzyków: Przyczynki do dziejów polskiej kultury muzycznej.* Cracow: PWM, 1977.

Zaremba, Marcin. *Komunizm, legitymizacja, nacjonalizm: Nacjonalistyczna legitymizacja władzy komunistycznej w Polsce.* Warsaw: TRIO, 2001.

Zerubavel, Eviatar. *The Elephant in the Room: Silence and Denial in Everyday Life.* New York: Oxford University Press, 2006.

Zimmerman, Joshua D. *The Polish Underground and the Jews, 1939–1945.* Cambridge: Cambridge University Press, 2015.

Zubrzycki, Geneviève. *The Crosses of Auschwitz: Nationalism and Religion in Post-Communist Poland.* Chicago: University of Chicago Press, 2006.

———. "Narrative Shock and Polish Memory Remaking in the Twenty-First Century." In *Memory and Post-War Memorials: Confronting the Violence of the Past,* edited by Marc Silberman and Florence Vatan, 95–115. New York: Palgrave Macmillan, 2013.

———. *Resurrecting the Jew: Nationalism, Philosemitism, and Poland's Jewish Revival.* Princeton, NJ: Princeton University Press, 2022.

Zymer, Izabela. "Zofia Lissa i Włodzimierz Iwannikow: Polska muzykolog i radziecki kompozytor we wspólnej walce o nowy, lepszy ład." *Polski Rocznik Muzykologiczny* 20 (2022): 53–79.

Zysiak, Agata. "Hysteresis, Academic Biography, and Political Field in the People's Republic of Poland." *Theory and Society* 48, no. 3 (2019): 483–508.

Żarnowska, Anna. "Women's Political Participation in Inter-War Poland: Opportunities and Limitations." *Women's History Review* 13, no. 1 (2004): 57–68.

Żarnowska, Anna, and Andrzej Szwarc, eds. *Równe prawa i nierówne szanse: Kobiety w Polsce międzywojennej.* Warsaw: Wydawnictwo DiG, 2000.

Żarnowski, Janusz. "Inteligencja polska, jej ewolucja historyczna przed wojną i w dobie powojennej." *Roczniki Dziejów Społecznych i Gospodarczych* 79 (2018): 127–63.

———. *State, Society and Intelligentsia: Modern Poland and Its Regional Context.* Burlington, VT: Ashgate, 2003.

Żółkiewska, Agnieszka. *Zerwana przeszłość: Powojenne środowisko żydowskiej inteligencji twórczej: Pomoc materialna i organizacyjna ze strony CKŻP.* Warsaw: Żydowski Instytut Historyczny, 2017.

Index

acculturation, Jewish, 2, 4, 7–9, 26, 30; antisemitism and, 9, 10, 12, 41; classical music as avenue of, 46; concert music and, 42; Holocaust survival and, 172; music as vector of, 19; Nazi definition of Jewishness and, 111; Polish modernism and, 52; "Polish of the faith of Moses," 12, 39; in Warsaw Ghetto, 118–19

Advisory Council for the World Centre for Jewish Music, 48

Ajzensztadt, Marysia, 126

aleatoric composition, 234, 237

Alexander, Jeffrey C., 3

Anders, Władysław, 155

Anders Army, 155, 156, 157, 175

Andrzejewski, Jerzy, 17

Anointed, The (Kassern, 1951), 239

antisemitism, 47, 148, 193, 238, 252–53n29; among progressive composers, 42–44; anti-Polishness compared with, 84; communism associated with Jews (Żydokomuna), 10, 137, 149, 153, 157, 163; as cultural code, 10; institutionalization of, 61–66; Polish ethnonationalism and, 9–15; of postwar Polish state, 175, 239; rhetoric as administrative tactic, 11; right-wing politics and, 42; Soviet rule and, 162; trope of Jew as rootless cosmopolitan, 61, 153; trope of Jewish unmusicality, 44, 46, 60, 153

Arizona (café in Warsaw Ghetto), 125

"artist-activist" (*artysta-społecznik*), 32

aryjska strona. See Polish Warsaw, under Nazi occupation

assimilation (*asymilacja*), 7, 47, 252n17; Judenrat (Jewish Council) and, 118; Yiddish language against, 121. *See also* acculturation

Association of Enthusiasts for Early Music (Stowarzyszenie Miłośników Dawnej Muzyki), 62, 187, 189

Association of Jewish Musicians and Composers in Poland, 173

Association of Polish Composers, 177, 282n64

Association of Young Musician-Poles in Paris (Stowarzyszenie Młodych Muzyków Polaków w Paryżu), 52, 56, 62, 72, 246; competition hosted by (1928), 58–59; manifesto of, 57; in postwar period, 182; wartime underground and, 92

Association of Young Musicians in Cracow, 70, 75, 160, 263n108

associations (*stowarzyszenia*), 50

atonality, 39, 62, 97, 150

audiences, 1, 19, 52; concert etiquette and, 103; eagerness to attend concerts, 6; mixed Polish and Polish Jewish, 8, 129; Mycielski's "expression" and, 212; under Nazi occupation, 86; Polish

323

324 | Index

audiences *(continued)*
 national identity and, 130, 131;
 postwar, 209; presence of Nazi Germans
 in, 104; in Warsaw Ghetto, 126
Auerbach, Rachel, 119
Auschwitz camp, 105, 203, 217, 222
Austria, Polish partition ruled by, 29, 31,
 38, 87. *See also* Cracow; Lviv
avant-garde, 18, 22, 184; cafés and, 99;
 Cold War and, 234; emotional
 expressivity and, 54; as "formalism,"
 171; in France, 29; modernization and,
 233. *See also* modernism

Babbitt, Milton, 234
Babiracki, Patryk, 160
"Baby, ach te Baby" (Girls, oh girls; song,
 1933), 35
Bacewicz, Grażyna, 27, 106, 190, 192, 217,
 235, 241; Concerts of Wartime
 Compositions and, 268n104; Festival of
 Contemporary Polish Music and, 194;
 ORMUZ and, 67; on Paris versus
 Warsaw, 53–54; popularity in early
 postwar years, 209; as refugee from
 German invasion, 81; Trio for oboe,
 violin, and cello (1936), 53*ex.*, 54
Bach, Johann Sebastian, 101, 116
Baird, Tadeusz, 232
Bakman, Józef, 271n41
Baltic Philharmonic, 178
Bandrowska-Turska, Ewa, 100, 209
Barbag, Seweryn, 132
Barbag-Drexler, Irena, 93–94
Barcewicz, Stanisław, 118
Bard, Jakub, 154
Barrès, Maurice, 57
Bartek Zwycięzca (Sienkiewicz), 32
Bartók, Béla, 238
"Bartoszu, Bartoszu" (O Bartosz, O
 Bartosz; song), 159
Baruch, Wacław, 271n41
Baruch, Witold Hugo, 118–19, 133, 176,
 271n43
Barvinsky, Vasyl, 143, 145
Beethoven, Ludwig van, 116, 119, 145, 201
Bejgelman, Dawid, 121
Belarusians, as percentage of prewar
 population, 2
belonging, 49, 66; boundaries of belonging
 and exclusion, 49; Jewish belonging to
 Polish institutions, 26; Jews and
 European musical culture, 119; Nazi
 racial ideology and, 86; "peoplehood"

as ethnic belonging, 44; Polish
 ethnonationalism and, 163, 232
Bełżec death camp, 2, 82
Bem, Czesław, 271n41
Berent, Wacław, 135
Berg, Alban: *Wozzeck*, 39
Berg, Mary, 129
Berman, Jakub, 163
Bielińska, Irena, 103
Bierdiajew, Walerian, 93, 191
Bierut, Bolesław, 221–22
Biess, Frank, 16
big band music, 33, 35
Birnbaum, Zdzisław, 42
Biuletyn Informacyjny (Information
 bulletin), 93
Bizet, Georges, 46; *Carmen*, 101
"bloodlands," 13
Blumenfeld, Diana, 121, 174
Bodo, Eugeniusz, 35, 140
Bogucki, Andrzej, 132
Bohemian Brethren songbook, 197
Boléro (Ravel), 101
Borejsza, Jerzy, 188*fig.*
Borodin, Alexander, 145
Boruński, Leon, 126, 128, 202
Borwicz, Michał, 110*fig.*, 129
Boulanger, Nadia, 27, 31, 81, 241;
 Mycielski and, 59*fig.*, 180, 181, 182,
 213; students of, 53; visit to Union of
 Polish Composers, 59*fig.*
Boulez, Pierre, 234
bourgeoisie, 30
Brahms, Johannes, 101; Piano Quintet,
 103
Braun, Pola, 128
Breskin, Oleksandr, 143
Broniewski, Władysław: "Żydom polskim"
 (To the Polish Jews), 222–23
Bundism, 44

cabaret, 8, 34, 71; in prewar Warsaw, 128;
 in Warsaw Ghetto, 109
Café Club (Warsaw), 105
cafés, music performance in, 2, 15, 20, 86,
 89; earnings of musicians, 99–100,
 269n118; intelligentsia's ambitions and,
 28; Polish–Jewish bifurcation and, 195;
 in Polish Warsaw, 97, 99–101, 131;
 popular music, 34; in Warsaw Ghetto,
 109, 123–26, 131, 132. *See also* Café
 Club; Dom Sztuki; "Kawiarnie"
 (Różycki); Lardello café; Lira; L'Ours
 café; Nowa Gospoda; Splendid; Sztuka;

Sztuka i Moda; U Aktorek; Zachęta café; Ziemiańska

Calico, Joy H., 13

"Campo di Fiori" (Miłosz), 213

Cantional albo księgy chwal Boskych to jest Pieśni Duchowne (Königsberg, 1554), 197

capitalism, 140, 141, 146, 171, 180, 187

Caprice for Solo Violin, twenty-fourth (Paganini), 101, 102*ex.*

Captive Mind, The (Miłosz), 237

Carmen (Bizet), 101

Carnet de bal, Un (film, 1937), 130

Carroll, Mark, 234

Casanova (Różycki, 1922), 130

Catholicism, 196, 217; Jewish conversion to, 8, 66, 85; Marian imagery, 197–98, 199, 206

Cello Sonata (Debussy), 103

censorship: in occupied Polish Warsaw, 88; in the Warsaw Ghetto, 114; in Soviet Lviv, 141

Central Committee of Jews in Poland (Centralny Komitet Żydów w Polsce; CKŻP), 173–74, 222, 246

Central Institute of Culture (Centralny Instytut Kultury), 284n193

Chmielewska, Katarzyna, 238

Chomiński, Józef, 227

Chopin, Fryderyk, 47, 55, 60, 79, 191; "Chopin under the Occupation" article (1945), 201–2; grave in Père Lachaise Cemetery (Paris), 56*fig.*; Liszt transcriptions of, 72; Nazi view of, 87; performed in Soviet-occupied Lviv, 145; piano concertos, 48; Polish national identity and, 130, 131; "race" and Polishness in relation to, 56; recordings destroyed by Nazis, 86; synthesis of the national and the universal in, 61; Szpilman as interpreter of, 129; works performed in underground concerts, 95, 96*fig.*

Chopin Competition, 126

Chowrimootoo, Christopher, 33

Chromiński, Adam, 188*fig.*

Chwila (The moment; Jewish daily paper), 44

Chybiński, Adolf, 38, 39, 39*fig.*, 41, 150, 185, 241; antisemitism of, 64, 65, 66, 261–62n66; German-occupied Lviv and, 153; Jews and Ukrainians associated with Soviet occupation by, 149, 277n71; Lviv musicological institute and, 140; Lviv State Conservatory and, 142,

143–44; Soviet occupation of Lviv and, 81; State Music Publishing Council and, 190–91; at war's end with fellow survivors, 168

cinema, 8, 40

civil society, 84, 140

Cizmic, Maria, 17

CKI (Centralna Komisja Imprezowa; Central Commission for Entertainments), 121, 122–23, 247

classical music: broad social recognition of, 195; centrality of acculturated Jews to, 2; disseminated in eastern borderlands, 67; German classical repertoire, 119; Nazi cultural policy toward, 87–88; Nazi occupation policies and, 19; popular music in competition with, 34; selective narrative about the war and, 21. *See also* concert music

Cohen, Brigid, 26

Cold War, 22, 234, 236–38

Commission for Contemporary Music, 63

communism, 2, 22, 26, 228; Cold War and, 238; Communist Party of Western Ukraine, 40, 257n70; consolidation over postwar state, 171; Jews associated with, 10, 137, 153, 163, 174; nationalism and, 159; Poles of aristocratic origin and, 180, 181; Polish communists in the Soviet Union, 155

concert music, 185, 194, 240; canon of, 233; continuity project and, 1, 6; historiography of, 251n4; interwar division of, 27, 28*fig.*; Jewish acculturation and, 7; in Soviet-occupied Lviv, 140–41. *See also* classical music

Concerto for Orchestra (Lutosławski, 1954), 233

Concerto for Voice (Kassern), 218

Concerts of Wartime Compositions, 96, 104

Conference of Composers and Musicologists (Kyiv, 1941), 140

Connelly, John, 84

conservative composers, 28*fig.*, 42, 49, 54, 191, 234

continuity of Polish culture, 21, 36, 91, 195, 231; concert music and, 1, 5; "double occupation" and, 139; Holocaust and, 3; as ideological project, 6; interwar organizations reconfigured into state institutions, 187–92; Jewish absence and, 105–7; musical intelligentsia and, 6, 15, 231–32; social basis of continuity and rupture, 3–7

326 | Index

Copernicus, Nicolaus, 89fig.
Courrier musicale (French journal), 45
Cracow, 20, 26, 139; Festival of Contemporary Polish Music in (1945), 194, 197, 217–18; ISCM festival in (1939), 79; musicology program in, 38; Nazi General Government and, 83–84, 88, 89fig., 196; reconstruction and, 169
Cracow Conservatory, 178
"Crisis of Musical Modernism, The" (Palester, 1932), 35
Cud mniemany, czyli Krakowiacy i Górale (The would-be miracle, or the Cracovians and Highlanders; Bogusławski and Stefani, 1794), 146
cultural capital, 4–5, 6
"cultural-political guidelines," 86–87
Czarnecki, Maciej, 127, 128
Czerniaków, Adam, 116

Dąbrowski, Mirosław, 178
death camps, 2, 82, 85, 288n66
Debussy, Claude, 145; Cello Sonata, 103; Prelude to the Afternoon of a Faun, 101
Delegate's Bureau, 91, 105, 134
Dent, Edward, 80
Dies Irae (Penderecki), 233
Dmowski, Roman, 10
Dobrzycka, Stella, 201
Dobrzyniec, Adam, 271n41
dodecaphony. See twelve-tone composition
Dołżycki, Adam, 93, 104
Dom Sztuki (House of Art) café, 88, 100, 101, 103–4, 104fig., 127
Dorabialska, Helena, 38, 40
Drobner, Bolesław, 160
Drobner, Mieczysław, 75, 160–61, 162, 163, 179, 187, 241
Drzewiecki, Zbigniew, 28fig., 45fig., 178, 179, 191
Dutkiewicz, Zofia, 119
Dvořák, Antonín, 201

ecosystem, musical (ruch muzyczny), 5, 105, 109
"Educational Role of Musical Culture in Society, The" (Szymanowski, 1930), 67–68
Efebos (Szymanowski, 1918), 31
Eichmann, Adolf: trial of, 254n62
Ekier, Jan, 188fig., 218, 227
emotion, 126, 218, 236; centrality to postwar aesthetics, 195; coded in

national terms, 54; containment of wartime emotion, 16, 211–16, 215ex.; realism and, 220, 221, 227
Engel, David, 252n29
Engel, Joel, 46, 48
Engelking, Barbara, 108
Era of the Witness, The (Wieviorka), 254n62
Erhardt, Mieczysław Jerzy, 100
ethnonationalism, 4, 9–15, 52, 64, 73, 163, 141, 195, 240
Europe, western, 4, 62, 68, 206; under Nazi occupation, 86; postwar skepticism toward, 218

Fairclough, Pauline, 220
Familier-Hepnerowa, Janina, 201, 202
"Farewell to the Fatherland" (Ogiński), 206, 207ex.
fascism, 19, 48, 52, 72–75, 169
Feicht, Hieronim, 39fig., 191
feminism, 38
Festival of Contemporary Polish Music (Cracow, 1945), 194, 197, 217, 221
Filar, Marian, 11–12, 85
First Division army. See Polish Army in the USSR
Fiszman, Henryk, 271n41
Fitelberg, Grzegorz, 2, 27, 42, 176, 241
Fitelberg, Jerzy, 59, 60, 61, 183
Flatau, Artur, 271n41
Fogg, Mieczysław, 100
folk music, 27, 79, 143, 233; as nationalist resistance, 146; recordings destroyed by Nazis, 86; Soviet modernization of, 151; Ukrainian, 150, 152
"formalism": communist rejection of, 171, 191, 192; "Formalism and Realism in Music" (Sokorski), 221; shift in definition of, 227. See also socialist realism
Fosler-Lussier, Danielle, 234
foxtrot dances, 33, 35, 99, 130
"Fragments of a Memoir from the Years 1939–1945" (Palester), 135
France, 210, 218; Dreyfus affair, 29; "Latin culture" shared with Poland, 57, 58; pledge to support Polish independence, 80; right-wing politics in, 57–58. See also Paris
Frank, Hans, 83, 86, 88
"Freedom and Gagging" (Szeligowski), 75
Freemasons, 66
Fuks, Marian, 118

Index | 327

Fund for National Culture, 63, 64, 65
Furmański, Adam, 118, 119

Gadejski, Gerard, 113, 128, 130, 188
Galicia, 50, 144
Ganche, Édouard, 45
gay men, 18, 26, 31
Gazeta Żydowska (Jewish newspaper; Warsaw Ghetto), 115, 117, 120
Gebirtig, Mordechai, 121
General Government, 83–84, 99, 169; cultural policy in, 87; Jewishness defined in, 85. *See also* occupation, Nazi
generations, discourse about, 17, 51, 233–34, 237, 254n68
Germans, 83, 94; German Jews, 12–13, 85; as percentage of prewar population, 2; Volksdeutsche, 83, 94. *See also* Nazis/ Nazi Germany
Germany (German lands): musical culture of, 68, 87
Gesellschaft zur Beförderung der Musik in Galizien. *See* Polish Music Society
Gestapo (Nazi secret police), 122, 133, 134; cafés in Warsaw Ghetto and, 123, 127, 129; rumors of Gran's collaboration with, 210–11; Zarzycka case and, 203
Gilels, Emil, 141
Gliński, Mateusz, 2, 46, 176–77, 242; escape from Nazis, 84, 176; on French influences in Polish music, 57; ISCM and, 45; *Muzyka* journal and, 5, 44–45, 45fig., 64, 176, 193
Gnessin, Mikhail, 46
Godlewska-Bogucka, Janina, 88, 132
Goebbels, Joseph, 86
Goethe, Johann Wolfgang, 56
Gold, Artur, 33, 34, 126
Gold, Henryk, 33, 155
Goldberg, Amos, 109
Goldberg, Halina, 7
Goldfeder, Andrzej, 130
Gombiński, Stanisław, 114–15, 120, 126
Gorbaty, Jan, 153, 154
Gordon, Avery F., 16
government-in-exile, Polish (London), 91, 92, 141, 142, 155, 222
Górecki, Henryk, 18; *Symphony of Sorrowful Songs*, 233
Gradstein, Alfred, 61
Gran, Wiera, 85, 113, 122, 140, 242; escape from Nazis, 133; as memoirist, 272n70; postwar trials of, 210–11; in

prewar Warsaw cabaret scene, 128, 129; on Soviet censorship, 141; as star performer in café Sztuka, 127, 209–10
Great Depression, 63
Grochowski, Stanisław, 197
Gross, Jan T., 14, 141
Grossman, Ludwik, 7–8
"Grupa 49," 232
Gulag system, Soviet, 13, 154, 155
Günsberg, Henryk, 153
Guthrie, Kate, 33

Hába, Alois, 75, 79
HaCohen, Ruth, 7, 10
Hahn, Reynaldo, 72
Halpern, E., 173
Halvéy, Jacques, 46
Harris, Albert, 140
Haubenstock-Ramati, Roman, 175, 238
Hebrew language, 8, 175
Hebrew Suite, op. 8 (Wolfsohn, 1926), 47–48
Heisman (pianist murdered by Nazis in Lviv), 153–54
Helman, Zofia, 54
Her First Ball (Jej pierwszy bal; Szlengel and Szpilman), 129–31, 209–10
Hermelin, Artur, 153
Higher School of Music (Cracow), 217
Hindemith, Paul, 27, 72, 202
Hindemith, Rudolf, 202–3
Hitler, Adolf, 80
Holcman, Ludwik, 271n41
Holmgren, Beth, 33
Holocaust, 7, 12–15, 109, 154, 177; as central event of modern Polish musical culture, 3; cultural production of continuity and, 3; de-Judaized memory of, 240; documentation of, 174; "double occupation" and, 162; inability of ghetto internees to conceive possibility of, 211, 288n66; lived through music, 15; musical intelligentsia's responses to, 15–17; musical memorializations of, 238, 239; percentage of Polish Jews lost in, 1; in Polish cinema and literature, 16–17; Warsaw Ghetto Uprising and memory of, 196. *See also* death camps; Warsaw Ghetto
Holy Week (Andrzejewski), 17
Home Army (Armia Krajowa; AK), 91, 133, 167, 178, 197
homosexuality, 31
Honegger, Arthur, 58, 72

328 | Index

Horenstein, Jascha, 44
Huberman, Bronisław, 173

Idelsohn, Abraham Tzvi, 47
"Ideological Situation among Polish
  Composers, The" (Lissa), 192
"Instructions for Culture Workers"
  (underground publication), 90
instrumental music, 17, 220
intelligentsia (*inteligencja*), 4, 9, 18; appeal
  of fascism and, 73; café performances
  and, 100; comparison with French
  intellectuel class, 29; comparison with
  Russian intelligentsia, 255n15; in
  Nazi-occupied Polish Warsaw, 83, 105;
  nobility and, 29; as percentage of
  interwar population, 28; provincial, 71;
  as self-proclaimed vanguard of the
  educated, 25–26; as targets of Nazis, 81;
  urban professional classes, 8, 28–29; in
  Warsaw Ghetto, 122, 123, 127. *See also*
  musical intelligentsia
interwar period (1918–39), 2, 4, 18, 26, 49,
  109, 233; cabaret, 209; centralization
  and education as focuses, 231; civil
  society in, 19; classical music scene in,
  73; conservatives versus progressives in,
  27, 28*fig.*; cultural continuity project
  and, 21, 91; discrimination against Jews
  in, 11, 157, 163; elitism of musical
  intelligentsia, 5; female musicologists in,
  38, 41; high and low musical genres in,
  36; intelligentsia in, 28; interethnic
  relations in Lviv, 140, 144; interpersonal
  networks in musical organizations, 20;
  musical internationalism in, 61, 186,
  232; musical organizations and
  institutions of, 46, 50, 51, 187, 189,
  190, 193; musicology journals of, 62;
  neoclassicism of, 217, 235; Polish
  Jewish identity in, 41, 44; politics of,
  9–10; popular song in, 34; racial
  imagination in, 55; tensions in musical
  intelligentsia during, 67. *See also*
  Poland, Second Republic
ISCM (International Society for Contemporary Music), 34–35, 40, 63, 134, 247,
  282n64; festival held in Poland (1939),
  79–80; founding of (1924), 45; Lviv
  branch, 140; Polish Jewish musicians in,
  65
Israel, 175, 210
Italy, fascist, 73, 74, 75
Iwaszkiewicz, Jarosław, 31, 95, 204

Jachimecki, Zdzisław, 11, 25, 38, 61, 176,
  242
Jackowski, Aleksander, 221
Jakelski, Lisa, 234
Jakubczyk-Ślęczka, Sylwia, 50
Jakubowska, Longina, 29, 231–32
Jarecki, Henryk, 59
Jarzębska, Alicja, 97
Jasiński, Roman, 105, 106
jazz, 34, 71, 101
Jedlicki, Jerzy, 29
Jemnitz, Sándor, 80
"Jesienne róże" (Springtime roses; Gold and
  Włast, 1932), 34
"Jew," capitalization of in Polish, 65, 149,
  261–62n66, 277n71
Jewish Artistic-Literary Society, 48
Jewish Association for the Promotion of
  Fine Arts, 173
Jewish Music Society (Żydowskie
  Towarzystwo Muzyczne), 46, 48,
  259n2
Jewishness, 9, 21, 48, 224, 252n24; debate
  over role in artists' identity, 49;
  downplayed as self-preservation
  strategy, 163, 176; ethnic belonging as
  basis of, 44; fluid border with
  Polishness, 85–86; interwar Polish
  musical culture and, 27; Nazi definition
  of, 111, 203; as private religious
  confession, 12. *See also* Polish Jews
"Jewish question," 11
"Jewish Question, The" (Szymanowski,
  1922), 43
Jewish Society for Public Welfare
  (Żydowskie Towarzystwo Opieki
  Społecznej), 121
Jewish Symphony Orchestra (Żydowska
  Orkiestra Symfoniczna), 20, 66, 133,
  201; acculturation and, 118–19;
  formation of, 116; Jewish Council and,
  117, 118; pay of musicians, 116–17;
  sealing of Warsaw Ghetto and, 113;
  works by non-Jewish composers played
  by, 114, 116, 117
Joyous Overture (Koffler), 149
Judaism, 8
"Judaism in Music" ("Das Judenthum
  in der Musik"; Wagner, 1850),
  10, 47
Judenrat (Jewish Council), 116, 117, 118,
  128, 131
Judeo-Bolshevism. *See* Żydokomuna
Jüdischer Kulturbund (Germany), 114

Index | 329

Kaczerginski, Shmerke, 174
Kaczyński, Tadeusz, 237
Kaden-Bandrowski, Juliusz, 63
Kaplan, Chaim, 123
Karczewski, Kamil, 31
Kassern, Tadeusz Zygfryd, 59, 66, 175,
    242; canon of concert music and, 233;
    conversion to Catholicism, 198;
    defection and emigration of, 238–40;
    escape from Holocaust, 196; evacua-
    tions between German and Soviet
    occupation zones, 84–85; State Music
    Publishing Council and, 191
—WORKS: *The Anointed* (1951), 239;
    Concerto for Voice, 218; *Tryptyk
    żałobny za śpiew z fortepianem* (1945),
    196, 197–99, 200*ex.*, 201, 206
Kataszek, Szymon, 33
Kawiarnia Prof. Woytowicza (Professor
    Woytowicz's Café). *See* Dom Sztuki
"Kawiarnie" (Cafés; Różycki), 123–26
Kazuro, Stanisław, 28*fig.*, 178
Khan, Shamus Rahman, 4
Kisielewski, Stefan, 5, 97, 179, 216–18,
    220, 242; on the Festival of Contempo-
    rary Polish Music, 194; *Muzyka Polska*
    journal and, 62; on Palester's *Ogiński
    Polonaises*, 206–7; postwar reconstruc-
    tion and, 220; PWM and, 188*fig.*; *Ruch
    Muzyczny* journal and, 191, 194, 217;
    twelve-tone polemics and, 257n65
Klechniowska, Anna Maria, 38
Klecki, Paul, 61
"Knights of ORMUZ, The" (Kondracki),
    68, 70
Koc, Adam, 73
Koffler, Józef, 2, 8, 48, 60, 61, 148*fig.*, 242;
    murdered by Nazis, 149, 154; *Muzyka*
    journal and, 45; performed in
    Soviet-occupied Lviv, 145; in Polish
    section of ISCM, 65; in Soviet-occupied
    Lviv, 147–52; twelve-tone polemics and,
    257n65
—WORKS: *Joyous Overture*, 149; *Ukrainian
    Sketches* (*Szkice ukraińskie*; 1940), 150;
    *Variations sur une valse de Johan
    Strauss*, op. 23 (1935), 150
Kołacze, poemat weselny (Wedding cake,
    epithalium; Palester, 1942), 135
Kondracki, Michał, 36, 54, 59; "The
    Knights of ORMUZ," 68, 70
Koneczny, Feliks, 57
Konopnicka, Maria, 159
Konrad Wallenrod (Mickiewicz, 1828), 208

Korwin-Szymanowska, Stanisława, 67, 72
Kościuszko Uprising (1794), 146, 158, 206
Kosenko, Viktor, 145
Kowalska-Trzonkowa, Halina, 132–33, 203
Kowalska-Zając, Ewa, 175
Koźmińska-Frejlak, Ewa, 210
Kraków. *See* Cracow
Krenz, Jan, 97, 232
Krewer, Cecylia and Fanny, 201
Kronenberg, Leopold Julian, 8, 42
Kultura (Polish émigré publication in Paris),
    236, 237
Kupfer, Jerzy, 125–26
Kwartalnik Muzyczny (musicology journal),
    62, 65
Kyiv State Conservatory, 144

Lachs, Dawid, 201
Laks, Szymon, 58, 59, 238
land reforms, 29
Lardello café (Warsaw), 104, 269n129
Laskowski, Aleksander. *See* Baruch, Witold
    Hugo
Latoszewski, Zygmunt, 178, 191
Latvia, 137
Lebow, Katherine, 169
Legend of St. George, op. 9 (*Legenda o św.
    Jerzym*; Rytel, 1918), 27
Lewak, Izydor, 271n41
Lira (The Lyre) café, 99
Lissa, Zofia, 2, 8, 15, 38, 140, 179, 243,
    280n148; communism supported by, 40,
    147, 162, 257n70; excluded from
    Muzyka Polska, 65; as Holocaust
    survivor, 154, 158; as interpreter of
    Soviet policy for Poland, 160; Jewishness
    downplayed by, 176; Lviv State Conser-
    vatory and, 143–44; on Palester's
    changes, 236; on physical destruction of
    Warsaw, 169; politics of Jewish omission
    and, 162–63; socialist realism and, 221;
    in the Soviet Union, 157*fig.*, 158–59; on
    Turski's "Olimpica" Symphony, 227;
    on twelve-tone music, 39–40
—WORKS: "The Ideological Situation among
    Polish Composers," 192; "Music during
    the First Five Years of People's Poland,"
    185; *Śpiewnik żołnierza polskiego*
    (Songbook of the Polish Soldier),
    158–59
Liszt, Franz: Piano Sonata in B Minor, 103;
    Wagner transcriptions, 72
Lithuania/Lithuanians, 2, 137
lived experience, 12, 17, 22

330 | Index

Lorentz, Stanisław, 91
Lotto, Izydor, 7
L'Ours café (Warsaw Ghetto), 125
Lublin, interim pro-communist government in, 160, 161
Lublin Music Society, 161
Lutosławski, Witold, 67, 100, 105, 168, 218, 243, 283n86; popularity in early postwar years, 209; transition to avant-garde and, 233; works published by PWM, 190, 192
—WORKS: Concerto for Orchestra (1954), 233; Trio for oboe, clarinet, and bassoon, 218, 288n86; *Variations on a Theme by Paganini*, 101
Lviv, 20–21, 26, 28, 39*fig.*; German occupation of, 132, 152–54; Jewish Artistic-Literary Society, 48; as major prewar cultural center, 137; as multiethnic city, 144; musical culture built by Jews, 46; music and politics of nation in, 144–52; musicology institute in, 38, 39, 41, 140; music schools in, 68; Sovietization of musical life, 140–44; Soviet occupation of, 12, 84, 124, 196
Lviv State Conservatory, 142–43, 146–47, 152, 154, 158
Lyatoshynsky, Borys, 145, 151–52
Lysenko Institute (Lviv), 143, 146
Lyudkevych, Stanislav, 145

Łabuński, Feliks, 57
Łabuszyński, Józef, 271n41
Łagów Lubuski, congress of the Union of Polish Composers in, 171, 224–28
Łobaczewska, Stefania, 40, 140, 179, 236, 243, 257n65; Chybiński's undermining of, 41; on creation of "Polish School" of composition, 205; Lviv State Conservatory and, 143–44; mixed attitudes toward Jews, 11–12; racialized notion of Polishness and, 60–61; State Music Publishing Council and, 191
Łoboz, Piotr, 154

Maciejewski, Roman, 235
Mahler, Gustav, 145
Maklakiewicz, Jan, 34, 42, 72, 224
Malawski, Artur, 188*fig.*, 218; Symphony No. 1, 218, 288n86
Maliszewski, Witold, 263n116
Mała uwertura na orkiestrę (The little overture for orchestra; Palester, 1935), 36, 37*ex.*

Mannheim, Karl, 51
Marek, Tadeusz, 54, 59*fig.*
Markiewiczówna, Władysława, 38
Maurras, Charles, 57
mazurkas, 130
Medaliony (Medallions; Nałkowska), 288n81
Mehrer, Artur, 46
memory, 2, 15, 22, 229; collected memory and collective memory, 196; of Holocaust, 196, 240; memory politics of communist state, 14; nationalized, 13; place of victimhood and survivorship, 16; rumors and war memory, 201–5; socialist realism and war memory, 220–24, 223*fig.*, 227–28
Mendelsohn, Ezra, 7
Mendelssohn, Felix, 201
Messiaen, Olivier, 235
Meyerbeer, Giacomo, 115
Michalski, Stanisław, 64
Mickiewicz, Adam: *Konrad Wallenrod* (1828), 208
Mierzejewski, Mieczysław, 224
Miłosz, Czesław: *The Captive Mind*, 237; *Ocalenie* (Rescue), 213; "A Poor Christian Looks at the Ghetto," 17
Minc, Hilary, 163
Ministry of Culture and Art (Ministerstwo Kultury i Sztuki), 178, 184, 187, 189, 239, 247
Mitelman, Ignacy, 271n41
modernism, 18, 27, 171; Festival of Contemporary Polish Music and, 194; middlebrow, 33–36; modernization and, 51–52; Paris as center of, 52–55. *See also* avant-garde; progressive composers
modernization, 33, 52, 72, 182, 233
Molotov-Ribbentrop Pact, 80, 81, 137
Moniuszko, Stanisław, 115
monumental works: vision of stability and, 220
Monument to the Ghetto Heroes (Rapoport, 1948), 222, 223*fig.*
Moralność pani Dulskiej (film), 130
Morawski, Eugeniusz, 27, 28*fig.*
Moss, Kenneth B., 263n11
Mozart, Wolfgang Amadeus, 101, 116
Münchheimer, Adam, 7
Münzer, Leopold, 65, 66, 154
musical intelligentsia, 4, 5, 107, 109, 135; border of Jewishness and Polishness, 85–86; civil society and, 51; concert music defined and promoted by, 26;

conservative branch of, 42, 49, 179; continuity project and, 6, 15, 231–32; creation of musical elite, 27–33; displacement in the Soviet Union (USSR), 154–59; historical narrative of war defined by, 205–11; Jewish members of, 44, 109, 177; liberation from Nazi rule and, 160–61; mass culture perceived as threat, 33; musical edification of the masses and, 32–33; musical institutions and, 51; musicology and gender in, 38–41; as postwar force, 177–82; postwar rupture and consolidation of, 192–93; progressive branch of, 35, 42–43, 49, 62, 67, 177, 178–79; reconstruction and, 169–70, 180; responses between silence and witness, 15–17; rumors and war memory among, 201–5; as social network and ideological project, 18; underground activities under Nazi occupation, 91–94; war memory and, 229; Warsaw as main center of activity, 19; women and gay men in, 18. *See also* conservative composers; continuity of Polish culture; intelligentsia; progressive composers
—BIFURCATION OF POLES AND JEWS IN, 170–71, 195, 232; among refugees in USSR, 156–58, 159; definition of wartime past and, 205–11; ethnonationalism and, 12; postwar view of Warsaw Ghetto cafés, 209–11. *See also* Polish Warsaw, under Nazi occupation; Warsaw Ghetto
musicalization (*umuzykalnienie*), 32, 70, 185
"Music at a Turning Point" (article in underground press), 89
Music Chamber (Izba Muzyczna), 73
music critics, 1, 3, 30, 44, 57, 96
"Music during the First Five Years of People's Poland" (Lissa), 185
"Music in Lviv and Jews" (Plohn, 1936), 46
musicologists, 2, 13, 231; female, 26, 38–41, 39*fig.*; nation as organizing category, 26; rehabilitation of émigrés and, 238; Soviet, 143; State Music Publishing Council and, 191
"Music on the Street" (Wars, 1941), 142
music schools, 68, 69*map*, 146, 160, 161
Mussolini, Benito, 75
Muzyka (Music; journal), 5, 176, 247, 255n26; antisemitic criticism of, 65–66;

based on French journals, 44–45; downfall of, 48; funding denied to, 64–65; *Muzyka Polska* founded as alternative to, 64, 65; polemics over twelve-tone music, 40; sympathetic articles on jazz, 256n38
Muzyka Polska (Polish Music; journal), 45, 187, 247, 255n26; anti-Jewish exclusion policy of, 65, 66; antisemitism in, 44; appeal of fascism and, 73; coded anti-Jewish positions expressed in, 66; conceived as alternative to *Muzyka*, 64; contributions of Polish Jews erased from, 65; ISCM festival (1939) and, 79; as a main venue to discuss new music, 62; polemics over twelve-tone music, 40; *Ruch Muzyczny* as continuation of, 191; "totalistic" organization of musical life endorsed by, 74
"My, Pierwsza Brygada" ("We, the First Brigade"; Polish military song), 159
"My, Pierwsza Dywizja" (We, the First Division; Pasternak), 159
Mycielski, Zygmunt, 5, 31, 32, 53, 177, 179, 217, 243; antisemitism denounced by, 174; canon of concert music and, 233; evolution into critic of state socialism, 236; friendship with Boulanger, 59*fig.*, 180, 181, 182, 213; on new aesthetics from cataclysm of war, 211–13; *Ocalenie* (Rescue), 213–14, 215*ex.*, 216; in Polish army, 81; on postwar avant-garde music, 235; postwar reconstruction and, 180–82, 220; on race as national essence, 56–57; on realism in art, 220–21; response to proposal of "totalism" in music, 74, 263n116; skepticism of the masses, 33; turn away from Francophile internationalism, 182, 183; on wartime transformation of musical culture, 208–9; on young generation of composers, 232–33

Naliwajek, Katarzyna, 251n4, 265n15
Nałkowska, Zofia, 288n81
Naszkowski, Marian, 158
Nasz Przegląd (Our review; Jewish daily paper), 44
National Democrats, 10, 26, 42, 73
nationalism, Polish, 4, 26, 38, 252n17; German and Soviet views of, 146; "homonationalism," 31; Nazi occupation policies and, 90
"nation-centered" historiography, 26

332 | Index

Nazis/Nazi Germany, 12–15, 48, 74, 162; Czech lands taken over by, 79; German Music Chamber (Reichsmusikkammer), 73; nonaggression pact with Soviet Union, 20, 80; official antisemitism of, 75, 84. *See also* occupation, Nazi

Neighbors (Gross), 14

neoclassicism, 54, 217, 235

Neumark, Irena, 113

Neuteich, Marian, 66, 118, 201

Niekraszowna, Ilza Sternicka, 38

Niewiadomski, Stanisław, 72, 115

Nikodemowicz, Andrzej, 84, 141

NKVD (People's Commissariat for Internal Affairs), 140, 142, 152

nobility/gentry, hereditary (*szlachta*), 29, 231–32

Nono, Luigi, 235

nostalgia, 129, 176, 206

Nowa Gospoda (New Tavern), 27

Nuremberg Laws, 85

Nussbaum, Klemens, 156

Nutcracker Suite (Tchaikovsky), 101

Ocalenie (Rescue; Miłosz), 213

Ocalenie (Rescue; Mycielski), 213–14, 215*ex.*, 216

occupation, Nazi (1939–45), 2, 4, 19, 138*map*, 198, 239; Ministry of Public Enlightenment and Propaganda, 86, 88; musical composition as resistance to, 86–90; musical organizations and, 51; music and national survival under, 90–94; policy toward art and entertainment music, 86–87. *See also* Polish Warsaw, under Nazi occupation; Warsaw Ghetto

occupation, Soviet (1939–41), 81, 82, 84; "double occupation," 137–39, 138*map*; Jews and Ukrainians under, 21, 146, 149; music and politics of nation in Lviv, 144–52; Sovietization of Lviv's musical life, 140–44

Ochlewski, Tadeusz, 5, 31, 34, 183, 186, 188, 243; Association of Enthusiasts for Early Music and, 62; Concerts of Wartime Compositions and, 268n104; *Muzyka*'s crumbling as benefit to, 193; occupation-era activities of, 92, 93; ORMUZ and, 66, 70; PWM led by, 187–90, 188*fig.*, 191; Stalinist campaign against "formalism" and, 191–92

Ogiński, Michał Kleofas, 135; "Farewell to the Fatherland," 206, 207*ex.*

Oistrakh, David, 141

Olick, Jeffrey K., 196

Operation Barbarossa, 137, 152

operetta, 71

ORMUZ (Organizacja Ruchu Muzycznego; Organization for Musical Culture), 52, 66–68, 70–72, 75, 185–86, 248

Ostatni etap (The last stage; film, 1948), 203

Ostjuden ("East Jews"), 47

overtures, 17

Oyneg Shabes (Ringelblum) archive, 110–11, 110*fig.*, 114; contributors' views on assimilation, 127; Różycki's writings for, 123, 124–25, 211

Paderewski, Ignacy Jan, 72, 88

Padlewska, Nadzieja, 199

Padlewski, Roman, 90, 196; a capella Stabat Mater (1939), 199; death in Warsaw Uprising, 197, 198, 199, 201; "The Gorget" (1933), 286n16; String Quartet No. 2, 196

Paganini, Niccolò, Caprice for Solo Violin (twenty-fourth), 101, 102*ex.*

Palester, Barbara. *See* Podoska, Barbara

Palester, Henryk, 112–13, 134

Palester, Małgorzata, 134, 135–36

Palester, Roman, 34–36, 60, 106, 190, 243; arrest of, 105; canon of concert music and, 233; Cold War and, 236–38, 291n29; Concerts of Wartime Compositions and, 268n104; family exposed to blackmail, 133–34; Festival of Contemporary Polish Music and, 194; Jewish family passing as Polish in Warsaw, 112–13; as Jew raised Catholic, 85; on musical intelligentsia and the postwar state, 178; in Paris, 183, 184*fig.*; on Polish compositional parity with western Europe, 205–6; on popularization of Polish music, 186; on postwar audiences, 209; PWM and, 188*fig.*; relations with family, 134–36; saxophone concertino, 80; State Music Publishing Council and, 191; traces of Jewish experience in war-related compositions of, 203–5; at war's end with fellow survivors, 168–69; works smuggled out of Nazi-occupied Poland, 90

—WORKS: Concertino for piano and orchestra (1942), 135; Concerto for viola and orchestra, 291n35; "The

Crisis of Modern Music" (1932), 35; études for piano (1943), 135; "Fragments of a Memoir from the Years 1939–1945," 135; *Kolacze, poemat weselny* (Wedding cake, epithalium; 1942), 135; *Mała uwertura na orkiestrę* (*The little overture for orchestra*; 1935), 36, 37*ex.*; *Metamorfozy*, 291n35; Piano Sonatina for four hands (1940), 135; *Polonezy M.K. Ogińkiego* (Ogiński Polonaises; 1943), 206, 207*ex.*, 208; Requiem, 204, 228, 236; String Quartet No. 3 (1942–44), 135, 192; Symphony No. 2 (1941–42), 134, 135, 218, 219*ex.*; Symphony No. 4, 291n35; Symphony No. 5, 291n35; Violin Concerto (1939–41), 134, 135

Panufnik, Andrzej, 100, 105, 168, 188*fig.*, 189, 283n86; *Pięć polskich pieśni wiejskich*, 218; *Symfonia Pokoju* (Symphony of peace; 1951), 228; works published by PWM, 190, 192

Paris, 27, 31, 283n86; diminished significance in postwar period, 182; as epicenter of Polish musical modernism, 52–60, 59*fig.*; *Kultura* (Polish émigré publication), 236; Polish composers and performers studying in, 52, 55; Russian émigrés in, 58

Pasternak, Leon, 159

peasantry, 29, 32, 68

Penderecki, Krzysztof, 18; *Dies Irae*, 233; *Threnody for the Victims of Hiroshima* (1961), 235

Perkowski, Piotr, 27, 52, 113, 167–68, 178, 244; at Chopin's grave in Paris, 56*fig.*; Concerts of Wartime Compositions and, 268n104; Festival of Contemporary Polish Music and, 194; Lira (The Lyre) café of, 99; performed in Soviet-occupied Lviv, 145; State Music Publishing Council and, 191; *Swantewit* ballet, 218; on Turski's "Olimpica" Symphony, 227; underground activities of, 92, 177

Person, Katarzyna, 118, 210

Petersburski, Jerzy, 155

Philharmonic of the General Government (Philharmonie des Generalgouvernements), 88–89, 89*fig.*, 93, 202–203

Pianist, The (film, 2002), 11

Piasecki, Stanisław, 263n116

Pięć polskich pieśni wiejskich (Five Polish peasant songs; Panufnik), 218

"Pieśń z nad Odry" (Song from the Oder), 159

Piłsudski, Józef, 10, 11, 73, 159; coup led by (1926), 30

Plohn, Alfred: "Music in Lviv and Jews" (1936), 46

Podoska, Barbara, 105, 134, 188*fig.*

"Poem about Music" (anonymous), 153

pogroms, 14, 21, 138; in Kielce (1946), 174–75; in Lviv, 144, 152

Poland: as bulwark of "Latin civilization," 57; as Catholic nation, 57, 58; Constitution (1921), 10–11; ethnic diversity in prewar period, 2; London government-in-exile, 91, 222; partitions (period of statelessness; 1795–1918), 4, 29, 159, 197; population loss in World War II, 82; postwar shift of borders, 1

Poland, Second Republic (1918–39), 18, 26, 91, 257n67; concert culture of, 185; demise of, 49; eastern borderlands (*kresy*), 68, 69*map*, 70–71; establishment of, 30; Ministry of Art and Culture, 63; Ministry of Religious Denominations and Public Education, 63–65, 72; religious and ethnic diversity of, 58; Soviet/communist view of, 146, 187; Soviet seizure of eastern territories, 137, 138*map*; Ukrainian identity in, 140, 276n34. *See also* interwar period (1918–39)

Poles (non-Jewish, Catholic Poles), 12, 51, 253n46; in Anders Army, 155, 157; antisemitism and, 9; brutal treatment by Nazi Germany, 13; conflict with Ukrainians after World War I, 144; deported to Soviet labor camps, 137, 140, 155; evolution of listening habits, 33; expropriation of Jewish property during the war, 174; Holocaust witnessed by, 213, 222–23; Jewish musicians saved by, 132–33; Jewish spouses of, 93; Jews in hiding blackmailed by, 14, 112, 133–34, 204; as the most "Latin" of the Slavs, 58; music as means of national survival, 2; as percentage of prewar population, 2; range of responses to Holocaust, 14; reduced to unskilled labor for Nazis, 83, 87; required to leave Warsaw Ghetto territory, 85, 111; in Soviet-occupied Lviv, 146–47; Soviet power in confrontation with, 10; tensions with Polish Jewish refugees in USSR, 156–58, 159, 162

334 | Index

Polish Army in the USSR (Kościuszko Division, First Division), 155, 156, 158, 160

Polish Committee of National Liberation (Polski Komitet Wyzwolenia Narodowego; PKWN), 160, 161

Polish Jewish musicians: aided by non-Jewish colleagues, 14, 107; converts to Catholicism, 66; "double occupation" and, 139; Franco-Polish synthesis and, 59, 60, 61; in German-occupied Lviv, 153–54; Holocaust survivors and rebuilding of Jewish Poland, 172–77; persecution and murder of, 1–2; postwar emigration of, 175; postwar return to Poland from the West, 176; in Soviet-occupied Lviv, 147–52; as in-between subculture, 8–9; unemployed musicians in Warsaw Ghetto, 119–23; in Warsaw Ghetto, 20. See also acculturation, Jewish

Polish Jews (Jewish citizens of Poland), 12, 19; deported to Soviet interior, 154–59; despair of, 73, 263n111; in eastern borderlands (kresy), 67, 70; in German-occupied Lviv, 152; homophobia and, 31; imprisoned in ghettos, 81; Jewish assimilation and the concert hall, 7–9; as members of intelligentsia, 30; percentage of loss in Holocaust, 82; politics of Jewish omission after liberation, 162–63; postwar emigration of, 224; refugees in Soviet Union, 15, 21; search for Jewish music, 41–49; sequestered in ghetttos, 2; in Soviet-occupied Lviv, 144, 146–52

Polish language, 7, 12, 124; acculturated Jews and, 8; cabaret in, 130; capitalization of ethnic groups, 261–62n66; ethnonationalism and, 10; Jewish cultural identity and, 47; Oyneg Shabes archive documents in, 110; replaced by Ukrainian in Lviv, 140; spoken in Warsaw Ghetto, 111, 120, 127

Polish-Lithuanian Commonwealth, 29

Polish music, 5, 12, 72, 79, 169, 231–32; antisemitism and, 9, 11, 12; broadcast on Soviet radio, 156; as contested and fragmented category, 26; evocations of "Latin" culture and, 57, 58; genres banned under Nazi occupation, 87; Jewish musical culture separate from, 27; in Lviv concert programming, 145, 146

Polish musicians, 2, 14, 180, 282n68; acknowledgment of Jewish suffering and, 3; censorship under occupation and, 88; continuity project and, 3; ethnonationalism and, 26; fascist or totalitarian arts policy and, 52; in German-occupied Lviv, 152–53; identification with France and "Latin" culture, 57, 58; Nazi cultural policy and, 87, 88; reconstruction and, 21; relocation to cities in postwar state, 141; relocation to Warsaw during occupation, 83; Soviet occupation and, 142; underground (podziemie) and, 20

Polish Music Publishers (Polskie Wydawnictwo Muzyki; PWM), 179, 187–92, 188fig., 193, 237, 238, 248. See also Ochlewski, Tadeusz

Polish Music Publishing Society (Towarzystwo Wydawnicze Muzyki Polskiej; TWMP), 19, 52, 63–64, 66, 186, 248; antisemitism in, 61–62, 71, 75; appeal of fascism and, 74; Music Chamber (Izba Muzyczna), 93; postwar transformation of, 187; publications of, 62–63; PWM and continuation of objectives of, 189–90; state socialism and prewar aims of, 192. See also Muzyka Polska; ORMUZ

Polish Music Society, 50

Polishness, 21, 94; based on citizenship, 10; fluid border with Jewishness, 85–86; as inherent racial quality, 56; liberal version of, 55; racialized notion of, 52, 60–61; unmarked, hegemonic status of, 253n46

Polish People's Republic (1952–89), 14, 51, 139, 280n148

Polish Radio, 40, 92, 147, 282n68

Polish Radio Orchestra, 88, 118, 119

Polish Socialist Party (PPS), 40, 160

Polish United Workers' Party (PZPR), 179, 192

Polish Warsaw, under Nazi occupation, 19, 20, 131, 188, 202; as aryjska strona (Aryan side), 82, 113, 132, 133, 210; café performances, 97, 99–101, 103–6, 131, 211; continuity project and Jewish absence, 105–7; General Government and, 83–84; German cultural policy in, 83; Jews passing as Poles, 112; Warsaw Ghetto comparisons with, 108, 110, 114

Polish Workers' Party (PPR), 178, 181, 282n68, 283n75. See also Polish United Workers' Party polonaise genre, 206

Polonezy M.K. Ogińkiego (Ogiński Polonaises; Palester, 1943), 206, 207*ex.*, 208

Polonization, 9

polytonality, 39

"Poor Christian Looks at the Ghetto, A" (Miłosz), 17, 213

popular music (*muzyka lekka*; "light music"), 33–34, 35, 49, 67, 95, 100, 129, 140, 155

Porter-Szűcs, Brian, 9

Potocki family, 31

Potter, Pamela M., 13

Poznań, city of, 26, 38, 68, 69*fig.*, 139

Poznań State Opera, 178

Prelude to the Afternoon of a Faun (Debussy), 101

private apartments, music performance in, 2, 94–97, 96*fig.*, 131, 268n97

Prizament, Shloyme, 173

Professional Union of Musicians, 161, 177, 179; verification committees of, 202

progressive composers, 28*fig.*, 42–43, 49, 62, 178, 282n64; audiences and, 34; Festival of Contemporary Polish Music and, 194; neoclassic aesthetic and, 54; ORMUZ and, 67; Polish Music Publishing Society and, 62; in space between high and low musical genres, 35–36; State Music Publishing Council and, 191. *See also* modernism

Prussia, Polish partition zone ruled by, 29, 87, 159

"Przedmowa" (Dedication; Miłosz), 213, 214

Przekrój (Cross section; journal), 217

Przypkowski, Tadeusz, 135

publishing houses, 5, 49. *See also* Polish Music Publishers, Polish Music Publishing Society

Puccini, Giacomo, 115

Pulikowski, Julian, 64, 65

Pullman, Szymon, 118, 119

Quintet for clarinet, bassoon, violin, cello, and piano (Régamey), 97, 98*ex.*

Qui Pro Quo cabaret, 127

"race": interwar concept of, 55; Jews and, 9, 47; modernist composers and, 56–57

racism, 48, 59, 60, 223

radio, 33, 40, 172, 257n67; Jewish music on, 173; Yiddish-language broadcasts, 175

Radio Free Europe, 237

Radkiewicz, Stanisław, 175

Radziwiłł family, 100

Rajchman, Aleksander, 8

Rapoport, Nathan: Monument to the Ghetto Heroes (1948), 222, 223*fig.*

Raschèr, Sigurd, 80

Rathaus, Karol, 60, 61, 65

Ravel, Maurice, 58, 60, 72; *Boléro*, 101

realism. *See* socialist realism

reconstruction, postwar, 180–82, 188, 193, 212, 221–22; building of state socialism and, 231; defining the past and, 195; generational shift and, 178–79; of Jewish culture, 172, 173; Polishness–Jewishness division and, 21, 170–71; role of musical intelligentsia, 169–70; as transformation, 182–86

recording industry, 33

Régamey, Konstanty, 28*fig.*, 34, 36, 106, 183, 218, 244; canon of concert music and, 233; Concerts of Wartime Compositions and, 268n104; ISCM festival (1939) and, 80; on neoclassicism in "Polish style," 54; participation in Warsaw Uprising, 167; Quintet for clarinet, bassoon, violin, cello, and piano, 97, 98*ex.*; Tansman dismissed by, 59–60; on turning away from radical experimentation, 216; twelve-tone polemics and, 257n65; underground activities of, 91; on underground concerts, 96–97; on wartime café concerts, 208; works smuggled out of Nazi-occupied Poland, 90

Rehding, Alexander, 220

Reich, Steve, 15–16

Reich (-Ranicki), Marcel, 117, 119, 132

Reiss, Józef, "The Soul of Jewry in Music" (1928), 46, 47

Ringelblum, Emanuel, 110, 123, 270n22

Ringelblum archive. *See* Oyneg Shabes archive

Rocznik Muzykologiczny (musicology journal), 62

Rodziński, Artur, 291n29

Rogers, Jillian C., 17

Rogowski, Ludomir, 263n116

Rohr, Hanns, 88

romanticism, 27, 54

Rosenbaum, Ignacy, 201

Roussel, Albert, 58

Różycki, Ludomir, 45*fig.*, 72, 106, 211; *Casanova* (1922), 130

336 | Index

Różycki, Stanisław, 114, 123–24, 127
Ruch Muzyczny (Musical currents; journal),
179, 191, 194, 237, 249; circulation
figures for, 192, 285n141; Padlewski's
letters to mother published in, 201;
"right-wing elements" at, 178; rumors
in, 201–2
Rudnicki, Edmund, 91, 93, 94, 282n68;
Concerts of Wartime Compositions and,
268n104
Rudziński, Witold, 205, 216, 227–28
rumba dance, 130
Russia, imperial: Polish partition ruled by,
29, 31, 87
Rutkowski, Bronisław, 32, 33, 64, 179,
186, 244; Association of Enthusiasts for
Early Music and, 62; changing views of
organization in musical life, 178;
Concerts of Wartime Compositions and,
268n104; *Muzyka Polska* journal and,
92; ORMUZ and, 67, 71; participation
in Warsaw Uprising, 167; *Ruch
Muzyczny* journal and, 191; underground activities of, 93, 94; on young
generation of composers, 234
Rydz-Śmigły, Edward, 73
Rytel, Piotr, 28*fig.*, 179; antisemitism of, 42;
Legend of St. George, op. 9 (*Legenda o
św. Jerzym*; 1918), 27; State Music
Publishing Council and, 191; Szymanowski as archenemy of, 43

Sabbatai Zevi, 239
Saminsky, Lazare, 47
Sanacja ("healing") regime, of Piłsudski, 30,
71, 73
Schmitt, Florent, 58, 145
Schoenberg, Arnold, 13, 15–16, 74;
ORMUZ programs and, 72; *A Survivor
from Warsaw*, 238–39; *Verklärte Nacht*,
39
Schreker, Franz, 129
Schubert, Franz, 101, 115
Schumann, Robert, 115
Scriabin, Alexander, 39
Sendler, Irena, 134
serialism, 234, 237
Serocki, Kazimierz, 232
Shore, Marci, 17
Shostakovich, Dmitri: *Song of the Forests*,
228
Shreffler, Anne, 234
Sienkiewicz, Henryk, 32
Signale (French journal), 45

Sikorski, Kazimierz, 62, 94, 145, 202, 244
Sikorski-Maiskii Pact (1941), 155
silence: critiques of in Holocaust studies,
15, 240, 254n57
SiM café. *See* Sztuka i Moda
Singing Fool, The (film, 1929), 40
Snyder, Timothy, 10, 13, 137
Sobibór death camp, 2, 82
social circles (*środowiska*), 5, 6, 51, 72–73
socialist realism, 171, 175, 192, 193, 233,
235; avant-garde in revolt against, 235;
centrality of emotion to aesthetics and,
195; heroic aesthetic of, 228; music in
mandate to rebuild Poland and, 172;
war memory and, 220–24, 223*fig.*,
227–28
societies (*towarzystwa*), 50
Society for Jewish Folk Music, 46, 48
Society for the Promotion of Jewish Music
(Towarzystwo Krzewienia Muzyki
Żydowskiej; Cracow), 46
Society for the Promotion of Jewish Music
(Verein zur Förderung jüdischer Musik;
Vienna), 47
Sokorski, Włodzimierz, 221, 227, 228
Sołtys, Mieczysław, 145, 152–53
Song of the Forests (Shostakovich), 236
"Soul of Jewry in Music, The" (Reiss,
1928), 46, 47
Soviet Union (USSR), 1, 67, 74; Cold War
and, 234; German invasion of, 81, 137,
150, 154; invasion of Czechoslovakia
(1968), 236; nonaggression pact with
Nazi Germany, 20, 80; Poland's "loyal
collaboration" with, 181, 182; Polish
Jewish refugees in, 15, 21; wartime
atrocities of, 13. *See also* occupation,
Soviet
Spisak, Michał, 58
Sprigge, Martha, 17
Splendid (café in Warsaw Ghetto), 126
Srokowski, Jerzy, 28
Stalin, Joseph, 140, 149, 155, 158; borders
of Poland and, 160; death of, 233;
Shostakovich's paean to, 228
Stalinism, 17, 21, 162, 182, 193, 221;
pressures on PWM and, 191–92;
Stalinist era in Poland (1948–56), 171;
unwinding in Thaw (1956), 235,
280n148
Stanisław Moniuszko Music Institute
(Lublin), 161
State Higher Music School (Katowice),
178

Index | 337

State Music Publishing Council (Państwowa muzyczna rada wydawnicza), 190

state socialism, 21, 229, 234; critical stances toward, 217, 236; end of, 14; musical intelligentsia and advocacy for, 182; musical modernization under, 233; prewar aims of TWMP and, 192; reconstruction and, 231

Steinberg, Edward, 153

Steinlauf, Michael C., 13

Stockhausen, Karl, 234

Strauss, Johann: *Emperor Waltz*, 150

Stravinsky, Igor, 56, 72, 74, 201, 218, 238

String Quartet No, 3, op. 19 (Zemlinsky), 40

String Quartet No. 2 (Padlewski), 196

String Quartet No. 3 (Palester, 1942–44), 135, 192

String Trio, op. 20 (Webern), 40

Suchowiejko, Renata, 60

Survivor from Warsaw, A (Schoenberg), 238–39

swing music, 33

Symfonia Pokoju (Symphony of peace; Panufnik, 1951), 228

symphonism, 27

Symphony No. 2 (Palester, 1939–1941), 134, 218

Symphony No. 2 "Olimpica" (Turski), 224, 225*ex.*, 227–28

Symphony of Sorrowful Songs (Górecki), 233

Szajewicz, Iso, 121

Szałowski, Antoni, 27, 58, 183, 190, 217

Szczepańska, Maria, 39*fig.*

Szeligowski, Tadeusz, 53, 74, 235, 263n116; "Freedom and Gagging," 75; on Turski's "Olimpica" Symphony, 227

Szlemińska, Aniela, 188*fig.*

Szlengel, Władysław, 128, 129

Szpilman, Kazimierz, 271n41

Szpilman, Władysław, 11, 80–81, 167, 244; as performer at café Sztuka, 129–130, 209; sealing of Warsaw Ghetto and, 113; survival owing to help of non-Jewish Poles, 132

Szpinalski, Stanisław, 67, 74, 264n116

Sztompka, Henryk, 67, 70, 72

Sztuka (Art; café in Warsaw Ghetto), 126–31, 209–11

Sztuka i Moda (SiM; Art and Fashion) café (Warsaw), 88, 100, 101, 103, 104, 105, 127

Szulc, Jakub, 271n41

Szymanowski, Karol, 18, 25, 72, 79, 191, 244; antisemitism of, 43; "The Educational Role of Musical Culture in Society" (1930), 67–68; *Efebos* (novel, 1918), 31; as elder statesman of progressives, 27; elite background of, 31; ISCM and, 45; "The Jewish Question" (1922), 43; *Muzyka* journal and, 45*fig.*; performed in Soviet-occupied Lviv, 145; on race and musical creation, 55–56; sexuality of, 31; on synthesis of the national and the universal, 55, 61; works performed in underground concerts, 95

Śpiewnik żołnierza polskiego (Songbook of the Polish Soldier; Lissa), 158–59

tango dances, 33, 35, 99, 130

Tansman, Aleksander, 2, 45, 60, 61, 175, 245

Tarnowski family, 31

Taruskin, Richard, 54

Tchaikovsky, Pyotr Illyich: *Nutcracker Suite*, 101

Thirteen, the, 128, 210

Threnody for the Victims of Hiroshima (Penderecki, 1961), 235

Toeplitz, Henryk, 7

totalitarianism, 19, 52, 73–75

trauma, 6, 22, 208, 233, 251n4; acknowledgment of, 212; in coexistence with seeming normalcy, 213; expressed through music, 17; limits of representation and, 17, 254n67; personal and national responses to, 201; Polish Jews and Cold War schism, 238; sense of self shaped by, 109; social crisis as cultural crisis, 3; of war, 21

Treblinka death camp, 2, 82, 85, 111, 132

Trio for oboe, clarinet, and bassoon (Lutosławski), 218

Trio for oboe, violin, and cello (Bacewicz, 1936), 53*ex.*, 54

Tryptyk żałobny za śpiew z fortepianem (Mourning triptych for solo voice and piano; Kassern, 1945), 196, 197–99, 201, 206; "Płaczy dzisiaj duszo wszela" (Weep today, every soul), 197, 199, 200*ex.*; "Stała pod krzyżem [Stabat Mater]" (Under the cross stood the grieving mother), 197; "Stała się jest rzecz dziwna" (A strange thing occurred), 197

Trzonek, Henryk, 133

Turkow, Dina, 121

338 | Index

Turkow, Jonas, 123, 127, 132, 172, 174, 245; on language of performance in the Warsaw Ghetto, 120–21; on postwar antisemitic violence, 175
Turkow, Zygmunt, 121
Turski, Zbigniew, 178, 179; Symphony No. 2 "Olimpica," 224, 225*ex*., 227–28
Tuwim, Julian, 129
twelve-tone composition, 2, 27–28, 236; Koffler and, 150, 151*ex*.; Lissa's writings on, 39–40; polemics over, 40, 257n65; Régamey and, 97, 98*ex*.
Tygodnik Powszechny (The universal weekly), 217

U Aktorek (The Actresses' Café; Warsaw), 99, 100–101, 104
Ukrainian language, 140, 143, 144; Lviv Opera performances in, 144; musical press in, 150
Ukrainians, 21, 139, 263n94; in eastern borderlands, 67; enrolled in Lviv State Conservatory, 146–47; liberated from Polish lords in Soviet propaganda, 140; as percentage of prewar population, 2; response to German takeover of Lviv, 152; Soviet occupation of Lviv and, 145, 146
Ukrainian Sketches (*Szkice ukraińskie*; Koffler, 1940), 150, 151, 151*ex*.
Ulica graniczna (Border street; film, 1948), 203–4
Umińska, Eugenia, 67, 188*fig*., 191
Unchosen People, An (Moss), 263n11
underground (*podziemie*), 20, 91–94, 131, 203; concerts organized in private apartments, 94–97, 96*fig*., 268n97; connections with Warsaw Ghetto, 113; Council for Aid to the Jews (Żegota), 134, 135; musical sounds associated with, 94–97
Undzer gezang (Our song; Kaczerginski, 1947), 174
Union for Artists of the Jewish Stage, 173
Union of Composers of Soviet Ukraine, 148, 150
Union of Polish Composers, 161, 171, 174, 178, 182, 204, 235, 249; Association of Polish Composers subsumed into, 177; Festival of Contemporary Polish Music sponsored by, 194; Łagów Lubuski congress (1949), 171, 224, 227, 228; Palester expelled from, 237;

reconstruction and, 185; socialist realism and, 220–21
Union of Polish Patriots, 155, 156, 158, 160, 162
Union of Soviet Composers, 151
Union of Yiddish Literati, Journalists, and Artists in Poland, 172
Union of Yiddish Writers and Journalists, 173
unions, professional, 49
United Kingdom, 80
United States, 142, 239
upowszechnienie ("making universal or common"), 183–85, 186
urbanization, 33
Urbański, Jerzy, 204
USC Shoah Foundation, 135

Variations on a Theme by Paganini (*Wariacje na temat Paganiniego*; Lutosławski), 101
Variations sur une valse de Johann Strauss, op. 23 (Koffler, 1935), 150
Verdi, Giuseppe, 115
Verklärte Nacht (Schoenberg), 39
Vest, Lisa Cooper, 6, 51–52, 183, 220, 233
Vilnius, 68; Vilnius Ghetto, 174, 201
Violin Concerto (Palester, 1939–41), 134, 135
Volkov, Shulamit, 10

Waghalter, Józef, 271n41
Wagner, Richard, 56, 84, 176; "Judaism in Music" (1850), 10, 47; Liszt transcriptions of, 72; in Warsaw Ghetto, 115
Wajner, Leon, 173, 222, 223–24
Wajnkranc, Romana, 127, 128
Waldorff, Jerzy, 11, 31, 169, 236, 245; antisemitism of, 43–44; PWM and, 188*fig*.; as "totalitarian," 75; on wartime productivity of Polish composers, 106
Walenty z Brzozowa, 197
Wars, Henryk, 33, 35, 140; Anders Army and, 155; "Music on the Street" (1941), 142
Warsaw, 19–20, 139, 275n3; cafés, 28, 101; feminism in, 38; German bombardment of (1939), 167; ISCM festival in (1939), 79; music schools in, 68, 69*map*; in newly independent Poland, 25; Polish Jews' leading role in musical institutions, 7; ruins of, 213. *See also* Polish Warsaw, under Nazi occupation

Warsaw Autumn Festival of Contemporary Music (1956–), 234, 235, 238, 291n35

Warsaw City Theater (Theater der Stadt Warschau), 93

Warsaw Conservatory, 94, 118, 142, 178, 202, 250

Warsaw Ghetto, 2, 106, 108–11, 112*map*, 188, 202; café performances, 109, 123–26, 132; courtyard concerts, 119–23, 131, 132; creation of, 85, 111; Grossaktion deportations (1942), 85, 111, 132, 133; house committees in, 120–23; Jewish Symphony Orchestra in, 66, 113, 116–19; life inside, 111–14; mixed marriages and cross-wall connections, 113; musicians rumored to have died in, 201; music making in, 20, 82; postwar view of cafés in, 209–11; reduced to rubble, 169, 170*fig.*, 171*fig.*; Różycki on cafés in, 123–26; sonic transformations in, 114–19, 116*fig.*, 131–32; Sztuka (Art) café, 126–31, 209–11

Warsaw Ghetto Uprising (1943), 85, 132, 167; commemorations of, 196, 222, 224; film about, 203; Kassern's opera proposal and, 238–39

Warsaw Institute of Musicology, 41

Warsaw Music Society, 8, 50

Warsaw Opera, 86, 88, 93

Warsaw Philharmonic, 2, 8, 20, 44, 88, 119, 147, 249; concert hall destroyed by German bombs, 81, 86; concerts of 1920s, 27; former members in Jewish Symphony Orchestra, 118; musicians of, 43*fig.*; plans to rebuild, 93; prominence of Jews in, 42; surviving music volumes in basement of, 190; Wajner's cantata and, 224

Warsaw Uprising (1944), 82, 93, 101, 167–68, 181; death of Padlewski in, 197, 198, 199, 201; musical scores lost in destruction of war, 189; Palester's stepbrother killed in, 168, 204

"Warszawianka 1831" (Song of Warsaw, 1831), 159

"War Topics" (Kisielewski, 1945), 217

Wasilewska, Wanda, 158

Wasser, Hersz, 110*fig.*

Webern, Anton, 80, 235; String Trio, op. 20, 40

Weinberg, Mieczysław, 175–76

Weprik, Alexander, 48

Werner, Ryszard, 202

West Ukrainian People's Republic, 144

Wiadomości Literackie (Literary news), 127

Wiechowicz, Stanisław, 32, 59, 185; on war and representation, 216; works smuggled out of Nazi-occupied Poland, 90

Wielopolski family, 31

Wieniawski, Józef, 7

Wieviorka, Annette, 16, 254n62

Wilczak, Tadeusz, 188*fig.*

Wiłkomirski, Kazimierz, 132–33, 209

Wisłocki, Stanisław, 227

witness, musical, 15–16

Wlodarski, Amy, 13, 15–16

Włast, Andrzej, 34

Wohlfeiler, Erwin, 126

Wolfsohn, Juliusz: *Hebrew Suite*, op. 8 (1926), 47–48; "New Jewish Music" lectures (1933), 48

women, 18, 26, 31, 257n75; collaboration charges against, 210; female musicologists, 26, 38–41, 39*fig.*; recitals in trade schools for, 92; work of mourning and, 198

World Centre for Jewish Music, 148

World War I, 25, 27, 144, 159

World War II, 11, 19, 29, 180, 208; composers' turn away from representational content about, 216–18, 220; continuity and change across, 17; as heroic episode, 195; lived through music, 15; Polish population loss, 1; socialist realism and war memory, 220–24, 223*fig.*, 227–28

Woytowicz, Bolesław, 53, 60–61, 88, 179, 190, 245; Dom Sztuki café run by, 88, 100, 101, 103; ORMUZ and, 67; popularity in early postwar years, 209; postwar activities of, 178; State Music Publishing Council and, 191; on turn away from formalism, 221

Wozzeck (Berg), 39

Wójcik-Keuprulian, Bronisława, 39*fig.*, 41

Wyka, Kazimierz, 83

Yiddish language, 7, 8; Bundism and, 44; national Jewish culture based on, 121; Oyneg Shabes archive documents in, 110; radio broadcasts in, 175; spoken by unacculturated Jews, 172; spoken in Warsaw Ghetto, 111, 118, 120; theater in, 121, 173

340 | Index

Zabawka (Just a toy; film, 1933), 35
Zachęta café (Warsaw), 269n129
Zak, Yakov, 141
Zakazane piosenki (Forbidden Songs; film, 1947), 95, 96fig., 203
Zakopane, 168
Zalewski, Teodor, 32, 33, 62, 65
Zarzycka, Helena, 202–3
Zemlinsky, Alexander von: String Quartet No, 3, op. 19, 40
Zerubavel, Eviatar, 213
Ziemiańska (literary café in prewar Warsaw), 127

Zionism, 44, 224
Zygielbojm, Szmul, 222

Żydokomuna (Judeo-Bolshevism) 10, 137, 149, 153, 157, 163
"Żydom polskim" (To the Polish Jews; Broniewski), 222–23
Żywe kamienie (The living stones; Berent, 1918), 135
Żywy Dziennik (The living newspaper), 129

Founded in 1893,
UNIVERSITY OF CALIFORNIA PRESS
publishes bold, progressive books and journals
on topics in the arts, humanities, social sciences,
and natural sciences—with a focus on social
justice issues—that inspire thought and action
among readers worldwide.

The UC PRESS FOUNDATION
raises funds to uphold the press's vital role
as an independent, nonprofit publisher, and
receives philanthropic support from a wide
range of individuals and institutions—and from
committed readers like you. To learn more, visit
ucpress.edu/supportus.

www.ingramcontent.com/pod-product-compliance
Ingram Content Group UK Ltd.
Pitfield, Milton Keynes, MK11 3LW, UK
UKHW030627180325
456381UK00001B/1/J